THE FIGHT
FOR HISTORY

THE FIGHT FOR HISTORY

75 YEARS OF FORGETTING, REMEMBERING, AND REMAKING CANADA'S SECOND WORLD WAR

TIM COOK

ALLEN
LANE

ALLEN LANE

an imprint of Penguin Canada, a division of Penguin Random House Canada Limited

Canada • USA • UK • Ireland • Australia • New Zealand • India • South Africa • China

First published 2020

www.penguinrandomhouse.ca

LIBRARY AND ARCHIVES CANADA CATALOGUING IN PUBLICATION

Title: The fight for history : 75 years of forgetting, remembering,
and remaking Canada's Second World War / Tim Cook.
Names: Cook, Tim, 1971- author.
Identifiers: Canadiana (print) 20190144467 | Canadiana (ebook) 20190144513 |
ISBN 9780735238336
(hardcover) | ISBN 9780735238343 (HTML)
Subjects: LCSH: World War, 1939-1945—Canada. | LCSH:
Collective memory—Canada. | LCSH: Memorialization—Canada.
Classification: LCC D768.15 .C66 2020 | DDC 940.53/71—dc23

Cover and book design: Five Seventeen
Cover images: (front) Lt Richard G. Arless / PA-142714, (spine, top) Lieut. Ken Bell /
PA-135956, (spine, bottom) Lieut. Ken Bell / PA-162648; all courtesy of Canada. Dept. of
National Defence / Library and Archives Canada

Printed and bound in Canada

10 9 8 7 6 5 4 3 2 1

Penguin
Random
House

FOR PAIGE, EMMA, CHLOE, AND SARAH.

CONTENTS

INTRODUCTION

"Nobody would be interested in reading about the Second World War after 1948," said Canadian minister of national defence Brooke Claxton shortly after Hitler and his Nazis were defeated.[1] Claxton's flippant comment was made to Colonel Charles Stacey, who was the army's official historian and who would become Canada's most influential military historian. At the time, Stacey was frustrated by the government's lack of interest in publishing an official history—one based on government and military records during the war that would have been closed to civilian researchers because of security concerns—and he would come up against this political ambivalence for years to come. He found that politicians were worried by, even afraid of, what a historian might uncover and reveal to the public. But Stacey refused to let Canada's war effort be forgotten, and he railed against the politicians, eventually overseeing or writing several foundational army histories, as well as *Arms, Men, and Governments*, a crucial 1970 study on Canada's wartime policy. Despite such successes, Stacey and other historically minded Canadians who wished to chronicle the country's wartime story would also find themselves struggling against inertia, fear, and apathy among the general public. It was not only distrustful politicians but also many Canadians who were uninterested in celebrating or commemorating Canada's role in the Second World War.

One of the challenges that Stacey and others faced was that even as war had shaped Canada's destiny over centuries, Canadians did not see themselves as a warrior people. From Indigenous conflicts to the wars of empire that made Canada a British colony, and from the pre-Confederation colonies resisting the incursions of the United States to the shattering effects of Canada's Great War, armed conflict had transformed the nation time and time again. War would determine whether we would be ruled by the English or French or Americans; it would forge a reputation for Canadians on the world stage, and it would nearly rend the country apart before ushering in developments like income tax or the federal vote for women. And yet despite these epic changes, some joked, Canadians didn't pay much attention to the legacy of war because they were too busy trying to stay warm. Others concluded that although Canada's destiny was shaped by war, without a revolutionary war or a civil war to define itself, its leaders emphasized gradual constitutional changes in explaining the country's political character. Canada's isolated geography and alliance systems certainly allowed it to avoid spending huge sums on defence. Stacey offered a famous dictum on the country's condition: "Canada is an unmilitary community: Warlike her people have often been forced to be; military they have never been."[2]

And yet the suggestion that somehow Canadians would be indifferent to reading about the Second World War only a few years after it ended seemed absurd given Canada's enormous contributions. Canada mobilized early for the long fight against Hitler, his Nazis, and other fascists, and by war's end the country of 11.5 million

Almost 1.1 million Canadians served in uniform during the Second World War. They contributed to the Allied victory in battles and campaigns around the world. But they left behind loved ones for several years, and some 45,000 were killed and never came home.

had close to 1.1 million men and women in uniform. Choosing to declare war independently against Germany, Canada had raised substantial formations to fight in the air, at sea, and on land in the global war. For six years, Canada supported its allies—primarily Britain and the United States—as a junior if equal member of the Western alliance. Canada's participation was all the more important after France, Belgium, and the rest of Western Europe were defeated and occupied by the Germans. The price of victory had been high, with 45,000 Canadians killed and another 55,000 physically wounded. Thousands more suffered from wounds to the mind and spirit. The survivors came home and were rewarded with generous benefits from the government that enabled them to build new lives and a new country.

With veterans making up one in three adult males in the 1950s, along with the more than 50,000 women who served, it would be easy to assume that the aftermath of the Second World War would permeate Canadian society. But that was not the case. In fact, the war was rapidly pushed aside, evoking little relevance in the fast-changing postwar years and for much of the twentieth century.

This book seeks to track and untangle the complicated, contested, and ever-shifting meaning of that war over the past seventy-five years. Canada's commitment to winning, whatever the cost to its citizens, forever changed the trajectory of the nation. The gears of the war effort drove massive political, economic, social, and cultural transformations across society. Government intrusion into the lives of Canadians was furthered by the war through the massive mobilization of resources and, in the immediate postwar period, through an unparalleled effort to help service personnel integrate back into society. The war created a million new veterans who needed to be treated with respect; the injured had to receive care. Meanwhile, Canada's dead were honoured to assuage the grief of next of kin and the soldiers' communities.

Over time, a particular form of social memory emerged surrounding Canada's war effort. Social memory is the constellation of thoughts, ideas, and key events that people create and embrace to make sense of their society. Often this involves forging an agreed-upon version of the past that resonates in the present. The past may not change, but how we view it does.[3] And while there are many strands of memory, not all are dominant. As part of the interplay of ideas, historians uncover new evidence that slowly makes its way into the school texts, although often popular culture is more effective in shaping our understanding of history. A novel like Joy Kogawa's *Obasan* (1981), a film like Steven Spielberg's *Saving Private Ryan* (1998), an exhibition at the Canadian War Museum—all read, seen, or visited by hundreds of thousands or millions—can have a tremendous impact on what Canadians know about their history.

After Canada's monumental contribution to victory, it is surprising that Canadians' engagement with and interest in the Second World War faded in the postwar years. This "Necessary War" had been fought against an evil regime—Hitler's Thousand-Year Reich—and large segments of the country's citizenry bore almost any burden to win the war. While some were unmoved by the war effort, often for political or religious reasons, and sometimes because of distance from the front or isolation in rural areas, most Canadians stood behind and firmly supported the war effort. But within a decade, the war's meaning changed dramatically, losing its potency to move Canadians as a galvanizing symbol of pride and sacrifice. How memory shifts can be difficult to decipher; harder still is understanding why. Often controversy is involved, as groups fight over a new meaning or hold fast to old ones, and that is certainly the case with Canada's disputed war memory. Of course, these discussions and debates often tell us more about the present than the past. In the late 1960s, for example, some Canadians, disaffected by the toll of the Vietnam War, clashed with veterans over the relevance of Remembrance Day, a day with sacred origins in 1919. As novelist Viet Thanh Nguyen once said, "All wars are fought twice, the first time on the battlefield, the second time in memory."[4] As this book will show, the past rarely lies still in its grave; it is continually dug up, reanimated, and occasionally even weaponized.

All nations reconstruct meaning around their wars: telling battle-field stories, creating symbols, and, over time, situating those wars within the country's social memory. In Canada, the erection of monuments—or their absence—tells us something about how Canadians envisioned the war effort. Films, plays, and novels can illustrate how the war resonated among artists. The discourse sur-rounding conflict and how it is taught in schools or appropriated by politicians shows how some stories are infused with weighty meaning while others are discarded or forgotten. The key role of anniversaries in focusing the media's attention or gathering veter-ans together—or their failure to do so—reminds us that what we mark, honour, and celebrate is not constant over time. And, cer-tainly, controversy and disagreement reveal the contours of a war's invoked memory, which shifts from generation to generation and differs from nation to nation.

For the United States, the Second World War is the great cru-sade, the "Good War" in which the Americans defeated their evil enemies in the Pacific and in Europe. While there are no uniform views among the more than 320 million Americans, any sustained questioning of the war's righteousness—by raising such issues as the use of atomic bombs or the racialized nature of combat in the Pacific—has been attacked vigorously as wrong, even disloyal, by politicians, veterans, and citizens.[5] War has always occupied a central place in American history. The Second World War is the fulcrum upon which the United States emerged as a superpower, while the disastrous Vietnam War left Americans discouraged and haunted. After a decline in public interest through the 1970s, the Second World War was invoked again more forcefully in the 1980s, its image reinvigorated by politicians to tell new stories of American exceptionalism. It continues to be an important narrative within that country's history.

The Second World War is obviously depicted as something quite different in Germany. It is the darkest event in that nation's history, a period of madness and humiliation. At first, the survivors tried to forget, even while standing in the ruins of their country's shattered cities and blasted countryside. But once some of the pain receded, Germany began to examine its past. This reflection took different forms in the divided country where the West embraced democracy and the East was stifled by being shackled to the Soviet Union. From the 1960s onward, the new generation in both West and East Germany questioned Hitler's rise to power, and how he corrupted democracy and made the German people complicit in wars of aggression, genocide, and the Holocaust. This examination turned to action in West Germany, where the enduring dishonour led to financial restitution being made to Israel and to a strong desire not to repeat the past.

And yet, in the 1980s, a new strand of memory emerged that portrayed the German people as victims. In this scenario, Germans suffered at the hands of the Nazis, who, oddly, were seen as somehow apart from German society; they also endured the Allied bombing campaign that killed over 593,000 people.[6] Of course, accepting this depiction of themselves as victims required Germans to actively forget much of their aggression against others, an act of historical revisionism that was forcefully questioned outside of the country. Since the early twenty-first century, German leaders of the reunified country have taken part in commemorative ceremonies with the nation's Western allies as an equal partner, hoping to ease the lingering hurt of the war in a modern, industrialized, and very prosperous Germany.

For Britain, the dominant memory of the war is that of the lone island standing up against overwhelming Nazi forces, fighting as the underdog at Dunkirk, enduring the Battle of Britain, and bravely withstanding the German aerial bombardments known as the Blitz. The fact that more than half a billion people in dominions and colonies within the British Empire contributed masses of service personnel and war supplies is conveniently downplayed in favour of celebrating Winston Churchill, the pugnacious war leader who rallied the beleaguered British to defy and defeat Hitler. This was Britain's "finest hour" and the unified war effort is deeply embedded in the nation's psyche. For many years, the British put far more emphasis on the relatively insignificant Desert War in North Africa than on the Italian campaign or even the all-out battles in Europe, seemingly because, in that desert arena, the British were underdogs who ultimately won. And, of course, it was a victory that did not have to be shared with the Americans, who came late and initially were badly outfought. By the time of the D-Day landings in the summer of 1944, it was the British who were the junior partners to the Americans. Victory in those battles was more difficult to situate within the central narrative of the underdog.[7]

The French have their own fraught relationship with the war, agonizing over their inglorious defeat in the summer of 1940, after which Germany occupied France. To assuage the shame, a post-war myth emerged that most French citizens had supported or fought within the Resistance against their Nazi oppressors. Only in the late twentieth century did intellectuals and politicians undergo a painful public conversation about the large number of collaborators in French society and the compliance of the Vichy regime with the Nazi occupiers. [8]

Russia labelled its struggle as the "Great Patriotic War," a searing memory that helped fuel the Soviet Union's leaders' hostile actions throughout much of the Cold War. The desperate need to avoid another costly invasion—at least twenty-seven million Soviets died as a result of direct assaults and genocidal German policies beginning in June 1941—motivated the Soviet Union to create a strong buffer zone of Communist satellite countries. Framing the war as one in which they were victims of German aggression, the Soviets used their wartime losses to justify abhorrent behaviour towards weaker nations. [9] The Second World War was, of course, not the sole reason for the Soviet Union's aggressive policies, but the catastrophic wartime damage became an important element of Soviet, and later Russian, identity.

Japan's story of the war was difficult for generations of that country's citizens to address. Cultural codes created an enforced silence within a complex interplay of willed forgetfulness, wounded pride, and national disgrace. Like many other citizens of war-torn countries, Japanese people believed that their war effort was a defensive one, forced on them by Western encroachment. [10] A strange story indeed, especially considering Japan's war of aggression in China, but a perspective that was easier to embrace after the United States used atomic bombs against Hiroshima and Nagasaki in August 1945. While Germany made restitutions and Mussolini's Italy was largely ignored as a pathetic junior partner, Japan was condemned by much of the world for failing to address its wartime atrocities.

Other countries created their own wartime legacies, choosing to diminish and to forget, to elevate and celebrate. And it is not only countries that continue to struggle to make sense of the war. Jews have had their own unique and agonizing reckoning with this period in history, and the Holocaust, an event that was barely discussed until the 1960s, is now forever intertwined with attempts at understanding the war and perhaps the very nature of humanity.

Given Canada's significant contribution to the Allied victory, it was surprising, even shocking, that the war faded rapidly from social memory. Only a decade after victory, the Necessary War lost its ability to inspire within Canadian society. There were many reasons why Canadians pushed the war aside, and why they chose not to tell war stories that defined and gave shape to the nation—certainly, the dark shadow of the Great War had a significant influence. Canada's Great War of 1914 to 1918 had seen 630,000 Canadians in uniform from a population of eight million. The struggle nearly tore the nation apart along existing and new fault lines, especially with the enactment of conscription in late 1917. And yet it also thrust the country forward into the international arena. The Canadian Corps—Canada's primary fighting formation at 100,000 strong—was an icon for the young country. But the cost of an unlimited war effort was terrible, with more than 66,000 killed. The loss of those fallen soldiers, airmen, sailors, and nurses weighed heavily on the nation.[11] The Great War marked Canada's coming of age. It was described as the birth of the nation by some, with the Battle of Vimy Ridge—an April 1917 victory in northern France and the site where Ottawa would build its striking national monument—becoming a useable symbol of how

Canada was forever changed. There was much more to the war effort, but Vimy, where Canadian soldiers captured an almost impregnable position, became a kind of shorthand for how the war propelled Canada to nationhood.[12] In contrast, there was no similar symbolic Canadian battle during the Second World War. The December 1943 Battle of Ortona was not on the same scale, the catastrophe at Dieppe was something quite different, and Canada's heroic actions at Juno Beach on D-Day were shared with other nations. This book will look at why some Second World War battles were elevated in importance over others, but also why there was no Vimy-like battle to anchor the war's social memory.

The Great War's traumatic losses haunted the young nation. They marched through Canadians' imaginations, demanding recognition and remembrance, a message captured in John McCrae's popular poem *In Flanders Fields*.[13] Although that poem was written in 1915 as a clarion call by the killed soldiers to continue resisting

Canadian soldiers marching away from the trenches of the Western Front in the Great War. The terrible exertion and sacrifice of that war haunted Canada.

the Germans, in the war's aftermath the dead were interpreted as passing on the torch to the living, urging them not to put out the light of that generation's sacrifice. The Great War became a touch-stone—functioning as a warning, as a symbol of grief, and as a coming of age event—and the thousands of community monuments erected across the country, along with symbols like the poppy and Remembrance Day, were part of the quasi-religious fervour of promising never to forget.

If one of the strongest narratives of Canada's Great War was that the young dominion came of age and moved to full nationhood, what then was the meaning associated with the Second World War? The image of the Canadian Corps and of Vimy, where all four Canadian divisions fought together for the first time, allowed for the fastening of memory on one story. Canada's global Second World War, longer and even greater in scope, somewhat ironically left the constructed memory unfocused.

From 1939 to 1945, and immediately afterwards, Canadians knew that the Second World War was a struggle against the evils of fascism. Moreover, while Canada did not go to war in 1939 to save the Jews, by the end of the hard fighting, the revelation of the death camps showed that the terrible battles and campaigns had been justified. While the armistice of November 11, 1918, stopped the Great War in an anti-climactic manner and the subsequent peace treaty led to unrest in the defeated nations, the Second World War was a total victory for the Allies, with the Axis powers of Germany, Italy, and Japan utterly defeated. The Canadian army's fighting units ended the war primarily in the Netherlands, where tens of thousands were involved in freeing the starving Dutch. Welcomed as liberators and celebrated as heroes, Canadians understood that it had been a just war.

And yet, quite rapidly, the idea of the Necessary War was pushed to the periphery and largely made irrelevant in the modern Canada that emerged after the war. Canadian veterans were silent and silenced, often unable to tell their stories because of the trauma they had experienced or because they felt that no one would understand. Amplifying the problem, Canadian novelists, playwrights, and filmmakers mostly ignored the war. While Canadian culture has always been overshadowed by the size and vigour of American culture, and Canadians in the mid-twentieth century still carried a colonial mindset about the worth of telling their own stories, the war had mobilized Canadian culture and artists and engendered tremendous pride in the country's service. This could and should have been our story to tell. But we failed. After the war, both the United States and Britain inundated theatres with films and stores with books that celebrated their wartime roles. And so when Canadians wanted to understand the war, they were forced to turn to other countries' accounts.

The Americans have always been better at commercializing memory, but Canada barely tried from the 1950s onward. Within twenty years, the emergence in the nation of a different youth culture, student activism, sexual politics, race issues, and an angry and outspoken antiwar movement contributed to the sweeping of the Second World War further into the dustbin of history. Concerned citizens and veterans railed against this diminishment— especially the Royal Canadian Legion, the largest and most influential veterans' organization—and a battle was waged to preserve the war's importance.

But not all those who served in uniform cared. More than a million veterans survived the Second World War, and most came back and were recognized as heroes. They were proud of their service, feeling it was the most significant thing they had ever done. Others, though, were missing body parts and suffered a lifetime of agony. Many survived physically but carried mental scars that plagued them daily or, more commonly, rose periodically to the surface, never letting a man or woman be free of the war. Under such circumstances, many wished to bury the war—or bury it for a time—in order to move ahead with their lives. It's important not to homogenize the veterans' experiences, but historians must draw out broad narratives and story arcs, even while acknowledging and embracing the messiness of history. There was no single story for Canada's million veterans, but we can determine the dominant experiences and narratives while also valuing the peculiar and marginalized.

By the 1970s, the significance of the Second World War for Canada had faded. Canadians had been saturated for years with news of the dreadful and unwinnable Vietnam War, and as successive generations shaped the new Canada, they embraced multiculturalism, bilingualism, and other national symbols that rose to replace or sideline the country's remarkable war effort. The rise of Quebec nationalism during this period also made it more challenging to describe Canada's participation in the war as a nationalizing force in the country's history. Remembrance Day receded from the public stage. Canada was represented at key commemorative ceremonies in Europe, such as the fortieth anniversary of D-Day in 1984, but the Canadian veterans who returned to the historic beaches found that the Americans and British—and even the French, who did not land on D-Day in any significant numbers—talked proudly of their soldiers' deeds and sacrifices, while their leaders neglected the Canadian story. It was as if Canada had not fought in the war.

The Second World War retreated further from social memory by the late 1980s because many Canadians feared its divisiveness.

For some groups—such as Japanese Canadians who had been forcibly relocated, interned, and ill-treated during the war—they were not part of Canada's struggle against fascism. In fact, they had been targeted as part of the war effort. While it took decades to come to grips with the hurt, Japanese Canadians were empowered by the 1982 Canadian Charter of Rights and Freedoms, and they began to fight for their history. Other veterans, such as Indigenous people and merchant seamen, pressed the state for greater recognition, recompense, and rights. These were important battles to redress old wrongs, but they left contemporary Canadians unclear about Canada's contributions in the once proud Necessary War.

A decade later, in the early 1990s, Canada's part in the war was largely presented throughout Canadian society as a sequence of defeats, disasters, and disgrace, which culminated in the much-seen television series *The Valour and the Horror* (1992). The series enraged veterans, who wondered how the Necessary War could have been reduced to shame and scandal. In the history books and media, there was little positive discussion of Canada's vital role in the Battle of the Atlantic or the air war against Germany, the success of its armies in Italy and Western Europe, or the weighty production of war materials on the home front. No other victorious nation underwent this bizarre reframing of the war, remaking victories into defeats, scorning its war years in a weird display of misplaced self-loathing.

And then it changed. After years of neglecting veterans, the Canadian government celebrated the nation's wartime record to mark the fiftieth anniversary of D-Day in 1994 and the end of the Second World War the next year. Canada had long been seen as a country of peacekeepers, but here in France were thousands of veterans who had fought a desperate and legitimate war in defence of liberty and freedom. The next year in the Netherlands, there was

Canadian soldiers in victory holding a captured Nazi flag.
The Second World War was a necessary war, one that had to end
in victory no matter the cost.

a second celebration that focused on the Canadian liberation of the Dutch. That was largely a Canadian event, and those back home were astonished to watch on television as hundreds of thousands of grateful Dutch, cheering and crying, welcomed back the aged heroes. Many Canadians were ashamed that they had neglected their veterans for so long. Since 1995, there has been a concentrated effort by veterans and other Canadians to restore the Second World War to a prominent position in the country's social memory landscape.

How we remember and what we remember matters. There are many gaps in the fragmented historical record. Some groups and events are marginalized, while others are celebrated and sanctified, but that process is fluid. These narratives of our past, including the story of the Second World War, rise and fall on their own tide, but they are also carried along as society changes. Each generation has new heroes, icons, and symbols, with its own reconfigured meanings. The malleable past is reflected through the ever-shifting present.

Hundreds of books have now been written about Canada's participation in the war, covering almost every aspect of the conflict. I have provided my own interpretation in the two-volume history *The Necessary War* (2014) and *Fight to the Finish* (2015).[14] In *The Fight for History*, I explore the many battles to control the interpretation of Canada's Second World War history—a subject that has been virtually unexplored. The explosive debates over the meaning of the war create the spine of this narrative. Veterans and historical actors are front and centre, with each generation engaging with the war or turning away from it. Over the last seventy-five years, change agents, cultural provocateurs, and guardians of the heritage have been crucial to shaping the history and creating new ways of seeing the past.

The Fight for History is a story of struggle and loss, of neglect and reclamation. It is not a sentimental, nostalgic, or mawkish plea for more war in our history, but an attempt to track the rise, fall, and rise again of the relevance of the Second World War to Canadians. The unfolding of Canada's social memory of war also reminds us that if we do not tell our own stories, no one else will. If we do not embrace our history, it will be forgotten. And without our own history, we run the risk of becoming unmoored and ungrounded. This is our story, a war story that is essential to the unfinished narrative of what it means to be Canadian.

CHAPTER 1

WHY WE FOUGHT

How wars end shapes the way they are remembered. Unfinished or ambiguous endings allow for dissent and anger, the shifting of blame, and the creation of counter-narratives to explain defeat. The Great War ended abruptly, even strangely, on November 11, 1918. After four years and three months of intense battle, of armies and nations fighting well past any rational point, the Central Powers rapidly collapsed. Austria-Hungary and Turkey sued for peace in the weeks before the end, forced to that grim conclusion as the German armies were soundly beaten in battle after battle in what has become known as the Hundred Days campaign. And yet the Germans ended the war on occupied terrain and Germany was largely untouched by enemy armies, although food shortages from the naval blockade caused hundreds of thousands of deaths from malnutrition and disease. Despite millions of dead, the uncertain ending allowed some in Germany—most notably Corporal Adolf Hitler—to claim in its aftermath that the front-line soldiers had not been defeated and that instead they were stabbed in the back by Jews, socialists, and other "undesirables."

A generation later, by May 1945, Germany's defeat was unequivocal. There would be no stabbed-in-the-back conspiracies,

Allied bombers smashed German cities throughout the war, eventually reducing most of them to burned-out husks. The defeat of Germany was total.

as its armies were defeated in the east and the west, its cities reduced to charred ruins by relentless aerial bomber attacks. Millions of civilians were on the run from the east, terrified of being caught by the Soviet armies who were carrying out cruel acts of vengeance against Germans caught before its advancing forces. Those in the west prayed that the Western Allies would extend mercy. The German people had paid a terrible price for following their nation's mad leader, Hitler, into the abyss.

Canada had declared war separately from Britain on September 10, 1939, and fought as part of the Western alliance to bring about Germany's defeat, as well as Italy's; it had also had a minor role in Japan's downfall. Of the Canadians who served in the Great War, about half had been born elsewhere, but most of those who fought in the Second World War were born in Canada.[1] From a country of

11.5 million, eventually 1,081,865 were in uniform. Of the 2,474,000 Canadian men between the ages of eighteen and forty-five, some 42 percent of those eligible answered the call or, near the end of the war, were conscripted.[2] Before conscription, Canadians were motivated to fight for many reasons: to stand shoulder to shoulder with Britain; to earn a steady paycheque while seeing the wider world; and to stand up to the unfettered aggression of Germany. All those who volunteered—including the 50,000 or so women who served in uniform—had their own reasons to leave behind their loved ones and put themselves in harm's way, but perhaps Claude Châtillon's explanation of his decision to enlist with the Royal 22nd Regiment offers some insight: "Something is happening over there that has profoundly touched me, my convictions and my principles. It's a reality I can no longer avoid . . . it's a war of ideas . . . of freedom, of rights, without discrimination as to origin, age, or colour . . . in Europe, it has gone out of control with cruel savagery."[3]

A Canadian soldier who knows why he is fighting: to knife Hitler and end his odious regime.

Canadians fought around the world in the desperate clash to free oppressed peoples from fascist tyranny, and they paid a terrible price in the attritional battles and campaigns. At home, the country was slow to mobilize for the war, but with the shocking fall of France to German armed forces in June 1940, the country rapidly accelerated its efforts. It increased its production and shipping of food and raw materials, and built munitions and weapons of war as quickly as possible. In raw numbers, some 8,655 ships and small vessels were manufactured, along with over 16,000 aircraft, 42,966 artillery guns, 800,000 military vehicles, and over 1.7 million small arms. Canada became an arsenal of democracy.

Canada's defences on the east and west coasts were strengthened early in the war, but geography was the country's greatest protector. And yet even as it was far from the fighting in Europe or the Pacific, Canadians were directly threatened when German U-boats slipped into the St. Lawrence River in the summer of 1942, inciting fear in eastern Canada and Quebec as twenty-three ships were sunk, with even more ships savaged on the east coast. In the increasingly desperate struggle, victory came at a high cost. An intrusive government reached into the lives of Canadians through rationing, taxation, and censorship. Civil liberties were curtailed for many and trampled on for a minority. The fight against tyranny overseas came with some outrages at home in the name of victory, although they paled in comparison to the mass murder and cruelty abroad.

Anxious to defend Britain, a first division of 20,000 Canadian soldiers arrived on English shores starting in December 1939, to be joined by half a million others over the course of the war. Canadians were also sent to defend Iceland, Jamaica, and Bermuda, while 2,000 were lost in the battle for the doomed British colony

Canadian war poster depicting a determined British lion and a
Canadian beaver ready to do battle. Canada fought in the war as
a British ally, albeit a junior one.

of Hong Kong in December 1941, when Japan launched its surprise offensives against the Western Allies. The Dieppe raid of August 19, 1942, which saw significant Canadian involvement, was a day of infamy and loss. It was also the point when the Allies were reminded starkly that invading Europe would be harder than anyone imagined, especially the naive Americans who badly wanted to dispose of the German forces in the main theatre of battle so they could win their war in the Pacific. Dieppe showed that victory would only come with better planning, more resources, and much blood.

The first and longest-serving Canadian Army commander, General Andrew McNaughton, oversaw an army in training for years and eventually succumbed to political pressure in Ottawa to send his soldiers into action in the Mediterranean. McNaughton did not want to divide his army, aware that the four divisions of the Canadian Corps in the Great War, almost always fighting together, had become a recognized symbol for the nation and an effective fighting force. But his objections were overridden, and he agreed to split his force to take part in the invasion of Sicily in the summer of 1943. After defeating Axis forces in North Africa numbering about 230,000, the Allies moved northward through Italy, hoping to siphon off German strength from the Eastern Front, where Stalin's forces were exchanging hammer blows with the Germans. The 1st Canadian Division and a tank brigade fought well in Sicily from July 1943 as the Canadians cut their teeth in combat. The invasion of mainland Italy in September of that year drove the Italians from the war and sucked in German resources from the Western and Eastern Fronts, but campaigning was difficult and costly in the mountainous terrain. There would be no breakthrough of the enemy trench positions, and eventually nearly 100,000 Canadians would serve in Italy.

With Germany fortifying its positions in Europe, bracing for the Allied invasion from the west, the Wehrmacht was slowly driven back by Soviet forces in the east that had survived the crushing battles of 1941 and 1942. Meanwhile, the Western Allies tried to relieve the pressure on Stalin's forces by wearing down the German war machine through aerial bombardment of its cities and infrastructure. It was one of the few ways to hurt the enemy. Responding to the need to train new airmen, Canada established a massive air training program, which welcomed its first recruits in April 1940. It expanded rapidly, with 107 schools and 231 sites operating across the country to allow the aircrew from Canada, Britain, the Commonwealth, and even the United States to learn their difficult trade. Eventually some 131,500 airmen would be trained in what became known as the British Commonwealth Air Training Plan. By war's end, about 250,000 Canadians would serve in the Royal Canadian Air Force (RCAF) in many aerial campaigns, both in the air and on the ground—in jobs ranging from working as radar technicians, to flying supplies to the British and Indian armies in Burma, to patrolling the sea lanes. Fighter squadrons defended Britain, supported coastal shipping, and ranged over Europe to engage the Luftwaffe. Most importantly, bombers took the war to German industry and citizens. The two-engine bombers in the early part of the war were death traps, but the larger four-engine beasts, the Halifaxes and Lancasters, which carried more bombs and were equipped with better technology, began to turn the tide by 1943 as German cities were punished in nightly raids. The bomber crews paid a high price by being the striking arm of the Western Allies, but they took the fight to the heart of Germany.

The bombs these crews dropped and the supplies that kept Britain in the war came through the crucial lifeline from North America—a route kept open by the Royal Navy and the Royal Canadian Navy (RCN), which underwent a massive expansion in sailors and warships. The Canadian sailors resisted the German U-boats attacking in wolf packs, hampered by the lack of airpower that left their convoys of warships and merchant vessels vulnerable, and always struggling against the merciless weather. In fact, the Battle of the Atlantic was the longest campaign of the war, running from the first day of the conflict to the last, and from mid-1940 to mid-1943, it was a constant struggle for the Canadian naval forces to fend off the slashing U-boat attacks. The sailors pressed on as new tactics, better ships, and increased numbers of bombers patrolling for U-boats disrupted the threat by May 1943, forcing the Germans back to safer waters near their European bases. The navy served in other theatres of war, too, securing crucial oil in the

Caribbean, carrying soldiers to their beaches in landing craft, and running supplies to the Russians in the cold, dreary, and dangerous Murmansk Run. And there were also the civilians in uniform, the merchant seamen who served on commercial vessels carrying war supplies, food, and oil. Braving the gauntlet of U-boats, sailing in convoys with scant protection, they faced the cruel sea and a skilled enemy, somehow finding the courage to keep steaming across the pitiless sea, delivering the supplies to Britain. The convoys also carried the hundreds of thousands of soldiers from Canada and the United States in preparation for the invasion of Europe.

Beginning with the epic landings of June 6, 1944, when some 15,000 Canadians clawed their way ashore on Juno Beach beside American and British divisions, the invasion of Western Europe would be a gruelling, costly battle of attrition. While D-Day became an important symbol of victory, it was but the beginning of the end, and the Canadian forces would fight with the massive Allied ground armies non-stop from that day. RCAF fighter and

Canadian Sherman tanks firing at the enemy.

bomber squadrons took the war to the enemy, while the RCN continued to participate in minesweeping operations, transport troops, and pound enemy fortifications with shellfire. The less glamorous but essential convoy work also continued, although most of the U-boats had been driven from the Atlantic. In Italy, I Canadian Corps, close to 100,000 strong, had delivered victory after victory, defeating the Germans at Ortona in December 1943, crashing the Hitler Line in May 1944, and in August of that year breaking the heavily defended Gothic Line. The Canadians in that theatre had been fighting longer than those in Northwest Europe, even as their accomplishments and deeds were overshadowed by D-Day and First Canadian Army.

After defeating two German armies in Normandy, where 400,000 Germans were killed or captured by August 21, 1944, the Allies pushed on to liberate the French. The Americans and British fought among themselves for the glory and gas to keep their armoured vehicles driving through the enemy, while the Canadians were given the task of overcoming the Long Left Flank. Clearing the Channel ports along the French coast meant a difficult fight against an entrenched enemy, but the Canadians succeeded throughout September, even as they were denuded of artillery and shells that were diverted to the bigger British and American campaigns. The Canadians opened up the Channel ports and then pushed northward, grimly fighting through the flooded, low-lying polders of the Scheldt to free up the key shipping route to Antwerp. Again they were successful, opening the route by early November at the cost of some 6,000 casualties, and this was among the Canadians most important contributions to Allied victory during the war, as Antwerp allowed for the movement of crucial war supplies to the overextended armies.

In 1945, victory involved steamrolling the German army out of existence and reducing most of the nation's cities to fire-swept carcasses. After the war, armchair generals would condemn the continued bomber sorties, even as the Canadian infantry at the sharp end praised the airmen directly above them. For them, the air force was striking hard to end the war before more soldiers died. Though the early 1945 army operations, with names like Veritable, Blockbuster, and Plunder, had rolled forward behind massive artillery barrages and aerial bombardments, it had always fallen to the infantry and armoured divisions to dig out the Germans. More than 5,300 Canadians were killed or wounded in those final operations against the crumbling Third Reich. At the same time, thousands of British citizens died under the rain of rockets that Hitler ordered against civilians in a vengeful last gasp in 1944. These rocket attacks concerned the Allied high command, as did the introduction of two feared German superweapons, the Type XXI U-boat and the Messerschmitt 262 jet fighter. Though the war seemed won, they couldn't help worrying—how many more of these weapons did the Germans have?[4] And so the Allies kept smashing the enemy in a war that could only end in "unconditional surrender," a decision made several years earlier by British prime minister Winston Churchill and American president Franklin Roosevelt to convince Soviet dictator Joseph Stalin that the Allies would not abandon him.

With the Soviet Red Army battling through Berlin from April 16 onward, the end came fast after Hitler's suicide on April 30. After the Führer's death, the German forces in Italy downed arms on May 2, with a ceasefire in the First Canadian Army sector in the Netherlands on May 5 and the final surrender two days later. Victory in Europe—VE Day—would be celebrated in the Western world on May 8. General Harry Crerar, who commanded the largest Canadian army in the country's history, issued a message to all ranks as the fighting ended: "Crushing and complete victory over the German enemy has been secured. In rejoicing at this supreme accomplishment, we shall remember the friends who have paid the full price for the belief they also held that no sacrifice in the interest of the principles of which we fought could be too great."[5]

The final Canadian operations of the war, in which the nation's regiments fought alongside British, American, Polish, and other Allied forces, had been costly, as the Germans resisted fiercely to the end. Between May 1 and May 5, 114 Canadians were killed in action in Northwest Europe.[6] They were among the last casualties of the almost 45,000 Canadians killed in the war, although more would die in the conflict with Japan until the atomic bombs forced that nation to sue for peace and officially surrender on August 15. The Allied victories in the multiple theatres of the war had come at a heavy cost: some 60 million people had been killed around the world, and countless more were wounded and maimed.

Canadians contributed to the Necessary War and its armed forces consisted largely of civilians who had put down pen or plough, left cities and farms, to fight the enemy in the all-out war of survival. James Alan Roberts, a prewar ice cream salesman who rose to the rank of brigadier, wrote after the war that while "Canada is not a warlike nation . . . we played an unbelievably important role . . . in the defeat of Hitler's Germany."[7]

Canadians had followed the final battles of the war closely in their newspapers, on their radios, and in newsreels and feature films. They knew that Germany was steadily being hammered from the air in the bomber war, and that it was besieged on all fronts by the Soviets and the Allies. Anticipation of the end had been building for weeks. On May 7, when news of the "unconditional surrender" broke, Canadians took to the streets for two days. In cities, towns, and villages, they flew the British Union Jack, the Canadian Red Ensign, and their provincial flags; they waved and cheered and hugged and kissed. Bands stirred the crowds with martial music, while individuals played flutes, guitars, or garbage-can-lid cymbals in raucous jubilation. The favourite songs of the war—"Hail, Hail, the Gang's All Here," "Bless 'em All," "Roll Out the Barrel," "En avant"—were belted out until throats were raspy and sore. But there was plenty of liquid to loosen up the vocals for another round. For two rollicking days, bonfires burned, occasionally consuming the effigy of Hitler, and the excitement carried forward into the night hours, fuelled by wild abandon and alcohol. In some places, streetcars were damaged and store windows shattered into shards of glass. Away from the partiers, soldiers' parents and widows quietly observed the celebrations, some carrying photographs of their sons and husbands who would never come home.

After the many battles and campaigns, months of hardship and loss, long periods of anxiety and terror, the Canadian soldiers, airmen, sailors, and all others in uniform also embraced the victory. There were celebrations of song and drink in the many air bases, camps, and hospitals in Canada and England. Yvonne Jukes, who served with the RCAF's Women's Division in England with No. 6 Bomber Group, had seen many airmen disappear or die in the bomber strikes. She later recounted, "It was a great feeling of relief that we were not going to lose any more of our young friends."[8] In the field, there was a more muted response. C.L. Jackson, serving with the 1st Canadian Signal Security Section, remembered the intense "feeling of relief that the whole thing was finally over," and he stood around with a few buddies, each savouring a lukewarm bottle of beer in a muddy forest near Hengelo in the Netherlands.[9] With many Canadian units still quite close to the enemy in the Netherlands and Germany, some battle-wise soldiers refused to reveal themselves for some time, worried that enemy snipers had not heard the war was over or that they would take no heed. No one wanted to die in the minutes after the formal end of the global war.

For most of the war-weary Canadians in uniform, it was hard to summon the strength to see far into the future. They had anxiously watched the skies for bombers that never returned, or waited for ships lost at sea, or buried too many comrades in the final months of the land battle. Most had expected at some point that they too would catch a bullet. But they had survived. These young men had spent much of their twenties learning to kill people in between marching and polishing buttons. They were toughened, but they faced an uncertain future.

Canada's army ended the war in places both of goodness and of evil. Since 1944, information about the Nazi genocide of Jews and others deemed undesirable had filtered through the fighting armies, but the Western Allied forces could not have imagined the horror of the death camps they encountered in the final weeks of the war. As part of the systematic desire to eradicate Jews in Europe, Hitler and his henchmen had devised the Final Solution, an efficient and industrialized means of executing those caught in their grasp. Dedicated kill teams known as Einsatzgruppen had travelled the Eastern Front, shooting and gassing hundreds of thousands, but even those shocking numbers of murders had been carried out with too much inefficiency for Hitler's liking. The Reich ordered the creation of concentration camps where trainloads of Jews would be sent to be exterminated in specially built gas chambers. The Holocaust saw six million Jews murdered, along with hundreds of thousands of others the Nazis deemed to be racially or socially inferior, including the disabled, Roma (Gypsies), and gay men.

The Allies overran Bergen-Belsen on April 15, 1945. Within the 55-hectare camp, the stench of the thousands of decomposing dead wafted over the area from huge mass graves. The evidence of the Nazi outrage was everywhere: mounds upon mounds of starved, broken bodies, their pale skin looking like wax paper, stringy strands of hair, legs and arms folded in on themselves. There were about 60,000 prisoners, barely alive, still in the camps. There were no ovens or gas chambers at Belsen, but starvation, inhumane treatment, overcrowding, and executions had achieved

The unimaginable sight of the dead at Bergen-Belsen being bulldozed into an open grave.

the same result. The great killer was typhus, with some 18,000 inmates dying in March 1945 alone, including teenaged sisters Margot and Anne Frank. The latter's diary remains a poignant testimonial to the lives of Jews in hiding in the Netherlands under the monstrous Nazi occupation.

Maurice Victor, who served with the Royal Canadian Army Medical Corps, later recounted that there had been rumours of systematic German attacks against Jews, but none of the Canadians were prepared for "the unprecedented scale and savagery of the annihilation."[10] The full horror of the Nazi Holocaust was revealed to the Canadians by the almost 30,000 unburied, emaciated, naked corpses thrown into huge open pits throughout Belsen. It was here, more than any other place, that Canadians would be exposed to the stark realities of the war.

The dead took soldiers' breath away, but the living were an agonizing gut-punch to Allied eyewitnesses. Wrapped in rags, crawling with lice, thin to the point where bones jutted sharply from parchment-like skin, the prisoners were the living dead. In the hours after liberation, if that is the word, typhoid-ridden skeletal survivors shuffled out of the dark buildings. Men, women, and children with glazed, sunken eyes rocked back and forth, unable to talk, let alone cheer. The Allied soldiers began to hand out rations and offer medical care to camp inmates, but prisoners died by the hundreds over the next couple of days. It was yet another sick irony in a mad war through which some of the Jews had held out for years.

Bergen-Belsen may have lacked the gas chambers of Auschwitz, but for the Canadians and British soldiers who arrived there, it was still a death camp that was synonymous with the Third Reich's crimes. Devastated by what they saw, the liberators were compelled to record this small fraction of the Nazi atrocity. Many tried to write about it, if only to make sense of the sights that assaulted them. Others took photographs, sketched, or painted. There was a need to document. Larry Mann was at Belsen, and he remembered his near disbelief: "Nobody is ever going to believe this in a million years," he wrote. "I better take some pictures."[11] British and Canadian film units were also sent to the camp to officially record it. The Allies were not gentle with the German SS guards; they ordered them to carry the corpses to the mass graves, and then filmed them stacking the bodies. Canadian Leo Heaps raged, "I looked at these beasts who had once been men. . . . No matter how degenerated they had forced, by starvation and indignity, the people of the camp to become, the SS guards had reached, by their own crimes, untouchable depths of degradation."[12]

Canadian official war artists Alex Colville and Aba Bayefsky created paintings of the camp to establish a permanent record. Colville created several works, including *Bodies in a Grave, Belsen*, which captures the jutting ribs, pelvis, and impossibly thin legs of the dead in mass graves. The twenty-two-year-old Jewish-Canadian Bayefsky was haunted by the nightmare before him. Overwhelmed by the experience, it took him a long time even to put brush to canvas. But when he started, he could scarcely stop. Bayefsky later recounted that seeing the evidence at the camp "was the determining factor in everything I have done since."[13] Throughout his long career as an artist, he would continue to grapple with his shock and revulsion, painting aspects of the atrocity.

At Belsen and other camps, long after the bodies were buried, the sense of repulsion would live on. Supreme Allied Commander Eisenhower had demanded official documentation of the evidence so that future generations of Germans could not deny the genocide and so that those at home would know why the Allies had fought. Local Germans were force-marched through the camps to witness what they had contributed to or allowed to happen. Charlie Hancock had flown in a Halifax bomber as a wireless operator with No. 408 Squadron, RCAF, and he visited Belsen. In his mind, after seeing this glimpse of the Holocaust, "the validity of the war could never again be denied, it seemed to me, insofar as that war was fought to prevent or avenge a human tragedy such as this one."[14]

While it took some time to lodge its way in the world's consciousness, and there was always a minority of loathsome deniers, the Holocaust came to have many meanings. It was to stand as proof of the monstrousness of Hitler's regime, which had engaged in a genocidal race war. "What we saw," recounted British lieutenant colonel J. Douglas Paybody, "was a nightmare which beggars description."[15] It was also a nightmare that confirmed that the struggle against the Nazis had been a necessary war.

Just as the encounter at Belsen had shaken Canadians, the liberation of the Dutch was an equally important capstone to the end of the war. For the Canadian units driving forward into the Netherlands in the final weeks of the war, it had been a race against time to free the starving Dutch. It was a dangerous push, as many of the Dutch settlements were held in strength by fanatical enemy soldiers who still believed that Germany might win. But Canadians rarely played it safe, and many risked their lives to free the Netherlanders.

The Dutch people had suffered under the cruel occupation, with the rapacious Germans looting everything they could pry loose for their war machine or the personal gain of individuals. Meanwhile the Gestapo, the Nazis' secret police force, mercilessly tracked down Dutch Jews to transport them to the death camps, eventually rounding up over 120,000 Jews, most of whom did not survive the war.[16] Estelle Tritt-Aspler, a Jewish-Canadian nurse in Montreal before the war, went looking for other Jews in the Netherlands to offer aid, but could not find any. "The Jewish population," she noted, "was just destroyed."[17] In addition, at least 2,800 Dutch men and women were executed in reprisal for offences against the Germans or for being caught as part of the Dutch underground resistance. The executions were often carried out in public, with a bullet to the head and bodies left in the streets for days as a warning.[18]

Another 18,000 people died from starvation during what became known as the Hunger Winter of 1944–1945, although thousands more succumbed to illness induced by malnutrition and lack of care.[19] About half of the nine million Dutch citizens in the Western Netherlands were subsisting on 500 to 700 calories a day, and many were reduced to eating toxic tulip bulbs. The old succumbed first, with the very young following them into the grave. Elly Dull, a Dutch girl who lived in the south of Amsterdam, remembered seeing desperate people slowly pushing their dead family members in handcarts, using up the last of their energy as they tried to find a place to bury them in the frozen ground. The cemeteries were largely filled, in her words, with "children and older people."[20] The morgues and churches contained stacked corpses, and sometimes entire households perished, left for weeks or months before they were discovered. Dutch men enslaved by the Nazis for forced labour succumbed from overwork and neglect, dying far from their communities. In the months before liberation, hope bled away. Teenager Maria Haayen, who lived through the bleak period, recounted, "Every day was a fight for life."[21]

The cheering Dutch greet their liberators.

Just as the dark, cold months of winter were coming to an end, light and hope appeared. In the early days of May, the smiling Canadians rolled through town after town in Fortress Holland, as the Germans called the area, bringing food and cheer. Within minutes of entering the first towns and villages, Canadians were garlanded with flowers, their vehicles covered with what seemed like a strange herbal camouflage. The jubilant crowds waved flags, screamed themselves hoarse, and wept with joy. Mothers held up their babies; old men clutched at the sleeves of the Canadians in uniform; women threw themselves at the surprised soldiers, hugging and kissing them. "The Dutch are a staid race," observed Farley Mowat, an officer in the Hastings and Prince Edward Regiment and a future acclaimed Canadian writer, "but when they broke loose, they simply flung off all restraint and went berserk."[22]

The flotilla of grinning Canadians, soon with young ladies and children riding on their jeeps, Staghound armoured cars, and Sherman tanks, felt like the victors they were.

As the ground forces liberated the Dutch, Royal Air Force (RAF) and Royal Canadian Air Force bombers were dropping food across more isolated parts of the country in Operation Manna. The grateful Dutch waved flags and banners, and even painted signs on barns and house roofs: "Thank you, Canadians!" Pilot Colin Friesen, a Canadian who flew in No. 150 Squadron of the RAF, was only too grateful to switch from bombs to dropping food, relieved that he "no longer had to be destructive."[23] Turning from grinding warfare to humanitarian aid, and being thanked for it, left a lasting impression on the Canadian airmen and ground-pounders. Sydney Frost of the Princess Patricia's Canadian Light Infantry later recounted that the unbridled love that the Dutch showed to the Canadians would remain with him forever: "All the wounds and the suffering, suddenly it seemed very much worthwhile."[24] Canadians who had become cynical or hollowed out after years of combat snapped to the realization that they had been fighting a just war. They had saved these people, by the millions. Their sacrifices, collectively and individually, had been worth it, and that realization was reflected back to them in the gaunt but cheering Dutch faces.

The 170,000 Canadians of First Canadian Army settled into Dutch life during that 1945 summer, meeting and mingling with the country's citizens in the cities, parks, and bars. A close relationship developed. From the first days, encountering the famished, mewling little street urchins, the Canadian soldiers shared their food and chocolates. John Drummond of the Regina Rifle Regiment remembered seeing the "people starving and children just so thin and hungry looking," often waiting patiently outside the Canadian camps at lunch and dinner, hoping that some extra food or even scraps might be sent out to them.[25] Many fainted and collapsed from the smell of the cooking. Canadian soldiers took it upon themselves to go hungry and to feed the desperate Dutch in the first weeks of liberation before regular food supplies arrived. Many young people who survived the Hunger Winter remembered eating chocolate for the first time in months that summer. For the Dutch, it would forever be a symbol of liberation.

Dutch parents of soldiers invited the Canadians to stay in their houses. Fresh bread and some home-cooked meals—usually using the food supplied by the Canadians—cemented friendships. Many of the Dutch told of their trying experience of being compelled to billet German soldiers in their homes, men who came to lord it over the family and displace the father within his own house. John Spurr, a wartime historical officer with the 4th Armoured Division and later a librarian at the Royal Military College of Canada, wrote of how the Dutch "hatred of Germans was almost tangible."[26] The Canadians would be welcomed as second sons, even when they wore muddy boots into the house or came home late the worse for drink.

The Canadian liberators were much loved, but not all were saints. The tired warriors, many fighting hard for the better part of a year, spent their money freely in the safe and welcoming bars and restaurants. They drank and danced, using their near limitless cigarettes as currency in bars. They had no problem finding female partners, and after the dreariness of the war, there was a new sexual freedom among the Dutch. This was largely a result of the pent-up urges and newfound independence that came with the removal of the Nazi jackboot from the nation's throat, and there was much mutual affection between the young Canadians and Dutch, even as some lecherous Canadians used their wealth or access to goods, even promises of a new life, to entice sex.[27] More often, though, there were deep and fulfilling relationships, some of which led to marriage.

Beginning in late 1945, as the Dutch re-established their government and rebuilt their economy, local journalists led the way in suggesting, increasingly forcefully, that the Canadians had to go. At some point liberators become occupiers, even friendly ones. There were appeals to women to stop cavorting with the Canadians. The 260,000 adult males who had been conscripted into slave labour by the Germans filtered back to their communities, and were increasingly unhappy with the Canadian male presence there. But the Dutch women exerted their own agency, refusing to curtail their fun or youth for the sake of discomfited journalists, embarrassed elders, or jealous men. "In twenty years, when another world war may have broken out, it will not be necessary to send a Canadian Expeditionary Force to the Netherlands," went one widely circulated joke. "A few ships filled with uniforms will suffice."[28] A new crop of Canadian-fathered babies were born in early 1946. By that point, however, most of the Canadians had been sent back to Canada. Some did the right thing, marrying out of love or duty. Others fled with no forwarding address. Decades later, hundreds of those children sought out their fathers in Canada.[29] Some dropped the idea after a few letters to the Canadian government or the Legion brought no information; others spent decades trying to find the Canadian fathers who had left them behind.

———

After liberating the Dutch, Canadian signaller Norman Penner believed, "there was no doubt that we had been fighting a just war."[30] The initial wild greetings had settled into a long friendship between the soldiers and their hosts through 1945, and despite some discomfort and challenges, a remarkable bond had been forged between the Dutch and the Canadians. At the other end of the spectrum, some Canadians had taken part in the liberation of Belsen, a symbol of evil. News of the camp and others like it were spread through film, photographs, and art, documenting the unthinkable acts for future generations. The world must not be allowed to forget. And yet, this idea of the Necessary War—a fight for good and against evil—would fade rapidly in the postwar years, losing its impact for most Canadians. This would be a bitter pill for those who had fought so hard and sacrificed so much.

Two Canadians who fought in the Necessary War.

CHAPTER 2

GOING HOME

Rifleman Les Wagar, a twenty-two-year old who served with the Queen's Own Rifles in the Scheldt campaign, wrote an essay in the Canadian Army newspaper, *The Maple Leaf*, about what changes he'd like to see made in Canada after the war. "There is not one of us who has been away from home for any length of time who does not look forward to a better Canada than that which he left," he wrote. [1] The learned Wagar offered ideas on how to do this, including a fundamental change to the Constitution regarding federal and provincial powers, a topic on which he had been influenced by reading the 1940 Rowell-Sirois Report on federal-provincial relations. The vast majority of Canadian soldiers likely had never heard about the report and had no idea of how federal and provincial powers would be renegotiated, but all had a desire for the war to forge a different Canada. They had left a nation that was mired in the Depression, but now they returned from the great crusade in the hope that Canada would be a fairer society.

They were not alone in their fear that the country would slip back into a devastating economic depression. The bleak 1930s had gouged deep and left scars. Canadians had sacrificed too much during the war to let their lives be ruined again in a country of ruined crops, locust hordes, and bread lines. The war had been a true "people's war," involving most Canadians. Both overseas and on the home front, the nation's citizens had sacrificed and bled for victory. They deserved a peace dividend, and they turned to their government to act. The war had conditioned Canadians to believe that Ottawa could effectively control, intervene, and set public policy.

Prime Minister William Lyon Mackenzie King transitioned Canada from a warfare to a welfare state. But King was a cautious, plodding politician, and while he always professed to care for the needy and the downtrodden, and indeed wrote about such concerns in his diary and publications, he was unsure if Canadians believed that the state should help those in need. Despite his almost fifteen years as prime minister before 1939, it took the war to transform King's thinking. Though key reports written by Canadian and British intellectuals and social scientists argued for state intervention, perhaps the more urgent motivator was the popular Co-operative Commonwealth Federation (CCF) on the PM's left flank. King had always been adept at holding the large centre political ground and he was convinced by 1943 about the need to appropriate some of the CCF's social programs, much as he had done in the 1920s to first gain the support of the Progressives and then to make them irrelevant.

One of the most radical ideas circulating in government circles at the time was to offer a monetary stipend to all Canadians with children. The family allowance scheme—known as the "baby bonus"—would put money in the hands of Canadian mothers (in all provinces except Quebec, where it went to fathers). King was initially reticent to implement this program, writing in October 1943, "To tell the country that everyone was to get a family allowance was sheer folly,"² but his conservative fiscal views were overcome the next year and the fusty prime minister grew to embrace the idea of raising the living standards for Canadians. The war had changed King and many Canadians, who now felt that citizens should not be left to drift and fend for themselves in a Hobbesian capitalist society that would grind out the workers and the weak.

The Liberals' cornerstone legislation, the baby bonus, would provide a guaranteed income to families—on a sliding scale by age, but consisting of around $7 per child per month. With the average wage of workers at around $120 a month, the baby bonus

A Dutch war bride with children, preparing to be reunited with her husband.
These babies, and millions more, would benefit from the baby bonus and
other forms of state intervention in the postwar years. Canadians had
sacrificed much for victory; now they deserved peace and prosperity.

was not insignificant; it might mean new clothing, fresh milk, and some additional vegetables for growing children. One of the advantages of the family allowance benefit was that Ottawa could give it and not interfere in, or even have to work with, the provinces. It was also an effective political platform on which to build for the coming election after the war. The Conservatives raged against it, but ineptly so, when they accused the Liberals of buying off Quebec because French-Canadian families often had many more children than Anglo families. King rightly saw a useful wedge issue with which to portray the Progressive Conservatives, as they had renamed themselves, as the old heartless party that had left Canada floundering in the early years of the Depression under Prime Minister R.B. Bennett.

The Liberals ran in the June 1945 election on the basis of their steady wartime leadership and their forward-thinking social programs, which included the baby bonus but also a limited form of unemployment insurance. Canadians wanted change; they wanted to know that their sacrifice in defeating Hitler would create a more equitable country. The electorate turned again to the wizened King, who never inspired but offered steadiness and safety. Canadians entered the war under the Liberals, won it under them, and now faced an uncertain peace with the same Liberals at the head of the country.

Some Canadians in uniform had been out of the country since 1939. Even those who arrived late in the war wanted to leave Europe once Germany was defeated. They missed their families and were tired of the annoying discipline of following orders and the heavy-handed punishments for the slightest offences. They worried, too, that if they did not get home quickly, they would lose out in the job hunt. The Department of Veterans Affairs—a new government department set up to care for the million veterans—stated publicly that the keenest desire of service personnel overseas was to get home as soon as possible. "Feeling their job was done," wrote veteran and administrator W.S. Woods, "they were anxious to rejoin their loved ones, and pick up the threads of Canadian life which had been interrupted by their service."[3] There was much unease about the future.

Industry in Canada petitioned the government to release skilled workers first, and to let the others come back gradually. But fairness prevailed. "First in, first out," was the only policy that made sense, with some exceptions made for married men or others in special categories, such as the badly wounded or those facing hardship with children or parents requiring care. A complex system of points based on time served overseas and other factors resulted in the first service personnel returning home shortly after victory in Europe, followed by tens of thousands each month that followed.[4]

Though Canada was not deeply involved in the war against Japan, about 8,000 Canadian personnel served in the Pacific theatre of war. Two squadrons flew supplies to the Allied armies in Burma, while fewer individuals were involved in Special Operations behind enemy lines, and an intelligence unit was stationed in Australia. But Canada's greatest worry in that region was for its roughly 1,500 prisoners who had been captured during the Hong Kong battle in December 1941 and who had spent the war in camps in Hong Kong and Japan, where they were beaten, starved, and tortured. After securing victory over the Germans, Canada was planning to contribute more forces to the American war effort against Japan. Thousands of

*Canadian service personnel waiting around for a series of
tests and interviews as part of the demobilization process.
A sign above them reads, "Back to Civvy Street."*

Canadians still based in Europe volunteered for service in the
Pacific, as they were promised a month of leave first in Canada.
Those who did so moved to the front of the line, enjoyed their
leave with loved ones, and were saved from the expedition to
East Asia when the war was ended by the dropping of two
atomic bombs on Japan. Hiroshima was levelled on August 6,
and, three days later, Nagasaki was shattered by a second atomic
blast.[5] Japan formally surrendered on August 14 and the Western
world celebrated the end of the war against Japan on August 15,
known as VJ Day.

By the time Japan surrendered, tens of thousands of Canadians
had already returned to "civvy street." With about 30,000 service
personnel coming home each month, most Canadians were back

in their communities by early summer of 1946. While most were anxious to reconnect with their loved ones, they also carried a heavy burden. They had left comrades and chums behind, buried or lost on battlefields around the world. The *Regina Leader-Post* said of the returning soldiers, "It means the end of one long march and the beginning of another. . . . The long trail which stretches behind them is strewn with memories; and the road ahead shines bright with hope."[6]

Servicemen who had been away from families for half a decade struggled to reconnect. They grieved parents who had died in their absence and wondered what had happened to family heirlooms that had disappeared. Though most of those who served were single, husbands and wives faced the challenge of reintegration. Not all families survived the strain. War is very much about loss and loneliness, and sexual infidelity had occurred overseas and at home.[7] Some couples made it work, finding ways to move past the hurt. Others could not. "My wife has changed," said one veteran. "Everything has changed."[8]

Newspaper advice columns offered a way forward. One woman who had been told her husband was killed had remarried, only to discover that her first husband was alive and returning home from a PoW camp.[9] In another case, a woman with four children whose husband had been killed during the war wrote to the *Windsor Star* for advice on remarrying. She felt agonizing guilt but wondered if "loyalty to the unknowing dead requires the sacrifice of the living."[10] The columnist told the widow to start living. Other widows never found a way to move past their bereavement.

After years of absence, it is not surprising that the divorce rate rose significantly from 1945 to 1947, as men damaged or savaged by war could not find their place in society or the family.[11] There were other challenges, too. A returning father could be a mystery to young children, who scurried for cover from the uniformed outsider who had arrived out of the blue. One man who was a child in 1945 recounted years later his uneasy relationship with his father who returned from the war, noting, "He always felt like a stranger [who] had come and taken over my life and my mother's house."[12] Having kept food on the table and the family afloat for years, a wife was not always willing to hand over all responsibility to a coarse man who returned with a dim view of the challenge of domestic life.

But most veterans were young and single. They went it alone in a country that had given them significant back pay upon their release. Ex-service personnel talked openly of being restless and unsure of the future, uneasy at parting with their best friends in uniform who had acted as a surrogate family, and the uncertainty of returning to a society that had moved on without them. Flush with money, men drank out of boredom, in a boozy search for comradery, and to forget.

Those who had waited at home through the war were filled with questions for the returning service personnel. Often the veterans could only respond with half answers, grunts, or avoidance. Many simply focused their accounts on the exotic places they had visited, good-hearted adventures, and other positive memories. Métis veteran Euclide Boyer recounted how he did not like to talk about the war, "especially with people who don't know anything about it. I find it much easier talking to a man who's been there; then we both know what the other guy is talking about."[13] Great silences intruded into families. The chasm between veteran and loved one was not easy to overcome. *The Legionary*—the Canadian Legion's magazine for members—warned veterans and those closest to them of the trials ahead: "Although the war has just recently ended, there are thousands of Canadian infantry men, whose only thoughts a few brief months ago were to kill or be killed, mingled with a homesick longing, who have taken civilian jobs and are trying hard to prove their worth and their stability. These men are not strange, queer, dangerous persons but boys who are more than a little sick of bloodshed, fear, privations."[14]

And yet not all men were broken and scarred; many—perhaps most—had had good wars. They were proud of their service, be it at one of the many fronts or far from the action. They had seen and done things that they never could have experienced if they had stayed in Canada. These Depression era kids had been to London, Paris, Rome, and other great cities. And the strangeness of the return was soon left behind, pushed to the past by the many joyful reunions resulting in a generation of postwar babies. The baby boom of 1945 to 1947 saw more than one million babies delivered, and that trend continued in the coming decade.[15] With new wealth, prosperity, and relative peace, millions of Canadians rapidly replaced—in cold statistics—those lost in the war. But the fallen were not forgotten. Their absence would be felt in Canada for decades to come, and indeed, is felt to this day.

Women had powered the war effort on the Canadian home front, with 1.2 million at work in industry. They had white- and blue-collar jobs, and were especially involved in building the weapons that won the war: warships, tanks, bombers, shells, cartridges. What was to become of these women as the men in uniform came home? Most lost their jobs to make way for those returning from the services. Women who had stepped up in the Necessary War were discarded rapidly, and with little acknowledgement of their accomplishments and even less concern for their well-being.

Some 50,000 women also served in uniform in the army, navy, and air force, and as nurses. During the Second World War, there was no full equality of opportunity, and women did not participate in active combat, but they played an important support role in bases and training areas. Some faced discrimination and had to ignore a nasty rumour campaign that women in uniform were somehow in it for the money or to engage in sexual promiscuity.[16]

Wartime poster for the Canadian Women's Army Corps, whose members served shoulder to shoulder with men in uniform.

Those ideas were firmly rebutted by the government, but they revealed just how destabilized some people felt as women broke gender barriers. Despite those hardships, most of the service women derived great satisfaction from playing a part in the Allied victory, and said so at the time and afterwards.

During the massive reduction of the military forces in 1945, the women's services were abolished. Few women desired to make a career in the military, although many stayed in touch through veterans' groups and periodic reunions. The demobilized service-women were also eligible for veterans' benefits. A higher propor-tion of women than men enrolled in the job training programs offered to veterans, but almost 85 percent chose traditional jobs and occupations, like nursing, hairdressing, and sales work, partly in response to the programs' inherent bias that urged them to pursue those careers. By 1946, about 16,000 ex-servicewomen were married and about 20,000 had jobs.[17] Yvonne Jukes of the RCAF's Women's Division recounted how she missed her friends when they were demobilized, but she took satisfaction from her role in the war, and felt that those in uniform, both men and women, had "a right to be proud of the part they played in defeat-ing the greatest evil the world has ever known."[18]

No one had gone to war in September 1939 thinking that Canada's involvement in the conflict might lead to a new, wealthier nation, but that is exactly what happened. Canada's GNP, at $5.6 billion in 1939, had risen to $11.8 billion by 1945.[19] Other economic indicators showed that buying power and household income also rose during and after the war. Jobs had been for the taking since 1940, when war production had allowed the country to shake off the last stultifying effects of the decade-long Great Depression. Buying power remained stable during the war, a result of Ottawa's revolutionary and successful freeze on wages and prices to contain inflation, but there were not a lot of consumer goods available for purchase, and a great deal of money had been saved. Canadians had also been encouraged to buy war bonds—which they did in staggering numbers, with over $10 billion raised for the war effort.[20] And now that the future looked brighter, Canadians began to spend. The great upswell of purchasing created new jobs, higher salaries, and a profitable cycle for many across society.

Ottawa wisely decreed that veterans would have a claim on their prewar jobs. But many had been out of work in 1939, and few war heroes yearned to return to stocking shelves or make-work manual labour projects. As one wounded combat veteran said after returning to his Alberta family farm, "I had been in London and Amsterdam. . . . I didn't come back to be a stupid farm boy!"[21] Civil servant jobs were opened up first to veterans, with temporary workers dismissed in favour of veterans who were given permanent positions.[22] The war had seen an expansion from 46,000 civil servants in 1939 to 116,000 in 1945, and an additional 26,730 veterans were hired by the end of 1946, including some 940 women.[23] Preference was given to those with overseas service, which, according to government reports, accounted for the lower number of women. The offer of civil service employment was an important step, but the opportunities were limited. More would have to be done for the veterans, and the government felt the need to intervene.

War provides many lessons, and one that had been learned from the Great War was the need to generously aid the returned service personnel. In 1919, as the country floundered in debt, the state understood its obligation to provide pensions to the wounded, but many veterans felt that they had not been adequately compensated for their long service and adversity.[24] Perhaps indicating the complexity of adequately caring for the veterans—and signalling the evolving government thinking in its responsibilities to its citizen-soldiers—in the twenty years after the Pension Act was passed in 1919, it was amended sixteen times.[25] A generation later, in late 1944, more serious planning was undertaken to help citizen-soldiers and service personnel make the transition back to civilian life. The King government had created a more interventionist state that was necessary to run the war, using an army of bureaucrats to impose regulations, higher taxation, and wage and price freezes. Canadians across the country worried that the wartime victory could be diminished if veterans came home to unemployment, strikes, and despair.

Politicians, civil servants, academics, and veterans from the Great War—represented most forcefully by the veterans who banded together to form the Canadian Legion—pushed King's cabinet to enact forward-thinking legislation for the newly returning veterans. "It is nothing less than a moral right," argued the Legion, "that a man who has served his country shall, as far as possible, be re-established in society."[26] Three new government departments were formed—Reconstruction, National Health and Welfare, and Veterans Affairs—with influential ministers at their helm. The war had cost $16 billion from 1939 to 1945, and billions more would be spent in the coming decades for veterans' benefits and support of dependents. But the government could afford to be generous to the women and men coming home, and so it enacted the Veterans Charter, which, like the American G.I. Bill of Rights, was a compendium of legislation aimed at helping veterans transition from war to peace. It was among the most influential set of acts and programs ever created in Canada.

The Charter included a clothing allowance of $100, which was useful since most men had bulked up in service and no longer fit their old clothes. Moreover, it offered a war-service gratuity that rewarded personnel with a tax-free bonus of $15 for every thirty days served outside the hemisphere, and half that sum for those who served on the home front. Prime Minister King had said of the payment that it represented "an attempt to recognize a service upon which no price can ever be placed." Monetary payment was both "an acknowledgment and an encouragement; an acknowledgment of burden borne and sacrifice endured; and an encouragement to the men and women who have voluntarily given their services, have survived the vicissitude of this, the most terrible war in world history."[27] Compensation came in other forms, too, and in total, a private who served overseas for two years and another in Canada would stand to leave the military with about $500. Much of the money went immediately back into the economy as veterans purchased goods to start a new life.

The administrators of the Veterans' Land Act, a component of the Veterans Charter, also offered low-interest loans for veterans to acquire land and equipment. Eventually, about 120,000 vets would receive a loan to purchase property, animals, and equipment for their existing farms, while another 33,000 acquired land.[28] This trend was a reminder that while Canada had become more urbanized, many men sought solitude and silence in the countryside after the cacophony and chaos of war.

Records show that another 6,902 veterans received loans to start a business. The Veterans Charter created many opportunities for ex-servicemen and -women, although not all veterans took advantage of them or even knew they existed, despite the government's promotional efforts. Some men, like conscripts, were excluded from many programs, while others, such as the Indigenous veterans, either were not told about the programs or were denied access by paternalistic "Indian agents," the federal government's representatives on the reserves. It would be decades before those veterans—and others, like the merchant mariners—would receive full veterans' rights. But while not all veterans benefitted from the Veterans Charter, most did, and there was, on the whole, equality under the legislation.

The civil servants in the new Department of Veterans Affairs were enthusiastic about training men and women for future professions; the programs were seen as a means of empowerment rather than as a hand-out from the state. The government paid for over 80,000 veterans to pursue vocational instruction; they could choose from among more than 100 different fields, and many would become plumbers, machinists, electricians, and the like. One slogan was "jobs for the fit—and fitting the unfit for jobs."[29] Almost all would be established in a profession or vocation, and the newly trained veterans added to the country's prosperity. Others turned their sights to higher learning. Before the war, attending university was a luxury that most working-class families could not afford, save for a gifted young man or, more rarely, a woman, who secured a scholarship. Wartime surveys of RCAF personnel found that a surprising 45 percent desired education or specialized training.[30] An astonishing 54,000 veterans—including 2,300 women—would eventually head towards the university classroom, forming about half the student body in Canada in the late 1940s. As one veteran remarked years later, with pride, "There were opportunities for everyone, such as the chance to go to any university or college in Canada. You didn't have to be the son of a banker to go to university. . . . There was an opportunity to better yourself."[31] Another education specialist observed that "a grateful country" sought to reward "a large number of students now released from the services, who would otherwise have had no such opportunity."[32]

Some of the veterans attended university with their new wives. Within weeks of landing on English soil at the beginning of the war, Canadian soldiers were marrying women, and they continued to do so over the next six years as half a million friendly Canuck invaders moved in among the British population. The army tried to discourage the practice, but it was a losing battle. The vast majority of the women were British, although there were some 1,886 Dutch war brides, followed by 650 Belgians and 100 French.[33] Love was easy during a time of war, with all its desperation and dreams, but there were difficult realities to be faced once the drama of war stopped and ordinary daily routines resumed.

When the war ended, the war brides (as they were called) prepared to leave behind their parents and siblings and make a new life in the northern dominion. Eventually, 44,886 war brides set off for a strange land, along with 21,358 children, the majority emigrating between August 1944 and the end of 1946. They did not travel with their husbands, and so most war brides banded together on the ships taking them across the Atlantic. Some realized during the week-long voyage that they had little idea—other than the name of the city, village, or hamlet—as to where their new homes were located. After arriving in Halifax, their train trip westward seemed to go on forever. Slowly the number of war brides dispersed, with tearful farewells and calls of good luck.

At the platforms and stations, sometimes a husband was there to welcome his wife; sometimes he had not yet come home and it was his parents greeting a daughter-in-law they had never met. One English war bride recounted that she had not seen her husband for several years and had no photograph; she did not recognize him when he hailed her in Winnipeg, out of uniform and looking altogether dissimilar after passing through the trials of combat. "He was a different man from the one who had courted me, and we were very strange with each other, at first."[34]

The brides left behind the dreariness of Britain or the wreckage of Western Europe to make a new life in Canada. A surprising number of marriages survived the test of war and peace. Later in the century, some of the war brides would seek each other out, and many stayed in touch via mail. There were occasional encounters at clubs, stores, or within the community. History books would be written about these women's amazingly hard journeys to establish a new life—at first oral histories to capture their experiences, then, later, more detailed studies.[35] In the twenty-first century, hundreds of thousands of Canadians have a direct link to these wartime marriages, and they are a living legacy for the modern Canada.

The war brought other legacies. One significant issue was that the many returning soldiers and their families needed homes. During the war, there had been a well-publicized struggle to secure lodging in the large cities, but most young people were willing to share flats, with two to a bed and sleeping in shifts not uncommon. But after the war, the heroes from overseas felt angry and embarrassed that, despite having served their country and now enjoying full bank accounts, they could not find suitable homes. A year after the end of hostilities, 400,000 housing units were still needed.[36]

The Legion created housing committees in communities across the country and pressed all levels of government to engage in a sustained home building program.[37] The "deplorable" situation, in the words of General C.B. Price, Dominion President of the Legion, had left veterans "discouraged and demoralized."[38] In 1946, Ottawa responded by creating the Central Mortgage and Housing Corporation, now the Canada Mortgage and Housing Corporation. The National Housing Act was to be administered by the new Crown corporation, and $275 million was earmarked to build tens of thousands of houses, including new suburbs across the country. The program was a symbol of the country's new wealth that allowed more of its citizens to own homes—an unexpected legacy of the war.

There was a significant housing shortage in Canada after the war and one of the enduring wartime legacies was the building of new communities for veterans, their families, and other Canadians.

The wartime government had imposed new taxes on individuals and businesses, with most of the profits from the latter returned to the state. These high taxes were necessary to finance the war effort, but the postwar federal government wanted to retain them to help fund the emerging welfare state.[39] The British North America Act delineated federal and provincial powers in the Constitution and made it difficult for the federal government to influence matters of education and health, but Ottawa set itself to solving the tax question. A number of royal commissions over the years had argued that Ottawa needed to reform the Constitution for taxation purposes, but this move was fiercely opposed by provincial premiers guarding their powers. At the first meetings to discuss the tax revolution, there was blood on the carpet—most of it King's—but the old leader had grown used to losing battles while winning the war. He faced down Ontario and Quebec, with their intransigent premiers—Progressive Conservative George Drew in Toronto and the Union Nationale's Maurice Duplessis in Quebec City—and he eventually beat them, allowing the federal government to control direct taxation and redistribute funds back to the provinces. Ottawa secured the victory by dangling comprehensive national social security programs to care for the sick, the elderly, and some of the unemployed. The language of the war years—emphasizing the need to mobilize society and strain against injustice—was often used in this new fight to ensure fairness for all Canadians, not just those living in wealthy provinces.

As government transformed basic societal structures, organized labour also sought new rights. Labour unions had been strengthened during the war when worker shortages occurred as a million men went into uniform. Working-class men and women understood that they were called upon to support the Canadian industrial war machine that would help defeat the Nazis. And yet wages were often stingy. As the long war dragged on, labour was increasingly alienated, and the number of strikes increased to more than 400 in 1943. The government was forced to compromise because it desperately needed to ensure a continuous flow of raw material and finished weapons of war. In February 1944, Ottawa sat down with labour leaders and agreed to collective bargaining. It was a huge win for labour when workers were guaranteed the right to form unions. Other foundational aspects were established, too, such as defining unfair labour practices and the right to strike.[40] Recognizing that organized labour deserved more rights was a revolutionary concession by those holding the power, even though there were many more battles to be fought by the working class. The laws, the state, and the courts were still weighted against labourers, but the war resulted in a seismic change in labour rights.

Canadians in uniform exchanged their rifles for riveting guns and hammers, achieving another kind of victory. The country's economy improved as veterans returned to industry, as wartime savings fuelled purchases, and as new housing was built. But Canada faced other challenges as cheap American products poured across the border to be snatched up by eager Canadians. It was good for consumers, but the country experienced a shocking trade deficit with the United States. As a result of Britain's weakness in the aftermath of the war, especially because of its nearly depleted gold reserves and its reliance on American aid, the United States' undeniable strength was drawing Canada into its orbit.[41] During the war, King had successfully staved off economic disaster by appealing to his friend Franklin Roosevelt for a trade deal in which the Americans bought Canadian war goods to counter imbalances and trade deficits. The Hyde Park Declaration of April 20, 1941, announced an agreement between the two countries, which meant that North American manufacturing, especially the aircraft and shipbuilding industries, became integrated in the production of war goods as natural resources easily passed back and forth over the border. As a result, Canada's industries vastly expanded during the war and became increasingly tied to the North American economy.

Canadians and Americans had fought and died together to defend the western hemisphere. Canadians warships protected the east coast of the United States, especially as the Americans reduced their navy presence from early 1942 to build up the Pacific force. Long-range bombers from both air forces protected the convoys, which contained American and Canadian merchant seamen. Canadian soldiers took part in the Kiska campaign in late 1943 to drive the Japanese from the Aleutian Islands off the Alaskan coast. In turn, Americans served in Canadian forces overseas, with many enlisting before December 1941 when the United States was neutral. Canada's wartime fear of enemy invasion and the nations' shared wartime economy had bound the country more firmly to the United States, an absolute necessity during the war but a bond that had far-ranging consequences.

This North American mindset was no easy thing to reverse, and Canadian politicians were worried about US industry dominating and destroying domestic factories. The solution came from the Americans, who had been thrust into the role of defender of the Western world because of Britain's weakness and the Soviet Union's aggression. To stave off Communist insurgencies in Western Europe—while acknowledging that Eastern Europe was lost to Stalin—Washington poured billions of dollars in aid money into the ruined economies. The Marshall Plan, named after the

US general and secretary of state, eventually dispersed $18 billion to war-shattered Western Europe. The Americans allowed Canada to contribute to the Marshall Plan with wheat and industrial products, and let Europeans use aid money to purchase Canadian goods, all of which stimulated the economy in the form of $1 billion in sales. Canada's economy expanded during the troubled period of reconstruction, rising from $11.8 billion GNP in 1945 to $18.4 billion in 1950.[42]

With the British colonial empire collapsing as the bankrupt island kingdom abandoned India, Pakistan, Burma, Ceylon, and its other territories, it was only the United States that could stand against the new Soviet threat. And yet English Canada's heart remained with the gutted and no-longer-Great Britain when the former motherland turned to Canada for financial assistance. King's government pondered its response to London's request—really a plea—for a loan to keep its economy afloat. Some of the Canadian ministers harrumphed, feeling that London had not always been kind to Ottawa during the war; it had haggled over paying for the British Commonwealth Air Training Plan, opposed Canadian representation on certain strategic boards, and generally taken the Dominion for granted. But King knew that English Canadians would want to make the loan, and so did he. The cabinet agreed to a low-interest loan to Britain of $1.25 billion—more than one tenth of Canada's gross national product. This was in addition to the more than $2 billion in munitions and food that Canada had sent to Britain during the war under the Mutual Aid Program, as well as the cost of the British Commonwealth Air Training Plan, most of which Canada had swallowed.[43] Some complained that the country was beggaring itself to aid Britain, but the ties of blood and history remained strong, even if Canada was now more deeply linked economically with the United States. The billions of dollars in loans also illustrated how the war had remade Canada into a wealthy middle power.

Increasingly urbanized, industrial, and wealthy, Canada was set on a new trajectory as a North American nation. As most veterans moved on with their postwar lives, thousands of other veterans would have no easy re-entry into Canadian society. Some 55,000 Canadians had been wounded during the war, and an unknown additional number would suffer from invisible, mental wounds. Medical treatment was provided for injured personnel, and by October 1946, some 13,020 veterans were patients in long-term care facilities, with the Department of Veterans Affairs operating forty-four hospitals, homes, and wings of hospitals across the country.[44] In addition, there was about the same number of badly disabled veterans, with internal injuries and blindness, and many needing multiple operations and care that stretched for years. Some 2,000 ex-servicemen suffered amputations, and in the postwar years their stumps were fitted and refitted for prosthetic limbs, as newer, more comfortable, and more flexible models became available.[45] Men learned to walk with new legs or to work without a hand. Those who lost an eye realized that the vision in the other one often also dimmed over time. The Canadian National Institute for the Blind and the Sir Arthur Pearson Association of War Blinded played a heroic role in retraining blinded veterans.[46]

Many of the mentally wounded recovered with rest and rehabilitation, but often those with serious psychiatric issues were cut off from society. They were shuttered in isolated hospitals, sometimes with the Great War veterans who had never escaped the ghastly legacy of their own war. One distressed father, Charles S. Napier of Stratford, Ontario—whose son was shuttered away in a hospital—lamented the horrible "prison-like wards, with barred windows and locked doors" and grey-skinned patients from both wars who act "practically like dead men."[47] Many more veterans were untreated for what we now call post-traumatic stress disorder. The nation's newspapers occasionally reported on veterans' suicides. Leslie Crocker, a thirty-two-year-old veteran who served four years in the forces, shot his wife after an argument and then turned the shotgun on himself.[48] She survived; he did not. As the veterans were no longer part of the military system, the Canadian military could not track these suicides, and it is unclear how many veterans ended their lives in the immediate postwar years or decades later. Many veterans dealt with their psychological wounds by trying to drown them with alcohol, but the memories and nightmares would periodically rise to the surface to stalk survivors.

Pensions were provided for the badly wounded. But as with those who served in the Great War, the veterans had to register their injuries as they were leaving the services. Many of these tough men were used to dealing with their pain in silence and had refused to delay their demobilization after the war to seek proper treatment overseas. They limped back to a wife or a job. But over time, as blown-out knees, crippled backs, the lingering effects of metal passing through flesh, or the steel that veterans carried in their bodies from shrapnel, shell, and bullet wounds resurfaced—literally pushing through the skin—they turned to the state for pensions. The Department of Veterans Affairs had the difficult job of assessing the men, and occasionally women, ultimately deciding if they qualified for a pension and then how much they should receive. The Great War had revealed that even a decade after the armistice, many who

*The transition from serving Canada in uniform to becoming
a civilian was much anticipated by men and women. While that
transition came with tremendous challenges, these million Canadians
would forever be known as veterans.*

had worn the uniform came forward with new or lingering injuries
exacerbated by age or lack of medical care. The same occurred after
1945. Meanwhile, there were special cases of service personnel,
especially the Hong Kong veterans who had been tortured and
starved in the Japanese prisoner-of-war camps, whose ailments
proved unconventional and difficult to treat. The Veterans Affairs
officials were often strict, remaining unmoved by these complicated
cases, so that too many suffering men were denied benefits. That
said, from 1945 to 1948 the federal government spent $1.6 billion
on veterans' programs, with billions more dispensed during the
next few decades.[49] While the Second World War veterans were
treated more generously than their fathers and uncles who returned

from the Great War, the fight for better pensions and more aid did not stop. The veterans would engage in a prolonged battle that continues to this day and that likely will continue until the last warriors are gone from this earth.

"The many thousands of service men, in all branches, now pouring off steamers cannot possibly be quite the same individuals as they were when they left Canada," warned *Saturday Night* magazine in the fall of 1945.[50] All men carried ghosts of the departed, and most learned to live with them. May Croft-Preston of New Westminster, British Columbia, wrote to *The Legionary*, which published her letter in March 1946, "Our boys are returning home and thousands of them are sick and tired of that ugliest thing in the world—war!" But those who fought for freedom, argued Croft-Preston, had been affected by the war. "We must learn to understand these boys, many of whom return perhaps gloomy, contemplative, irritable at times and difficult to understand. It will take time, readjustment and reabsorption into civilian and social routine, but if they are loved and understood and properly taken care of by us, for whom they have done so much to save us from nameless horrors, most of them will recover and recapture all the old joys of their pre-war lives."[51] Indeed, they needed love and understanding, and the burden often fell to their families.

David McIntosh, a decorated wartime RCAF navigator in No. 418 Squadron, was just one of many veterans who struggled to find his place in the new Canada. He felt guilty about having survived while so many of his comrades were denied the gift of a future. McIntosh ran into the father of his friend John, who was killed in action. The grieving father was looking for answers to an impossible question: "'Why isn't John here instead of you?' 'I was just lucky, I guess,' I said, fidgeting with my cap. 'Why should you have the luck and not John?'"[52]

And yet many understood that the next war—waged at the personal level and after the uniform was put away—was a fight to move on, to stride forward, and to find solace in the new Canada. The survivors knew they had defeated the evil regime of the Third Reich and had earned their peace dividend. Many felt the need to create a better, more equitable society. They had survived while so many comrades had not. They would not waste their lives. But they would always be a breed apart. Mavericks and misfits, heroes and winners—they were united by the uniform, bound by their service. They would forever be known as veterans.

CHAPTER 3

THE FALLEN

C anada's memorial landscape was forever changed by the
Great War. Some 61,000 Canadians were killed in action,
died of wounds, or succumbed to illness between 1914 and 1918,
and another 5,000 died in the next three years from accidents,
suicide, lingering injuries, the pandemic flu of 1918–1919, and
other diseases. Amid this raw postwar sorrow, almost every city,
town, and village established committees to raise funds, select a
sculptor or architect, and erect a monument to the fallen.[1] These
memorials usually occupied a place of pride at the centre of a town
or near a city hall. By the end of the 1920s, they numbered several
thousand across the country. Even though millions of citizens on
the home front had worked in factories or farms, thereby contributing to victory in the total war, the monuments were devoted to
those who served in uniform, and were often only for those who
had died. The unprecedented nature of the sacrifice demanded
unique treatment of the dead.

Britain and the dominions agreed that no bodies would be
returned from the battlefields or overseas training areas—but the
dead could not be left unattended. The Canadian government
agreed to participate in and to financially support the Imperial War

Graves Commission, which was established in 1917 to care for the dead in thousands of cemeteries around the world.[2] The memorials in Canada were therefore cenotaphs—empty tombs that represented the absent bodies. The monuments, which ranged in size, shape, and grandeur, usually displayed a list of names accompanied by short inscriptions to mark glory, loss, and sometimes the major battles, such as the Somme, Vimy, and Amiens.[3]

Many other forms of commemorative icons took shape beginning in the 1920s, from gardens to stained glass windows, and from plaques displayed by businesses to school tablets listing

Canada's Brooding Soldier monument in Belgium marks the Battle of Second Ypres in April 1915. It is among the most evocative of the many memorials overseas and in Canada to memorialize the service and loss of Canadians in the Great War.

those "old boys" who served and fell in service. Streets, parks, and geographical sites were named after war heroes. War trophies had returned from overseas, too, with captured German artillery pieces and machine guns standing as symbols of victory.[4] Those monuments, in their many forms, ensured that the Great War would not easily be forgotten. Reflecting the grief of hollowed-out communities, they acted as haunting reminders of dreams shattered and lives lost.

This anguish was reinforced by prominent death symbols like the poppy and by the observance, starting in 1919, of two minutes of silence across the country on Armistice Day, renamed as Remembrance Day in 1931. The Great War also created powerful legacy words. The appellation "Great" underscored the war's massive and shocking nature. The phrases "To our Glorious Dead" and "Lest We Forget" came to be associated with the graves and cemeteries of the fallen. "The passing of the torch" and the promise that we "Will remember them at the going down of the sun, and in the morning" were recited like prayers. Canada's most prominent Great War memorial overseas was unveiled in July 1936 on Vimy Ridge. Walter Allward's striking limestone monument invited visitors to stare out over the Douai Plain; it was a towering beacon on a ridge that would be forever Canadian. On the monument are the engraved names of 11,285 Canadians who died with no known graves in France, this inscription serving as a moving act of reclamation. Twenty allegorical figures, including those on the two pylons that jutted skyward and represented Canada and France, added new layers of meaning. At the monument's emotional core is "Mother Canada," officially known as *Canada Bereft*, who stands, head bowed, mourning her sons in the empty cenotaph below her.[5] The Vimy monument, seemingly un-Canadian in its size and splendour, would draw generations of pilgrims seeking to honour the nation's Great War dead.

In the heart of Ottawa, the war was also represented at Canada's seat of democracy. The Peace Tower, initially known as the Peace and Victory Tower, emerged in 1927 from the ashes of the Parliament Buildings, which had burned down in 1916. The tower was the architecturally dominant element of Parliament, and it enclosed the Memorial Chamber, a sacred space built to commemorate those killed in the Great War. In an ornately decorated room, graced with stained glass windows and an altar, the story of Canada's war effort is told in carvings.[6] Atop the altar, in the centre of the room, rests the Book of Remembrance, containing the names of Canada's staggering number of war dead.

In the aftermath of the Second World War, with Canada's landscape both geographically and imaginatively populated by the Great War monuments, memorials, and gardens, what was to be done to mark this more recent war's dead? Would Canadians build thousands of new monuments? There would be a fierce debate across the country over how to honour the fallen of the Necessary War.

Canada paid a high price for the Allied victory against fascism in the Second World War. The nation's largest service, the army, suffered the most fatalities, with 22,917 dead. Another 18,517 were killed while serving in the Royal Canadian Air Force, the majority of them in Bomber Command. Meanwhile, 1,990 sailors were lost while serving in the Royal Canadian Navy.[7] An additional 1,629 Canadian and Newfoundland mariners of the Merchant Navy, the "fourth arm" of the military, as they were called during the war, were slain during their crucial mission of running supplies in convoys or in other naval disasters. Decades of struggle followed before the merchant mariners were finally deemed veterans—a fight recounted later in this book. In the twenty-first century, the Government of Canada's official statistics state that Canada lost 45,000 killed in the Second World War.

But this loss, though huge, paled in comparison to the devastation suffered by other major nations, with the war's overall toll estimated at some 60 million combatants and civilians. The United States' claim of 418,000 deaths and Britain's 449,000 killed were low numbers in comparison to Germany's 6.9 million dead, of whom 5.3 million were combatants.[8] The Soviet Union, which bore the brunt of the German war machine in the vicious battles of the Eastern Front, suffered some 27 million dead, the majority of them non-combatants. The high number of civilian deaths accentuated the inhumane nature of the fighting on the Eastern Front and the regularity with which civilians were targeted and

A wounded Canadian infantryman being cared for on the Normandy battlefield. Canada paid a terrible price in the Necessary War.

killed by the German forces. Any country that had enemy armies fighting on its own soil also saw crushing losses to the civilian population. China, whose war against Japan started in 1937, is thought to have lost 15 million, including millions of civilians starved or slaughtered [9]

Canada was lucky to escape with its comparatively low number of losses, but there remained thousands of widows and orphans in the country, along with many more grieving parents, grandparents, and extended family. For them, the war against fascism resonated in different ways than it did for those who had served and come home. The memory of the war would always be steeped in terrible grief. The bereaved mothers were issued the Memorial Cross (often known as the Silver Cross), following the Great War tradition of acknowledging a mother whose son had been killed overseas. [10]

But although it mourned those it had lost in the Necessary War, Canadian society did not remember the struggle through the prism of death, as it did with the Great War. While the losses in families never faded, the country did not long dwell on the carnage. This had been a great crusade against fascism—an idea cemented by how the war ended, with Canadians as the liberators of the Dutch and the revelation of the Nazi concentration camps. The Canadian deaths weighed heavily on some in the immediate postwar years, but they did not destabilize the nation. Instead, the country moved forward and refused to dwell on the past.

Just as in the aftermath of the Great War, the authorities in 1945 worried over the challenges of moving the huge number of dead, some many years in the ground, buried in mass graves and in

locations spread around the world.[11] Ottawa journalist Douglas
How broke the story in October 1945—an announcement issued
simultaneously in Britain and all the dominions—that "no bodies
would be brought home from Europe for the same reasons that those
of their fathers were not brought home after the war."[12] With that
decision made, there were many new cemeteries to be built overseas.
And the global nature of the war meant that there would be Canadians
buried from Jamaica to the Baltic, from the Middle East to East Asia,
from Iceland to Ceylon, in tropical jungles and on mountains, in
farmers' fields and along waterways. However, most of the slain lay
in Italy and Northwest Europe, the main battlegrounds for the
Canadian forces, as well as in Britain, where many wounded succumbed to their injuries and were buried.

Canada's dead were usually buried close to the battlefields
where they fell. In one unique case, a trooper had been cremated in
a fiery tank explosion while fighting near Falaise in August 1944,
and his ashes were returned to Canada before Ottawa decided that
all the fallen should be left overseas; the urn and ashes were brought
back to Bretteville-sur-Laize cemetery and reburied.[13] Officiating at
the ceremony was Major the Reverend J.W. Foote, who had been
awarded the Victoria Cross at Dieppe for choosing to stay behind
during the withdrawal to minister to the wounded on the beach and
later in prison-of-war camps. One commentator observed of the
ceremony that the Canadian soldier's ashes would be buried at "the
scene of his supreme sacrifice."[14]

The terrible fighting conditions of the Great War, with the
glutinous mud and the annihilating shellfire, left over 18,000
Canadians with no known grave because their bodies were lost or
blown out of existence. The missing of the Great War left a haunting legacy, but the Second World War losses seemed to register less

in the public consciousness. Within the British Commonwealth, a staggering 226,000 troops had gone missing from 1939 to 1945, a number that included 8,063 Canadians.[15] With enormous Great War memorials already situated on the Western Front—Thiepval, Vimy, Tyne Cot Cemetery, and the Menin Gate—and many other national memorials to the Australians, New Zealanders, Indians, Canadians, and other dominion soldiers (not to mention those commemorating the French, Belgians, and Americans), the British Commonwealth nations decided that they would not build separate national monuments for the missing of the Second World War.

Instead, the names of the missing Canadians were inscribed on Commonwealth memorials around the world, although primarily on five memorials—the Bayeux Memorial in Normandy; the Groesbeek Memorial in the Netherlands; the Cassino Memorial in Italy; the Brookwood 1939–1945 Memorial in Surrey, England; and the Air Forces Memorial at Runnymede, also in England. The Canadians would be listed with their Allied comrades. In November 1967, a solely Canadian memorial was erected in Halifax, dedicated to the 3,141 Canadian and Newfoundland sailors and soldiers from the two world wars, some of whom were formerly commemorated on an older memorial standing on Citadel Hill. The globe-shaped memorial in the nation's capital, known as the Ottawa Memorial, remembers the 798 men and women who died in Canada while serving or training for the air war. Finally, Canadian names are also inscribed on Commonwealth monuments around the world in smaller numbers, with, for example, 213 airmen named on the stone panels of the El Alamein Memorial in Egypt, 191 missing Canadians' names inscribed on the Singapore Memorial in the Pacific theatre of war, and 51 Canadians among the 26,875 names of Commonwealth missing on the Rangoon

Memorial erected to those who fought in the jungle campaign in Burma or those who flew supplies to them.

Given that Canadians had served, fought, and died around the world, there was no sensible way to build separate national memorials. However, the lack of a centralized memorial would come to affect the nation's memory of the war. With no separate national monuments being erected to commemorate the many Canadian Second World War victories, and with the Canadian missing grouped with other Commonwealth nations, there was more absence than presence in the country's memorial landscape. Lacking a unifying symbol like Vimy—impossible for this war because of the global nature of the fighting—it became difficult over time to focus on a single region or victory to use as an anchor for the Canadian story.

Though the missing were to be accounted for on the Commonwealth memorials, cemetery construction began shortly after the war as body reclamation units scoured the many battle grounds, seeking out the fallen. Sometimes the dead were clumped in small groups under a temporary cross slung with a helmet; other times they were alone, along a road or near a farm-house where a civilian had buried them. The location was marked as the body was exhumed. Identifying information on a grave was checked against identification of the remains. Some bodies had no markings or identifiers to use in determining a soldier's name, but most did, often a paybook, identification tags, or even letters from home.

"We don't expect to find more than half of the total number of missing," claimed Group Captain Roger Burges, the senior British officer charged with locating 40,000 British Empire missing airmen, in January 1947. Burges would deploy 440 men, criss-crossing the world but focusing on Europe, to work with local authorities in searching for the graves. "We don't wish any parents or wives to be misled into thinking that their sons or husbands are wandering through Europe with lost memories."[16] He was responding to the powerful myths that emerged during and after the Great War, and which loved ones grasped onto, that suggested a missing son or father was not dead but simply an amnesiac in a hospital or an unidentified prisoner in a PoW camp. Some families spent years walking Europe, searching for a missing soldier whom they hoped was alive. Burges wanted to avoid giving these desperate loved ones false hope, although his dedicated men found about a quarter of the missing from the flying services within a year of the end of the war.

"Where feasible," reported *The Legionary* in November 1946, "it has been the policy of the RCAF to exhume bodies of Canadian airmen, especially from graves in enemy lands, and reinter them in the new Canadian cemeteries. However, it also is RCAF policy

Canada's fallen service personnel were buried around the world.
This is the Groesbeek Canadian War Cemetery in the Netherlands,
where 2,331 Canadians forever rest.

not to break up flying crews by removing the bodies of the Canadian airmen from the company of the British or other allied airmen with whom they flew and died."[17] The RCAF members were often left where they fell, even in Germany and East Asia. There are over 500 Canadian airmen buried in the 3-hectare Berlin 1939–1945 War Cemetery, along with more than 3,000 Allied service personnel, most of them aircrew who crashed after being shot down during the bombing campaign. Several hundred additional Canadians lay in the German centres of Hanover, Hamburg, Kiel, and Soltau. In Malta, local residents made a public pledge in September 1945 to care for the more than thirty graves of Canadian airmen who were downed in the defence of that island fortress.[18] In Britain, often near the RCAF air bases, there are many cemeteries, including Harrogate (Stonefall) Cemetery in West Riding, where most of the 666 Canadian airmen who are buried flew in No. 6 Group Bomber Command squadrons. The assaults against the German war infrastructure, the smashing of cities, and the struggle for mastery over the skies of Europe came at a heavy cost.

The army's dead were also spread across the world, and Canadian newspapers tracked the stories of the Imperial War Graves Commission and its impressive work cultivating what one paper called the "Gardens of the Dead."[19] There were eleven new "all-Canadian cemeteries" erected after the war, in which the majority of those buried came from Canada.[20] One of the first was the Dieppe Canadian War Cemetery, finished in 1949. After the failed Dieppe raid in August 1942, the Germans had moved the Canadian slain from the beaches and buried them about 4 kilometres inland. Should they be left there, wondered the commission members, or moved to a new cemetery, to be reinterred by Allied hands? As the bodies had been laid out with respect, it was decided to keep the fallen where they were first buried. There are 765 graves at that site, of whom 582 are Canadian soldiers, sailors, and airmen. Most of the Canadians killed at Dieppe lie here, including the dead who never made it off the landing crafts, the stalwart sailors who carried them in, those who died on the beach, and those who fought into the town. Of the raid's total 907 dead, the others are buried in different sites, having succumbed to their injuries in prisoner-of-war camps, or in Britain, where an incurable wound or an infection ended their lives.

Some 2,043 Canadians lie buried at Bény-sur-Mer Canadian War Cemetery near Juno Beach, a bloody portal to battle and liberation. Most of the dead were from the 3rd Canadian Division, which had landed and fought so tenaciously for the beaches and then held the beach-head against enemy counterattacks. Twelve pairs of brothers lie in that cemetery. The Westlake family of Toronto lost one son on June 7, and then two more boys within the week; all are buried at Bény-sur-Mer.[21] Further inland, Canadian cemeteries and memorials bearing Canadian soldiers' names follow the path of the Allied armies as they liberated Europe.

There are too many cemeteries to name, but the many sites of loss and sorrow attest to the terrible combat during the Battle of Scheldt in October and November 1944, during the drive to the German borders in February and March 1945, and during the final campaign to free the Dutch. Near Nijmegen, 2,331 Canadians lie beneath the maple leaf at Groesbeek Canadian War Cemetery, a poignant symbol for all time of the cost of liberating the Dutch. The First Canadian Army fought its way into Germany during the immense offensives through the Rhineland, but army commander General Harry Crerar ordered that no Canadian army dead would be left buried on German soil. After the war, those killed in the last

The Dieppe Canadian War Cemetery where 582 Canadians are buried,
almost all killed during the August 19, 1942 operation.

six weeks of fighting, numbering at least 1,482, were disinterred and moved to Groesbeek or Holten cemeteries in the Netherlands.[22]

Thousands of other Canadians lie in Italy and Hong Kong.[23] Lotta Dempsey made the arduous trip to Italy to see the grave of her husband in the fall of 1955. "As one leaves the cemetery to return to Ravenna and then back home to Canada, the thought comes—is it wise that our sons' and husbands' graves should lie in this foreign land?" she pondered. "Then one remembers that side by side are buried comrades from all over Canada, related to each other in that they were mates in the supreme sacrifice, that their last weeks and months were spent together and they had grown into a unit. So, on reflection, it seems better to think of them there together—peaceful in beautiful surroundings."[24]

Leaving the Canadian fallen to rest together forever was a powerful idea, but the multiplicity of cemeteries and their location around the world also ensured that none would act as a single focal point of remembrance. Over time, key battles at Dieppe, Ortona, and Juno Beach would take on special significance and be singled out as Canadian sites of memory, especially as the cemeteries gave power to those places, but none would equal Vimy's impact as an anchor for the Great War's memorial landscape overseas.

At least 559 cemeteries and 36 new memorials were erected for the Commonwealth fallen of the Second World War, with most construction finished by the mid-1950s. In addition to paying a

A sculptor of the Imperial War Graves Commission
carving a Canadian headstone.

share of the costs, Canada had sent thousands of trees to line many of the cemeteries, especially red, sugar, and white maples.[25] The Canadian known dead lay buried under the headstones of Portland stone, carved to a uniform length and slightly curved at the top to better withstand the harsh weather.[26] Some thought the stone should be a cross, but not all who had served in the forces were Christian. The shaped stone also allowed for more symbolic designs and writing, and a crest of a maple leaf was displayed for Canadians and a caribou for Newfoundlanders. Name, regimental number, rank, decorations, unit, and birthdate were included, along with date of death, when known. Simply finding the stone for hundreds of thousands of slain service personnel, then cutting the stones to size and inscribing them with the proper information was a daunting task. In 1946, it was expected to take fifteen years to produce the 350,000 headstones for the new Imperial War Graves Commission cemeteries, but the commission had become more efficient, and new tooling machines sped up the work.[27]

One of the most heartrending tasks for the next of kin was choosing or composing a short epitaph, limited to sixty-six characters, for their relative's headstone. While including this personalized inscription would slow the production, it was deemed necessary and was in keeping with the Great War tradition.[28] Grieving families turned to scripture, poetry, and slogans in an attempt to capture a loved one's spirit, and many of the epitaphs were agonizingly raw.

"TO THE WORLD HE WAS JUST ANOTHER ONE. TO US, HE
WAS OUR DARLING SON."
Private Lawrence Burton Perkins, SDGH, 7.6.44 (age 26)

"SOMETIME WE'LL UNDERSTAND. ALWAYS REMEMBERED
BY WIFE AND FOUR CHILDREN."
Sergeant Murray Louis Burns, RCA, 5.8.44 (age 31)

"HE WENT FREELY TO FIGHT BESIDE OTHER FREE MEN
FOR THE FREEDOM OF US ALL."
Trooper Hugh Hjalmar Michael Lismore,
1st Hussars, 6.6.44 (age 21)

This was mourning in stone.

Canadians killed in the Second World War are buried in more than seventy countries, although largely in Western Europe and Canada.[29] There are no cemeteries at sea. Sailors in uniform and merchant mariners told stories of harrowing escapes from torpedoed ships and of floating in small lifeboats for weeks in the harsh Atlantic, praying for rescue. But when vessels went down, sailors were often swallowed by the depths. And yet not all bodies were lost. When the Royal Canadian Navy Tribal Class Destroyer HMCS *Athabaskan* engaged in a fierce surface battle along with its sister ship HMCS *Haida* against German destroyers along the coast of France on April 29, 1944, it was torpedoed, even as two German destroyers were pounded into submission and driven aground. The night battle was fought under flares, fires, and punishing naval shell strikes, and it left *Athabaskan* burning brightly in the water. Finally, the ship shattered as a series of explosions took it down. *Haida* risked being sunk by the U-boat sharks that closed in on the battle. Thirty-eight sailors were pulled aboard, but in a gut-wrenching decision, *Haida*'s captain, Lieutenant-Commander Harry DeWolf, had to turn the vessel away, even as Canadians were left in the freezing, oil-slick sea. DeWolf had been urged on by his friend, Lieutenant-Commander

John Stubbs, captain of *Athabaskan*, who called out from the water, "Get away, *Haida*, get clear," even as the other ship's escape sealed his doom. Some of *Athabaskan*'s sailors were taken prisoner by German boats, but fifty-nine lifeless bodies washed ashore and were buried in a coastal plot of Plouescat Communal Cemetery, 25 kilometres northeast of Brest.

In 1924, a memorial was erected on Halifax's Citadel Hill to the 415 sailors lost at sea in the Great War, and in 1955 an additional 2,852 names of sailors—both those in uniform with the Royal Canadian Navy and the merchant mariners—were added to it. But lashed by the Maritime storms that blew in off the Atlantic, the memorial gradually deteriorated. Over a decade later, in November 1967, the Halifax Memorial was built by the Commonwealth War Graves Commission (as the IWGC was renamed in 1960) and the Government of Canada to commemorate some 3,141 Canadian and Newfoundland sailors, soldiers, and nurses who lost their lives at sea in the First and Second World Wars but who had no known graves. A great Cross of Sacrifice, 12 metres high, emerges from a granite base that bears the names of the missing on bronze panels. The

HMCS Haida: *warship, memorial, and museum.*

original panels from the Citadel Hill memorial, upon which the names of the dead had been inscribed, were consigned to the sea.[30] The inscription on the Halifax Memorial reads: "THEIR GRAVES ARE UNKNOWN BUT THEIR MEMORY SHALL ENDURE."

Another means of honouring Canada's naval contribution in the Second World War is the observance, each year on the first Sunday in May, of the Battle of the Atlantic Day, marked with national and local ceremonies. And as of 2003, Merchant Navy Remembrance Day has been observed each year on September 3 to recognize the first loss of SS *Athenia* and the start of the Battle of the Atlantic, the longest campaign of the Second World War in which the Merchant Navy played a key part. At the same time, with so few naval cemeteries, naval vessels hold a special place as memorials for naval crew. In 1964, after the government announced it would be scrapped, the 115-metre *Haida* was saved by a group of concerned citizens and towed to Toronto, where it was restored and opened to the public the next year. In 2002, *Haida* was moved to Hamilton, where the warship is a memorial, museum, and National Historic Site. Now located at Pier 9 near Bayfront Park in Hamilton, Ontario, *Haida* was one of Canada's twenty-seven Tribal class Second World War destroyers, and is the only one still in existence.

The decision having been made to leave Canada's dead overseas, a fierce debate arose in 1945 over how to mark the country's 45,000 fallen on home soil. In the 1920s, most communities erected memorials to the Great War dead, with several thousand eventually standing as silent witnesses across the country. Grieving communities wondered, should they engage in a new series of monument building? This seemed impractical, and so the majority decided against it. The names of the Second World War dead were instead inscribed on the existing war monuments. However, there was often a difficult melding of two world wars, as some Great War cenotaphs proudly displayed battles and campaigns from 1915 to 1918; they were also sometimes topped by statues of soldiers in the uniform of that earlier war. The Second World War names occasionally looked like the late addition that they were.

Some people proposed instead the creation of "functional" memorials. In contrast to the stone and marble monoliths and cenotaphs of the Great War, these new, "useful memorials," as the *Calgary Herald* called them in early 1945, included community halls, sports stadiums, ice rinks, student scholarships, auditoriums, and health clinics, with even tennis courts and camping sites offered as possible options.[31] Utilitarian memorials would be used by the local residents and would become, it was hoped, active, vibrant places where the dead would be remembered as they had lived—animated, laughing, and part of a community. A Gallup poll published on Remembrance Day of 1944 determined that an overwhelming 90 percent of respondents favoured "living memorials" over traditional monuments.[32] This result underscores the secondary place the fallen service personnel from 1939 to 1945 held within the landscape of commemoration at the time. The new Canada was more interested in the future than in the past, in the living instead of the dead.

One successful commemorative act, supported by the Legion, was the naming of geographic features after the fallen. In 1947, the federal government's Geographical Names Board of Canada, which approves all nomenclature in Canada, began working with the provinces to survey unnamed lakes, islands, and geographical features, and to name them after slain service personnel. Saskatchewan and

Manitoba have the largest numbers of water bodies—with over 100,000 lakes in Manitoba alone—and the names of the Second World War dead, and later the Great War and Korean War fallen, were applied throughout those provinces in this worthy pursuit that combined history and geography. "The names published on future maps of the province," said one government body, "will serve as a monument for all time to Saskatchewan men who gave their lives in defence of democratic ideals in the Second World War."[33]

Though naming hockey arenas and libraries after the generation who had died during the war appealed to many, the Canadian Legion challenged the idea of functional memorials. Its members argued that the act "belittled" the stone memorials of old, and that the new functional memorials were places that would have little permanence or sacredness.[34] To cite one extreme example they offered, young people engaged in hitting a tennis ball around a memorial court would not be thinking of honouring fallen Canadians. Moreover, the idea that traditional stone monuments were no longer relevant rankled the veterans in the Legion, whose high command rejected the notion that monuments "in stone and bronze were outmoded and quite inappropriate for commemorating the valour and sacrifice of Canada's fighting men who had laid down their lives in the Second Great War."[35] The memorials were sites for Remembrance Day, they insisted, and without them, where would the ceremonies be held? Were the Second World War veterans and their families expected to gather in a pool? Others were angry too. Journalist Robert W. Thom, writing in *The Globe and Mail* on July 11, 1945, sneered that these functional memorials allowed the Canadians to "capitalize on the suffering and sacrifices of our soldiers, sailors and airmen so that life may be easier and more pleasing for those who remained at home and did little worth mentioning."[36] The *Edmonton Journal* followed this line of argument, lamenting the movement to "solve the war memorial problem by giving that name to some utilitarian project we meant to complete anyway, war or no war."[37]

Despite such scathing commentary from the Legion and other opponents, these concerns were largely ignored, and communities continued to commemorate the dead by adding the names of the fallen service personnel to the existing Great War monuments and by creating utilitarian spaces where those who gave their lives could be celebrated through social gatherings and leisure activities. Many communities turned to creating special gardens, with trees planted to mark the service of fallen personnel. Money was raised for hospitals, and in Toronto a special Dieppe room was established in the Hospital for Sick Children.[38] The town of Hanna, Alberta, raised funds through public subscription to build a swimming pool that would be dedicated as a memorial.[39] A playground was unveiled in October 1945 at Cowansville, Quebec, "in memory of those who fought that children might play."[40] Schools named spaces after the fallen, with Eglinton Public School in Toronto, for example, dedicating its new audio-visual education room to all its graduates who served in the war.[41]

Literary critic W.A. Deacon echoed the appeal for these new functional memories, arguing that "the cenotaph is a gate closing on the past," while a commemorative library "is an open door to a better future."[42] Living memorial libraries and other structures benefitted communities, he observed, and who would object to an ice-skating rink or scholarships for children named for killed service personnel? While some communities, schools, or businesses also erected small stone memorials or plaques, the functional memorials were a different form of reverence. They were indeed useful to communities, but they lacked permanence, and almost all of the commemorative, functional arenas or gardens are no longer in existence in the twenty-first century, having been replaced by newer buildings, structures, and spaces. Furthermore, adding a plaque or the names of those lost in service has done little to turn these functional places into spaces of reflection. While the door to the past seems to have been shut, as one critic foresaw, many communities have been left with few permanent "shrines" that hold the fallen of the Second World War "in reverence and honor."[43]

After the war, in Britain, Canada, and across the Commonwealth, discussions arose about Remembrance Day. Was November 11 a useful day on which to honour the fallen now that the Second World War had been won? Should it be June 6 (D-Day); or perhaps it might be moved to May 8 to mark victory in Europe? The problem was that there were multiple dates that were equally relevant for the commemoration of the Second World War, with victory against Germany in May, D-Day in June, and Japan defeated in August. A warm-weather commemoration date had the advantage of veterans not being forced to stand in the sleet, snow, and biting wind, but Great War veterans were adamant about not changing the date. After fierce discussion in the veterans' community and in Parliament, November 11 remained the day on which to observe Canadians' sacrifice in war.

In early 1945, even before the war ended, the Canadian Legion urged that Remembrance Day remain on November 11, but it argued, as a body and through its editorial mouthpiece, *The Legionary*, that the national memorial in Ottawa was too closely associated with the Great War to be useful in honouring the next generation of warriors. Veterans of the second war adopted the Great War's structures of grief almost universally, but they drew the line at the national monument. Editor John Hundevad wrote in February 1945, "The heroic uniformed figures which form part of the National War Memorial depict fighting men of the First Great War so faithfully as to make the March brothers' fine monument quite unsuitable as a memorial to our Glorious Dead of the present conflict."[44] The Second World War veterans wanted their own national memorial.

The King government was surprised to hear this demand. Vernon March's national monument had been unveiled in May 1939, only six years earlier. Formally known as The Response, it was an overtly First World War memorial, with its twenty-two figures from almost every arm of service passing through an 18-metre-high granite arch, atop which rested the allegorical figures of "Peace" and "Freedom."[45] The sculptor had died in 1930, but

Rare photograph of the National War Memorial's construction. This image captures the mess around the monument some two months before its unveiling in May 1939.

Unveiling of the National War Memorial in Ottawa on May 21, 1939 by King George VI before thousands of Canadians.

his six brothers and sisters, all sculptors themselves, had completed the monument. It had been created to commemorate the war that many hoped would be the last one fought by Canadians—"the war to end all wars"—but when it was unveiled in May 1939, a new war, against Nazi Germany, loomed on the horizon.

Prime Minister King had pressed civil servants and fellow politicians to place the Great War monument near Parliament. It was a symbolic gesture to erect the memorial within sight of Canada's physical and imagined representation of democracy. Ottawa had emerged from the nineteenth century with few protected green spaces and little of the national cohesion associated with capital cities like Washington, London, or Paris. In the 1920s, the future site of the memorial was a busy intersection of roads, foot bridges, light rail, and businesses. It was no easy task to reroute streets, demolish buildings, and create a suitable area around which to frame the monument, but for two decades, King slowly remade this crucial spot in the heart of Ottawa. He saw Confederation Square, as it would later be called, as one of his great achievements.[46] King had even written large parts of King George VI's speech at the unveiling, where the monarch had called The Response "the very soul of the nation."[47] Not surprising, then, that King was little inclined to build a new monument in 1945.

Ottawa suggested to the Legion that perhaps adding "1939–1945" to the National War Memorial would suffice. Simply embracing The Response and defacing it with new dates was wrong, countered the Legion, as "this would not be practicable, because the uniformed figures which form an integral part of the monument, as well as the arms and equipment, are definitely 'dated' as being from the First Great War period."[48] In effect, The Response was simply too closely associated with the Great War.

As the waves of veterans were returning from overseas in the fall of 1945, *The Legionary* alerted its readers to the fight on their

The temporary wooden cenotaph on Parliament Hill that was used for memorial services during the Second World War. In 1945, veterans hoped for a permanent memorial like this to honour the fallen of the Necessary War.

behalf for a monument, observing, "For many months past a great controversy has been going on in all parts of the country on the question of war memorials."[49] The Legion called publicly for a new national cenotaph that should be erected at the base of the Peace Tower of the Parliament Buildings. It would be a simple, even stark structure, a cenotaph based on Edwin Lutyens's famous memorial at Whitehall in London. But the Legion's hopes were dashed in September 1945, when King announced that there would be no second national monument. He instead proclaimed that a beautification program in Ottawa would be a living, functional memorial to the Second World War fallen. He had gone on record before and during the war with his desire to create more beauty and coherence in Ottawa by adding green spaces and walking paths and tearing up old railway lines, and he even brought famed French architect Jacques Gréber to the capital to plan for such a program. King believed that the beautification of Ottawa itself would be the greatest monument and that "no form of a memorial could be more worthy of the service and sacrifice given in the war than to give the Capital of our country as worthy a place amongst the national capitals of the world."[50] King was joined by M.J. Coldwell, leader of the Co-operative Commonwealth Federation, who also did not endorse a new national monument, suggesting instead a national art gallery, library, ballet theatre, or even an opera house—all of which were missing from Canada's desolate national artistic landscape. One or more of these national arts centres would honour the "memory of Canada's sons and daughters who have freely given their lives in this war."[51]

The concerned veterans were nonplussed by the politicians' ideas. While the Legion encouraged the government to beautify Ottawa and to create national cultural institutions, it stressed that these initiatives would not be enough to mark the sacrifice of the Second World War generation. The Legion was not alone in its disappointment with the King government. The *Edmonton Journal* eviscerated the beatification plan with this withering accusation: "It is difficult to see just how a scheme of his kind could possibly provide a suitable monument to the Canadians who fought and died in the conflict just ended. Whatever may be said against conventional memorials, such as cenotaphs and statues, they at least compel the beholder to think about the dead." King's plans for "huge, pompous government buildings, miles of ornamental driveways and acres of formal park," the paper scoffed, were little more than "Babylonian extravagances" and had little to do with those who served and never came home. The *Journal* gave a final twist of the dagger, suggesting King's plan was more a monument to the "glory of the living politicians" than that of fallen military personnel.[52] There were other critics, too, and most felt that King's plan for the capital was an attempt to masquerade an urban planning project as a commemorative site.

The Legion continued to press for a new cenotaph into 1946, but now it had shifted the desired site to Major's Hill Park, overlooking the Ottawa River. The memorial would be in a position of pride and importance, and the cenotaph would "inspire real remembrance and sincere reverence."[53] "Real" and "sincere" were not abstract adjectives here, but words being used with intention, as a point of contrast with the beautification program being fobbed off as a living memorial.[54] However, in the face of politicians' lack of interest and polls suggesting that Canadians were not enthused about sacred memorials, the idea of the national memorial faded, especially as the Legion was kept busy fighting for veterans' rights and pensions. Nonetheless, the *Ottawa Citizen*

Canada's National War Memorial, The Response, was so directly linked to the Great War, with its 22 service personnel passing through the arch, that the Second World War veterans demanded their own memorial.

noted in early 1946 that King's beautification program as a form of memorial continued to be "emphatically opposed" by the organized veterans.[55] The possibility of a new Second World War national monument disappeared from public discussion, although the Veterans Memorial Buildings were raised in 1949 and 1955 in honour of the Second World War dead, opposite the Supreme Court of Canada and with a memorial arch between the two buildings. But the debate would resurface a decade later, with new demands being made for a monument to honour those who had given their lives in the Necessary War.

The Great War dead traumatized Canada in a way that the fallen from the Second World War did not. The losses from the Great War were larger in sheer numbers, and even more so when the size of the country was factored in: some 66,000 killed from a population of 8 million, compared to 45,000 killed from a country of 11.5 million in the later war. But perhaps more important, the Great War was a colossal and unexpected rupture to Canadian society, one that could never be matched. Innocence had been burned away in the cauldron of the Western Front. Terrible sacrifices were again made during the Second World War, but in 1939 no one was naive enough to think that the war would be short or that it could be won without an appalling blood offering by the country's youth. The Great War had hardened Canadians to the grinding cost of industrialized warfare, and the Depression years imposed further hardships. And yet those who lost daughters, sons, brothers, uncles, and fathers during the Second World War felt no less sadness than the generation earlier. They were no less grief-stricken and hollowed out. So why was there not a similar emotional outpouring to mark the losses?

Across the country there was an acknowledgment—especially when the death camps were discovered and the Dutch were saved from starvation—that the fight against Hitler had needed to be won, no matter the cost. Mourning and sorrow were allowed, of course, but they would not dominate the narrative in commemorating the crusade against tyranny. The Second World War had mattered in a profound way, and had laid the foundations for the modern Canada, but the war's fallen did not haunt Canadians like those of the Great War. This was a war where victory meant a focus on the living, not the dead. Ironically, this would make it more difficult for later generations to understand the meaning of the Necessary War.

CHAPTER 4

ABSENT FROM THE HISTORICAL RECORD

The Canadian Legion's call for "Total Victory" went out in 1941. The veterans of the trenches demanded that the government engage in an unlimited war effort. Any cost must be borne, and that included conscription. The overseas forces must be supported. In December 1945, the Legion issued a new call to all Canadians: "Total Victory demands a total effort for a new world, worthy of the sacrifice our comrades have made. We, as veterans, believe that we must fight for this new world here in Canada."[1] The Legion sent personalized messages to every member of Parliament and to many business leaders across the country. The goal was to ensure a country that valued its veterans, caring for those who needed assistance and easing the way forward for the able-bodied. "Winning the Peace," proclaimed one September 1945 editorial in *The Legionary*, "is as important an objective as winning the war."[2]

The Canadian Legion, the conglomeration of several veterans' groups, had been formed by the Great War veterans in 1925, and chartered early the next year. Canadian humorist Stephen Leacock wrote of war veterans, "When the war ends they are welcomed home under arches of flowers with all the girls leaping for their necks, and within six months they are expected to vanish into thin air, keep out of the public house and give no trouble."[3] He was not wrong. In the harsh postwar years, the living veterans increasingly banded together during the 1920s, sometimes in unit associations and often in the newly built Legion Halls. These were sites where veterans could gather and talk, where they could share their difficult memories, hoist a pint to absent comrades, or sing nostalgic songs.[4] The veterans' spaces allowed the survivors to deal with the enduring strain and profound scars of mental trauma, while also processing their stories of service and comradery.

During the Second World War, the Great War veterans fought for their sons and daughters to have a fair shake from Ottawa. Knowing that their lobbying efforts had resulted in the progressive Veterans Charter, the older ex-soldiers wanted to bring this new generation into the Canadian Legion to strengthen the position of veterans in society. While former service personnel never spoke as one unified voice, and there were smaller groups—for example, the Sir Arthur Pearson Club for Blinded Sailors and Soldiers, Tubercular Veterans, the Army and Navy Veterans in Canada, the Canadian Pensioners' Association, and the War Amputations of Canada ("War Amps")—the Legion was the largest, the most influential, the most recognized, and the group that most often dealt with Ottawa.

The Legion advertised widely and encouraged its members to recruit their friends and neighbours. Each month, thousands of Second World War ex-service personnel, their average age in the mid-twenties, joined the organization. As one of the older veterans observed, these new men offered innumerable "shots of plasma into the Legion blood stream."[5] By the end of 1945, some 200,000 veterans were a part of the Legion. Captain J. Harper Prowse wrote in September 1945 in *The Legionary* that veterans could become a "powerful group" in society if they banded together and avoided being divided by politicians and other groups "as part of a sinister plot to keep them [veterans] politically impotent."[6]

But the Legion was much more than just a lobby group; it sought to reinvigorate the wartime cohesion that sustained service personnel through years of hardship and, in the postwar years, to renew that "priceless and unforgettable thing called comradeship."[7] Many joined for that reason, but there were more ex-service personnel who did not, being either too busy, preoccupied with settling in, focused on recovering from wounds, or simply wanting to get away from anything related to the war. "I used to like hunting," recounted Private Norman Latender of the Loyal Edmonton Regiment towards the end of the war, "but when I get

A Canadian stretcher bearer (as they were known, instead of the American term, "medic") caring for an injured child during the liberation of France. After the war, veterans found it necessary to bind together in unit associations or national organizations like the Legion to care for one another.

home I never want to see another rifle."[8] Another veteran, Jeffrey Neff, recounted that "most of us who survived went back to our homes after the war, and tried to bury the horror of things we had to do as soldiers."[9] There had been too much marching, too many friends lost, too much killing. Another officer, Donald Pearce, who served with the North Nova Scotia Highlanders, kept a diary through much of the fighting from the Battle of the Scheldt in October 1944 to the end of the war. In the aftermath of the fierce combat, he burned several of his diaries, explaining, "Since I had survived the war, the record, which was supposed to have survived me, now seemed rather pointless, and what was left of it quickly dropped out of sight and out of mind, where it remained for many years."[10] It took twenty years, and his son expressing curiosity about his war experience, for him to rewrite his story.

In July 1946, the Department of Veterans Affairs enlisted the Dominion Bureau of Statistics to interview 5,000 returned service personnel. It was found that 31 percent were twenty-five to twenty-nine years old; 28 percent were twenty to twenty-four; and 18 percent were thirty to thirty-four. Almost 60 percent of the veterans were in their twenties, and about the same number—60 percent—were married. About half of these veterans went to the altar during the war or shortly after discharge. The veterans also accounted for a noted shift from the rural to the urban. The movement to the cities had been a part of the war, and with jobs in the urban areas because of the booming postwar economy, few felt the pull back to the land; only about 12 percent of the interviewed veterans lived on farms. Some 31 percent were engaged in manufacturing; 17 percent were in trade, finance, and insurance; another 17 percent were in service jobs—defined as stores, laundries, or garages; 11 percent worked in transportation; and 9 percent were employed in construction. Most had jobs: 82 percent of those interviewed were in paid employment, and most of them—86 percent—had found a job within two months of discharge.[11] Veterans were getting on with their lives, and many wished to leave the war behind. Ken Carvers from Ottawa was one of them. He had joined the navy at age eighteen and had served on corvettes. When he returned home in his early twenties, he had no interest in staying connected to the war, going to reunions, or talking about it.[12] It would take him fifty years to find his voice and tell his stories. And he was not alone. Many veterans felt a strong desire to move forward with their lives, already having given too much to the war, no matter how necessary or just it may have been.

Not all Canadians who had served in uniform during the war were treated fairly or equally by the state, or by other veterans. There were fierce debates after the war, and for much of the Legion's existence, over who should be allowed to join the veterans' organization. Some veterans thought membership should be reserved only for those Canadians who had served overseas. However, as hundreds of thousands of men and women had been involved on the home front—in roles ranging from air training to hemispheric defence—the Legion decided to accept all veterans, except those who had been conscripted.

The conscripts had been forced to serve under the National Resources Mobilization Act (NRMA) of June 1940, legislation that had been passed during the calamitous period after France collapsed in the face of the German lightning attacks. Canada's limited conscription program trained young men for combat but did not force them to go overseas. Prime Minister King had made that promise to Canadians, and especially to Quebec, but the NRMA men, who

Infantry from Le Régiment de la Chaudière landing on Juno Beach, June 6, 1944. The survivors and most of the Canadians who served in uniform were welcomed into the Legion. But not all. The conscripts—of which some served with the "Chauds"—were denied admittance for years.

trained in the same camps as other recruits, were pressured to "go active"—in effect, to serve overseas. Some did, browbeaten with insults or literally beaten with fists and boots. But most did not go, having conscientious objections, either moral or religious, or simply not wanting to leave their families and their loved ones to be killed overseas on some muddy battlefield. The NRMA soldiers were abused for years in Canada during the war, often by men and women who were not serving in uniform. They were called "zombies"—men with no souls, in reference to the popular Hollywood horror movies of the time. As one conscript, a young French Canadian stationed in Sydney, Nova Scotia, later remarked, the girls "shunned" him, and others who were not in uniform made it clear that he was "despised and scorned."[13]

During the depths of the conscription crisis in November 1944, King eventually succumbed to the enormous pressure to address the manpower shortage in the army in Europe, and some 13,000 soldiers were forced overseas, with 4,881 conscripts reaching the battlefields.[14] While at the front, 61 conscripts were killed or listed as missing, and 226 were wounded. The 157,841 NRMA soldiers came from all linguistic, ethnic, and religious backgrounds; most were never sent overseas.[15] The conscripts had few champions and many enemies, but General Crerar, upon his return to Canada in late 1945, described them as having "fought extraordinarily well," and noted, "There was nothing wrong with them at all . . . and I'm quite sure a number of them won decorations for gallantry."[16] Those who were drafted into the depleted fighting units were usually accepted by their comrades, who got over their distaste toward the conscripts quickly as they dug the same slit trenches, huddled together for warmth, and fought together for survival.

And yet after the war, the NRMA soldiers were stigmatized. They were not issued a sterling silver discharge button, even if they had served overseas, been wounded, or received a gallantry medal.[17] At the May 1946 Legion convention in Quebec City, attended by some 2,000 Legionnaires and Field Marshal Alexander of Tunis, the war hero and new governor general of Canada, there were many discussions and debates about various veteran-related resolutions. However, the most controversial of these, reported *The Legionary*, and "certainly the one that caused the sharpest cleavage of opinion on the floor of the Convention," was the proposal that NRMA veterans who had served overseas in theatre be allowed to join the Legion.[18] An hour of angry denunciations raged forth, some of which were recorded. One Legionnaire from Manitoba yelled, "Only a few hundred of them reached us late in the war . . . they had the whole war to make up their minds. . . . Keep them out." The speaker had his facts wrong, as close to 5,000 NRMA soldiers had served at the front, but the actual number was not well publicized. A Nova Scotian commented that if the conscripts were admitted, "We'll all be dishonoured." A Vancouver member was more positive, opining, "They did what their country compelled them to do." Another favourable response came from a war leader from the front, Lieutenant-Colonel Lucien Lalonde, who commanded Le Régiment de Maisonneuve. The regiment had received a large influx of conscripts to keep up its strength in 1945, and the colonel declared, "When they fought, they fought damn well. . . . We originally didn't want anything to do with them, but on the field of battle they proved themselves good Canadian soldiers." He urged the Legion to "let them in." The arguments raged back and forth, heated and furious, but the voters eventually sided with the sentiments expressed by Legionnaires like Harry Caminer of Verdun, Quebec, who warned, "You'll split the Legion wide open if you let them in." The NRMA veterans were denied the opportunity to join the Legion.[19]

There was also an erroneous perception that the conscripts were mostly French Canadian, and as part of this fierce debate, much open anti-Quebec sentiment was aired. Many of the Legion's veterans derided French Canada's wartime contributions. This hurt in Quebec, where it was felt that French Canadians had con-tributed significantly to the war effort. Some of the Legionnaires' anger was left over from the time of the Great War, when English and French Canadians had argued over the same issue. But in the Second World War, Quebeckers enlisted in much higher numbers (although never equal to those from English Canada), and many identifiable French-Canadian units were involved. Nonetheless, the rancour over the NRMA veterans was often focused on French speakers not having done their duty, a perspective that both diminished the role of those who had served and confirmed for Quebeckers that they had never been wanted in the first place. It was not until the 1950 Dominion Convention that the Legion agreed to extend membership to the NRMA veterans who had served overseas. The resolution was finally passed, but the anger festered and NRMA veterans were rarely welcomed into the Legion Halls; some provincial commands held out until the 1970s before allowing the conscripts to apply for Legion membership.[20]

Though the concept of veteranship was contested, both in the military community and in wider society, the 1.5 million or so veterans from the two world wars made up a significant segment of the Canadian population of 12 million in 1945. "There are many thousands whose bodies bear the mutilation and scars of war," observed one concerned veteran.[21] The Legion rapidly expanded in size and influence, and it promised to fight for able-bodied veterans, for the wounded, and for their dependants. D-Day infantryman Cliff Chadderton, who served with the Royal Winnipeg Rifles of Canada and lost his lower leg in battle, reminded the survivors that they owed a debt to their comrades whom they had left behind on the battlefields. "We who served and fought, and lived to return to our Homeland, have brought back a torch to carry," he wrote in *The Legionary* in 1946. "A torch which was flung to us as our buddies, facing death and fearing for their loved ones, turned over a Heritage to those of us who were still unscathed. They left their wives, their children, their mothers and fathers in our hands—hands they hoped desperately would not fail."[22] Chadderton stayed true to those sentiments and he would become a force for veterans' rights in the postwar decades.

One of the Legion's most productive sections was a small office that engaged in legal and bureaucratic battles with civil servants. These experts knew the pension guidelines inside and out, and they often advocated on behalf of the widows and elderly parents of slain service personnel to ensure there were proper payouts from the Department of Veterans Affairs. By January 1947, Richard Hale, the chief pension officer for the Legion, reported that his bureau had intervened in 102 pension claims from the Second World War and another 15 from the Great War. "Every member of the Legion can feel proud of being a shareholder in this great work of service to disabled comrades and to the dependents of those who have given their lives in the service of our country," he wrote.[23] Tensions arose between veterans and civil servants who seemed intent on creating an adversarial process: when assessing pension claims, these gatekeepers would often demand evidence of wounds that could not be given except by pointing to scars. Veterans looked in vain at their service files, which often contained only sparse notes on wartime medical procedures and sometimes failed to contain detailed information about their wounds. And yet many of the civil servants were veterans themselves, and one suspects there was more than a little generosity afforded to their former comrades. But perhaps it only took a few dozen cases to sour the relationship; as one Canadian veteran exclaimed in print, for many ex-service personnel, it was necessary to "fight every inch of the way."[24]

To intervene on behalf of veterans and next of kin, the Legion needed money. The organization gathered limited annual dues from its members, but its primary source of income was the sale of red poppies worn around the time of Remembrance Day. The poppy had become a recognizable symbol of remembrance during the Great War because of the immense reach of John McCrae's *In Flanders Fields*.[25] The much reprinted poem was often accompanied by illustrations of red poppies, drawn from the imagery of its opening lines, and starting in 1922 the Legion sold poppies as an emblem of commemoration and as a means of fundraising. During and after the Second World War, poppies were manufactured by disabled ex-servicemen in Vetcraft shops and distributed by veterans from the Legion's 1,500 branches. Sales of the poppy around Remembrance Day in 1945 produced profits of more than $128,000.[26] And the next year the Legion took out advertisements imploring Canadians to purchase a poppy to "Honour the Dead . . . Remember the Living."[27]

As soldiers, airmen, and sailors left the services, some were thinking about how to keep alive the bonds of comradery with the men who had sustained them through the war. The Legion was a national organization with provincial commands and regional branches in almost every community, but individual units—regiments, medical formations, warships, and squadrons—also set about creating post-war clubs. Many of these units had been formed during the war, drawing from the local communities—especially units in the army, the largest branch of service. It was more difficult for sailors to be anchored to a single unit, as they served on many warships; aircrews, meanwhile, were posted to all manner of squadrons after their training, with as many sent to the RAF as the RCAF. Even with these obstacles to overcome, unit-based formations and clubs emerged after the war to meet the needs of veterans.

To highlight but one example, the Regina Rifle Regiment came together in early 1946 to create a regimental association. Organizers from the unit advertised widely in local papers in Saskatchewan to gather a list of names and addresses. Captain W.F. Ferris, chairman of the membership committee, noted in *The Legionary* that most of the regiment's veterans living outside Saskatchewan could not attend the annual meetings, but he believed the association, "when formed, will evolve some system of maintaining contact with them."[28] The association produced a regimental history and the "Johns," as the Reginas were sometimes known because many of the unit's soldiers were farmers ("Farmer Johns"), worked with the City of Regina to add an inscription plaque to the cenotaph in Victoria Park. That cenotaph, originally erected for the Great War dead, became the site of an annual ceremony at which the Reginas honoured their fallen comrades and marked their June 6 assault on Juno Beach.[29] Wealthier units in Toronto and Montreal, some of which had a long historical lineage, already had drill halls and buildings in which members would meet several times a week. Some units published newsletters, filled with information about members as well as stories of wartime service and articles on veterans' rights. Most formations marked the anniversary of major battles—some from the Great War, like Second Ypres on April 22 or Vimy on April 9—but there were newer engagements to be recognized too. Most often it was momentous occasions like the anniversary of the Juno Beach landing or the August 19 Dieppe date, or other days when a unit had fought with distinction. And even those veterans who lived too far away to attend the reunions, or who did not want to be reminded of the war, sometimes put on their medals and marched with their regimental comrades on Remembrance Day.

———

Despite the absolute necessity of the war against the fascists, many veterans remained ambivalent about whether to continue to associate themselves with their service. Many simply wanted to move on with their lives; others would never be able to outrun the memories, and so they buried them deep. In 1945, however, it was clear that millions of Canadians who had not served in uniform were interested in the war experience. Almost everyone had been touched by the war. On VE Day, the *Charlottetown Guardian* rejoiced over the end of the war—as indeed all the nation's papers did—noting, "It seems difficult to believe that at long last the guns have been silenced." The newspaper also observed that after the celebrations, there would be time to learn more of "the achievements of our gallant Canadian forces on land, sea and in the air. It is a record of which every Canadian should be proud."[30] In the war's aftermath, as censorship eased, Canadians yearned to understand the war that had shaped their lives for six years.

One of the most successful early histories came from Ross Munro, a wartime correspondent who published *Gauntlet to Overlord* (1945). Munro had been present for important battles and invasions: Dieppe, Sicily, and Juno. *The Legionary* called the book an "instant classic," and observed of Munro that "in an unusual sense his name is a household word in Canada."[31] During the war, Munro had travelled alongside the fighting units, reporting on the battles and life at the front for the Canadian Press, which printed his stories in more than ninety newspapers across the country. "With the world literally coming to an end and the ground shaking, he sent colourful despatches from a slit trench, pounding out his stories on a type-writer," said one reviewer.[32] *Gauntlet to Overlord* sold widely, won the 1945 Governor General's Award for non-fiction, and was on its third printing by the summer of 1946.

After reading the book, a reviewer in *The New York Times* described the Canadians as "the unsung heroes of the war."[33]

Other wartime Canadian journalists, too, were feeding the demand from a hungry public. Lionel Shapiro penned a history of the Italian campaign, *They Left the Back Door Open* (1944), while Captain Peter Simonds, the brother of Lieutenant-General Guy Simonds, offered *Maple Leaf Up, Maple Leaf Down* (1946), which focused on the Canadian Army and highlighted the "rugged individuality" of the soldiers aching to take the fight to the enemy.[34] Simonds's book was likened in reviews to Munro's *Gauntlet to Overlord*, although Munro's evocative pen was contrasted with Simonds's more stilted and sometimes misleading retelling of operations.

Additional history books were written, usually based on newspaper accounts, but none has stood the test of time. Memoirs

Journalist Ross Munro reporting from the frontlines in Italy in August 1943. He was Canada's best-known journalist as he wrote the story of Canada's army during the war, and immediately afterwards.

fared better, offering eyewitness narratives of events and individuals. Richard Malone, staff officer and editor of the army newspaper *The Maple Leaf*, wrote the gossipy and provocative *Missing from the Record* (1946), which offered insight into Montgomery, McNaughton, and other senior generals. The first round of books emerged from the desks of journalists, although some veterans offered their thoughts too. Raymond Hickey, a much-loved padre with the North Shore Regiment, wrote *The Scarlet Dawn* (1949), a haunting story of men in battle that explored camaraderie, service, and death. His account of giving the last rites to soldiers, some with glazed eyes as death overtook them, some whispering pleas for their mothers, was particularly wrenching. Hickey described the crucifix that he passed over the battered bodies of the Canadians, noting, "it could tell of things my pen won't write—better that it can't, for it might speak of things a war chaplain tries to forget, things he may hold in his memory, but will carry down with him unspoken to his grave."[35]

After that brief postwar deluge, the memoirs dried up for many decades. It was never easy for those who had been there to draw the disparate stories together to create a narrative, and most military personnel preferred to leave the memories as their own— or simply tried to banish them.[36] Pilot Officer Ron Laidlaw of the RCAF described the challenge of wrestling his wartime experiences onto the page, confiding, "For years I've been trying to face up to this. But my mind is like a jigsaw puzzle with many of the pieces either fuzzy or they won't fit into place or are lost. . . . As I now ponder how to handle this, with the same shudder I have had for ensuing years, I find I'm able only to put swatches of scenes together—never the whole picture."[37]

A Canadian soldier in a slit trench writing a letter, a few kilometres beyond Juno Beach. After the war, veterans had a difficult time writing about their war experience.

It was perhaps easier for some men to convey their war experience through the medium of fiction. The best writers drew upon their service, amplifying, shifting, and rearranging the narrative, but all with an eye to exploring the many contested meanings of service. Poet and wartime personnel officer Earle Birney's popular novel *Turvey* (1949), about a rogue hero, drew inspiration from Old Bill, the anti-hero cartoon character from the Great War.[38] Veterans delighted in reading about one of their own who pushed back against authority, and they embraced Birney's sad-sack soldier who lacked patriotism and warfighting skills. *Turvey* won the Stephen Leacock Medal for Humour, and the story would be periodically mounted on the stage over the years. Other fictional accounts of the Second World War similarly drew interest, and yet the two classics to emerge from the war—Hugh MacLennan's *Barometer Rising* (1941) and *Two Solitudes* (1945)—were about the Great War.

———

Official histories have sometimes been criticized as being little more than court history. Because they are sponsored by military and civilian authorities, the official historians have access to records or participants in a way that others do not. But at the same time, that access comes with censorship that can strangle the historian's voice. "Official but not history," military historian Sir Basil Liddell Hart condemned, dismissing the British official histories of the Great War.[39] Other historians concede that while official histories may be flawed by a lack of openness and by being written too close to events and sometimes under the sway of people in power, no real alternative exists, as governments refuse to open up the archives or documents for the professional historians for at least several decades after events occur.

In Canada, only one of a planned eight official volumes about the Great War was ever published, as the series was started too late and had a veteran at the head of the project instead of a professional historian. When it came to officially capturing the Second World War, the military authorities were better prepared and more aware that their experiences were worthy of recording for posterity.[40] During the war, the army and RCAF historical sections published several best-selling histories that were snatched up by Canadians desperate to know about the conflict. Among the most notable: *The RCAF Overseas*, a two-volume work about the air force, with a third book published after the war, all of which were national best-sellers. *Canada's War at Sea* (1944) was a fast-paced naval history written by civilians, journalists Leslie Roberts and Stephen Leacock, the latter one of Canada's most recognizable writers, although the authors were aided by the Canadian navy, which gave support to the project.

Major Charles Stacey, a prewar Canadian history professor, was appointed early in the war to chronicle the army's history as it unfolded, and to ensure that records were created and archived. He won over the senior army command with his argument about the importance of documenting the Canadian army's exploits, and his work at Canadian Military Headquarters in London harnessed contemporary lessons from the battlefield for the generals.[41] He also laid the foundation for writing a multi-volume official history series of the army. Dynamic, knowledgeable, and politically minded, Stacey knew that an official historian would bear a "heavy responsibility" and that passing judgment on victories and defeats would be "in some respects an unpleasant job," but he also felt he had a duty to chronicle the complex story of the army at war.[42]

Though Canada's three military services had invested in historical officers during the war to gather war records, arrange them, and write preliminary histories, the postwar cutbacks to the defence budgets forced difficult choices on the high command. In this climate of retrenchment, the senior officers found the pen-wielding uniformed historians easier to target than the traditional military personnel heading into the new Cold War. The air force and naval history-writing programs were served up for cuts, with little support for them being offered from outside their small sections, but Stacey had made a wide range of friends during the war, and he mobilized support for his work. Lester B. Pearson, then the undersecretary of state for external affairs, eventually intervened and convinced military authorities that Stacey should be allowed to complete the work for the good of the army, and the country. The army history was saved: a one-volume summary would be published soon after the war's end for the public, followed by three more in-depth volumes and, finally, an all-encompassing history of wartime policy and strategy. But this result paled in comparison to the output of the British and the Americans, who were working away on their series that spanned dozens and dozens of books, with each service clamouring to tell its story.

Because of the cutbacks, only two volumes of dense, encyclopedic history of the Canadian navy were published by Gilbert Tucker—a civilian in an official historian position who had been commissioned by the senior naval brass and who felt compelled to start his history from the time of New France. The minister of national defence, Brooke Claxton, found the result to be useless academic tomes, and he refused to allow Tucker to work on the third volume, about operations in the Atlantic, instead giving the job to a talented writer, Joseph Schull.[43] *The Far Distant Ships* (1950) was stirring history, but it lacked a basis in British or German archival records and was very much a heroic and derring-do account of the Canadian navy's contribution to victory. Meanwhile, the RCAF historical section was "shot down in flames," as C.P. Stacey put it years later, "leaving a disgraceful gap in the national historiography."[44] Claxton had little interest in seeing the story told, despite being a strong nationalist, and the minister offered the naive view that because "the RCAF fought with the British . . . it was up to the British to tell the story."[45] Not surprisingly, the British showed little inclination to single out the tens of thousands of Canadians who served in RAF units, or the independent contributions of RCAF squadrons in multiple theatres of war.

Only Stacey managed to keep the official history program going. Working non-stop with a small team of historians who had to wade through millions of pages of documentation, Stacey published his one-volume summary in 1948. *The Canadian Army, 1939–1945* was a history for all Canadians, and it was strikingly good. Stacey had fought the British for access to strategic records, and while he was partly successful, some areas remained shrouded. So he was cautious when describing why the Dieppe raid was launched, or when writing about the confusion around the Hong Kong fighting, or when discussing the highest level strategic decisions that had an impact on the Canadian forces. But *The Canadian Army, 1939–1945* was a best-seller, esteemed as the recipient of the 1949 Governor General's Award for non-fiction, and recognized by international historians as a model work.[46] Stacey had shown that official history was not court history. His work was lauded by *The Legionary* as "masterful study of care and precision, a monument worthy of the brave men whose deeds it records."[47]

Stacey was guided by the need to share the inspiring story of Canada's achievements during the war. "We have to tell, for the Canadians of today and of days to come, the story of a tremendous human enterprise—the part played by Canada in the defence of freedom against the bloodiest tyrannies of modern times. It was the greatest undertaking in our national history. . . . Someday, perhaps, the poet will arise who can do it justice; in the meantime, the historian can only do his best."[48] However, Stacey also warned his superiors that, after a 1946 visit to Washington, he was surprised to find that the Americans were using both civilian and military historians to write their hundred-volume series, noting, "It is possible that this may result in our history carrying somewhat less weight."[49] Canada's single volume on the army three years after the war's end would rise to the task and carry much historical weight, even as the British and Americans—flush with resources and pride—told their stories in book after book after book.

———

Official historian Colonel C.P. Stacey struggled for years to write a multi-volume official history of the Canadian Army during the Second World War. While the first volume was published in 1948 to much acclaim, subsequent books were delayed by fearful politicians who worried about what secrets he might reveal.

French President Georges Clemenceau had once quipped that "war was too important a matter to be left to the generals."[50] The same appeared to be the case for the writing of war, and in Canada only a thin gruel had been forthcoming from the senior Second World War commanders. The Canadian military high command—army, navy, and air force—was not a group that leaned towards crafting a literary legacy; amazingly, almost none of them chose to write a memoir. In this regard, the commanders were following in the steps of most of the senior Canadian leaders in the Great War, including Sir Arthur Currie, who failed to put pen to paper in defence of his reputation or to stake out his view of history.[51]

General Harry Crerar might have been expected to write his memoirs of the Second World War, since he had proved to be a literate officer, and he was a champion of history who supported Stacey's efforts to create a truthful account of the war. But at fifty-seven years old, he had served in two world wars and he now retired from public service in 1946. Canadians never warmed to Crerar, and they certainly did not venerate him in the same way that they did General McNaughton, who had been the First Army commander and had been elevated early in the war to hero status. Crerar's retirement ensured that he would not have a platform to give voice to the national war effort, unlike outspoken generals such as the United States' Eisenhower and Bradley, or Britain's Montgomery. Crerar was offered a number of minor appointments, none befitting his stature, and he was not even considered for a Senate seat, an indication of how little Canadian politicians thought of the generals. While Crerar remained in Ottawa after the war, occasionally contributing to the national debate, arguing in support of veterans' rights, and advocating for the unpopular idea of compulsory service (limited conscription), according to his biographer he "faded into obscurity."[52]

General Crerar might have solidified his place in history if he had written his memoirs. Canadians would have been interested in his insights into aspects of the war, especially the challenges of command and fighting in Western Europe. Like previous generals—especially Currie—Crerar was offered large sums of money to pen his story, and was even given the option by publishers of hiring a ghostwriter, but Crerar knew that any true account would hurt other key players in the war, not the least being Field Marshal Bernard Montgomery, with whom he had had a difficult relationship and whom Canadians greatly admired. Any memoir would also have had to include his own inglorious undermining of McNaughton as army commander, his pressure on Minister of National Defence J.L. Ralston to send troops to Hong Kong, and his involvement in the Dieppe operation. When prolific author Kim Beattie suggested to Crerar that he had a duty to share his impression of the war to counter that of US general Omar Bradley, who published his memoir, *A Soldier's Story* in 1951, Crerar again demurred. A disappointed Beattie responded that by not writing a history—which "all the American generals are doing"—Crerar was missing a chance to tell the Canadian war story.[53] Brigadier-General Denis Whitaker, a veteran and historian of the war, wondered if Crerar's failure to write was a sign of "Canadian timidity, or modesty."[54] Towards the end

General Harry Crerar, Canada's last army commander,
might have been better known to Canadians and in history if he
had written about his war experiences.

of his life, Crerar was arranging his archival papers and thinking of an autobiography, but he died in 1965. A few of the nation's generals wrote later in life, but in the three decades after the war, when interest was likely to be strongest, the Canadian senior commanders' literary legacy was largely absent from the historical record, remaining so until the end of the century, when historians turned to studying them.[55]

In this postwar battle of reputations, Canadians ceded the field to the American and British senior commanders. The public ate their accounts up, with readers most interested in the inside history of Field Marshal Bernard Montgomery. After an illustrious military career, which he ended as commander of NATO military forces, the cantankerous Montgomery settled old scores against the Americans with his memoirs in 1958. Never shy to express his opinion or bend the truth, Monty accused the Americans of poor strategic thinking and blamed them for many of the failures in Northwest Europe. Montgomery hated an untidy battlefield, and he was no less fond of untidy history: he "cleaned up" some of the stories to make them more presentable and especially to allow himself to appear in control of the chaos of battle.[56] *Memoirs* (1958), an international best-seller, was popular in Canada, where most veterans loved the rascally old showman, and the book was especially favoured because it enraged the Americans. President Eisenhower, whose own memoir, *Crusade in Europe* (1948), had aided his successful bid for presidency in 1952, bit back his fury but felt betrayed by Montgomery. Throughout the war, Eisenhower had shielded Montgomery from his many enemies who ached to remove him from command. Sharpened daggers in the form of pens were broken out after the war to do in rivals and shape the history, but Canada's senior military command was absent from this new battlefield. And so was Canada's story.

Field Marshal Montgomery visited Canada shortly after the war and *The Legionary* reported, "It is no exaggeration to say that he is one of the two most popular war-leaders in the Second Great War as far as the fighting men and the common people throughout the British Commonwealth Empire is concerned. Winston Churchill is the other, and it is significant that they are the only two in comparable positions of responsibility and authority who have become known to all and sundry by an affectionate nickname. 'Good old Winnie' and 'Good old Monty' will be remembered and honoured long after most of the other wartime statesmen and military leaders have been forgotten."[57] Perhaps betraying the nation's colonial mindset, Canadians took to British political and military leaders more than to their own, and how could they not be drawn to the charismatic Montgomery and the pugnacious Churchill? British prime minister Winston Churchill's words made Canadians shiver. His command of the English language and his mastery of projecting an underdog's scrappy self-confidence had made him a symbol of the West. Canadians cheered to see him defiantly standing against the Nazi thugs and taunting the tyrant of Europe from behind his jaw-clamping cigar.

And then there was William Lyon Mackenzie King. Long-serving and suffering, and yet revelling in his service to the Canadian people whom he had guided to a prosperous future, Canada's unlikely warlord offered his platitudes and vague remarks that started in one direction and ended up somewhere else. King could stand resolutely on his principles, but he was not the type to fight to the death over an issue, save in the rarest of circumstances.[58] He almost always ensured there was a compromise or, if that failed, a back-door escape from whatever pledge he offered. His slipperiness was his strength, but it was a quality that made it difficult for most Canadians to see

The brilliant orator and master of the pen Winston Churchill presented his view of the war in a series of histories, while Canada's wartime prime minister, William Lyon Mackenzie King, was overlooked, and then further cast aside after his death in 1950. King was not as dramatic or charismatic as Churchill, but he carefully guided Canada through the war. Historians and Canadians writ large have not treated King with much reverence or respect.

him as the leader to rouse the nation. However, one of King's great assets was in building a strong cabinet, perhaps the most talented in all of Canadian history.[59] While the rotund, uninspiring, and slightly wheezy King was not the leader to fire up Canadians, he had been the right leader at the right time, ensuring that English Canada's passion for an unlimited war effort did not tear the country apart. He was most proud of avoiding reckless actions, and was known for crowing about what he prevented as opposed to what he accomplished. This approach was not glamorous, although it was perhaps necessary in the Canadian context and after the terrible national scars wrought by the Great War. And yet, whereas Churchill promised to fight on the beaches and in the city streets to the death against a Nazi invasion, King gave us the trickster words of "conscription if necessary, but not necessarily conscription." The British lion roared; the Canadian beaver chewed away at the details. Churchill, the pre-eminent historian of the twentieth century, wrote millions and millions of words in international best-sellers that cemented and presented the history he made, shaping it to reflect his views on the war. King also wrote millions of words in his secret diaries that spanned more than fifty years—petty, small-minded comments mixed with a record of nearly every key event in the first half of the twentieth century.[60] Churchill defined the contemporary history of the war; King seemed absent from it, although his diaries would later come to inform the Canadian historical record.

German generals, too, as they were released from prison, shared their memoirs and actively laboured to shape history. Field Marshal Albert Kesselring penned two influential accounts in 1953 and 1955, while General Heinz Guderian and Field Marshal Erich von Manstein offered their expurgated exploits in presentations at American and British veterans' associations. The two German generals worked with historians to present their understanding of the fighting, and all the while downplayed their compliance with the Nazis and the systematic slaughter of civilians on the Eastern Front. These messages, in books, films, and presentations, were read and studied in the English world.[61]

Those who fought against the Germans had long been fascinated by their fighting exploits and aggressive attack style, and despite devastating defeats in the world wars, their generals and soldiers were held up as ideal soldiers. During the Cold War, the Americans even employed German generals to write their own history of the war, hoping to pick up clues on how to defeat the Soviet Red Army. These works, not surprisingly, also attempted to restore the reputation of the Wehrmacht. The American fascination with the German way of war was something akin to hero worship, and some Americans felt that the German generals might have won the war if they had not been hamstrung by the incompetent and mad Hitler.[62] There were many meanings to unpack in the German generals' exculpatory writings, but by producing their works they shaped and controlled the narrative, especially by highlighting the German fighting soldiers' prowess and downplaying the army's culpability in Eastern Front atrocities.

In the global war, Canada had contributed to victory far beyond the Allies' expectation of the poor and small-minded dominion that had stumbled its way out of the Depression, entirely unready for the war to follow. But having significantly aided the Allied victory, in the war of reputations to follow, Canadians reverted to their colonial ways. The Legion was focused on gathering veterans into its fold and on fighting for tangible pension and dependants' rights. The veterans' organization saw its role as primarily encouraging remembrance and commemoration, and it hoped others would tell the country's war stories. Most did not. The failure of the Canadian military and civilian high command to write their personal histories, along with the reticence of the million veterans to commit thoughts to paper beyond the first couple of years, meant that Canadians did not have much of an opportunity to read about Canada's war experience. This historical absence would grow and continue through the 1950s and 1960s, as American and British films, television shows, and books took up that space, mapping those national memories onto the history and offering little mention of Canada's wartime contributions. Canadians had only themselves to blame.

CHAPTER 5

SHIFTING MEANINGS AND FADING MEMORIES

"**L**et the man be forgotten," pleaded *The Ottawa Journal* in 1947. The paper directed its appeal to Canadians, with the hope that SS general Kurt Meyer would be left to rot in Dorchester prison in New Brunswick. The Nazi war criminal had become well known to Canadians in late 1945 for having ordered the murder of Canadian soldiers when he was a senior commander in the 12th SS Panzer "Hitler-Jugend" Division, the Canadians' adversaries from the first days of the Battle of Normandy in June 1944. The division was filled with adolescents indoctrinated with the murderous Nazi ideology and trained to revel in self-sacrifice.[1] The Hitler Youth were led by hard-bitten non-commissioned officers (NCOs) and officers, many of whom had seen brutal combat on the Eastern Front. Under the command of SS-Brigadeführer Fritz Witt, the 12th SS had failed to drive the Canadians back in the first week of battle in June, with both sides inflicting and suffering heavy casualties.[2] Two of Witt's regimental commanders, Brigadiers Kurt Meyer and Wilhelm Mohnke, were Nazis to the core, and they ordered and oversaw the execution of dozens of captured Canadians in the first week of June.

When Witt was killed in an airstrike on June 14, 1944, Meyer took command of the division. Meyer was a well-seasoned soldier: he joined the National Socialist Party in 1930 and was soon a member of Heinrich Himmler's Schutzstaffel (SS), the Nazi internal security force known for its ruthlessness. Meyer fought in the 1939 Polish campaign, in which he was slightly wounded—later receiving the Iron Cross second class for bravery under fire. He received another Iron Cross, this time first class, for combat against British forces near Dunkirk. A senior officer, SS-Obergruppenführer Sepp Dietrich, assessed Meyer's qualities as an officer, writing that he "possesses an unusual level of maturity in relation to his age. Hard upon himself, he puts personal well-being behind concern for his subordinates. . . . Meyer showed unheard of dash and considerable bravery. He was an example to his men in personal conduct and contributed substantially to the success of the *Leibstandarte* as leader of the advance company."[3] Small in build, he was explosive in command, an aggressive, charismatic leader who fought his way in and out of desperate situations on the Russian front. Meyer's command style epitomized the German strike doctrine of attacking hard and fast, and one superior noted that he had a "fanatical combat spirit." He was also a mass murderer and he talked freely of killing prisoners on the Eastern Front and laying waste to villages full of the elderly, women, and children.[4]

In Normandy, the second brigadier, Wilhelm Mohnke, commanded the 26th SS Panzer Grenadier Regiment. Whereas Meyer was cool and brave, Mohnke was a tyrant who frightened almost everyone who met him. A morphine addict after having a foot amputated from grievous injury while fighting in Yugoslavia, he was prone to outbursts of inexplicable rage. Mohnke's soldiers had also been unable to break the Canadian front on June 8 and 9,

Kurt Meyer, the commander of the 12th SS Panzer "Hitler-Jugend"
Division, was an arch-enemy for Canadians.

and he took his rage out on captured Canadians. Along the farmers' fields lay the bodies of unarmed Canadians who had been captured and shot in the head or machine-gunned in small groups. In all, at least 156 Canadians were murdered after capture in the first week of fighting in Normandy, attesting to the ferocious nature of battle and the wanton bloodlust of the 12th SS.[5]

More is known of Meyer's war crimes than of Mohnke's. In the aftermath of a clash of arms on June 7, almost two dozen members of the North Nova Scotia Highlanders and the Sherbrooke Fusiliers were taken prisoner and brought for interrogation at Meyer's headquarters at the ancient Abbaye d'Ardenne, on the outskirts of Caen. Most of the Canadians refused to give any useful information to the SS troops, and Meyer was present at some of these rough interrogations. Witnesses later testified to his ordering that there were to be no prisoners. One by one, the Canadians were taken away and shot. As each man was selected for execution, he would shake the hands of his comrades and walk to his fate.[6] It wasn't until the Canadian forces drove the 12th SS out of the Abbaye on July 9, during the capture of Caen, that the mass graves were discovered.

The once 21,000-strong 12th SS Division was destroyed in the Normandy fighting, reduced to about 500 soldiers, although Meyer survived and was captured in early September 1944. The Canadian forces wanted Meyer and the deranged Mohnke to stand trial for mass murder, but Mohnke disappeared after the war into a Russian Gulag.[7] Solely focused on bringing Meyer to account for his crimes, the Canadians built their case throughout late 1944 and early 1945, with Lieutenant-Colonel Bruce Macdonald, a prewar lawyer from Windsor, Ontario, and former commander of the Essex Scottish

Members of the 12th SS Panzer Division, who fought the Canadians from June to August 1944, before being annihilated as a fighting force by the end of the Normandy campaign.

A Canadian soldier armed with a Sten gun entering Caen after driving back the 12th SS forces. Afterwards, the Canadians discovered the bodies of their executed comrades across the battlefield and at the Abbaye d'Ardenne.

Regiment, eventually appointed as lead prosecutor. After victory in May 1945, the Allies prosecuted a small number of senior Nazi leaders, both political and military, in trials at Nuremburg starting in November of that year. Some felt it was too generous to give the murderous Nazis the opportunity of a trial, and that only summary execution was justified. Nonetheless, Allied authorities considered it important for the Nazis to be tried in a court of law. It might have been a victor's justice of sorts—although most scholars, both at the time and since then, have considered the trials fair within the historical context—and the justice they received was far better than the Nazis gave their millions of victims.[8] The trials would also create a formal record of the atrocities for the public and for history, while reinforcing the concept of the Necessary War.

The Canadian military and civilian authorities played no part at Nuremburg and instead focused their legal efforts on their personal enemies, the 12th SS. The numbers of Canadians murdered in the first week of battle with the Waffen-SS Hitler Youth—at least thirteen different incidents across many kilometres of battlefield—were sufficient to suggest that enemy soldiers were acting on orders or with tacit approval from their senior officers. The imprisoned Meyer was interrogated and, not surprisingly, denied giving any order to kill prisoners.[9] Macdonald and his small team searched through captured war records and interviewed German prisoners to find justice for the executed Canadians. Few of the Nazis in the 12th SS who survived chose to talk, but Macdonald doggedly pursued leads across the many prisoner-of-war camps. He eventually found a Polish conscript, Jan Jesionek, who was no friend of the Nazis and who testified that Meyer had told his soldiers he did not want any prisoners. Macdonald thought he had enough evidence to try Meyer for the murder of almost two dozen Canadian soldiers.

A hesitant federal cabinet in Ottawa, unsure of whether it should be involved in prosecuting a war criminal and initially hoping the British might do it for them, eventually agreed to allow the trial to go ahead. At the heart of the matter in the Meyer case was the idea that the Nazi general was responsible for the actions of his soldiers, even if he did not take part in the crimes. This was the new concept of command responsibility—in effect, being held accountable for subordinate soldiers under one's command. The basis for the Canadians' approach was in this sense much like the principles that would be established during the Nuremburg trials to prosecute the senior German political and military commanders for the war's atrocities.[10]

———

The trial took place in Aurich, a small German town by the North Sea. The Canadian military tribunal was formed by a group of senior officers who had seen combat and borne the weight of command. Major-General Harry Foster, president of the tribunal, had commanded the 7th Infantry Brigade on D-Day and fought throughout Normandy in some of the most vicious battles of the war, finally leading the 4th Armoured Division. The four other judges were all Canadian brigadiers: H.A. Sparling, Ian Johnston, H.P. Bell-Irving, and J.A. Roberts. Defending Meyer was Lieutenant-Colonel Maurice Andrew, a prewar lawyer from Stratford, Ontario, who had commanded the Perth Regiment in battle, for the most part fighting in the Italian campaign.

On December 10, 1945, the trial commenced and was without precedent in Canadian law. It attracted widespread attention in Britain and the United States, and was covered by Canadian journalists who reported daily from the courtroom. The German people also watched closely as they waited to see what form of justice might befall one of their former generals, most of them believing that this would be a show trial.

Macdonald had built a strong case over six months, gathering forensic evidence indicating that the Canadians had been murdered with bullet shots to the heads while their hands were bound. While the prosecutor had not been able to locate any of the 12th SS trigger men—most of them had likely been killed in the fighting in Normandy—he had found several key witnesses. The most important was Jesionek, who testified that he had witnessed cold-blooded murder on June 7 and 8, 1944, at the Abbaye, the site of the worst Canadian massacre. He claimed that Meyer, upon seeing a number of captured Canadians, had asked his troops, "Why do you bring prisoners to the rear, those murderers only eat off our rations?"[11] Jesionek recounted that, shortly thereafter, the prisoners were stripped of their papers and taken away, one by one, and shot in the head.

During the two-week case, Meyer's lawyer, Maurice Andrew, offered little in the form of rebuttals. But throughout the trial most eyes were on the German general, who sat still and soldier-like but continually glared at witnesses, intimidating some into stutters and silencing others with his cold gaze.[12] When Meyer finally took the stand, he refuted Jesionek and remained unrattled by Macdonald's questions. Clipped, professional, and selective in what he recounted, he was very much the SS general who had come through the fire of combat. He refused to admit to giving any orders that might have led to the murder of the Canadians. If such acts had happened, he suggested, they were carried out by a rogue few.

Canadians followed the trial thousands of kilometres from the courtroom, through daily reports from a number of journalists, including Ralph Allen in *The Globe and Mail*. The headline of his front-page story in the December 12, 1945, issue read: "Canadian Troops Shot With Their Hands Up."[13] A few days later, Allen

Kurt Meyer on trial in Aurich, before the Canadian military tribunal, December 1945.

wrote about the Canadians who courageously walked to their deaths: "A story of sadism and mental torture that sounded like an oriental horror tale entered the records today."[14] Ross Munro, Canada's most famous wartime journalist, told his readers on December 13 how Jesionek had offered eye-witness testimony to Meyer's order to murder Canadian prisoners.[15]

The arguments ended before Christmas, and after a short break for the holiday, on December 27 the Canadian senior officers on the bench deliberated the case and its many facets. While it was undeniable that Canadians had been murdered, the senior Canadian generals came to the conclusion that Jesionek's testimony to Meyer having ordered the executions was not believable. This was a blow to Macdonald's case, although there were six charges against Meyer, and the lesser ones—pertaining to his allowing the actions to occur under his command—could still result in the death sentence. The judges' deliberations were not recorded, but General Foster later noted that two of the senior officers—Johnston and Sparling—believed Meyer to be guilty of all charges. The final verdict found him guilty of only three of the six charges he faced; the most serious conviction was for allowing his troops to murder prisoners. Years later, Foster spoke of his own struggle over holding the Nazi accountable for the actions of his troops, acknowledging that his own soldiers had likely done similar acts, albeit in revenge for the initial executions.[16] That might have been true, and certainly Canadian infantrymen talked openly of revenge in Normandy once the 12th SS murders were revealed. Yet there was a difference between killing in battle, motivated by fear and pumping adrenaline within a confusing situation where some of the enemy were surrendering while others were still fighting, and carrying out cold-blooded executions hours or days later.

Putting aside the grim nature of battle, there is no evidence that Canadians did what the SS had done.

On the morning of December 28, 1945, the military court sentenced Meyer to death by firing squad. He had expected nothing less. Macdonald felt a grim satisfaction and, as he later wrote, "a profound sense of relief that it was all over."[17] He had come to respect Meyer for his toughness, courage, and dignity, but he felt a stronger debt to ensure justice for his murdered countrymen.

The rules of procedure for the court had ensured that the judges' final decision would be reviewed by a senior Canadian officer, and Major-General Chris Vokes, the commander of the Canadian Army Occupational Force in Germany, was chosen for the task. The hard-fighting, red-haired, barrel-chested Vokes had battled his way through Italy and Northwest Europe. He was a soldier through and through, and had been willing to accept significant casualties— some said too willing after the bashing affair at Ortona—to achieve a victory. Vokes was quite unsure about being involved in the trial, and he worried that the Canadian regulations for war crimes trials were among the first carried out by any of the Allied nations, and that Canada might be marching too far ahead of the Americans or the British. Nonetheless, he decided to allow the death sentence to stand, signing off on December 31, 1945. Meyer would die in a week's time. And with his execution, justice would be served and perhaps Canadians might find some sense of closure to the war against evil.

But although a firing party was detailed and Meyer said his farewell to wife and children, Macdonald had written the rules of procedure for the court to include not one but two reviews of the judgment by a senior Canadian officer. The final sign-off was to be completed by the senior Canadian theatre commander, then Lieutenant-General Guy Simonds, who was in the Netherlands. But a ruling by military justice officers at Canadian military head-quarters in London ordered that because the trial was in Germany, the task again had to fall to Vokes, who was stationed there. This was only a formality since Vokes had just signed off on the death sentence a few days earlier, but now the Canadian general returned to studying the transcripts during the first days of the new year, talking the trial over with officers. He wavered and decided to fly to London to consult with senior staff officers. To his surprise, most of them recommended a commuted sentence.[18] Vokes changed his opinion, reluctant to set the precedent that a commander in the field was "responsible with his life for the acts of subordinates," especially in the absence of written evidence of such an order.[19] Having passed the death sentence a few days earlier, Vokes now reversed his decision and commuted Meyer's punishment to life in prison. The Nazi general found out he would be spared on January 13, 1946, having suffered through a week of expecting every day to be his last. No Canadian shed a tear for him, and his reprieve was met by grinding teeth among most military personnel. It was, to say the least, a shocking reversal.

On January 16, three days after Meyer heard of his reprieve, Canadian papers reported the news, which was met with wide-spread outrage. Canada's war dead had been betrayed, argued several editorialists. A *Toronto Telegram* letter writer raged, "Our boys were innocent. This man should be made to suffer in the same way he made them suffer."[20] Others were furious on behalf of the families of loved ones who would never find peace with the knowl-edge that this Nazi monster lived while their sons and husbands lay buried. Rabbi A.C. Feinberg, writing in the *Toronto Star*, warned that the war against fascism might have been won, but if murderers like Meyer still lived, the fight was not over.[21]

Macdonald and the prosecuting team were shattered by Vokes's change of mind.[22] While Meyer had been convicted, the unexpected reversal and subsequent outrage left many regarding the trial as a failure. From that point forward, Canada gave up attempting to go it alone in prosecuting war criminals. At the same time, Meyer was now a problem for the Canadian government. Where would he be incarcerated for life? Canada had no overseas prisons, and military officials decided against sending him to a British military prison; and so he was committed to Dorchester prison in New Brunswick, becoming the only German war criminal to be held outside Western Europe. Three months later, and hoping to avoid journalistic scrutiny, the authorities put Meyer aboard S.S. *Aquitania* on April 24, 1946. During the week-long passage to Canada, the general wandered freely aboard the ship, interacting with the other passengers, most of whom were war brides and children soon to be reunited with their husbands and fathers. To remove him from the vessel without unwanted attention in Halifax, the military dressed Meyer in a Canadian private's uniform—the attire of the very men whom he had ordered or allowed to be executed.

Canadians forgot about Meyer for a time, but he resurfaced in February 1950, when Ralph Allen, the noted journalist who had covered the Meyer trial in 1945, wrote an incendiary article for *Maclean's* magazine, with the provocative title, "Was Kurt Meyer Guilty?" A sympathetic chronicler of the Canadian war effort, Allen dropped a bombshell, opining, "If the Kurt Meyer trial was unfair, its greatest unfairness wasn't to Meyer himself. It was the final over-riding unfairness to a set of precepts which, if we deny in the face of our enemies, we may yet deny to ourselves."[23] Allen argued that the trial was not in accordance with several principles of Canadian law, although he did little to include the context in which the trial was conducted. He portrayed Meyer as a heroic soldier and an inspiring leader, while downplaying the atrocities that he and his soldiers carried out on the Eastern and Western fronts.

With *Maclean's* boasting a readership of over 400,000, the article reverberated across the country. Meyer's former defence counsel, Maurice Andrew, publicly dismissed Allen's charges of unfairness, while others warned there would be hell to pay if the German general was released on a technicality.[24] A number of Canadians complained to *Maclean's*, and their letters were published in its pages. P.M. Wass of Newport Station, Nova Scotia, argued that there was no injustice and that the "strutting Nazi Meyer condemned himself by word and action." The Nazis followed no law, he said, and throughout the war they had "fattened their egos on mass murder."[25] Others seemed confused about why some acts of killing in the war were singled out, seeing war as

The prisoner Kurt Meyer in jail at Dorchester prison in New Brunswick.

inherently barbarous and therefore assuming that there was no difference between a killing on the battlefield and the post-battle execution of defenceless soldiers who had surrendered. In the reaction
to the article, one could see that the idea of the Necessary War had
already slipped a little from its central place in the public discourse.

In the harsh immediate postwar years, West Germans had survived the partition of their country in 1949 and now faced the
Soviet threat on their eastern frontiers. With the help of billions
of dollars in US Marshall Plan aid money, West Germany rapidly
rebuilt and regained prosperity, even as East Germany, under
Communist rule, became bleaker and greyer and was finally cut
off from the West with the erection of the Berlin Wall in 1961.[26]
NATO commanders argued that they needed a re-armed West
Germany as a forward defence in what many feared was the
coming World War III against the Soviets. However, the notion
of rebuilding a strong new German army produced tremendous
disquiet in France and other nations that had endured the Nazi
invasions. The Germans were aware that they needed to seek
redemption, but they also knew that if their country was to be
turned into a bulwark against the Soviets—not an immaterial
thing in a war that was expected to go nuclear—then its leaders
held some sway in the negotiations.

A key discussion point was the transfer of German soldiers to
the fatherland, which West German Chancellor Konrad Adenauer,
in power from May 1949, demanded as part of the process of
Germany's return to the Western alliance. In Meyer's case, as the
Cold War deepened and as the Second World War faded from
immediate memory, West German authorities argued that the general might be more useful in a soldier's uniform than in that of a
prisoner. He certainly deserved to be on German soil, authorities

from Bonn argued, as he was the only convicted war criminal who was being held outside Europe.

The Canadian cabinet agonized over what to do with the Nazi prisoner, even as it decided in late 1950 to send an air division and an army brigade to strengthen NATO in Germany against a possible Soviet invasion.[27] As Minister of External Affairs Lester B. Pearson later wrote in his memoirs, he told the cabinet, "The Korean War had increased our fears of Soviet military aggression; a contribution by West Germany to NATO forces and its acceptance of NATO responsibilities was held to be essential."[28] The enemy of my enemy is my friend, seemed the bitter phrase of the day.

Throughout 1950, the Canadian Liberal government was lobbied by German diplomatic representatives, who used the *Maclean's* article to bolster their argument that Meyer had suffered an injustice. They offered veiled threats implying that growing outrage in their country's media over Meyer's incarceration was souring Germans on returning to the Western sphere of influence. The Canadian cabinet debated the matter into 1951, discussing at length the political fallout that Meyer's release would create, but there were few political champions to defend the murdered Canadian soldiers. In early February, the *Ottawa Citizen* broke the story that the government was considering releasing the Nazi general. There were angry letters in newspapers across the country, and *Time* magazine reported that Hamilton's United Council of Veterans protested the clemency, which it said "would be a flagrant injustice to the families and comrades of . . . victims of inhumanity," while in Windsor, at Ford Local 200, there was a resolution passed opposing the release of "this butcher of defenseless prisoners."[29] Another Canadian fumed, in one of the many letters sent to Ottawa, that any leniency would be "an insult to the revered memory of the thousands who died to free the world of Nazi enslavement."[30]

In September 1951, the cabinet returned to the worrisome political issue and asked for advice from the chief of the general staff, Lieutenant-General Guy Simonds. As Canada's most effective Second World War battlefield commander, his voice carried weight, and he suggested that Meyer had not been tried fairly and that he could not be responsible for the actions of his men. This was an ill-informed recommendation, one perhaps shaped by Simonds's discomfort about generals being responsible for the actions of their soldiers, but it helped the cabinet extricate itself from the political nightmare.[31] With the cover of Simonds's recommendation, the cabinet ordered Meyer back to Germany.

On October 19, 1951, three men drove through a dark night to Dorchester prison. The orders from Ottawa were to ensure that the operation was carried out swiftly and with no publicity. Meyer was removed from prison, with the four men speeding off to Halifax and boarding a plane for Germany. Before Canadians had any clue about the sneaky manoeuvre, Meyer had left Canadian soil. The Nazi was sent to Werl and incarcerated in a British-run prison with other convicted war criminals, including General Albert Kesselring and General Erich von Manstein.

When news spread that Meyer had been released from Dorchester, a new round of controversy and public protests took place. *The Globe and Mail* charged the government with "an entirely false and unnecessary air of mystery" that had contributed to strong feelings of betrayal among Canadians.[32] Conspiratorial accusations related to Meyer's return to Germany emerged, one of the most popular being a published tract by well-known Vancouver journalist Ray Gardner, titled "Wanted for Murder."[33] Gardner presented the case against Meyer and even slipped in some deep-state musings suggesting that the general was being returned to Germany to take up a role in a new Nazi organization.

For his part, journalist Douglas How felt there was a story in Meyer's wife, Kate, and her reactions to the original death sentence, the commuted sentence, the prison term in Canada, and now her husband's return home to a prison on German soil. The journalist visited her on November 26, 1951, and to his shock, Kurt Meyer was there, granted a day pass from prison. The Canadian journalist interviewed the couple, and his published stories were carried in newspapers across Canada. When How asked Meyer if he regretted his association with the Nazis and his support of Hitler, the general evaded the question, replying, "The past is dead."[34]

How's article unleashed a new firestorm of controversy, with the government accused of misleading the public.[35] The past was not dead, Canadians insisted, and more than a few raged that the Canadians executed by Meyer's actions would have no future. A heated political battle erupted in Parliament, with the Conservative leader of the Opposition, Great War veteran George Drew, raking the government's front benches with verbal fire, decrying the betrayal of Canada's Second World War murdered soldiers even as the same government sent other young men off to war in Korea. "Kurt Meyer is more than simply another Nazi general," Drew roared. "He has become a symbol in the minds of Canadians, who have suffered from Nazi brutality, of the sort of thing that would raise doubts as to the clarity of our attitude toward conduct of that kind. I think that, at a time when other young men are being called upon to fight for their country, the people of Canada want some reassurance as to exactly what is going to be done."[36]

Over the next two years, the West German government negotiated with the Soviets, the British, and the French for the release of many of its soldiers from behind bars. With new Cold War politics to consider, reviews were put in place to examine the Nazis' trials and punishments, and few in London, Paris, or even Moscow had much stomach for continuing to pay for these war criminals in special prisons. As Meyer was now in a British prison, the Canadians were not part of the consultative process. Taking a cue from the now dead prime minister King's playbook, the Liberal cabinet liked it that way; plausible deniability allowed the Louis St. Laurent government to shift blame to the British should the Nazi be released. The Germans continued to petition for Meyer to be pardoned, and in January 1954 little protest was heard from the Canadian government when a doctor ruled that the war and incarceration had irrevocably damaged Meyer's health and that he should be released for compassionate reasons.[37] Following the recommendation, the cabinet reduced Meyer's sentence from life imprisonment to fourteen years with an Order in Council.[38]

"The Canadian public," declared the *Toronto Telegram*, "had been given no justification to justify leniency and the mitigation of his sentence."[39] *The British Colonist* condemned the government's conniving behaviour and insisted that while "Canada could not dwell on the war forever," Meyer had received a fair trial and a just sentence in light of his murderous complicity or his outright ordering of mass murder.[40] In less than a decade, the Allies had gone from prosecuting and seeking the death penalty for the worst of these Nazis to letting most of them go. No wonder some believed that the many victims of the Nazis were abandoned in the Cold War, sacrificed on the altar of defence—part of a process whereby old enemies became new allies against the old allies turned new enemies.

With the Germans and the British now leaning heavily on the Canadians and threatening them with public censure if Meyer died in prison, the cabinet was further pressured to give its assent for the prisoner's release. The Canadian body was saved that difficult political decision when the British high commissioner in Bonn granted Meyer his release for good conduct in prison. After fewer than ten years behind bars, Meyer was freed on September 7, 1954. He was given a hero's welcome in his home town, with children bearing torches, the streets lined with cheering people, and some 5,000 Waffen-SS veterans saluting him. Photographs of the events were published in Canadian newspapers, revealing a robust and healthy Meyer, far from the near-death condition that the Germans had claimed he was in, and which had been a factor in his release.

Many Canadians wept for the murdered Canadian soldiers, who had been abandoned by their government that had not fought for justice. A cartoon in the *Calgary Herald* depicted a jailor (who represented the politicians in Ottawa) pushing eighteen murdered soldiers out of the way as Meyer goose-stepped his way out of prison.[41] Bruce Macdonald, the lawyer who had prosecuted the Nazi, raged that "Meyer's release can be justified on the basis of international political expediency only," and he published a book that year, *The Trial of Kurt Meyer*.[42] Macdonald even predicted that Meyer, being relatively young and an exalted warrior raised to the status of martyr, would likely again rise to power in Germany in a new political role.[43] Others ruminated that he might be a likely candidate for senior general in NATO, and that in that role he would command Canadian troops.

Meyer remained unapologetic about his wartime actions, and he would go on to lead a right-wing organization. As head of HIAG (Hilfsorganisation auf Gegenseitigkeit der Waffen-SS), an association of ex-SS soldiers who fought to receive full veterans' rights and other benefits that had been denied to them as Nazis, Meyer became an advocate for his SS comrades. He lied about the SS's wartime actions and denied they had anything to be ashamed of, suggesting that they were little more than regular soldiers in the Wehrmacht.[44] Meyer's profile was further raised by the 1957 publication of his memoir, *Grenadiere*, a gritty if sanitized account of the war years.[45] He portrayed himself as master of the battlefield, denied the Canadians were murdered, and characterized the trial as a sham. The executed Canadians were but minor props in his own story of war, captivity, and martyrdom.

Meyer rehabilitated his reputation after being released from prison, denying SS soldiers' atrocities and publishing his memoirs, the cover of a later reprint which is seen here with slightly different title.

The general eventually took a job as a travelling beer salesman. Among his clients were Canadian soldiers in NATO stationed at Soest, who occasionally drank with him in their mess. Weakened in health, Meyer died at age fifty-one on December 23, 1961. He lived seventeen years longer than the young Canadian soldiers whom he ordered murdered in the fields of Normandy.

The Meyer trial had been an attempt to seek justice for the executed. Though 45,000 Canadians had died during the war, these executions in Normandy weighed heavily on the country. They did not fit easily into the notion of sacrifice in the Necessary War, although most soldiers knew that combat was never clean. Meyer represented a particular form of evil that Canadians could understand. He had been an aggressive warrior, but he also stood for all that was corrupt in the Nazi regime. Some respected his tenacious skills in battle, but he was regarded, too, as a mad dog that had to be put down. When his death sentence was reported, Canadians took solace in the fact that his grim actions were being punished. But the commutation of the death sentence infuriated most Canadians. Less than a decade later, Meyer's release from prison provoked a new round of controversy that not only tempered the idea of the Necessary War, but also destabilized it. Ten years after most of the boys came home and rebuilt the country, the release of Meyer laid bare the notion of a war that was slipping from relevance. The government of the new day had betrayed the slain soldiers.

One of the strongest critics of the government's handling of the Meyer case was the Canadian Legion. One journalist described the organization as "the watch-dog of veterans' rights."[46] This role also extended to preserving the memory of fallen comrades and to

ensuring annual acts of remembrance. The 1951 Census indicated
that there were 1,228,000 veterans in Canada, of which about
200,000 were Legion members. Other veterans belonged to additional organizations, including 3,000 in the War Amps, 50,000 in
the Canadian Pensioners' Association, and 70,000 in the Army,
Navy and Air Force Veterans in Canada.[47] Those groups were not
as effective in advocating on behalf of veterans with Ottawa, and
they would lose members over the years, though the War Amps
would become a prominent agent for change under their dynamic
leader Cliff Chadderton from the mid-1960s onward. And yet
RCAF veteran Norman Shannon of *The Legionary* wondered why
fewer than a quarter of all veterans had joined organizations like
the Legion; he speculated that perhaps when the veterans came
back, the demobilization package of money and Veterans Charter
benefits was too good.[48] Few veterans understood that the Legion
had been working on their behalf, even as they were happy to
leave the war behind and move forward into building the new
Canada. Shannon and many Legion members felt that those veterans who were not members were getting a "free ride" on the
backs of those who banded together. But the Legion continued to
fight on behalf of all veterans, and it was by far the most recognizable veterans' organization. The memory of the war was, however,
becoming less relevant across society, which was only natural.
Canada had contributed to the Allied victory on multiple fronts,
but by the early 1950s the country was prosperous and moving
forward, happy to leave the war and the Depression years behind.
The vast majority of veterans had got on with their lives and they
refused to dwell on the past. Memories dulled over time, and for
those who did not serve—which was most Canadians—the war
gradually lost its intense meaning.

Except in the Legion Halls. Most communities, whether large or small, had at least one, and as they excluded those who did not serve, the halls were places of sanctuary for veterans. Traumatic experiences could be worked through. While not all service personnel saw battle, they were part of a great tribe that had done important things together. There were as many individual experiences as there were men and women in uniform, but those who served were connected by communal elements—first enlistment, training, fear, exposure to death, and pride in service, to name but a few. And it was common for the ex-service personnel to struggle upon their return to communities and loved ones, especially with recounting the war and what it meant to them. Sometimes their painful memories were revealed in brief glimpses or brought to the surface by an event like the Meyer case that excited many to anger. More often, there was silence.

Unable to ask the questions and perhaps fearful of the answers, some families simply ignored the war. One Canadian veteran, who served two years overseas and came back when he was twenty, felt that his aged parents, never asking, never inquiring, simply did not care—that they were consigning the war to the past.[49] More than likely, this mother and father had no idea how to talk to their son who had gone away a boy and returned as someone very different. "I often wonder how many wives really understand how their husbands feel about the war," wrote Doug Smith, a veteran of the Normandy campaign. "How difficult it is for one person to transmit to another their innermost feelings about an experience so unique and different from any other occasion in his lifetime."[50] The connections between the men and women in uniform were forged in a strange and terrifying land, and they were often far deeper than those made in civilian life, sometimes even fuller and more emotional than their relationships with wives or children.

The Legion Halls tended to be modest buildings that were run by local Legion branches. They were places of military history, and within them were displayed wartime trophies and memorabilia, photographs and works of art, flags and colours. Such objects, along with commemorative plaques for fallen personnel and recognition of service, contributed to the culture of comradery, nostalgia, and, at times, reverence. For instance, the halls had a rule requiring that hats be removed as a sign of respect for comrades. Many of the Legion Halls had been built in the mid-1920s, as the Great War veterans sought each other out in civilian life. The Legion had prided itself on being a class-free organization, where for decades all men, regardless of rank, called each other "comrade." The halls were built for the Great War veterans; they were decorated to their tastes and filled with their music and images of their heroes. And when the Second World War ex-service personnel began to attend in late 1945, they found the Great War veterans—the "Old Sweats" as they were sometimes called—holding all the positions of influence.

It was not easy for that older group of veterans to accept the young guns and their different ways, and strife arose over all manner of things, from formal toasts and traditions to music and wall hangings. Veteran Bob Smellie of the Royal Winnipeg Rifles recounted of the Legion Hall in his community, "My father and his cronies ran the organization from a room over his store. They let us in, but they made all the decisions."[51] It took about a decade for this intergenerational friction to work itself out, and then more Second World War veterans stepped into positions of power.

By 1957, two thousand Canadian Legion branches were established around the world.[52] And yet these veterans' spaces were mysterious places, leaving wives and children wondering what happened behind the closed doors. Others sneered, describing them as clubhouses where old soldiers disappeared to sing, tell lies, and drink their worries away. As Douglas Fisher, a veteran of the 12th Manitoba Dragoons and a former CCF and NDP member of Parliament, recalled, "I have heard characters scoff at the Legion and sniffily refer to the body as a bunch of flag-wavers and beer-drinkers."[53] But the Legion and the halls were places where veterans could go to talk and work through the war in their heads. While they played a key role in many veterans' lives, they also ensured that much of the war was kept hidden from other sectors of society, in a sense becoming a cloistered history of those who served. Veterans, too, contributed to the silencing of the Necessary War, as they struggled to make sense of it long after victory.

Despite being a closed organization, the Legion, with all its members drawn from the wider communities, was far from cut off from society. And although much of the Legion's work was geared towards aiding veterans and their dependants, the organization saw itself as a pillar of modern Canada. It was a fiercely patriotic body and yet also one with strong ties to the Empire and the monarchy. The Queen's image was in every Legion Hall, as were the Union Jack and the Red Ensign—the latter the unofficial flag that Canadians fought under during both world wars. The Legion was also anti-Communist, with one 1947 editorial in *The Legionary* describing the ideology as "a wide-spread conspiracy to destroy our form of government and way of life," the way of life that they and their comrades had fought for during the war.[54] The Legion supported the government's decision to back the United Nations in the war in Korea, and it advocated for conscription, even as few Canadians paid much attention to that overseas conflict.

Throughout the 1950s, the Legion continued to fight on behalf of veterans, war widows, and orphans. About 900 veterans' cases a year were brought forward and advocated for by the Legion, usually to raise pension rates, and this included the new veterans of the Korean War, where some 26,791 served and 516 were killed.[55] One way of repaying the debt to those who fell during the world wars or Korea was to care for their dependants. The Legion offered scholarships for education, while some veterans "adopted" the children of killed comrades in a "big brother" relationship.[56] The organization also pressured the government to financially assist the families of the fallen and was instrumental in the passing of the Children of Deceased Veterans Educational Assistance Act. The act established the Education Assistance Program, through which, over twenty-five years, some 5,000 children received millions of dollars in funding. As one minister said of the program, "This is part of the continuing obligation the government recognizes towards children of Canadian war dead who gave their lives for their country."[57]

But there was a growing sense among Legion members that the war was being left in the past. In October 1955, the organization's Dominion president, John O. Anderson, a member of the clergy and a Second World War veteran, asked the readers of *The Legionary*, "Quo Vadimus?—Whither are we going?" Anderson advocated that the Legion needed to transform itself by becoming more engaged with non-veterans. Ten years after the war, and some thirty years after the enactment of the Legion's charter, Anderson stated that to this point, "the Legion's chief characteristic has been its devotion to the welfare of the veteran," but that he felt the organization needed to broaden its impact or run the risk of becoming obsolete. The Legion would continue to advocate for veterans, although Anderson felt that much of the groundwork with the government on behalf of ex-service personnel had been laid. What next? He argued that the Legion had a "moral duty" to create a better, fairer, and more equitable country for all Canadians. Those who had fought for their country, he believed, had a stake in raising that country to new levels. The Legion branches across the country should begin to look outward into their own communities and become a force for good. Legionnaires should promote "freedom and democracy," aid in education, and assist in the polio campaign. They should also, Anderson said, promote the education of new Canadians in civics and notions of democracy, and focus on youth, especially on finding ways for them to connect with the war effort and its ongoing relevance. If the Legion did not follow this path, he warned, it would become increasingly irrelevant and move into "gradual decline where members sit in the lengthening shadows, contemplating the lost days of their youth."[58] Increasingly, Legionnaires would accept this mantle, and Anderson's call to action was much cited for years to come as an important hinge point in the veterans' movement.

Despite this refocus, which began in the late 1950s, commemoration remained crucial for the Legion, with Remembrance Day as the central act of engaging with the Canadian public. The day of observance resonated deeply with both those who served and those who lost loved ones. In Ottawa in 1955, amid a day of military pageantry and sombre reflection, Silver-Cross mother

Regina Leboldus of Vibank, Saskatchewan, represented the tens of thousands of mothers who had lost sons in the war, a form of honouring first observed in 1936. After two minutes of silence and bands softly playing "O God Our Help in Ages Past," Leboldus laid one of the official wreaths on the National War Memorial before an estimated 6,000 spectators. Across the country, Canadians watched her on television; wearing a large fur coat, the aging mother was flanked by Governor General Vincent Massey and Prime Minister Louis St. Laurent. The Russian-born Leboldus had come to Canada with her husband in 1903, a family of new Canadians who helped build up the country and served in its wars. Leboldus still bore the weight of having lost three sons in action within twelve months, all of them serving with the RCAF. Her sons had gone missing from February 1943 to February 1944. Two brothers were in No. 418 Squadron. Martin, a member of the land crew, had helped see his brother Peter off on a sortie. Peter never returned, his plane going down over France. Martin remustered to aircrew, becoming a flight engineer, and nine months later he disappeared while flying with No. 419 Squadron. The third brother, John, was lost over Italy as an air-gunner serving with No. 142 Squadron RAF, and his body was never recovered. Regina Leboldus later said of her despair and her determination to move forward, "I didn't think I could do it. But then I thought of my boys, and I knew I had to do it."[59]

The poppy, too, continued as an outward symbol of remembrance. In 1956, *The Legionary* said that the "national poppy campaign is a debt to the dead and a duty to the living," and that wearing the poppy was an annual pledge to marking the sacrifice of war.[60] But there was a growing sense of anxiety among Legion members that the act of remembrance was losing its relevance. This was partially triggered by the ongoing Cold War struggle with the Soviet Union that could at any time degenerate into a nuclear holocaust. The hydrogen bombs that both superpowers, the United States and the Soviet Union, had in their arsenals were at least 500 times as devastating as the atomic bombs that had been dropped on Japan. Few put much faith in the pathetic air raid warnings or the drills involving children taking cover under their classroom desks to protect themselves against bombs that created a blast hotter than the sun, followed by a nuclear winter. One Canadian Press story printed in papers after Remembrance Day in 1957 thought it almost quaint that "Canadians took a moment out of the satellite age . . . to remember their war dead from other anxious times."[61]

With nearly 4.5 million Canadian children having been born after the war, veterans in the late 1950s wondered how to connect with these young people and share with them the "living grief of those who were left behind."[62] Canada was changing. The old ways were shifting. A societal drift away from remembrance was evident, and veterans recognized that more and more people were untouched by the war. Quite simply, the Necessary War was losing meaning. Ian Burnett, in reflecting on Remembrance Day, asked in *The Ottawa Journal* in November 1960 if "we, as individuals and as a nation, are in danger of losing by default all that this day means, losing it through a careless, laissez-faire thoughtless attitude?" While there were gatherings at monuments in cities across the country, Burnett wondered if the children or teenagers understood the importance of the day. He observed, "This year one religious group organized parties for its children. Elsewhere dances were held for young people. No one would object to such activities provided the true meaning and message of this day has been safeguarded in the memories and imagination of our youth." Echoing a sentiment circulating in veterans' organizations, he emphasized that the champions of memory had to work to make sure the war was not forgotten. "A young nation has a particular need to cherish its memories," wrote Burnett. "Out of these must grow the traditions which in turn gives the nation its own special ethos. And among the greatest and most sacred of our memories as Canadians is the part played by our sons, our brothers, our fathers in two world wars. At peril to ourselves we forget them."[63]

The Legionary's Norman Shannon also alerted his fellow veterans to the danger of minimizing the past, and lamented that millions of Canadians had forgotten the war's impact on Canada's development as a nation. "Today most Canadians would be hard pressed to distinguish a veteran from a non-veteran," he said—save for the visibly wounded. Shannon thought this was a sign of the government's immediate postwar success in aiding the transition back to civilian life. In 1960, it would have surprised many Canadians to know that over a million men and close to 50,000 women were veterans of the war, including more than 100 federal MPs. As Shannon noted with concern, "The assimilation of the veteran into our political, economic and social life has been so successful that the veteran now blends completely with his environment."[64] This also meant that veterans, their wartime accomplishments, and even the totality of the Canadian war effort was increasingly becoming invisible. R.B. Shaw, a veteran and executive in the Victoria Legion branch, also noted in 1960 that across society there was a "'forget-your-war-service' attitude," and that this meanness of spirit extended to those who openly derided veterans and sometimes displayed a "tendency to ignore, discredit, or discount the achievements and military service records of others."[65] Shaw and other veterans worried that the importance of the nation's contribution to the Second World War was being lost in the modern Canada.

By the end of the 1950s, the war was no longer a meaningful force in shaping the Canadian imagination. Even the sacred Remembrance Day was losing its power to move many Canadians. The Cold War also influenced the narrative: why focus on remembering the old war when we had to contend with a new, ongoing, and seemingly unending Cold War? The need to re-arm Germany in the face of growing Soviet power and the fear of nuclear annihilation was preoccupying many Canadians. Nazi general Kurt Meyer's release from prison had stunned Canadians and led to much outrage, but it was clear to many that Cold War politics had overshadowed justice for Canada's executed wartime soldiers. The handling of Meyer's case was a poignant symbol that the war's meaning was fading, and the Legion recognized that it had to actively engage within its many communities to stay relevant. Veterans feared that young Canadians no longer understood or really cared about the wartime sacrifice of their elders. Across society, the war was little talked about, except in the closed Legion Halls, and this isolation left stories shrouded in silence. The Necessary War against Hitler and his Nazis was rapidly fading from social memory.

CHAPTER 6

THE MEMORIAL THAT NEVER WAS

C harles Lynch, the celebrated wartime journalist and postwar columnist, returned to Juno Beach in June 1954, on the tenth anniversary of the invasion. "There are not many signs today either on the beaches or in the countryside of the battles which raged here a decade ago," wrote Lynch. "Today there was nothing to show that Canadians and Germans had fought and died on the beach, apart from four ruined concrete pillboxes. There is a simple stone monument which contains what even the Canadians might admit is a rather sweeping statement: Here on 6 June 1944, Europe was liberated by the heroism of the Allied forces."[1] Lynch wondered why there was no Canadian memorial at Juno. Indeed, it's fair to ask—why was there no Vimy-like memorial anywhere in Europe to display to Europeans the Canadian contributions to the Allied victory? It was the same in Canada. Less than a decade after the war ended, few remembered how the King government had avoided building any new national monuments in Ottawa or overseas and that it had refused to accede to the Legion's demands for one. At the same time, the Legion had other priorities in 1945—the most important being the reintegration and care of the returned men and women—and they had not thrown their full weight behind the fight for a monument, whether overseas or at home. But that would change a decade later, with the unveiling of the Book of Remembrance.

Canada's Second World War Book of Remembrance was, as poet Duncan Campbell Scott wrote, a testament to the "Immortals that saved the World."[2] The tome listed those who died in the service of the country, and a similarly ornate book had been created as a literary shrine for the fallen of the Great War. After nine years of work, the Second World War book was ready for presentation in mid-1957. In the volume are the names of those who fell from September 1939 to September 1947, with the end date set two years after the war to account for those who died of their wounds or illnesses following victory.

The book's 614 pages list more than 44,900 Canadians, with each of the servicemen and -women's rank, unit, and decorations delineated in alphabetical order, by year of death. The Merchant Navy veterans were at the time still considered civilians in the war zone and not recognized as veterans. The sacred task of creating the book was carried out by Lieutenant-Commander Alan Beddoe, Canada's foremost heraldic expert, who had also overseen the production of the Great War book. A staff of artists and calligraphers illustrated the pages with images of battles in the global war, from Hong Kong to Iceland, from Ortona to Hamburg.

On November 11, 1957, Governor General Vincent Massey unveiled the Second World War Book of Remembrance, which rested on an altar next to the First World War Book of Remembrance with its 66,561 names. These two hallowed commemorative objects testified fully to Canada's extensive service and terrible sacrifice during the world wars. Massey observed, "It is right and fitting that we, the living, should always remember the sacrifices of them who,

The Memorial Chamber, near the base of the Peace Tower, is dedicated to Canadians who died in wars and peace missions around the world. The chamber contains a central stone altar, surrendered by other altars holding the different Books of Remembrance.

on the field of honour, died to give to us, and to generations yet unborn, the privilege of living in freedom."[3] Prime Minister John Diefenbaker, a veteran of the first war, said in his address at the ceremony that the memorial chamber was a "national shrine to the unforgotten" and that "in these days of foreboding and fear, our dedication must be that we not prove unworthy of them."[4] The prime minister also talked of building another memorial to the fallen from the Second World War. This was required, he said, since the Memorial Chamber was so overtly dedicated to the Great War, with its carved inscriptions of battles and stained glass windows to those who did not come home in 1919. This new memorial, which was to be called the National Shrine, would be the long-awaited monument that the Legion had been asking for since 1945.

Two years earlier, in a brief to cabinet on November 10, 1955, the Legion had submitted a proposal for a separate and unique national cenotaph in Ottawa to honour Canada's fallen of all wars except the Great War. Prime Minister King was dead, and the Legion sought to re-engage the nation's leaders over the issue of memorializing the Second World War. The Legion mobilized to fight for a new national monument, writing to all members of Parliament, restating that this proposed cenotaph would "serve to commemorate the fallen of all wars."[5] This was also the time when more Second World War veterans were taking over the leadership of the Legion, both in the individual halls and at the national level, and were exerting more political influence. With one voice, the Legionnaires returned to their request for a separate memorial that they had made to the government in 1945, asking again for a simple but authoritative memorial, one like Sir Edwin Lutyens's cenotaph in London, England, which marked all of that nation's war dead. Lutyens's "empty sepulchre" had "inspired reverence to a higher degree than any other form of memorial," claimed the Legion. The strong veterans' push for a memorial, to be erected on the grounds of Parliament Hill beneath the Peace Tower in Ottawa, would have the desired effect, and the Liberal Louis St. Laurent government appointed an advisory committee made up of members from government, veterans, and the Legion.

To bolster its case, the Legion complained—as it had done in 1945—that the existing national monument near Parliament portrayed the "heroic figures . . . of Canada's fighting men of the First World War so faithfully as to render it unsuitable as a memorial to our fallen in World War II and the Korean War. Many widows, children, parents and comrades of the fallen of those later conflicts have expressed surprise and disappointment that the memory of *their* dead has not yet been commemorated visually by the nation."[6] There was implied criticism of architect Vernon March's monument, The Response, suggesting that it was too closely linked to one war. Toronto, Montreal, Winnipeg, Calgary, and Vancouver, the Legion argued, had all chosen more "wisely," selecting monuments that were timeless (and not adorned with figures in Great War uniforms).

On April 30, 1956, Minister of Veterans Affairs Hugues Lapointe, who had risen to the rank of lieutenant-colonel in the war, announced that the government would fund a new national cenotaph for the fallen of Canada's wars (save for the Great War, which would continue to be honoured by The Response) and that it would act as a structure that would store the Second World War Book of Remembrance atop an altar.[7] The announcement was front-page news across the country. Nepean Point, overlooking the Ottawa River and located to the north of the present-day National Art Gallery, would be the future site of this memorial.[8] The Department of Public Works began planning for the project, which would include a park and the forum for future Remembrance Day ceremonies. The First World War Book of Remembrance would remain in the Memorial Chamber of the Peace Tower, although a copy of it would be held at this new national memorial; and a new Book of Remembrance for the Korean War was to be created for Canada's 516 dead from that conflict. The government was aware of the delicate balance of erecting a new national memorial since The Response had been unveiled only in 1939, but it was committed to meeting the needs of the veterans.

The memorial idea percolated within Public Works, and plans were drawn up for a cruciform-shaped building with sculpted figures and stained glass windows, but not much further progress was made until an MP prodded the Diefenbaker government in February 1960.[9] A series of studies by the Federal District

Sketch of the proposed National Shrine, circa 1963.

Commission (the precursor to the National Capital Commission) delayed matters and led to a reduction in the size of the shrine and the height of the central tower. Still, the government again announced that the project would go ahead, with the unveiling set for November 11, 1962. The proposed unveiling date was missed, and the Legion pressed again but made little headway. The increasingly chaotic Diefenbaker government was suffering internecine battles, and the October 1962 Cuban Missile Crisis had put many projects on hold.

As a new election loomed, the Diefenbaker government surveyed its list of projects and looked to make good on its promise to build the monument. On February 19, 1963, Public Works Minister Davie Fulton and Veterans Affairs Minister Marcel Lambert unveiled the architect's drawings. Designed by E.A. Gardner, the 12-metre-high memorial was a relatively modest $1.5 million project. Minister Fulton, a Second World War company commander with the

Seaforth Highlanders who lost a brother in the war, was an ardent supporter of the shrine in cabinet and in public, declaring that it "represents, quite simply, a quiet and reverent tribute to those who laid down their lives for their country and for freedom."[10] The plans were unfinished but included a mural, sculptures, and stained glass windows to be designed by Canadian artists. The Second World War veterans were gratified to have finally secured their memorial, expecting it to become a focal point of commemoration that would allow a new generation of Canadians to renew their faith in the fallen. It was also anticipated that the shrine would emerge as a new symbol in the heart of the capital and perhaps shift the focus of remembrance from the Great War to the Second World War. But veterans soon found themselves charging into a new battle with the government over another Canadian symbol.

In 1962, the Legion pledged that its members were "committed wholeheartedly to the perseveration of democracy and to maintaining and strengthening our British-inspired institutions."[11] Two years earlier, the Legion had petitioned for the right to add the word "Royal" to the organization's name and had been granted it, marking an enduring link to the British Empire and monarchy. Douglas Fisher, an astute observer of veterans, wrote that the Royal Canadian Legion was a body that extolled the importance of remembrance and commemoration, and that as such it tended to be an "institute of heritage, [that] must be conservative in its social attitudes and in its political stances. Even though the Legion is proclaimed as non-political, it has had, and by its very makeup, must have a conserving, not a radical view of society. This means it is likely to lag behind currents in our society."[12] As a bastion of Britishness in the evolving Canada, the Legion saw itself as a fervent protector of old symbols.

While the strong emotional links to Britain survived the Second World War in many parts of English Canada, they had been tested during the postwar years in other areas: in French Canada, in enclaves where new Canadians lived, and also among those English Canadians who believed that Canada had grown up and must strike out on its own. For the nation's government, responding to these shifting demographics meant loosening many of the ties to Britain, which no longer "ruled the waves" or was even a great power in the new world divided between the United States and the USSR. The fighting forces from 1939 to 1945 were made up of many more Canadian-born citizens than had fought for Canada in the Great War, and while the country still had a strong attachment to Britain, it was clear that Canadian nationalism had been strengthened during this conflict in which Canadian units and Canadian commanders fought. The half million Canucks serving in Britain could see how the brave Britons withstood the Blitz, but there was also a growing awareness that many aspects of the old world—everything from its rail lines to its lavatories— were inferior to Canadian products and practices. The class-based hierarchy in Britain was derided as backward-thinking; for many Canadians, leaving Canada had reinforced their understanding of just how good a country it was.

The postwar years also saw Canada bailing out the bankrupt Brits—another indication of how the Dominion was emerging from its prewar crippled, catatonic, and colonial mindset. The nation was moving away from the British Commonwealth, although, ironically, it was being pulled into the waiting arms of the new American empire. While King and many subsequent prime ministers—especially Diefenbaker—had kept the ties to Britain alive, the bonds were more emotional than financial. By the 1960s, Canada was a very different country from the one that had gone to war in 1939.

Befitting that decade of change, a fierce debate broke out in Canadian society in the early 1960s over the adoption of a new flag. Many politicians, leaders, and ordinary Canadians believed that a new flag was needed to reflect the emerging country as a nation fully independent from Britain. The Red Ensign had bound Canada to Britain and the Empire, those who objected to its use felt that it looked very similar to the other Commonwealth flags, from New Zealand to the Virgin Islands, all of which featured the Union Jack in the upper left corner. After 1945, the Red Ensign was flown from all federal buildings and it was a heady symbol even in a Canada transformed, especially for veterans of the world wars.

Shortly after the Second World War, King had floated the idea of a new flag, but he had met with serious opposition. Caucus members from English Canada disliked the idea of severing the link to Britain, while those from French Canada felt that King's proposed flag, still with the Union Jack on it, did not go far enough in symbolically individuating the nation from Britain. King buried the issue, but it was revived by Lester B. Pearson in 1963, when he defeated Diefenbaker and became prime minister. Pearson had his own motivations. As minister of external affairs, Pearson had played a key role in the October 1956 Suez Canal crisis by de-escalating the potential for greater violence in a situation that saw Britain, France, and Israel aligned against Egypt, while at the same time alienating the United States and the Soviet Union. Pearson had been awarded the 1957 Nobel Peace Prize for his idea of creating a peacekeeping force in the Suez, but once peace had been established, the Egyptians had refused to allow the Canadian soldiers into the country because of their British connections, uniforms, and the Red Ensign flag. Pearson burned with anger over the slight, but he also understood that Canada's old symbols needed to be modified in the new nation.

One of Pearson's champions was John Matheson, a Liberal MP who had been grievously wounded in the Second World War and still walked with the aid of a cane. He recognized that the Red Ensign was an emotional symbol to many and that creating another would not be easy.[13] Pearson and Matheson felt that the image of the maple leaf might again be pressed into service. Canadians had fought proudly with the maple leaf on their uniforms during the world wars. It was also carved into Canadian headstones. The maple leaf was a recognizable icon, and a Canadian one, although other symbols were floated by Canadians when the flag design process was opened to the public. Some of the more innovative of the 5,000 submitted designs included the image of crossed hockey sticks, which had an admirable buccaneering style, although it was not likely to be endorsed by heraldic experts. Others tried using the beaver as the central motif, although this image never made it far in discussions, possibly because Canadians did not want a large rodent on their flag. Or perhaps the idea of the nation's symbol being an animal that was best known for having been skinned for profit was ill-suited to a country dealing, in the early 1960s, with a massive trade imbalance with the United States.

Pearson also thought the creation of a new flag, added to his efforts to bring more French-Canadian leaders into cabinet, might help to quell the growing unrest in Quebec. The Quiet Revolution was gathering strength, with prominent francophone intellectuals, business leaders, and politicians fighting for control of the economy, which had been dominated by English Canadians. These secular forces in the province also struggled to reduce the influence of the Catholic Church, which intruded into almost all aspects of Quebeckers' lives.

The Legion veterans were the greatest critics of abandoning the old flag, and beginning in late 1963 they mounted a sustained defence both in *The Legionary* and in the 2,000-strong Legion Halls across the country. The prime minister realized he needed to face down his old comrades. Pearson and Matheson went to Winnipeg on May 17, 1964, for the Legion's twentieth Dominion Convention, where the prime minister, wearing his First World War medals, faced an angry crowd of 2,000 veterans. Television crews covered the event, aware—and perhaps hoping—that there would be a confrontation.

When Pearson addressed the hostile crowd, he was first met with boos, hisses, and cat-calls.[14] Never a great orator, Pearson

Canadian veterans standing by their flag. Many veterans were outraged over the idea of a new flag displacing the one that they fought under in two world wars.

rose to the occasion, highlighting his government's positive record on medical care for veterans and then acknowledging the Legionnaires' opposition to the new flag. He freely talked about the importance of the Red Ensign but also stressed the significance of the maple leaf. "When I went overseas in 1915, I had as comrades in my section men whose name were Cameron, Kimura, English, Bleidenstein, O'Shaughnessy, De Chapin. We didn't fall in, or fall out, as Irish Canadians, French Canadians, Japanese Canadians, Dutch Canadians. We wore the same uniform with the same maple leaf badge and we were proud to be known as Canadians, to serve as Canadians and to die, if that had to be, as Canadians. I wish our country had more of that spirit today, of unity, 'togetherness,' and resolve."[15] But when Pearson told the veterans that a maple leaf flag would be a reflection of the "new Canada," one of the veterans shouted, "You are selling us out to the pea-soupers."[16] The move to a new flag was not in fact a sell-out to French Canada but a reflection that Canada was evolving and maturing. In the aftermath of the public event, it was widely acknowledged that Pearson won the showdown with his old comrades.

But the battle did not end there. The clash over the flag would play out across society, in all regions and in Parliament, with the Conservatives rallying to the defence of the old flag, as Sir John A. Macdonald had done in 1891 and Sir Robert Borden had again in 1911. It did not work a third time. While there remained millions of Canadians with strong British ties, they were becoming a minority.[17] Not all veterans were against the new flag, of course, but the Legionnaires joined the fight, firmly siding with Great War veteran and former prime minister John Diefenbaker, who derided the emerging single red maple leaf design as a "flag without a past, without a history, without honour and without pride."[18] Others MPs, like Gordon Churchill, who had served in both world wars, rose in the House and spoke passionately about the meaning of fighting under the old flag. He talked of seeing the Red Ensign raised over the French, Belgian, and Dutch towns as they were liberated by Canadians: "These are experiences which no one who has seen them can ever forget. This is what a flag means to people—a flag borne in battle. And our flag has been borne in battle."[19]

There was much agitated and feverish talk on both sides. Some argued that by abandoning the flag, Canada was turning its back on its fallen soldiers, while others preached that the new flag would free Canada from the colonial shackles of its past. These were competing visions, neither of which was easily abandoned by its champions: an old flag that represented history, service, loss, and pride versus a new flag for a changing nation of Canadians who found the old flag wrongly tied to a foreign country. After six months of fierce debate, parliamentarians voted on the flag design on December 15, 1964; the new maple leaf flag flew over Parliament for the first time on February 15, 1965.

The adoption of the new flag was a blow to many veterans, and certainly to their largest organization, the Royal Canadian Legion. While many veterans likely supported the idea of a new flag, during the ferocious debates some media reports had mocked their old-fashioned ways and imperialist arguments. And even worse for the Legion, at almost the same time as it lost the fight against the flag, the organization also suffered a decisive defeat in its pursuit of a national memorial.

Although Pearson's Liberal Party had fought against the Legion over the flag issue, it had promised to continue the work on the National Shrine, with Minister of Veterans Affairs Roger Teillet, an RCAF veteran, announcing publicly on August 5, 1963 that the project would go ahead.[20] The Legion was thrilled and it issued communiqués in support of the memorial, even suggesting the name "National Remembrance Shrine."[21] But soon there was unexpected opposition. The media and Canadians across the country voiced uncertainty over why the memorial was needed. A concerned citizen, G.F. Maclaren, complained to Pearson, "I have heard no one who has been in favour of such expenditure or an additional war memorial on that site or on any other, with our country's finances and other needs pressing."[22] This must have given Pearson pause, as did critically minded articles in *Maclean's* magazine and *The Ottawa Journal*. Others derided the project, too. In the October 1963 issue of *Chatelaine*, magazine editor Doris Anderson described the memorial idea as "unimaginative and wasteful."[23] Another stone memorial to those who died in the war was unnecessary, she wrote, and the wartime generation, which had been raised in the grim Depression years, was "painfully aware of the little opportunity offered [to] youth in the thirties, and cynical about expensive, hollow displays."[24]

The Canadian government has always wrestled with the tension between supporting veterans and spending on acts of commemoration. But in the 1960s the cost of a memorial was insignificant compared to the government's overall budget for veterans' care. However, those who objected to the memorial articulated another vision—that the funding might more usefully be put toward cultural endeavours not linked to war. Setting aside the erroneous rumours that the National War Memorial in Ottawa would be torn down in favour of the new shrine, which excited public anger for a brief period, a growing chorus of opponents were returning to the immediate postwar concept of functional memorials. The president of the United Church Women's Association, for example, commented that a theatre or an observatory would be more useful to the public.[25] Taking an even more practical approach, Arnold Edinborough, in an article in *Saturday Night* magazine, argued that the funds should be put towards low-rent housing and labour unions.[26] These were progressive suggestions for something—anything—other than a stone monument, with others voicing support for the existing national monument as being surely sufficient for all wars. As the *Montreal Gazette* editorialized, "It is true that the present Memorial Chamber, and the present war memorial, were built before the Second World War and the Korean War . . . but they have always been understood to stand for the sacrifices that Canadians have made in all the country's wars."[27] *The Globe and Mail* ran an editorial arguing that Canada did not need a memorial built nearly twenty years after the war's end, asserting, "We are surely beyond the stage in which we thought it appropriate to honor our dead by erecting elaborate structures which have no practical use."[28]

The Legion's high command and many of its members were stung by this criticism, even though the shrine was not without its supporters in the media. The *Calgary Herald* argued in September 1963 that Ottawa should go ahead with the plan, stressing that "what this country needs is to get away from the dead hand of utilitarianism and spread its artistic wings a little." The Second World War generation deserved this memorial, the paper urged, and all Canadians "need a tangible reminder of their great deeds to help keep us from forgetting."[29] And yet the Pearson government was wary about the public backlash and was not feeling generous with the veterans, who were fighting tooth and nail against the flag.[30] In October 1963, the Pearson government put the project on hold, pending a review.[31]

The Loyal Opposition, led by Diefenbaker, having agreed to the project and knowing that "review" was often code for delaying until a project could be quietly smothered, now used the memorial as a cudgel with which to beat the government and score points with veterans. Pearson and his cabinet were getting fed up with the multi-pronged opposition, and members of the caucus began to question whether the undertaking was worthwhile.[32] Why not just push the monument into the realm of discarded projects? For Pearson, a major turning point was reached when the Naval Officers' Association of Canada, a veterans group separate from the Legion, questioned the need for the project, suggesting that a "living memorial" might be more useful, and that if the building of the shrine went ahead, their group and others like the War Amps, should be involved in the process. This disunity within the ranks of the veterans was a little bewildering for the government, which did not relish the idea of bringing all the veterans to the table for a project that was increasingly seen as divisive rather than unifying. In fact, on the project file for the memorial, Pearson wrote, "I am disturbed at the volume of criticism that this decision has caused. Either it should be reconsidered or some effort should be made to explain why this 'shrine' is being erected."[33]

The Legion executive shrugged off the criticism as unrepresentative of Canadians across the country, and continued to press the government. Their campaign included one appeal to cabinet on November 11, 1964, in which Pearson and his ministers promised the National Shrine would be erected, albeit now as a centennial project. There was talk in the media throughout the year about

The Veterans Memorial Building in Ottawa, now known as the East and West Memorial Buildings and joined by a memorial arch and, pictured here, is a little visited or even acknowledged memorial to Canadian veterans on Wellington Street in Ottawa.

entwining the shrine with a tomb for an unknown soldier of the Second World War and a new Canadian War Museum. The latter idea abruptly ended when the small museum that had been erected in 1942 in a nondescript and insufficient building near what is today the National Gallery was moved to a site on Sussex Street that had been the Public Archives of Canada. (In turn, the Public Archives shifted down Wellington Street to a new, purpose-built structure next to the Supreme Court of Canada).[34] The tomb, to be located under the memorial arch between the twin Veterans Memorial Buildings on Wellington Street, was an intriguing idea, but one that did not make it through many news cycles. An increasingly frustrated Legion kept at the government, but there were other more pressing veterans' issues. Legion president Fred O'Brecht advocated for an increase in pension rates to accommodate the rising cost of living and to recognize that ailing disabled veterans needed more funds to survive. The government dragged its feet on these issues, eventually calling together a commission to study the claims, while also putting off developing a plan for the shrine.

In the 1964 pre-Remembrance Day meeting with cabinet, the Legion advocated for a series of organized tours to the Western Front to mark the anniversary of the First World War, which would culminate in a ceremony at Vimy Ridge in 1967 to commemorate the fiftieth year since that definitive Canadian battle. The organization also advanced a request for a Canadian Second World War memorial overseas. As the Legion president told the cabinet, "Dieppe has become a symbol of the participation of Canadians in World War II. It would appear most appropriate that a memorial be constructed to include and portray the contributions of Canadians in World War II."[35] The Pearson cabinet had little interest in an overseas memorial, especially when it was still struggling with the notion of a national shrine in Ottawa.[36]

With the country's centennial on the horizon in 1967, Ottawa opened the coffers to encourage communities to celebrate Canada's birthday. Progress and history were highlighted in a burst of national sentiment, and tens of millions of dollars were distributed from Ottawa for major centennial projects across the country. In the capital, Pearson's cabinet settled on building a new National Arts Centre (NAC) after being convinced of its merits by veteran G. Hamilton Southam, a former diplomat and a member of one of Canada's most influential families. He was an articulate champion of the arts centre, corralling, imploring, and fighting for funding. The NAC opened to much acclaim in 1969, although it was wildly over budget at $46.1 million.[37] Across the country, 6 performing arts centres and 200 cultural facilities, along with 428 community centres, were funded to create a legacy of the anniversary of Confederation.[38] But there was no money earmarked for the Necessary War. The idea of a second national memorial for the Second World War veterans faded from the public consciousness: it had no champion and it was out of step with the thinking of most Canadians, who had firmly turned their backs on war. Despite the promises to the Legion by a succession of governments, little progress was made on the shrine from 1965 to 1966, and by January of the next year the Pearson government had suspended work.[39] Canada's war veterans suffered another defeat.

In the flag debate, the Legion came down on the wrong side of history. The country was transforming, its demographics shifting significantly, and Quebec's increased autonomy needed sustained attention and substantial action. A new flag was required to reflect a new country, but the veterans felt keenly that they had lost a poignant symbol under which more than 1.6 million Canadians had fought and more than 110,000 had lost their lives. The veterans' public opposition was often regarded as retrograde and backward—the mumbling and grumbling of old men about their traditions as they locked themselves away in Legion Halls. It was an unfair caricature, not least because it obscured the thousands of female veterans, but the stakes and emotions were high in the fight over the flag. At the same time, for some champions of a new flag, the Legion's opposition also went hand in hand with steady demands by veterans for better pensions or medical care. While no one articulated the idea at the time, this notion of entitlement because of a long-ago war rubbed some Canadians the wrong way and made them ungenerous to veterans' demands.

The government's failure to follow through on its promise to build the National Shrine was another blow to Legionnaires. Ottawa made only a half-hearted case to the public for why a second war memorial was needed, and Canadians were uninspired by the project. While the Legion pushed hard for the memorial, Canadians were more preoccupied with the ongoing conflagration in Vietnam or their fear of thermo-nuclear annihilation. Perhaps in the early 1960s, the Diefenbaker government could have built the monument, but by 1967 Canadians had different priorities. War was not to be marked or commemorated—it was to be buried.

CHAPTER 7

FAILING TO TELL OUR STORY

B y the 1960s, Canadians had for years been neglecting to tell their own story of the war. True, there had always been a segment of the population that was fascinated by the war, reading books and comics, playing with toys and games, watching television and war movies. And yet with so little Canadian-produced content available, those who sought to know more about the war turned to British, American, and German cultural depictions of it.

There was, however, an important exception to the rule. The major historical achievement of the time came through the completion of the army official histories. Colonel C.P. Stacey and his small team of historians continued to arrange and study the official war records, while preparing foundational historical studies. In 1955, Stacey published *Six Years of War: The Army in Canada, Britain and the Pacific,* which covered the half million Canadians in England and the challenging battles at Hong Kong and Dieppe. The book had been delayed for several years as fretful politicians worried it would unearth secrets, pull the scab off old wounds, and embarrass the government. After two years of frustrating postponements, and Stacey's threat of resignation, the Liberal government, which was coming to its end after being in power since

1935, let the work be published.[1] There were no controversies. Stacey's history was praised, even though he had struggled to understand the Hong Kong battle because most of the records had been lost or destroyed.

Stacey's attempts at chronicling the ill-fated Dieppe operation were also plagued by problems. Many of the senior Canadian generals kept shifting blame onto each other for the botched operation, while the originator of the raid, Lord Mountbatten, either did not leave a paper trail or destroyed key documents. But more records had been opened by the early 1950s, when Stacey was trying to untangle the historical mess, and he found that there was enough blame to go around. Writing while all the senior Canadian and British generals were still alive, and knowing that these important military figures were wary of how their actions would be framed in history, Stacey offered careful assessments of the reason for the raid, but he claimed that Dieppe provided key lessons for Normandy.[2] While it was not easy to directly connect the spectre of Dieppe to the skilled planning of D-Day, the failed 1942 raid had illustrated the need for overwhelming firepower and for a deception plan to draw or slow the hurling of enemy reserves into the battle; it also acted as a reminder to the Allied forces to avoid a frontal attack against a fortified port, and as another warning that the Germans were a formidable foe. While some of these observations were self-evident, and not worth the cost of nearly 1,000 lives, sometimes the most painful lessons are the ones learned in blood.

The next year, Stacey's Directorate of History published G.W.L. Nicholson's *The Canadians in Italy, 1943–45* (1956), the official history of the Sicily and mainland Italian campaigns. Nicholson was a gifted writer and a former high school principal who had worked as a historical narrator at the end of the war.

Stacey gave him the requisite time to research and write, and he produced a fine history that laid out the Canadian contributions to the Allied victories in Italy; these were little known to most Canadians, as the home front focus during the war had been on Northwest Europe. The "D-Day Dodgers," as the soldiers fighting in the Italian campaign had been labelled by one ungenerous British politician, had their war service reclaimed from fading memory. The two histories received much praise, with American official historian Forrest C. Pogue noting that because of these works, Canada's role in the war would no longer be obscured by the exploits of the British and American forces.[3] The histories helped to finally carve out the Canadian contributions, and the sales were strong, with over 25,000 copies sold by 1960.[4]

In that year, Stacey published the final army history, *The Victory Campaign: The Operations in Northwest Europe, 1944–1945* (1960).[5] The distillation of years of research and writing, Stacey's book placed the Canadian operations within the Allied story of invasion, battles, and the liberation of Europe. Aided by access to Allied and German records, Stacey reconstructed the victories and failures. Like most soldiers of his generation, Stacey was impressed by the Germans' tactics, élan, and ability to recover from defeat, and while he lauded the Canadians' D-Day gritty victory and the desperate defence in the first week against the 12th SS Hitler Youth, he felt that the Allies were slow to drive the Germans back in July and August 1944. At this point, more than fifteen years past the end of the war, the politicians were not much concerned with the history. But Stacey remained wary of writing about the senior generals—especially Simonds and Crerar—who were still alive. "It seemed undesirable to pillory these officers [both senior and junior] by reporting these circumstances in public print," Stacey later wrote.[6] Instead, he went easy on the generals, being less kind to the junior regimental officers, who he believed had not been sufficiently aggressive in pressing the attack. Stacey wrote in his final judgment of Normandy, "There still remained . . . that proportion of officers who were not fully competent for their appointments, and whose inadequacy appeared in action and sometimes had serious consequences."[7] Official historians rarely criticized officers, and later in life, Stacey regretted calling out the junior leaders, but he also noted that his description would surely apply equally to the Americans and British. Stacey also wrote that the "vast majority of the rank and file did their unpleasant and perilous jobs with initiative, high courage and steadily increasing skill. . . . As for their officers, the Canadian regimental officer at his best (and he was very frequently at his best) had no superior."[8] While Stacey was only lightly scolded by some veterans who felt that blame—if there was any—should have been assigned up the chain of command, overall there was much praise for the history that sold 6,000 copies in the first three months. But future generations of British and American historians would single out Stacey's negative assessment, overlooking the positive.

From 1955 to 1960, the deeds of the Canadian Army were codified in professional official histories that were rigorous in their analysis and essential in laying the foundation for future study. In contrast, the stories of Canada's navy and air force were left to fade, even as American and British historians published dozens and dozens of volumes on almost every aspect of their war effort. As the Australian official historian Gavin Long observed, "The small partners in a great coalition war must write their own stories if they wish them to be told in reasonable detail. The larger partners . . . have no inclination to do this task for them."[9] The

Canadian Army was lucky to have Stacey as its chronicler, and his history books carried weight among the few cultural expressions produced for Canadians in the 1950s.

While Stacey was working on his histories, the 1950s saw a handful of Canadian novelists and playwrights produce fictional works, among them Jean Vaillancourt's *Les Canadiens Errants* (1954), Lionel Shapiro's *The Sixth of June* (1955), and Colin McDougall's *Execution* (1958). The most important of these was McDougall's novel, which channelled his own experiences as a decorated officer with the Princess Patricia's Canadian Light Infantry. His novel received the 1958 Governor General's Award for Fiction and garnered much praise, with one reviewer enthusing, "*Execution* shows war in all its brutal reality, touches with biting satire upon political behind-the-scenes bungling and concessions and sucks the reader into the vortex of man's inhumanity to man in a way few other war stories have done."[10] McDougall's plot centres on Canadian soldiers executing two docile Italian prisoners and illustrates how the violence of war was seared deep into the soldiers who were forced to fight in Italy. *The Globe and Mail* felt that, by depicting the killing of prisoners, the novel might lead to a "storm of controversy," but there was no uproar, and other veterans seem to have liked it.[11] Gregory Clark, a Great War veteran and much-respected journalist, wrote to McDougall in praise of *Execution*, remarking, "I cannot help but remind you that trying to put War into a book, as Tolstoy and many another found out, is close to impossible. How then, in 227 pages you have effected the epic and tragic sense, I cannot for the life of me figure out." Farley Mowat, who penned *The Regimemt* (1955), a literary regimental history of his unit, the Hastings and

Prince Edward Regiment, told McDougall, "*Execution* is the closest approximation of the matter [war] I have encountered."[12]

And yet far more Canadians were exposed to British or American television accounts of the war than to the few classic Canadian war novels. American culture was all-pervasive in Canada, and children in the 1950s and 1960s watched mostly TV shows that came from south of the border—including war-related programs. There were comedies like *McHale's Navy*, which, in 138 half-hour episodes airing from 1962 to 1966, followed the misadventures of a US Navy PT boat and its commanding officer, played by Ernest Borgnine. Comedy was also the way to approach the prisoner-of-war experience, as in *Hogan's Heroes*, another American production that ran from 1965 to 1971. In each weekly episode, the American prisoners in the fictional Stalag 13 outwitted the bungling German goons, who could never uncover the prisoners' plans of espionage, trickery, and assistance to the Allied war effort. Intense dramas were popular, too, like *Twelve O'Clock High*, a series that followed the bombing war of 918th Bombardment Group flying B-17s, with many of the aircrew killed during the three seasons it was broadcast from 1964 to 1967. *Combat* (1962–1967) was a *Band of Brothers*-eque one-hour American drama that focused on the lives of a US platoon of infantrymen from Normandy to Berlin. Each episode featured a core group of soldiers who took on the Germans and beat them in the slow grind to victory. There was a vivid human element to the drama, as it portrayed the stress and exhaustion of campaigning mixed with the fear and agony of death. Perhaps the most iconic American action series of the time was *The Rat Patrol*, filmed in colour from 1966 to 1968. It focused on a long-range desert patrol in North Africa, tasked with attacking and harassing Field Marshal Erwin Rommel's Afrika Korps. The central characters were three Americans and a British soldier crossing the desert in jeeps with mounted machine guns. During the war, the American forces had arrived very late and contributed very little to the North African struggle, but on television they seemed to be winning it singlehandedly. It angered some viewers in Australia and Britain that the Yanks had appropriated the Desert War.

British television series had wartime settings as well, the most enduring and endearing being *Dad's Army*, a sitcom that ran from 1969 to 1977, featuring the exploits of the Home Guard in Britain bumbling its way through training and the threat of invasion. A more substantial offering was the colossal twenty-six-part series *The World at War*, produced in 1973 by the BBC. Presenting

A Canadian infantryman in France. The Canadian story of battle and liberation had largely been forgotten by the 1960s.

multiple aspects of the war on land, in the air, at sea, and at home, it was the most expensive documentary up to that point in history. The series was rebroadcast the next year in the United States, Canada, and around the world. Canada was featured in it only briefly, although that was to be expected in the films that ranged across campaigns involving hundreds of millions of soldiers and civilians around the world.

In the postwar period, the saturation of Canadian culture with other countries' stories was also apparent in the preponderance in Canada of comic books that featured American soldiers, like *Sgt. Fury and His Howling Commandos*. Canadian wartime comic-book heroes had existed—for example, Johnny Canuck, a home-grown hero who had no superpowers but whose grit and toughness helped him defeat Nazis and win a lot of fist fights with Hitler—but these cartoons did not continue for long after victory in 1945. There were similar issues with toys—children played with GI Joe figures, not with Canadian Tommies or Canucks.

Though Canada's story of the war was neglected within this mass of cultural products, the representations sometimes encouraged young people to talk to their fathers, brothers, or uncles, and occasionally mothers, sisters, and aunts, about their war experience. Television in particular became a shared medium through which to break the silence. Jim Burant, while growing up in Ottawa, watched Second World War documentaries and television series with his father and would ask him questions about the war. A veteran in the Canadian Army's 28th (British Columbia) Armoured Regiment, John Burant would offer his recollection of the Juno Beach landings and of being a liaison NCO with the Polish division later in Normandy. His father's recounting of his time in the war remained a satisfying memory for Jim, even fifty

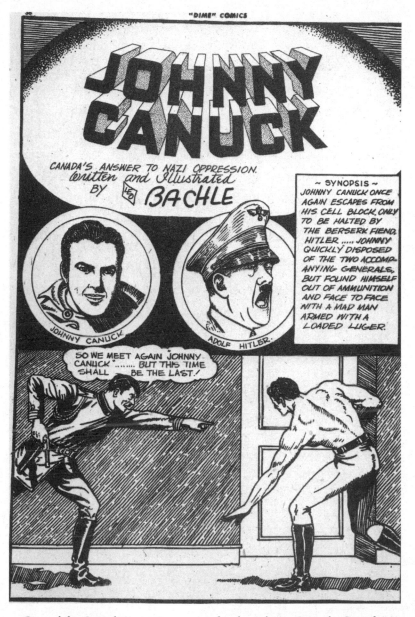

One of the Canadian wartime comic books, Johnny Canuck. Canada's
wartime comics could not compete with American culture after the war
that so fully dominated the northern dominion.

years later.[13] Bertram Frandsen, whose father served as a leading stoker on Royal Navy and RCN warships during the war, had as a young man an avid interest in war films, movies, comics, and books, and he would occasionally use the knowledge he gained from them to ask his father about the war. Most often, his dad refused to talk, unable to come to grips with his experiences. The absence of Canadian stories was noticeable to Bert even at a young age, and he wished to know more about his country's role in the war. He later recalled, "Most of my knowledge of the Second World War came from American sources—those that would have shed some insight into the Canadian experience were few and far between." His father only began to talk about the war in the 1980s, when Bert was nearing the end of his own thirty-seven-year career in the Canadian forces as a military educator and strategic analyst. Through his many years of travel and interactions with officers from other countries, Bert Frandsen came to the conclusion that "there was no thought given to the Canadian participation in the Second World War, and that Canada was merely a 'colonial appendage' to the larger British or American efforts."[14]

But even if there had been more Canadian films, novels, plays, or comic books, many veterans simply did not care to talk about the war in the 1960s, and had even less interest in reliving it. They were not blocked; they were not scarred; they were not suffering from PTSD. They simply dismissed their war experience. It was something they had done for a few years as young men or women, and it deserved to be left in the past. Eric Brown, who grew up in St. Catharines and was the youngest of five and who later made a career in the diplomatic service, had a brother who served in the RCN and a sister in the Canadian Women's Army Corps. His sister married a veteran of the war, a battery sergeant major who served in the artillery with the 23rd Field Regiment (SP). Whenever Eric asked him about the war, he would only grunt, "five bloody years taken from my life."

The avalanche of American and British popular culture that buried Canada's stories included those told on celluloid. Then, as now, movies had the greatest reach among the public, with one film able to inform millions. Hollywood churned out war films and the British followed suit, eager to present their history and allow audiences to relive the war, experience the fear, engage in nostalgia, and work through their emotions about the conflict.[15] Eighty-five British war films were produced from 1946 to 1959, and even more American ones.[16] Ranging from low-budget romances to expensive epics, they covered the experience of sailors, aviators, infantry, and prisoners in nearly every campaign. The movies were watched around the world, finding considerable box office success while forging myths and shaping the narrative for future generations.

During the war, the Canadian film industry was deeply involved in producing films about the Allied and Canadian war effort for theatres across the country. The National Film Board (NFB) was established in 1939 under the direction of the enigmatic British-born filmmaker John Grierson. Benefitting from a wartime injection of funds, the NFB publicized the national war effort through documentaries and historical series like *Canada Carries On* (released as *En avant Canada* for French-speaking audiences) that brought the war home. The board produced and distributed another 500 films across Canada during the war, documentaries that followed the Canadian forces overseas, often drawing on film footage shot by the Canadian Army Film Unit, which sent combat cameramen into battle from Sicily onwards.[17]

Canada had a robust documentary film industry during the war, with the National Film Board producing hundreds of films for Canadians and those outside the country. The Canada Carries On *series presented a myriad of war topics, including the one presented in this poster on wartime industry.*

The Canadian film industry also produced fictional films about the war, including a series of alarmist spy thrillers depicting German agents infiltrating the United States to engage in nefarious actions, the most popular of these being *Confessions of a Nazi Spy* (1939) and *49th Parallel* (1941).[18] The Royal Canadian Navy saw the advantage of publicizing its efforts in the war, and it worked with Universal film studio to release *Corvette K-225* (1943). Featuring Hollywood Western star Randolph Scott in the role of a Canadian corvette captain, the film captured the rough Atlantic seas, the German U-boat threat, and the tenacious bravery of the seamen struggling to keep open the supply line to Britain. The film ended with a dedication to "the officers and men of the Royal Canadian Navy, who have made the name Corvette a byword for endurance and sacrifice."

Perhaps the most successful war film was *Captains of the Clouds* (1942), which portrayed the British Commonwealth Air Training Plan (BCATP) and starred Jimmy Cagney as a tough, ill-disciplined Canadian bush pilot turned fighter. Produced with the support of the RCAF and filmed on BCATP air stations—with one segment including over 100 Harvard aircraft—the film dramatized the Canadian air effort, and it even had an appearance by Air Marshal Billy Bishop, the Great War flying ace, who plays himself in the film. The climax of the film sees Cagney's character fending off a German Bf 109 that is attacking a squadron of unarmed Lockheed Hudson bombers flying to Britain, and he sacrifices himself to save his comrades.[19] The film was lauded throughout

The British Commonwealth Air Training Plan was highlighted in Captains of the Clouds *(1942), one of several wartime films that showcased the Canadian war effort.*

the British Commonwealth, and the *Toronto Daily Star* film critic enthusiastically claimed it was "the first picture to show what Canada is doing in this war."[20] *Captains of the Clouds* ends with an ovation to the Royal Canadian Air Force and its battle against the Luftwaffe.

But after the war, Canadian cultural producers were drowned by the flood of American products. Even when the Massey Commission sent up a warning flare in 1951 about the difficulty of maintaining cultural autonomy in the face this onslaught, it was not easy for the Canadian film industry to revitalize.[21] And so while war films were a staple in the theatres across the country in the decades after the war, it was British and American films that were viewed by Canadians. The most acclaimed film from this period was the critically and commercially successful *The Longest Day* (1962). Based on Cornelius Ryan's 1959 best-selling history of the same name, producer and director Darryl F. Zanuck set out to tell the story of the Allied invasion on D-Day.[22] The epic ran three hours, had the largest budget ever for a black-and-white film, and showcased an international cast of hundreds. Gritty battles and costly losses flashed across the screen, and although liberties were taken with the history, the confusion of the D-Day paratrooper drop and the scattering of soldiers was captured evocatively, with many of the actors coached by Second World War veterans, some of whom handed over real artifacts from their war years to be used in the film.[23] *The Longest Day*, noted the *Ottawa Citizen*, "captured all the hell and hardship, grit and gore, bravery and sacrifice of men in war."[24]

While another Canadian reviewer of this larger-than-life film wondered if it was the "war movie to end all war movies," its unmistakable theme was that the battle for freedom and democracy was fought and won by the Americans. The success of the film firmly

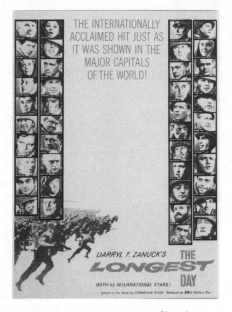

The Longest Day *(1962) was an epic film that reintroduced*
D-Day to a new generation, but it severely downplayed the
contributions of Canadians to the Allied battle.

ensured that D-Day was reinforced in consciousness as an event of
tremendous importance: it was the beginning of the end of the
Germans, and it had been the Americans who did all the heavy lifting
in the battle.[25] When the film premiered in Toronto on December 19,
1962, the Queen's Own Rifles held a celebratory viewing to mark
their own service on Juno Beach. They must have been disappointed,
however, as the Canadians were barely mentioned in the film. Frank
Morriss, who reviewed *The Longest Day* for *The Globe and Mail*,
rightly thought it a brilliant production and a "valuable historical
document," but he also noted that many viewers "may feel that the
Canadians have been slighted."[26] While Canadian troops were present a few times in the unfolding history on screen, no Hollywood
star played any of the Canadians, and the story of Juno Beach was

marginalized within the film's narrative. Veteran Conrad Drasse raged in the *Ottawa Citizen* that more credit should have been given to his countrymen, as "Canada was in the war before the U.S." Al Watson, also a veteran, pointed out that there were more "French-speaking Canadians" on D-Day beaches than "Free French," who received extensive treatment in the film.[27] Historian Terry Copp later observed that reviewers of the film "complained about the Americanization of D-Day," but that no production was made in response to tell the Canadian story.[28]

The Canadian Broadcasting Corporation (CBC) and the NFB were slow off the mark in creating homegrown war-related TV shows. It was not until 1962 that the NFB finally turned its attention back to the Second World War. Thirty-three-year-old Donald Brittain, who would become one of the most storied documentarists in Canadian history, wrote the script for a multi-part series known as *Canada at War*. Working closely with Colonel Stacey, Brittain drew upon official records, memoirs, and archives, and spent two years reviewing Allied, German, and Canadian footage, eventually studying some 16 million feet of film.[29]

Starting in April 1962, the thirteen-part series of half-hour episodes, which explored the story of Canada's fighting forces and the home front, was televised from coast to coast, in English and in French. "Those who were overseas," believed *The Legionary*, "will discover in these films that the home front was also actively making history—in politics, industry, and the nation's social fabric."[30] The NFB devoted considerable resources to ensure that, as one journalist noted, "this distinctively Canadian history of the war time period [was] both accurate and complete."[31] *The Globe and Mail* reviewed

Canada at War positively, but remarked that the series was late in arriving. The Americans and British had been broadcasting films for years, the paper observed, noting that the Canadian series "suffers from being a late entry into an overcrowded field of Second World War documentaries."[32] Much of the films' international footage, one critic claimed, had been shown previously. And yet, he conceded, this was a noteworthy series because it would finally show "the Canadian point of view, with emphasis on this country's participation in the conflict, and is therefore a welcome change from earlier presentations."[33] Another reviewer thought that with years and years of "films showing how the British and Americans won the war," it was time for our story and this was it. He declared it "distinctively Canadian."[34]

Despite the extensive praise for *Canada at War*, the CBC aired the episodes at 10:30 p.m. in most parts of the country. More than a few reviewers wondered why CBC had relegated the film so late in the evening, far beyond the bedtime of young people, with one noting that it "should be required viewing for all students."[35] In contrast, that same summer the US television network CBS produced its own D-Day documentary, largely about the Americans' role in winning the battle, airing it during prime time in the United States and Canada.[36] The story of Canada's war effort was trumped again by the Americans, although this time the defeat came at the hands of the state-funded Canadian television network. *Canada at War* left an evocative legacy on film, and it was rebroadcast over the years. But the NFB's poor handling of the priceless archival footage, which was abandoned to warehouses with no climate control, led to a devastating fire in 1967 that burned much of Canada's early film history, including most of the original Second World War footage.

The failure of Canadians to tell their nation's stories was made all the worse by American claims of the war as a defining event in the Republic's history. It was not unnatural that Canada would be pushed to the shadows when the Americans were playing for keeps, and one of the reasons why the memory of the Great War in Canada is so strong is that we never had to compete with the American will to dominate that war. In the United States, World War I has never resonated the same way as World War II and the American Civil War. But perhaps *The Great Escape* (1963) pushed absurdity to the limit. Based on actual events, the film told the story of Allied

National Film Board documentary, Canada at War *(1962), presented the Canadian Second World War experience, including the fighting in Normandy, as depicted in this image of three Canadian soldiers at the front.* Canada at War *was a ground-breaking series but it came late to Canadians and after years of British and American productions that focused on their own national war efforts and reduced Canada to an almost irrelevant partner.*

prisoners of war who, in the late hours of March 24, 1944, escaped from Stalag Luft III through a secret underground tunnel. In reality, seventy-six prisoners made it out beyond the wire, but they were captured, and the Gestapo ruthlessly executed fifty of them, including six Canadians.[37] However, in the film, the Canadian prisoners were replaced with American or British combatants, and there was the addition of the wonderful fabricated scene of Steve McQueen attempting to escape on a motorcycle. The Canadian contribution to the escape was erased from the story, even as Flying Officer Wally Flood, a Canadian who had worked in the mining industry at Kirkland Lake, Ontario, before the war and who had also taken part in the escape, acted as the film's technical advisor. The truth is that there were few Americans at Stalag Luft III in 1944, but that did not stop Hollywood from appropriating the story.

In 1968, *The Devil's Brigade* was released, featuring several American stars and focusing on the 1st Special Service Force (SSF), a joint American and Canadian unit that fought in Italy and southern France. Trained in mountain warfare and nicknamed the "Devil's Brigade," the unit was known for its effectiveness and for its willingness to take casualties. The film, which makes much of the American and Canadian rivalries before showing them banding together as an elite force, depicted the Americans as rough-and-tumble brawlers and the Canadians as spit-and-polish stand-up soldiers. Audiences liked it, even if some Canucks wondered how they had been given the traditional British role of the rigid, disciplined soldier in such films. The film at least did not write the Canadians out of the story, even if they were depicted as different than most veterans remembered. References to the 1st SSF have lived on, with Lieutenant Aldo Raine (played by Brad Pitt) in Quentin Tarantino's *Inglourious Basterds* (2009) wearing the unit's crossed arrows collar insignia, while Marvel's popular character Wolverine, a Canadian-born anti-hero with adamantium retractable claws, was said to be a member of the Devil's Brigade.

While present-day Canadians might feel a slight thrill upon learning Wolverine is Canadian, such tidbits were buried under the avalanche of films that rolled out of Hollywood and Britain during the 1950s and 1960s. Though admittedly it is not the task of Hollywood to offer accurate reflections of history, Canadians seeking to understand their own war during its aftermath would not find their story on the silver screen. A.R. Trimble even complained in a veterans' magazine that American terminology invaded Canadian journalistic stories, with "foxholes" replacing "slit trenches," "chow" supplanting "bully," "medic" substituting for "stretcher-bearer," and "GI" unseating "private."[38] The war was officially called the Second World War in Canada, but most Canadians took to the American term, whether it was "World War II" or "WWII." These linguistic differences were small but revealing details showing that Canadian stories were being subsumed by the American narrative. Though a handful of Canadian official histories and documentaries were produced, as well as a popular two-volume Reader's Digest history, *The Canadians at War, 1939/45* (1969), most Canadians learned of the war, if at all, through American mass media. The blockbuster Hollywood films built upon the deluge of histories, novels, and memoirs produced by American, British, and German senior officers. The Canadian war stories were left untold.

CHAPTER 8

"IT DOESN'T MEAN A THING"

In December 1968, a month after Remembrance Day, veterans were in a rage over a private member's bill that was before Parliament. Bill C-67 was crafted by Barney Danson, a Liberal MP from Toronto and a wartime lieutenant with the Queen's Own Rifles. Danson was worried about how Remembrance Day—drawing smaller crowds at national ceremonies and community memorials—was steadily losing its impact with Canadians and evidently mattering less to younger generations. Instead of holding the ceremony on November 11, Danson proposed, the event should be recognized on the Sunday before the 11th, in the hope of attracting more Canadians. Remembrance Day would be renamed as the National Day of Remembrance and it would be more inclusive and less directly anchored to the Great War Armistice Day.

Veterans railed at the thought of moving the ceremony away from November 11 and felt that a floating date would further erode the impact of Remembrance Day, which they acknowledged had indeed diminished over the decade. *The Globe and Mail* described Remembrance Day around this time as no longer a day of relevance but one of "public indifference."[1] But one veterans' group, the War Amps, through its journal, *The Fragment*, argued that "if we are allowed to pick and choose the day—or if it is moved to the nearest Sunday—we stand in grave danger of seeing this sacred and honorable day shoved around to suit the calendar—and it wouldn't be too long until we lost sight of it altogether."[2]

Along with the War Amps, the Legion fiercely rejected Danson's bill, which included a section advocating for allowing German and other enemy veterans to fully partake in the ceremony so that they or their children now living in Canada would not feel shame. Unwilling to fight the Legion, Danson eventually withdrew the bill, though he would later be a champion for veterans and the creation of a new Canadian war museum.[3] But there was no easy way to address the ambivalence shown by Canadians toward Remembrance Day and other acts of commemoration. For at least five years, warned the War Amps, there had been "bleats from the hippie-oriented citizens" about how Remembrance Day was about "the glorification of War." Alan Bowker, a student at the University of Toronto in the mid-1960s and a future high commissioner, recalled of the time, "We respected what the veterans had done, though we knew little of what they had gone through; but for a generation raised under the threat of nuclear annihilation, terrified by the Cuban Missile Crisis, and witnessing a society being torn apart by the escalating war in Vietnam, Remembrance Day seemed at best anachronistic, at worst a symbol of everything we opposed."[4] Some young people were downright vitriolic on the subject. The university newspapers and campuses were hostile to any marking of war, with one student-run paper claiming that veterans only observed Remembrance Day so that the old men could "recapture their lost image." More distasteful was the accusation by another university paper that "the wearing of medals was barbaric, in that it glorified killing."[5]

By the mid-1960s, Canada was undergoing a substantial transformation. A more radical youth culture emerged, one that saw young people pushing against the structures of society, their parents, and all they stood for. As one eyewitness from that time observed of his generation, "Growing up in the post-Second World War era, only vaguely or academically interested in wars long ago, and often thinking ourselves unaffected by them, younger Canadians have enjoyed the rare luxury of being able to pass judgement on their elders and neighbours without ever being involved in armed conflict."[6] The decade of disruption was shaped by activism for racial and gender rights, as well as for environmental causes and the need to address income disparity. The emergence of Quebec nationalism through the Quiet Revolution was viewed in English Canada first with uncertainty and then with worry that the country might be fracturing along linguistic fault lines.

A renewed sense of Canadian nationalism also arose in that discordant decade. The symbol of the nation's new flag and the energizing effects of Expo '67, the "Universal and National Exhibition" held in Montreal, generated tremendous pride among Canadians. Expo coincided with the celebration of Canada's centennial, and it was a rare period of sustained national excitement. The country was looking forward and not backwards, and at the same time was finding or forging new symbols with which to distinguish itself at the 100-year mark. Intellectuals, novelists, playwrights, and visual artists began a vigorous public commentary in their works, often marked with a nationalist tinge. During this period, Canadians frequently defined themselves by what they were not: Americans. It had always been popular among the

Canadian political and cultural elite to bash the United States and to contrast it unfavourably with Canada, but the hemorrhaging American military involvement in Southeast Asia and the disastrous Vietnam War that was playing out in sick detail on televisions made the republic an easier target for criticism. The unwinnable war had sucked in American resources and was spitting out a sickening regurgitation of soldiers in body bags and butchered Vietnamese civilians. The United States seethed with race riots, political assassinations, and student unrest. Beginning in the mid-1960s, Canadian antiwar protests mimicked those in the United States, and the uncompromising anti-Communist views of the 1950s and early 1960s were increasingly questioned, as they had led to the war in Vietnam. With more Americans disaffected and angry with the war, thousands of young men fled from the draft and crossed the country's northern border. They frequently added their voices to those of Canadians who charged that war was little more than an act of lunatics and murderers. Meanwhile, there was a gnawing fear that regional wars might spread into a global one, and then to thermonuclear Armageddon, in which life on earth would be consumed within a conflagration of fire and then frozen in a nuclear winter.

In this atmosphere, it is not surprising that the Necessary War of 1939 to 1945 appeared ever less relevant. Young people knew little about the war or those who had fought in it, and they were disinclined to study it or even understand why it had been fought. The poppy remained the primary symbol of remembrance during the 1960s, but the Legion observed ruefully that the numbers of poppies sold each year in the lead-up to Remembrance Day were fewer than during the 1950s.[7] However, the Legion hoped that the crimson flowers would remain a way to engage in "remembrance of those thousands of gallant Canadians and brother-Britons who in two world wars sacrificed their lives on the altar of freedom; remembrance of those days when human values were placed in sharp relief, with the multitude of quiet, decent-living people bending every effort to achieve victory."[8] By the 1960s, about a third of Canadians bought and wore the poppies, and veterans regarded that as another sign of indifference. They thought the numbers should be higher.

The gulf between veterans and the young continued to widen. Even the Legion's language distanced it from the next generation: references to lives given freely "on the altar of freedom" were mystifying to Canadians in bell bottoms, grooving to the new music and engaging in their own counter-cultural activities. Nor did any framing of the war to show Canada supporting "brother-Britons" have any appeal in French Canada. Increasingly, veterans faced a society that was aggressively turning away from all aspects of war, including the veterans themselves, who seemed like fossils from a bad, bygone time.

Veterans were not unaware of this identifiable shift in society. In 1960, one Legionnaire observed that the "crowds around cenotaphs and monuments, in the memorial halls and before the crosses of sacrifice are becoming smaller now."[9] It would only get worse as the decade wore on. In 1964, veteran R.G. Lovell of Glencoe, Ontario, wrote passionately in *The Legionary* that "between 70 and 75 percent of the people in Canada today have no actual association with or personal recollection of the First World War."[10] Moreover, time was winning its relentless war against those who had served in uniform: the average age of the Great War veterans in 1964 was seventy-three, and some 184,000 of that war's veterans died between the 1951 and 1961 censuses. In the steady march forward, warned Lovell, the world wars, the veterans, and what they stood for would be left behind in the past. It was true that Canada continued to have a robust if steadily diminishing Canadian forces, and that veterans were present in every community, but Lovell lamented that for most young Canadians, this was a "history of which they, personally, have neither direct knowledge nor actual association. To them, the men who fought, who suffered battle wounds, who died in action, will be unknown, for they cannot, of course, remember those whom they did not know."[11]

And while this anxiety over the war's memory and the veterans' place in society fell on one side of the generational divide, it is important to note again that not all veterans cared about such matters. A twenty-two-year-old combat veteran in 1945 would be in his mid-forties in the 1960s, and might very well have little interest in the war, its memory, or its legacy. Many veterans put on their medals and marched on Remembrance Day, reliving their youth and comradery, but not all did. Some remained vehemently opposed to war, with a good number becoming involved in the peace movement or in strengthening the anti-nuclear movement. Being against war, however, did not necessarily mean that one was against remembering and commemorating the past. The obvious waning of the Canadian memory and interest in the war remained a concern for many veterans in the 1960s, and the education of youth was a key tenet of passing the torch from one generation to the next.

Though many of the connections to the war were increasingly weakening within Canada, a strong bond endured between the Canadian liberators and the still-grateful Dutch. Veteran A.W. Harrison wrote to *The Legionary* about how indebted the Dutch remained in comparison to the neglectful majority of Canadians who seemingly neither realized nor cared that a million Canadians had fought in the war to ensure freedoms that they enjoyed daily. "I can't help wondering," Harrison remarked, "how many people realize how little the children of today actually know or care about Canada's wars, her fallen, or her living veterans? There is nothing taught in their school curriculum about either war until high school. Why don't we take an example from the Netherlands and have [war history] put into school curriculum in the early grades and have our youngsters grow up like Dutch children, realizing what their heritage is all about?"[12]

As early as the summer of 1945, Dutch families had begun adopting and caring for Canadian soldiers' graves through the Netherlands War Graves Committee (NWGC).[13] The Commonwealth body—the Imperial War Graves Commission—had a mandate to maintain the graves, but the next of kin in Canada could write to the NWGC with questions or requests for a photograph of a loved one's headstone.[14] In most Dutch communities, school children were taught about the liberators and instructed to lay flowers on the graves, especially on May 5, which was an official day of thanks. One Dutch man, Bruck West, wrote a sympathetic letter

The Dutch remembered their Canadian liberators.

in 1949 to the mother of a killed Canadian, which was published in *The Globe and Mail*. Describing the cemetery at Groesbeek and her son's grave, West affirmed, "He does not lie here alone and forgotten. He lies here in a certain kind of glory, deeply revered and cherished by the people who are free men and women today because he so nobly died four years ago."[15]

The strong relationship between the Dutch and the Canadians was forged by many instances of wartime generosity. One of the most evocative of these acts involved the Dutch royal family. After German forces overran the Netherlands in May 1940, the royal family fled to Canada. Enjoying the hospitality of the host nation, Crown Princess Juliana was a prominent member of society, with the royals bringing a new charm to Ottawa's drab social scene. On January 19, 1943, the Crown Princess gave birth in the Ottawa Civic Hospital to Princess Margriet, the only royal ever to be born in Canada. Before the event, however, the Dutch were frantic, as

With the Dutch royal family in exile, Princess Margriet was born at the Ottawa Civic Hospital on January 19, 1943. The Canadian government declared the hospital suite as temporarily extraterritorial, so that the princess arrived in Dutch territory.

the new princess had to be born on Dutch soil to retain the rights to the throne. The Canadian government engaged in a diplomatic wink and granted the four-room hospital suite the same legal footing as some foreign embassies and military bases, declaring it temporarily extraterritorial—outside of Canadian sovereignty. Princess Margriet came into this world in Dutch territory.

When the Dutch royal family returned home after the war, they did not forget their Canadian hosts' generosity. Sending 100,000 tulips to Canada in 1946, even as Canadian service personnel were still returning home, the Dutch created a new symbol of unity between the two nations. Tens of thousands of tulips followed in a yearly tradition. In The Hague, the seat of the Dutch parliament, the Canadians were offered the finest embassy building, a pride of place for the liberators. The gifts and acts of recognition continued, and in 1950 the Netherlands parliament passed a Special Act declaring the "earnest gratitude of the Dutch people" toward Canada. Three years later, Ottawa inaugurated the Canadian Tulip Festival, a spring event featuring dozens of varieties of tulips; the tradition continues to this day, with over 750,000 tulips displayed throughout the capital city.

In 1961, Dutch immigrant Karin Roos, who settled in New Westminster, BC, felt compelled to write to *The Legionary* about the living Dutch legacy in Canada. "I take this opportunity to remind those veterans of World War II who liberated the Low Countries how much they have contributed to inspire thousands of Dutch people to emigrate to Canada with their dreamy-eyed memories of God's own country."[16] From the year of liberation to the late 1970s, at least 200,000 Dutch emigrated to Canada. The first of these new Canadians were war brides; the tens of thousands who followed were drawn to the country that had saved them. One story

This sculpture, known as The Man With Two Hats, *was unveiled on May 11, 2002 by Her Royal Highness Princess Margriet in Ottawa, at Dow's Lake, as a sign of the enduring friendship between the Dutch and the Canadians. Artist Henk Visch sought to capture the terrible legacy of the war, where few Dutch men emerged from 1945 with more than one hat. The dual hats also represent Canada and the Netherlands, and the notion of duality continues with a second sculpted figure in Apeldoorn.*

involved eighteen-year-old Nijmegen native Betsy Heutinek, who had become friends with Private Thomas Gemmell of the North Shore Regiment before his death in February 1945. She continued to tend to the private's headstone, laying poppies and flowers, and she met Gemmell's father, Matthew, when he came to visit his son's grave in 1947 at Groesbeek. The senior Gemmell stayed with the Heutinek family and they became close, so much so that he offered to adopt Betsy and help her move to Canada, telling one reporter, "I feel Betsy would fill the void made by Thomas's death."[17]

Canada left behind thousands of its sons in the Dutch soil. In the immediate years after the war, small numbers of Canadians made the lonely pilgrimage overseas to their sons' graves, while others went to see where husbands, fathers, and uncles had fallen.

But for at least the first decade after the fighting, travelling to Europe was no easy task. Many countries remained war-torn, flights were expensive, hotels few in number, and maps to the new grave sites were rare.

Legionnaires recognized that a centralized effort would make the process easier, and as early as 1950 they urged the Legion Dominion Council to organize and lead a pilgrimage to the old battlefields and cemeteries. Veterans recalled the unifying effects of the 1936 voyage to Vimy, which had done much to bring ex-service personnel together on that sacred mission.[18] The Legion high command supported a new pilgrimage, but it raised the problem of how to properly acknowledge the global nature of the war effort of 1939 to 1945. "There is no single focal point or event, such as at the ceremony of the unveiling of the Vimy monument, upon which to base any specific date or time," organizers reported in *The Legionary*.[19] The Canadian war effort had extended to many continents, with the fighting taking place on land, by sea, and in the air. How could a pilgrimage range from the Pacific to the Mediterranean, from Hong Kong to the Netherlands? Of course, it could not. However, after studying the issue, the Legion suggested that there might be tours to different theatres of war, and within them, to specific sites of battle and memory. Pilgrimages might be offered to Sicily and the Italian mainland; to France and Northern Europe; to RCAF stations and RCN bases in Britain; and to localities and homes in Britain. A special tour might also be arranged for war brides to visit their former homes in Britain, France, Belgium, and the Netherlands. But after some research, the planners deemed it impossible to accommodate 6,000 Canadians in these tours, as had been accomplished in 1936 through a masterful feat of logistics, especially since many of the world's ocean liners had been sunk during the war. Europe was simply not ready for such an influx of Canadians.

A further issue was that veterans did not express much enthusiasm for the idea of the tours. In 1950, most of them were young and busy establishing themselves in their professions. They had started families, and there was no tradition yet of Canadians going on European summer vacations. And perhaps many veterans no longer cared about their war experience—certainly it defined fewer and fewer of them. Just as they had not written much about the war themselves or demanded that their own stories be told through the creative arts, most veterans did not want to revisit the battlefields.

Facing these challenges, the Legion shelved the idea of returning to Canada's global battlefields in the early 1950s, although there was talk of shifting the focus of the pilgrimage from veterans to next of kin still grappling with the loss of loved ones. Many Canadians felt compelled to see the graves of their kin, and they travelled overseas in small groups, hoping to ease the pain of their loss. With the Dutch accepting and greeting these grieving Canadians, there was a new push by the Dutch government from the mid-1950s to start a series of formal pilgrimages. Representatives from the Netherlands met with civil servants in Ottawa, but the Department of Veterans Affairs pleaded a lack of funds and did not make much of an effort to locate money. This official lethargy persisted even when the Silver Cross Mothers Association, consisting at that time of 3,500 women who had lost a son or husband in the world wars, asked the government in 1956 to arrange a formal pilgrimage to the Second World War battlefields. Ottawa again demurred.[20] The disgusted Legion stepped forward to facilitate and partially fund the tours, and it worked successfully with the Netherlands War Graves Committee to provide them. The pilgrims—they deliberately used the language of the sacred—would leave from Montreal by air. During the ten-day stay, the next of kin would be billeted by Dutch families, who would provide lodging, meals, and transportation free of charge.[21]

The first group, consisting of seventy Canadian mothers who had sons buried in the Netherlands, departed in September 1962. Many of the women were elderly, including Mrs. E. Gibbons of Kitchener, who was eighty-eight and yearned to see her son's grave before her death. Another mother, eighty-year-old Mrs. C. O'Leary of Pembroke, Ontario, was accompanied by her son, Jack, who had served and survived. Jack and his fallen brother had promised one another that "if one of them were to die the other would come back to Holland with their mother to visit the grave." Mrs. O'Leary, overcome with emotion, said during a personal meeting with the Netherlands' Queen Juliana, "Now I can die. I met my son and I know he found a peaceful place."[22]

Everywhere the pilgrims travelled, from cities to villages to towns, they were greeted by enormous crowds. The throngs were part of the grateful wartime generation, people who had lived through the liberation as well as school children who were born after the starvation years. Banners were hung with messages, among them: "Canada, we shall never forget what your sons did for our freedom."[23] This was the first of seventeen pilgrimages that would be made between 1962 and 1972, eventually bringing more than 2,000 Canadians to their loved ones' graves. Three pilgrimages were made in 1964 alone, and one reporter observed that they were "mothers and fathers, sisters and brothers, and widows, accompanied by sons or daughters who had never known their father."[24]

Canadian veteran Charles Barrett of the Highland Light Infantry suppressed his war experience when he returned home in

1945. He was not interested in exploring it with others and he confessed to bottling his memories up. But decades after the war, he returned to the Netherlands and was deeply moved by the gratitude of the Dutch and by their generosity to the Canadian dead. As he remarked of the experience, "It's too bad that we in Canada have never got that sense of respect for what was done for this country."[25] Indeed, there was little respect for the war's veterans in Canada at the time, and these tours to the Netherlands barely registered in the mainstream newspapers or in public discourse.

Doug Smith wrote worriedly in 1969 about how veterans across Canada had been not only forgotten but seemingly discarded. Smith often visited pawn shops and saw tarnished medals tossed haphazardly in boxes—pickings for pennies. It made him "sick at heart" to see a "one-time symbol of fame and heroism wind up" in a junk shop.[26]

Canadian society had accelerated its rapid transformation by the end of the decade. The war in Vietnam was a quagmire of death and defeat, and few spoke of any war in any positive way. Charles Lynch, a wartime reporter and the doyen of Canadian journalism, talked of his own engagement with Normandy, returning every five years or so to walk the battlefields and relive the memories. But by the late 1960s, he confessed, he and many veterans, and certainly almost all Canadians, "had wearied of the business."[27]

By the end of the decade, antiwar beliefs in Canada ranged from benign neglect to open hostility. "Make love, not war" was the sentiment of the time. To wear a military uniform in Canadian society was to risk being verbally abused, even spat upon. All soldiers were baby killers; all airmen were harbingers of nuclear annihilation; a navy was a waste of money when Canada had a coast guard. The unification of the three services between 1964 and 1968 had gutted the morale of service personnel, but this crisis scarcely registered with most Canadians, who did not understand the anger of service personnel and veterans about the loss of traditions, customs, and uniforms, and certainly did not care. By the late 1960s, anything related to the military was foreign to most Canadians. One Department of National Defence committee from that time urged the federal government to raise the profile of the military and the reserves, asking why Canadians believed that "a serviceman should be a hero in wartime and a curiosity in peacetime."[28] It might have been more accurate to call the Canadian military personnel and veterans in the 1960s an irrelevant curiosity, and the same report noted that most Canadians saw war and the armed forces "through a glass, darkly."[29]

"It was an invasion, that's it. It doesn't mean anything," a teenager told CBC reporter Norman DePoe, who interviewed a group of young people in June 1969 about the meaning of D-Day. "Nothing at all. War means nothing," another teen insisted.[30] A surprised DePoe, who came from a different generation, probed deeper, asking if this included "the fact that all those men died on the beaches? Some only a few years older than yourself?" The teens shrugged it off and remained unconvinced, responding, "Yes, it doesn't mean a thing." Throughout the 1960s, concerned veterans lamented that comrades who gave their lives for freedom were being banished from memory as Canadians turned their backs on the Second World War. For many, not only had the Necessary War ceased to be a touchstone of Canadian identity, but it no longer meant anything at all.

CHAPTER 9

"PORTRAYING OURSELVES CONTINUOUSLY AS LOSERS"

Veterans started the 1970s with a win. After a decade of battle with the federal government over the need to increase veterans' pensions, the politicians gave way to the Legion's relentless pressure. Up to that point, even a 100 percent disability pension, which was awarded only to those with the most hideous of wounds, was equal to the wage of untrained civil service labourers, such as cleaners and low-level clerks, although the payments were not taxed. "It is tragic that veterans have to battle so strenuously on behalf of their comrades," wrote Ernest A. Crosthwaite of Yorkton, Saskatchewan.[1] Another ex-serviceman, E.C. Box, expressed his appreciation for the Royal Canadian Legion's tireless work on veterans' behalf, remarking, "There isn't a veteran inside or outside the Legion [who should not] thank God for such an organization. Without it many Canadian veterans would have been no better off than the South African War veterans, many of whom died in the poor-houses of England."[2] The pensions were finally raised from near poverty levels in 1971.

Yet even as wounded veterans became more financially secure, veterans in general worried that they had lost their place in society, with one ex-serviceman arguing in *Legion* magazine, "Veterans have become conscious of something unrealized."[3] The splintering of society, which included the new youth movements extolling their own values and beliefs, had left some veterans adrift. Others simply did not identify as veterans—they were dads, hockey coaches, and golfers, and they further associated themselves with whatever profession they had found. And yet for those who still felt connected to the war of their youth, a sense of disillusionment prevailed. Though most veterans felt deeply linked to the Canada that they had helped to build into a wealthy, prosperous nation, it was increasingly a country unmoored from the Second World War. Few veterans wanted to continually relive the war, but its utter lack of relevance in the modern Canada was disconcerting for some who had once served so proudly.

Testifying to the steadily eroding importance of the war and veterans within the Canadian imagination, the numbers of attendees at Remembrance Day ceremonies continued to dwindle. More than half the population—55 percent—had no experience with war, and by the early 1970s at least two generations of Canadians were unable to easily conceptualize the loss that was to be marked each year.[4] As Brigadier Willis Moogk of Niagara-on-the-Lake noted ruefully, "We must face the fact that many Canadians now look on Armistice Day as just another holiday, rather than a day of grateful and thoughtful remembrance."[5]

The Legion was also aging, with most Great War veterans now over the age of seventy-five, past the life expectancy of men at the time. However, the veterans' organization remained a coherent body; by 1975, membership had grown to more than 450,000, and 200,000 wives belonged to the Ladies Auxiliaries. More veterans had joined the Legion in the late 1960s, perhaps because they found so little interest in the war throughout the rest of society.

But the aging crisis meant a projected sharp drop-off in the coming years, and there was no easy solution to the worry that, with the passing of the veterans, the memory of the war would go with them. "There is no doubt that the traditional Remembrance Day observance in some communities across Canada has lost its significance," lamented the Legion. "There are some who even decry it, and suggest that we forget the whole thing."[6]

While many Legionnaires were saddened by the diminishing emphasis on the importance of the war throughout much of Canada, there was a resurgence of the war's meaning in Quebec. This reconnection with the past was related to the Quiet Revolution in the 1960s, when French Canadians threw off the shackles of the Roman Catholic Church, embraced the new liberties of the age, and wrested economic and political power from English elites in Quebec. In this period of modernization, political groups redefined Québécois identity as a part of the goal of carving out a new French-speaking nation within Canada—and, for the most radical, a nation separate from Canada. To fulfill this goal of independence or identity construction, the world wars became a historical example of English Canada's subjugation of French Canada, one that was usefully redeployed in the new fight to break old chains.

Relations between the English and French in Canada had been severely damaged during the Great War. Prime Minister Borden had promised in late 1914 that there would be no conscription in the voluntary war effort. But the long, attritional campaigns of the Western Front had led to shocking losses, and more and more men were required to replenish the shattered units at the front. What was to be done? The French, Russians, and Germans had prewar conscription, while Britain was forced to turn to it in late 1915. Borden struggled with the dilemma, but after being lobbied by many influential English Canadians, and after making dozens of haunting visits to the wounded soldiers in the hospitals overseas, he changed his mind. A majority of Canadians supported Borden when he enacted conscription in late 1917, although a sizeable number of French Canadians, recent immigrants, and farmers were against the idea of pressing their sons and other young men into service to kill Germans. The introduction of forced military service pitted community against community, friend against friend.

During the Second World War, the King government wanted to avoid repeating the agony of conscription. In order to bring a united Canada into the war in 1939, with Quebec tacitly supporting Ottawa's declaration of war, King promised there would be no conscription. He also listened carefully to his influential Quebec lieutenants—Ernest Lapointe and then Louis St. Laurent—and let them run the Quebec wing of the caucus.[7] In fact, almost everything that King did as Canada's war leader was measured against the possible effects of conscription—to prevent another national rupture.

Throughout the war, King bobbed and weaved to avoid bringing in conscription, although he slowly lost control of his plan for limited engagement as Canadians demanded a total war effort. He could not dodge the issue of conscription, and when it looked as if his government would fall in late 1944, he pivoted and bowed to the pressure by instituting limited conscription. French Canada was unhappy, but it was clear that the King government had done all it could to avoid pressing men into service. Quebeckers did not exit the war with the same sense of grievance they had expressed after the Great War, but they were again harshly singled out by English Canada for not pulling their weight.

Despite such criticisms, French Canadians in fact embraced the Second World War more fully than they did the previous war. By March 1944, they formed 19.1 percent of the Canadian army, although critics noted that French-speaking Canadians made up about 30 percent of the population.[8] However, by war's end, about 132,000 French speakers served in the three services. The Second World War in Quebec was rightly positioned as a war against Hitler and his Nazis, who had overrun much of Europe, although there was still much disapproval among elites, intellectuals, the Church, and in rural communities.

Importantly, the Second World War had more identifiable French-Canadian units than the Great War, which had only the 22nd Battalion. The Van Doos were a meaningful symbol in French Canada during the Great War, and the unit also served in the Second World War as the Royal 22e Régiment, fighting primarily in Sicily and Italy with the 1st Canadian Infantry Division. It was joined by several additional French-Canadian infantry units, including Les Fusiliers Mont-Royal, who stormed the beaches at Dieppe; Le Régiment de Maisonneuve, which battled through Normandy; and Le Régiment de la Chaudière, which landed on D-Day. On the West Coast, Le Régiment de Hull served in Nanaimo and the Kiska campaign in 1943. There were warships named after French cities and French-Canadian RCAF squadrons, like No. 425 "Alouette" Squadron, which served in Bomber Command. Journalist Chester Bloom, writing in the *Winnipeg Free Press* towards the end of the war, offered his thoughts: "It does not seem to the writer that the fighting French-Canadians have been given the public acclaim that they deserve.

Certainly a man who braves not only death and wounds and hardship but also the disapproval of large elements of his own countrymen must carry a double dose of courage with him."[9]

French Canada complained that not enough French-speaking officers had been elevated to senior commands, with some notable exceptions like J-V. Allard and J.G. Gauvreau, both brigadiers in Northwest Europe.[10] The lack of militia units in Quebec, the shortage of young men who had attended the Royal Military College of Canada, and language barriers in an English-only army had contributed to the low number of high-ranking officers. But there were heroes like Major Paul Triquet, who had been awarded the Victoria Cross for his valiant actions during the Battle of Ortona, and who had returned home mid-war to mobilize support in French Canada. Georges Vanier, a decorated officer of the 22nd Battalion in the Great War and minister to France in 1939, was another key figure who also served in Canada as a brigadier, overseeing recruitment and training in Quebec and using his connections to ensure the Catholic Church hierarchy supported the war effort—or at least did not actively work against it.[11]

And yet Quebeckers were angry over the limited conscription in 1944, which again revealed the English domination of French Canada. The sense of betrayal was less over the actual effects of conscription (which saw only 13,000 men sent overseas and fewer still ordered to the front) and more over the seeming eagerness of English Canadians to again engage in forcing troops across the Atlantic against the will of French Canada. Conscription, with its war of words, caused a disruption to national unity that resonated throughout French Canada and was reflected in the creative output of the time. Gabrielle Roy's novel *Bonheur d'occasion* (1945), known in English as *The Tin Flute* (1947), and Gratien Gélinas's play *Tit-Coq* (1948) were both deeply influenced by the Second World War and its impact on French-Canadian identity. Roy's novel, a massive best-seller in Canada and the United States, explored the difficult working-class lives of Montrealers during the Second World War, via characters who question the meaning of the war even as it lifts them out of urban poverty. Gelinas's play, which reached a wide French-Canadian audience through a 1952 film of the same name, focused on the dislocated dreams of an overseas French-Canadian conscript who, wrenched from his society and oppressed by the army and religious mores, returns home to find that his girl has not waited for him. As one scholar has observed, "the majority of Quebecers did not have the same appreciation as did Canadians in other provinces for those who had volunteered; they remembered the war less for the united struggle for freedom that changed the world and more for the divisive conscription debate."[12]

The rise of French-Canadian nationalism in the 1960s came with a concomitant impulse for some Québécois to distance

While Quebec had contributed far more significantly to the Second World War than the Great War, there remained a sense of betrayal that was heightened by the films and novels that emerged from the war. This still image is from Tit-Coq *(1952), which presented the dislocating effect of the war on a French-Canadian conscript.*

themselves from English Canada. Not all proud Quebeckers or French speakers across the country felt this way, but the intellectuals and literati—pursuing a strident nationalist agenda that mobilized the past as one of the many new battle fronts—did. In the 1960s, *les patriotes* of 1837 were recast as freedom fighters against their English overlords, while Louis Riel, the martyred hero of Manitoba and the Métis, returned prominently to social memory as a tragic hero who died for his people opposing the English imperialists in Ottawa.[13] The Great War and the Second World War were also unearthed from their shallow graves, with conscription in both wars often conflated in French-Canadian memory. The wars became two more examples of how, since the Conquest of 1763, French Canada had been held back and put down by the rest of the country. A narrative of victimhood prevailed in Quebec, one that blamed others for both real and imagined subjugation.[14]

The French-Canadians' historical grievances came in many forms and provided additional ammunition in the ongoing battle between Quebec and the federal government to gain more autonomy for Canada's French-speaking province. Executing its nationalist agenda, Quebec created Hydro-Québec in 1963, established the Québec Pension Plan the next year, diminished the role of the Catholic Church, and demanded more power from the federal government. Meanwhile, the Front de libération du Québec (FLQ) was on the rise, a radical and ragtag organization that sought to carve out a nation by violence instead of negotiation. Within this stormy milieu, nationalists downplayed the story of French-Canadian service in the world wars, emphasizing instead the history of federal troops shooting civilians in the streets of Quebec City during the conscription riots on Easter weekend 1918. It was slaughter, not service, when talking about the wars.

Relations between Quebec and the rest of Canada were worsened by the October Crisis of 1970, during which the FLQ kidnapped James Cross, a British trade representative in Montreal, and murdered Pierre Laporte, the provincial minister of labour. Pierre Trudeau's government dealt decisively with the terrorists, invoking the War Measures Act and stationing thousands of soldiers in the streets of Montreal and Quebec City. The situation was sobering and scary, even as French Canadians supported the actions of the federal government.[15] But for some it appeared that history was repeating itself, with soldiers in the streets and federal action impacting French Canadians. It took considerable energy to twist the past into a weapon to be used in the present, but it was not the first or last time that history would be used or abused for contemporary goals.

Beginning in the late 1960s, school textbooks in Quebec reflected this newly politicized history, and Dieppe became another symbol of the oppression of French Canada. With Les Fusiliers Mont-Royal thrown into the second wave of battle at Dieppe—and controversially so—it seemed that they had been sacrificed in a witless plan. Textbooks exaggerated the French-Canadian losses and claimed that French-speaking soldiers were singled out and sacrificed by the British.[16] And even though, for Quebec, the Second World War was not as deeply wounding as the Great War had been, much of the cultural conversation about the war emphasized that those Quebeckers who served had been tricked into it. As one 1979 Quebec textbook declared, in reference to the French Canadians at Dieppe, "The colonized are always used as cannon fodder by those who colonize them."[17]

———

The shale stones at Dieppe, some the size of a small fist, offer an unsettling sound as they rub against each other. Footing is poor and the rocks move with pressure. The memory of Dieppe is like those stones, layered upon each other, shifting unsteadily, and disquieting. This is unsettled history. And yet it also dominates. The memory of Dieppe overshadowed the story of Canada's Second World War for much of the twentieth century.

Canadians were rivetted by the Dieppe Raid of August 19, 1942, from the start. In its immediate aftermath, officials in Ottawa and military authorities spun the operation overseas as a victory.[18] It was not. Slowly, news emerged of the terrible casualties and revealed the magnitude of the defeat: 907 dead, 586 wounded, and 1,946 taken prisoner. Despite the appalling results, Dieppe was one of the first major Canadian army operations in the war, save for the disaster at Hong Kong, and so the Canadian public latched on to it.

During the war years, communities that had regiments that fought at Dieppe marked the sad day with acts of remembrance held

Canadian prisoners of the Dieppe Raid of August 19, 1942
march into captivity.

in the shadow of the Great War local cenotaphs. At the 1944 ceremony in Toronto, the mayor spoke to the many Silver Cross mothers and wives in attendance who lost a loved one in the raid, averring, "In no engagement was valour shown better than in the Battle of Dieppe. . . . Canadians will remember Dieppe as they remember Vimy."[19] Calgary, Toronto, Windsor, Hamilton, and Montreal all held annual ceremonies, and after the war, veterans of the raid took part in these events.[20] Dieppe was an icon of sacrifice. Like the Great War's Battle of Second Ypres—the April 1915 attack where the Canadians were outgunned and outnumbered, but that became an important symbol of resilience until it was dislodged in the 1920s by the Battle of Vimy Ridge—the Dieppe Raid also occurred early in the war and was cemented into the commemorative landscape. But while Ypres was a gritty, fighting retreat, though one in which the Canadians were deemed to have emerged as a battered victor, Dieppe was more difficult to transform into a similar moral victory. However, death and defeat could be remade to reflect and infuse notions of national character, as the Australians did with the Gallipoli campaign in 1915 and early 1916, reshaping that failure as a symbol of Aussie toughness, grit, and soldierly mateness.[21] Other ingredients were infused in the alchemy of why Dieppe burrowed its way into Canadian consciousness. The raid's high cost in lives, the uncertainty of its goals, the possible value of its impact on future operations, and the conspiracy theories about whether the raid was cleared by high authorities—not to mention the raw heroics that were key components in the story of the raid—all came together to forge the idea of Dieppe as central to the Canadian war effort.

Often the wartime ceremonies on the anniversary of the raid—August 19—witnessed dignitaries speak about the "spirit of sacrifice" of the Canadians at Dieppe, which was evident in every way in the disastrous raid.[22] And yet some of the enduring interest in this brief moment in the war has been over that seemingly needless sacrifice. "Who bungled the Dieppe Raid?" asked an editorial in the April 1956 issue of *The Legionary*.[23] Over the decades, dozens of British, American, and Canadian historians, journalists, and veterans have struggled to make sense of the operation. Because of the scale of the catastrophe, Canadians looked for someone to blame. The alertness of the German defenders seemed to indicate that the enemy had prior warning of the raid. Many of the surviving veterans felt that this was the case. But it was not true. The Germans knew that the tides portended that raids were more likely on certain days and at certain times; and so, not surprisingly, they were at the ready in their positions on August 19, 1942. For many veterans, though, the frontal assault into a storm of fire from the waiting Germans could only be explained by an intelligence leak.

There were other, more significant, failures that contributed to the defeat at Dieppe, most of them emanating from Lord Mountbatten's Combined Operations Headquarters. Mountbatten was a member of the Royal Family with a less than stellar military career that included the loss of two warships under his command in the first years of the war. Churchill quipped that he might have had the good grace to go down with at least one of them. As commander of Combined Operations from October 1941, Mountbatten launched a series of raids along the French coast. These would successfully annoy the Germans and keep them on their toes, causing minimal damage but perhaps effecting psychological disruption. They also helped to hone amphibious operations and they showed Stalin that the Allies were doing something as his forces fought for their survival against the bulk of the German army.

This last point was crucial within the fragile alliance with the mistrustful Communists. Beginning with the German invasion of Russia in June 1941, the Soviets had been collapsing under the military might of the Wehrmacht, losing millions of soldiers and absorbing terrible blows. From late 1941 onwards, Stalin demanded repeatedly that the Allies launch an invasion of Europe to draw off German strength in a Second Front, but an invasion would have led to annihilation in 1942 and 1943, as the Allies did not have enough landing craft, trained forces, warships, or air force squadrons to support the assaulting force. At the same time, the British had to hold off the naive Americans, who also wanted to attack the Germans in Europe as soon as possible so they could get on with their war against the Japanese. The large-scale operation at Dieppe was launched for many reasons, but the most important of these was the desire to demonstrate to Stalin that the Allies were trying to aid him. It turned out that the raid's spectacular failure had little impact on Stalin, who cared not a whit about the death of thousands given that he was responsible for murdering millions, but it impressed on the Americans the challenges of a cross-channel invasion.

The Dieppe operation was so amateurishly planned by Mountbatten and his staff that, at that time and ever since, historians have looked for an explanation, possibly a conspiracy. There was none: the Canadians were not deliberately sacrificed; Mountbatten and his staff were simply incompetent. The raid suffered from multiple problems, but atop the list was Mountbatten's inability to convince the other service commanders to lend sufficient resources—primarily firepower from bombers and heavily armed warships. Another factor was the unrealistic goal of landing on three beaches (five, if one includes the commandos on the flanks) at staggered times. It was a shoddy operation, but it was also one that the senior Canadian high command, particularly Lieutenant-General Harry Crerar, at the time acting commander of First Canadian Army, wanted Canadians to be involved in. They had seen little action up to that point, other than guarding Britain from invasion, and it was a force in need of an operation.

One of the appeals of the Dieppe story over time has been how it fits into the narrative arc of a colony becoming a nation. Since Confederation, Canada's slow evolution to nationhood has been illustrated in many ways: through the creation of national institutions, railways, and cities; the development of economic and cultural autonomy; the influx of immigrants; and the country's changing relations with Britain and the United States. In the South African War, the Great War, and the Second World War, Canadians in uniform, politicians, and many on the home front felt motivated to carve out a distinct national identity, often in opposition to Britain, and this identity drew upon characteristics supposedly grounded in the dominion's harsh environment.[24] These images were embraced along with symbols and signs of independent service: from the maple leaf to the word "Canada" displayed on the uniform. And yet, as part of this process, Canadians also looked for someone to blame for the occasional defeats, failures, and losses. This was done sometimes to show that it was time for Canadians to take the lead. One of the underlying themes of Canada's Great War in much of the popular literature (and in a more nuanced form in academic scholarship) was the need for our forces to break free of the British influence and its seemingly incompetent, verging on homicidal, generals, a break that would ultimately lead to more Canadian soldiers commanding the fighting forces. Many of the survivors of Dieppe, and those who have written about the raid since, have followed a similar line, directly blaming the British for the operation's failure, and noting that out of this disaster came the need for Canadians to exert more control over their forces. While there was nothing nation-building about Dieppe, the defeat was a clear warning to Canadian politicians and soldiers—and those interested in the raid ever since—not to let the British throw dominion soldiers into forlorn operations as cannon fodder. In this "blame-the-British" narrative, the Canadian senior officers put their faith in Mountbatten and he betrayed them, although, in reality, the officers were not entirely without blame. Crerar and McNaughton had the right to call off the operation, but they failed to screw up their courage when the planning began to look wobbly. Instead, the divisional commander, Major-General John Hamilton Roberts, was scapegoated for the battle, first by his superiors and then by his own soldiers. Roberts had unwisely told his soldiers before the raid that it would be a piece of cake. For years after the war, on the anniversary of the raid, Dieppe veterans personally delivered a stale piece of cake to him—a reminder of his overblown confidence and the deadly cost to their comrades.

Another component of Canadians' fascination with Dieppe is the conspiratorial whispers that give new meaning to the operation. We are haunted by Dieppe because we don't understand it. Moreover, some of the operational and planning records related to the raid were destroyed, or were never created, and so some historians imagine that Mountbatten pulled off this foolish multi-service assault involving tens of thousands of Canadian, American, and British soldiers, sailors, and airmen without the knowledge of the British political leaders or the military high command. Writers who look for a hidden conspiracy point to how Mountbatten planned and launched the raid as Operation Rutter in July 1942, only to

cancel it and relaunch it a month later. The lack of planning documents for the second August raid has led to much speculation about
Mountbatten going rogue and ordering the operation without the
full knowledge of Churchill and other service commanders.[25]
Without conclusive records—as these were either destroyed or never
created—historians have continued to clash over this interpretation,
but the uncertainty of the operation and the lack of records combine
to bolster an enduring controversy.

Canadians have returned to the Dieppe beaches almost from the
first years of the war, standing on the shale rocks and studying the
cliffs that dominate the battlefield. We visualize the German machine
gunners in their impenetrable pillboxes, and we can almost hear and
see our countrymen cut down by fire and steel. This, too, is important to an understanding of the battle, and others like it. Vimy is
situated on an identifiable ridge. We understand the challenge. Even
today, we can see the craters. We can walk the rising ground and be
winded at the top, catching a glimpse of what the soldiers of 100
years ago saw, while under fire and while stepping over the bodies
of their comrades. Dieppe is like that. We can stand on the assault
beaches and shudder at the madness of the raid.

In contrast, the major armoured thrusts of the Totalize and
Tractable operations in August 1944, fought in what are now farmers' fields, are nearly impossible to imagine. The same might be said
of the August 1918 Battle of Amiens in the Great War, a moment
as equally important to the war effort as Vimy, and yet one largely
erased from the nation's public memory partly because it took place
in nondescript fields. These are lessons in how the memory of war
is constructed: fighting on identifiable terrain is often the first step;
the second is building memorials on that same ground, elevating it
in comparison to other battles or significant sites.

This iconic image captures the carnage of the Dieppe Raid, with burning landing craft, knocked-out Churchill tanks, and dead Canadians. It remains one of the most frequently produced images of Canada's war effort

Dieppe also produced Canada's most recognizable image of the war: the German propaganda photograph of several dead Canadians on the beach and knocked-out Churchill tanks. Why did Canadians reproduce this image over and over again? The American and Russian photographic counterparts depict victory, with the group of US soldiers raising their nation's flag at Iwo Jima and the Soviet soldier erecting his republic's flag over the Reichstag in Berlin. Over the decades, the haunting space of Dieppe has continued to demand justification, and we cannot look away from the slaughter. And yet we also turn to it, again and again, as the central emblem of the Canadian war effort.

In the mid-1950s, Dieppe veteran H.M. Woffindin of Mirror, Alberta, felt that the stories and histories that denigrated the raid, describing it as a wasteful operation with no redeeming value, were painful. "There are many relations and friends with us who lost loved ones," he wrote, "many wounded and still suffering from the raid; also prisoners-of-war who put up with a lot of hell.

Are we to believe that August 19th was just a flop like one of the schemes in England when the convoy landed up in a dead-end road?" He further remarked that, as a gunner there, "Nothing will ever convince me that those who suffered at Dieppe did not do something to help save others and make other landings a whole lot better."[26] It was an understandable sentiment—Woffindin needed to know that the sacrifice of his comrades had been worth something. The need to make meaning of the one-day raid also contributes to Canadians' continuing impulse to chew it over, generation after generation. This search for meaning plays out in many ways, but one critical aspect is how Dieppe forms a narrative arc leading ultimately to D-Day, from the wasteful carnage on that beach in August 1942 to the victory in June 1944. At Dieppe, the Allies limped away from the defeat, going on to implement the lessons learned in blood and, at Juno Beach, come back full force for the Normandy invasion. Many Canadian and British generals—including Crerar and Mountbatten—claimed that Normandy would have been lost without the lessons of Dieppe. Lord Mountbatten, speaking publicly in 1948, stated that "Dieppe was probably the most important and one of the most vital operations of the war," adding, "If I had the same decision to make again, I would do as I did before."[27] Others might have been less confident in such a reading of the history.

The legacy of Dieppe is complex, and it can be said with certainty that the spectre of the disastrous raid loomed over the D-Day planning. No one wanted to command another slaughter, especially one that could be twenty-five times larger. Concrete lessons were indeed learned from Dieppe and applied to the Normandy invasion. The D-Day plans incorporated better arms coordination, a multi-layered plan to divert and deceive, the realization of the need to avoid a defended port, and the acknowl-edged necessity of a massive array of logistics to sustain a force after the invasion. As well, Dieppe had taught the leaders to use bombers and warships to soften up enemy defences and to defend against counterattacking forces. But lessons had also been gleaned from other fronts, especially from the American fighting in the Pacific, as well as the amphibious assaults at Sicily and the Italian mainland. One of the challenges in examining Dieppe is to under-stand what victory meant in the context of all-out war. The Canadian D-Day landings on June 6 exacted a fearfully high cost in lives, with more than 1,000 Canadians killed or wounded on that day. But not a single credible person has ever voiced the question of whether it was worth it. The same cannot be said for Dieppe.

Returning to Dieppe in 1982 on the fortieth anniversary of the raid, veteran Cornelius Stapleton of the Essex Scottish Regiment remarked, "We have no memorial and no marker here. The only thing we left on this beach was blood."[28] In the ensuing decades, a few plaques and small memorials would be added, but the shock of the Dieppe losses had reverberated deep through Canadian his-torical consciousness. Even decades after the defeat, it is difficult to understand the Dieppe plan. It was so fundamentally flawed, and so devastating for the invading force, that we continue to look for a hidden meaning, or we seek lessons in the operation's entrails. Dieppe is also a truly Canadian story, like Vimy, but it is a defeat rather than a victory. Nonetheless, there is a strange desire to pos-sess it. For these reasons, the battle is prominent in every school textbook published since the war, where it features as a hinge event, confirming for some, particularly since the 1960s, the idea that war is a disaster and that those who fight for their country are pawns or victims. Almost from the first days after the raid, the nine-hour Dieppe operation edged out in importance the six year-long battle of the Atlantic, the month-long battle of the Scheldt, the eighteen-month Italian campaign, and almost every other Canadian operation in the war. Dieppe remains special, but the reason that it has loomed so large is that by the early 1980s Canadians lacked knowledge about the entire war effort. And for those who were taught about the war, especially in French Canada, it was weaponized for the fight in new sovereignty battles. A very strange story of Canada's war effort emerged over the decades, with so much shorn away but with repression in Quebec and a disastrous raid rising to the surface. It was mystifying to many, but with each media report, anniversary, and book, the one-day Dieppe battle came to overshadow the rest of the enormous Canadian contribution during the six years of the Necessary War. In the December 1983 issue of *Canadian Forum*, writer Mel Bradshaw lamented the "perverse" focus on the defeats at Hong Kong and Dieppe, observing that "portraying ourselves continuously as losers makes shaping our own destiny as a nation more difficult."[29]

CHAPTER 10

INSULTED, IGNORED, AND MARGINALIZED

As a result of the heightened focus on Dieppe within the country—on the part of both veterans and the general public—few other aspects of the war were known to Canadians. Canada's obsession with the Dieppe Raid must have seemed odd to the British and Americans, but there was in fact a Great War legacy that also worked against a more nuanced understanding of the army's role during the Second World War. Sir Arthur Currie's Canadian Corps was a national symbol, and the extraordinary achievements of this fighting formation loomed over Crerar's larger army during the Second World War. The Canadian Corps had defeated the enemy along the Western Front, especially at Vimy Ridge, Hill 70, and Passchendaele in 1917. And by the last year of the war, with four hardened divisions, the Canadians were a shock formation thrown into the most difficult battles in the Hundred Days campaign. At Amiens, Arras, Cambrai, Valenciennes, and the final liberation of Mons, the Canadian Corps delivered victory after victory, contributing significantly to the end of the war. It was not for nothing that C.P. Stacey said that "the creation of the Canadian Corps was the greatest thing Canada had ever done" to that point in the nation's history.[1]

The narrative of greatness that was wrapped around the Corps left the soldiers of the Canadian Army of the Second World War in its shadow, and they were often compared unfavourably with their fighting fathers. It didn't matter that the army served well on two major fronts: Italy and then Northwest Europe. The Canadian forces in Italy won at Sicily and Ortona in 1943 and broke the Hitler and Gothic Lines in 1944, though few Canadians took much notice of the army's contributions in this secondary theatre of war. But in Europe, where most attention has historically been focused, Crerar's army ran afoul of an important person: Field Marshal Bernard Montgomery. The British commander, slow in planning but quick in judgment, was supremely confident. The Canadians served under him first in the Mediterranean and later in Europe, and the charismatic diminutive general, with his famous two-badged beret, turtleneck, and corduroy pants, was much loved by the Canucks. They preferred him to most of their commanders, especially Harry Crerar, who was seen as a cold-fish paper-pusher. Crerar was that, but he was also a good manager of battle, even if he did not have Monty's easy ways with the soldiers.

Montgomery disliked Crerar, feeling the Canadian did not deserve to be an army commander since he had never led higher-level formations in battle. Not known for his manners or restraint, Montgomery frequently treated the Canadian formation as if it was a subservient colonial force and not an independent army. As a national commander, Crerar could not stand for this, and when he pushed back, the Canadian suffered Monty's slights, wraths, and undermining moves. Crerar absorbed most of the punishment, but he occasionally struck back, and in one famous case, after Monty demanded that Crerar come to a meeting, the Canadian

general decided instead to attend a parade celebrating the liberation of Dieppe on September 3, 1944. It was far more important
for him to be there at that site of loss and at the celebration of
triumphant return. When the British field marshal threatened to
fire him for this action, Crerar stood firm and said he would go
over Montgomery's head and make a direct appeal to the Canadian
government.[2] The chastised Montgomery mumbled an apology
and retreated.

The much-beloved Monty was waspish at the best of times, and
downright deceitful in blaming others for mishaps. A particular
instance was his shifting of the blame for his substantial failures in
the ground campaign in Normandy, during which he did not recognize early enough the opportunity to entrap and destroy the two
German armies in the Falaise Gap in mid-August 1944. When

Field Marshal Bernard Montgomery, seen here, was much loved by
the Canadian soldiers, but he condemned Crerar's forces in Normandy
for being badly led. His assessment was used by other historians and
commentators to also portray the Canadians as inferior soldiers in
comparison to the British, Americans, or Germans.

Monty failed to direct sufficient divisions and resources to the mission, it fell to the Polish and Canadian forces, worn down and short of fuel, to carry out the task. They did not ensnare the enemy as quickly as Montgomery hoped, so he blamed them and their commanders for being too slow. These were unfair charges, to say the least, especially as the Canadians had at that point participated in more days of active operations than any other British division in Normandy and had suffered more casualties than the other divisions in Montgomery's army group.[3]

The Canadians were not helped in their own cause when Major-General Charles Foulkes, after being soundly beaten by the Germans at Verrières Ridge on July 25, 1944, denigrated his own soldiers, admitting, "When we bumped into battle-experienced German troops, we were no match for them."[4] It was an unfortunate and decontextualized comment, and one that some historians have used to illustrate how the German soldiers handled the Canadians roughly throughout Normandy. Sometimes they did, but the Canadians chalked up far more victories than defeats in Normandy. Beyond that, the Canadians participated in clearing German forts along the coast in September 1944, in the Scheldt campaign the next month, and in the battles into Germany during 1945, all of which were clear-cut victories. And yet, with so few Canadians at home knowing anything about these battles, or how much the Canadian Army had improved through its experiences in Normandy, there was a sense among the Allied nations that Crerar's divisions did not fight as well as Currie's had in the previous war.[5]

The Royal Canadian Navy (RCN) was also derided by some of the officers in the Royal Navy. The Canadian sailors of the Second

World War had done a stellar job in the Battle of the Atlantic, with their meagre forces increasing at least thirty-three-fold during the war, from about 3,000 to 100,000 men. Not surprisingly, the RCN experienced growing pains, especially as it underwent a staggering expansion and agreed to build ships on a crushingly quick schedule. Moreover, its senior officers were too willing to accede to every request from the Royal Navy to send warships to other theatres of war, which left Canadian convoys increasingly vulnerable under the protection of thinner screens of warships.[6] The Royal Navy, in turn, was not generous about sharing the latest technological advances, with Canadian warships often being among the last to get the essential radar or weapons that saved lives by detecting enemy subs or holding them off in battle. The scurrilous Captain Donald Macintyre of the Royal Navy, only one of the British navy's critics of the RCN, described Canada's expanded wartime fleet as "travesties of warships."[7] And yet by war's end, the RCN was the fourth largest navy in the world and it had escorted half of the Merchant Navy ships across the Atlantic through convoy work. While the merchant mariners had suffered heavy casualties, 99 percent had made it through the U-boat gauntlet, with more than 25,000 Merchant Navy voyages arriving in Britain carrying full hulls of war supplies. The RCN did not excel at sinking U-boats, but strategic victory at sea was not about killing subs; it was about keeping Britain supplied. In this sense, the RCN was critical to the Allied victory by ensuring that Britain was not starved out of the war.

But the massive Canadian naval support was little acknowledged by either the British or the Americans, and in the postwar years Canada's ambivalent attention to its historical record—which included cancelling the RCN official histories—meant that

An ice-encrusted Canadian warship struggles in the harsh Atlantic.
The Royal Canadian Navy rapidly expanded during the war and played a
crucial role in guiding the merchant ships in convoys to their destination.
Without the RCN, the Americans and British would have had to
dangerously spread thin their naval forces.

the nation's navy was too often portrayed as the none-too-effective
county cousin to the Royal Navy. The failure to produce a proper
naval history, and the lack of academic writing on the RCN,
meant that other countries' historians and commentators defined
the Canadian naval war effort. That did not change until a series
of conferences in the early eighties, under the leadership of Alec
Douglas of the Canadian Forces' Directorate of History, who
brought together naval scholars to remedy the wretchedly bad
state of affairs.[8] The poor reputation of the RCN was most significantly redeemed by Marc Milner, first an official historian and
later a professor at the University of New Brunswick, who produced two ground-breaking books, *North Atlantic Run* (1985)
and *The U-Boat Hunters* (1994). They detailed the key work of

the RCN during the war, warts and all.[9] Milner's findings were surprising to both Canadian and international scholars, most of whom had written off the navy as a weak and pathetic service. It would take decades, and the publication of the detailed two-volume official histories *No Higher Purpose* (2002) and *A Blue Water Navy* (2006), for the Canadian navy's reputation to be fully rehabilitated and for the details of the RCN's contributions to the Allied victory to be laid out in full.[10]

The navy was not the only Canadian force to be disparaged by other nations. In the war's aftermath, American soldiers and historians diminished the contributions of the Canadian Army (as well as those of the British), while elevating the fighting prowess of the aggressive Germans. They were also both puzzled and concerned by the Red Army's ability to absorb punishment while mastering the operational level of war on the Eastern Front battlefields. Repeating the charges made by the wartime American high command that the British and the Canadians had not fought well in Normandy, later generations of historians felt that the British had been too tied to the set-piece battle of artillery, armour, and infantry, and not confident enough to let loose on the battlefield to exploit operational success.[11] But while the "tidy battlefield," as Montgomery liked to call it, of careful preparation and marshalling of resources was not glamorous, it was more judicious—and showed more concern for the fighting men's lives—than simply flinging units forward into the maw of the enemy guns. There was also little acknowledgment by the Americans of the combined-arms tactical evolutions achieved by the British and Canadians during the summer of 1944, which included the incorporation of bombers into the attack to soften up the enemy defences, the use of armoured personnel carriers, and even the execution of risky night operations.

The culmination of this dismissive thinking came with the publication of best-selling British journalist Max Hastings's *Overlord* (1984), which presented the Germans as an elite fighting force that was able to attack ferociously and defend vigorously, especially in comparison to the ponderous British army that lacked "aggression" in the face of the "glory of German arms in Normandy."[12] In his assessment, Hastings was building on years of American valorization of the Germans, which included much praise about their warfighting tactics that involved rapid exploitation and counterattack. It was not that the German forces were not good—they obviously were—but they did lose two world wars. And still, in 1984, it was Hastings's book that everyone talked about. *Overlord* was an international best-seller, and Hastings was particularly hard on the Canadians. He spent almost no time reading the primary archival sources and instead closely followed Stacey's interpretation in *The Victory Campaign* (1960), arguing that while the Canadian soldiers were good in battle, their officers were inexperienced and generally poor.

Other historians, both British and American, similarly felt that the Allies came off worse than the Germans in Northwest Europe.[13] This was sometimes true, especially in Normandy, where the Germans were fighting on the defensive and had stacked their best armoured formations against the British and Canadians. But it was less often the case from September 1944 to the end of the war, when many of the Allies' greatest challenges lay in overcoming logistics, geography, and weather. The Canadians fought a brilliant campaign in the Scheldt, battling through horrendous conditions to drive the Germans back in a sea of mud in October and November 1944. Yet little was known about those hard battles, either in Canada or outside of it. Indeed, most Canadians had little idea about what happened in the fighting beyond D-Day. Decades later, it seemed as if there had been an invasion on June 6, some muddled combat for eleven months, and then the surrender in May 1945. This downplaying of the Canadians' contribution was not helped by the country's historians, film-makers, and other cultural producers who had done little to tell these stories by the early 1980s.

Though the Canadian effort in the world wars was forgotten by most, denigrated by others, and weaponized for political ends by some in French Canada, many Canadians in the second half of the twentieth century did embrace one military symbol. The image of the peacekeeper as a different type of martial icon was taken up in the late 1960s by Canadians eager to distinguish themselves from the Americans, who were then mired in their unwinnable war in Southeast Asia.[14] As Canada made peacekeeping a central part of its defence policy, the idea of the nation as a force for peace became firmly lodged in Canadian consciousness by the early 1980s.[15]

The concept of the peaceable kingdom and its army of peaceful warriors was a seductive one that appealed to both English and French Canadians. After Canada's successful intervention to prevent war in the Suez Canal region in 1956, successive federal governments volunteered Canadian soldiers for mission after mission. The country's electorate and its politicians liked the middle ground, even if the act of peacekeeping was dangerous and dirty, requiring flexible engagement with difficult moral questions for those on the ground caught between warring factions. These issues were of little concern to most Canadians, and there was scarcely an international peacekeeping operation in the second half of the twentieth century in which Canada did not participate. The idea of Canada as peacekeeper was deeply embedded in the nation's popular imagination and was embraced, along with multicultural-ism and bilingualism, within the evolving symbolic landscape.

With peace eclipsing war in Canada's military mythology, the country's memorial landscape was also transformed in the early 1980s, as the once-promised Second World War monument reached its sad endgame. "After long years of discussion, the Legion has asked the department of Veterans Affairs to alter the National War Memorial in Ottawa to represent Canada's service losses since W.W.I," read a resolution passed at the 1980 Dominion convention in Penticton, BC, where the entire issue of a separate memorial was described as a "controversy."[16] The National Shrine for the Second World War had been quietly abandoned by the Pearson government in 1967, and while the Legion had periodi-cally raised the idea of a new memorial, few outside the veterans' community seemed interested in pursuing it.

The National War Memorial in Ottawa—The Response—had by this time been accepted by Canadians as the single monument to mark all of Canada's dead in all wars. Though it was an overt memorial to the Great War, it had, over the decades, come to embody the fallen of all wars, especially given that the national Remembrance Day ceremony was held there and broadcast live across the country. The monument had anchored the memorial landscape of Canada, being reproduced in posters, featured on stamps, and represented in all manner of media. By the early 1980s, the Second World War veterans' battle for their own memo-rial had been nearly forgotten, although in May 1982 the *Ottawa Citizen* dug through the ashes and reported that the failed shrine had been defeated by "a long story of backstage politics, obsti-nacy, bureaucratic inertia and, finally, indifference."[17] But few

*Plans for a separate Second World War memorial were finally buried
on May 29, 1982, when Canada's National War Memorial,
was modified with the dates of 1939–1945.*

cared, and on May 29, 1982, the dates of the Second World War
and the Korean War were added to the national monument.[18]

Memorials and monuments commemorate events that are
stuck in time, but their meaning is fluid, taking on new relevance
with each generation. Monuments also physically change, not
only eroding from misuse and weather but having new functions
given to them and occasionally new components grafted onto
them. They are not static in either form or interpretation. And yet
the Canadian government's decision to retain and add to the
nation's original war monument ensured that the Great War continued to dominate the wars that came before and after it, remaining a focal point of remembrance even as the dates of the South
African War (1899–1902) and the Afghanistan War (2001–2014)
were etched onto it in the twenty-first century. Before this, however, Second World War veterans who had demanded a separate

memorial understood that the meaning of the great crusade against fascism had long faded for most Canadians by the early 1980s. Capitulating to the inevitable, veterans recognized that the addition of the Second World War dates to the memorial was preferable to their continued absence.

The fortieth anniversary of D-Day brought fresh hopes for a renewed interest in the Second World War. World leaders planned to meet at the Normandy beaches on June 6, 1984, to mark the occasion. While French president Charles de Gaulle had been in power, from 1959 to 1969, D-Day celebrations had been all but ignored. The haughty and prickly wartime general had not liked the idea of acknowledging his nation's need to be liberated by the British, Americans, and Canadians, and the military operations were often called the "landings" as opposed to the "liberation."[19] For decades, the annual commemorations of the pivotal invasion had been left to local French authorities to organize; but now, on the fortieth anniversary, President François Mitterand's government was setting the agenda, and it was shaping up to be an impressive commemorative event. Tens of thousands of Allied veterans were set to join Queen Elizabeth II, President Ronald Reagan, and President Mitterand to memorialize this epic moment that marked the beginning of the end for the Germans in the West. The long-serving Canadian prime minister Pierre Trudeau had never taken much joy in these pageants of remembrance, but this was a major event—an opportunity for the Western nations to reaffirm their faith in one another and to offer a show of force during one of the darkest periods of the Cold War.[20] Trudeau would go to the Normandy beaches.

In the months leading up to the ceremonies, Canadian veterans and journalists were vehement in their demands that the Canadian government not let itself and the nation's veterans be pushed to the periphery. After decades of neglecting Canada's ex-service personnel, the government needed to seize this occasion to remind the world that Canada had contributed to the Allied victory—that its forces had landed on one of the five invasion beaches on June 6, 1944. It was not clear why journalists finally paid attention to Canada's history, but there was a strong anti-American theme to much of the writing. Charles Lynch, a wartime journalist and revered columnist, recounted a ditty popular in Canada after the Great War:

> The Yankees think they won the war, Parley Voo!
> The Yankees think they won the war, Parley Voo!
> The Yanks think they won the war.
> The [bleeping] [bleeping] [bleeps] of whores!
> Hinky, Dinky, Parley Voo!

Lynch argued that Canadians had experienced this same feeling during the Second World War and ever since, with the United States claiming all the credit for victory. In 1984, the Americans seemed intent again on ignoring the British and Canadians. "What the Americans tell their own people is one thing," sniffed Lynch, "but it's something else when they peddle their version of events in Canada, virtually eliminating our contributions to the victory in Normandy."[21]

The fear that Canada would be reduced to a second-rate player in France was exacerbated when the first posters and advertisements for the June event featured only French and American flags.

Canadian troops on the run-in to Juno Beach on June 6, 1944. Forty years later, the Canadian wartime contributions were largely ignored.

But rage fully erupted in Canada when a seventeen-page spread in *Time* magazine's May 28, 1984 issue, marking the anniversary of D-Day, focused almost exclusively on the role played by the Americans. Even in the Canadian edition of the US weekly, the editors claimed, "Never again, perhaps, would American power and morality so perfectly coincide. The Americans, from Eisenhower down, dominated the drama. The invasion, in a way, was a perfect expression of American capabilities: vast industrial energy and organizational know-how sent out into the world on an essentially knightly mission—the rescue of an entire continent in distress."[22] Canadians were roused to anger and bristled at the absence of their wartime contributions, but Lynch noted, "Perhaps the fault is our own, for not seeing to it that successive generations of Canadians were reminded of what our own armed forces accomplished."[23]

On June 6, eyes across Canada were focused overseas on the commemoration ceremonies. Many international television networks were in Normandy to cover the spectacle, with both CBC and CTV offering live broadcasts from the beaches and cemeteries.[24] The politicians used the high-profile event to speak of sacrifice and service, death and liberation, but they all had political messages. President Reagan addressed the world from Pointe du Hoc, the highest ground between Utah and Omaha beaches, and his message was timed to broadcast in the last hour of the morning TV shows in the United States. Brilliantly crafted, Reagan's speech described American bravery but also gave generous credit to the British, French, Poles, and even his neighbours to the north, applauding "the unsurpassed courage of the Canadians who had already seen the horrors of war on this coast," and noting, "They knew what awaited them here but they could not be deterred. Once they hit Juno Beach, they never looked back."[25] Canadians swooned at his words—as they do when anyone says something positive about the country on the world stage—and the American president dominated the day.

Reagan was at his best—magnanimous in speech and action but set against a backdrop of warships in the channel, helicopters circling above, and some 10,000 American veterans spread out before him. With the Cold War impossible to untangle from the Necessary War at this anniversary, the president used his speech also to rebuke the Soviet Union—reinforcing his denunciation the year before of the republic as an "evil empire"—and he vowed that the United States would continue to stand for the free-speaking world. From the West, the Americans had come to liberate in 1944, Reagan said; from the East, the Soviets had come to occupy, and they were still there as an unwanted, immoral force of oppression. Neither the West's wartime ally, now enemy, the Soviet Union, nor its wartime enemy, now ally, West Germany, were invited to the ceremony. As Chancellor Helmut Kohl had said earlier in 1984 upon visiting Jerusalem, "The stain left on German history by the Holocaust is the exception which proves the rule that time heals all wounds."[26]

Trudeau and Mitterrand used their TV time at the ceremonies to offer thoughts on the search for stability and made a pledge for peace, but Trudeau's voice was inevitably overshadowed by the other leaders. It was a challenging day for the French, as they had only played a minimal role in reclaiming their nation; but President Mitterrand, a member of the Resistance, spoke passionately about the sacrifice of the Allied soldiers, asserting, "We free men owe them what we are."[27] Thousands of French citizens lined the streets to cheer and wave flags. As an elderly woman told one group of Canadians, she had been twenty-four years old at the time of the invasion and had lived through five years of agony before being delivered from Nazi tyranny by the Allied soldiers. She vowed, "The French will always remember."[28]

Trudeau was seen with the other world leaders, but he paid little attention to the 3,000 Canadian veterans. The old warriors were unimpressed. "We didn't need him forty years ago and we don't need him today," seethed veteran Carey Adams.[29] Trudeau had not served during the war, despite being of age to do so, and as a young, wealthy intellectual in Quebec, he had been against the war and conscription. Veterans were particularly incensed about the stories of a brash Trudeau riding his motorcycle through Montreal during the war years, adorned with German First World War military regalia; during the next forty years, erroneous rumours altered the regalia into Nazi icons.[30] Be-medalled veteran Robert Thomas raged from Juno Beach that the supposed Nazi-loving prime minister "is desecrating the ground here," adding,

Canadian Prime Minister Pierre Trudeau (on far left) with other world leaders in Normandy. Canada's veterans were pushed to the periphery during the ceremony.

"He should have been lined up and shot. After all, we shot deserters."[31] Canada did not in fact do so, at least not during the Second World War, but the veterans' sentiments against Trudeau were strong.

The French authorities enforced strict security for the world's leaders during the ceremonies, to the point that most of the veterans were kept back from the beaches by the Gendarmerie police force. Those who had fought for freedom and watched their comrades die were now shunted aside as apparently unwanted and peripheral spectators. RCAF veteran Norman Shannon spoke angrily about the D-Day commemoration, which he said "generated more media hype than the original landings." Shannon raged that the "free-loading dignitaries and officials shoved the veterans so far back they couldn't see the wreath-laying at Beny-sur-Mer."[32] Throughout the spectacle, the mob of television, radio, and print journalists—estimated at 2,000—raced about, trying to capture the best images. Angry veterans nearly stormed the beaches again, especially when their view of the Queen was blocked by legions of photographers, some of whom trampled flowers or propped themselves against headstones in the war cemeteries to steady their shots.[33] "Move back, you media bastards," came the shouts from the veterans.[34] Many of the local French officials were so disgusted with the ill-treatment of the veterans that invitations were hastily extended to the Canadians or anyone wearing a maple leaf to visit their villages for impromptu celebrations. As the mayor of Tilly commented to one Canadian journalist, "In all this chaos, people seem to forget that it's not the chiefs of state we are honoring, it is the men who fought here."[35]

Don Thompson, a veteran from the Cameron Highlanders of Ottawa, returned to Normandy for the fifth time in 1984 and remarked, "It's not only a piece of your life. It's a piece of history. . . . There are men buried here who never returned home. They deserve to be remembered."[36] The men were honoured for a few days, but the event had little significant impact on Canadian acts of remembrance. In fact, the main message seemed to be contained in Reagan's stirring speech that once again portrayed D-Day as a battle in which the United States had dominated. This central theme was confirmed by the massive media coverage that frequently compared the Vietnam nightmare to the Good War of the 1940s. From June 1984 onward, US leaders made a sustained effort to use the victory of the Second World War to blot out the more recent American defeat in Southeast Asian jungles.[37]

At the D-Day ceremonies, Canadian veterans and politicians had again been marginalized, by both their own hand and others'. Trudeau saw himself as a man of peace and had no stomach for war-related speeches that might have raised Canada's profile inside or outside the country. And likely no one would have listened to a prime minister who was to leave office later that month. But he and others might easily have made the case for Canada's enormous wartime contributions, and for how the war propelled Canada towards prosperity and created a desire to move from isolationism to a policy of aiding countries in the international sphere. Instead, the prime minister offered only platitudes about peace. At this event of international importance, Canadian veterans felt that officials in Ottawa had once again refused to fight on their behalf.

CHAPTER 11

APOLOGY CAMPAIGNS

The Allied nations of the Second World War fought against tyranny and to liberate the oppressed. But in the all-out war against the Nazi evil, the Western Allies were themselves forced to embrace evil. They sided with the Soviet monster, Stalin, a mass murderer of his own people through starvation, executions, and purges. Canadians pursued victory like a crusade and there was little room for dissenters or those deemed as a threat to the war effort. In these circumstances, Canadians did not become a more tolerant people during the war.

As part of Canada's global war effort, a 2,000-strong force was sent to garrison the British colony of Hong Kong. This deployment—requested by the British government and urged on by Canadian senior military commanders—became a tragic focal point when Japan launched a military strike against the United States on December 7, 1941.[1] Canadians were shocked by the surprise attack on Pearl Harbor, but most soon learned that their countrymen were caught up in battle in Hong Kong, where the Japanese assaulted on December 8. The Canadians of C Force, largely drawn from Winnipeg and French Canada, engaged in intense and chaotic fighting that killed 290 and wounded 483, lasting until a surrender on Christmas Day, 1941. The British, Canadian, and other Allied survivors endured four years of hellish conditions in Japanese prisoner-of-war camps. Another 264 Canadians died in captivity from violence, malnourishment, deprivation, and execution. The men who survived the ordeal in the camps were forever damaged in health and scarred in spirit.[2]

At home, on Canada's weakly defended west coast, British Columbians felt vulnerable to a Japanese invasion. Fearing an assault, the Canadian government issued gas masks in BC to protect against a possible chemical attack, disseminated instructions about how to prepare for an air raid, and rushed ill-trained soldiers to crumbling defensive positions. Canadians searched the ocean for a marauding fleet, but any invasion was also expected to include fifth columnists, as had been the case in most of the successful Japanese offensives in the Pacific.[3] Caught up in this fear were almost 23,000 Japanese Canadians who lived on the west coast, of whom about two thirds were naturalized or Canadian-born.

Since the late nineteenth century, racist policies had been directed against Asiatic immigration to Canada, and Japanese immigrants were denied the full rights of citizenship. Despite the discrimination they faced—being denied certain jobs and experiencing outright violence—at least 222 Japanese Canadians enlisted in the Great War, fifty-four of whom were killed and thirteen recognized with gallantry awards. Those veterans were at the forefront of the campaign in the 1920s for voting rights for Japanese Canadians, which were finally granted in 1931 in British Columbia, although only to veterans. This did little to ease the racism.

In the aftermath of the Japanese attack on Pearl Harbor, President Franklin Roosevelt bowed to public pressure and fury over the 2,400 deaths, and issued an executive order on February

Canadian infantrymen in Hong Kong. They fought bravely during the December 1941 battle and endured horrific conditions in the prisoner-of-war camps. Their plight during the war left many white Canadians, already holding racist feelings, wary and vengeful towards Japanese Canadians.

19, 1942, that uprooted 120,000 Japanese Americans from the coast and relocated them to barbed-wire-enclosed camps where they were treated as prisoners of war. Less than a week later, facing pressure from the United States and cries for action from British Columbia, the Canadian cabinet authorized the forced removal of all "persons of Japanese racial origin" from the BC coast.[4] The Royal Canadian Mounted Police (RCMP) had already investigated Japanese Canadians and concluded that as a group they were not a threat to national security. But that assessment was not accepted by many white Canadians who regarded visible minorities as their enemy. The province's lieutenant-governor, W.C. Woodward, stated privately, "I have rarely felt so keenly about the impending danger as I do about the Japanese on this coast being allowed to live in our midst."[5] He was not alone in this opinion, and the widespread fear of war was stoked by rumour and racism. In fact, not surprisingly, many of the 7,200 Japanese nationals, who were not yet British subjects (there being no separate Canadian citizenship until 1947), were sympathetic to the Japanese Emperor, who was revered as a god. The Japanese consul, noted one Canadian intelligence report, "through his agents, and through the Japanese schoolmasters, and the Japanese patriotic societies, cultivates a strong Japanese spirit and a consciousness among the BC Japanese of being 'sons of Japan abroad' rather than Canadian citizens."[6] Stories circulated that Japanese Canadians were paving the way for invasion by enemy forces, and Canada's military intelligence officers' total lack of Japanese language skills left them in the dark about the situation in that isolated community.[7]

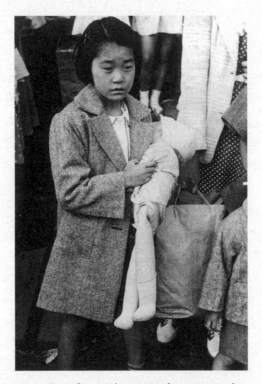

A young Japanese-Canadian girl, among the 23,000 who were forcibly removed from their communities during the war.

Following the cabinet's order, almost all Japanese Canadians—men, women, and children—were forcibly removed from their homes, often being given only a few days to pack up their goods and leave. They were moved to camps in the interior of British Columbia, or even farther east to work on beet farms in Alberta or in road-labour groups. Few resisted, but those who did were interned in camps in Ontario, far from their families. They were issued PoW uniforms like those of captured Germans in Europe, with a large target-like circle emblazoned on the back.

Japanese Canadians were placed in small interior communities or isolated camps that provided inadequate housing and schools, although many of the camps were upgraded and made more habitable by the efforts of Japanese-Canadian internees. Even then, life was hard. Many of those who were imprisoned pleaded that they, too, were British subjects and that, as one Japanese Canadian wrote in a letter to Ottawa, they were "no less loyal to Canada than any other Canadian."[8] Their appeals were ignored.

The Canadian cabinet went even further than relocation in its labelling of Japanese Canadians as "enemy aliens." The aim in doing so was to block the return of the internees to the west coast. The move violated existing Canadian law, but the cabinet, driven onwards by the minister of pensions and national health—the virulent anti-Asiatic Ian Mackenzie—created the Office of the Custodian of Enemy Property, which sold off Japanese Canadian–owned assets in early 1942 at far-below-market prices so that the internees would have nothing to return to after the war. About 1,200 fishing boats were seized—vessels that could be used to aid an invasion, according to the military. Farms, houses, and businesses were also auctioned off at criminally low prices without the owners' consent, sold to competitors and even former neighbours who took advantage of the Japanese Canadians' persecution. Attesting to the unlawful nature of this fire sale, the cabinet did not inform Parliament about these actions until months after the property had been sold. However, meticulous records of the dishonest dealings were kept, which would later be used in redressing the crime.[9]

Arthur Lower, a Great War veteran, civil libertarian, and historian, remarked in 1941, "We are fast losing whatever tolerance and magnanimity we once possessed."[10] The crusade for victory was steamrolling over all objections and all who were considered a hindrance to defeating the Fascists, especially during the terrible years of 1941 and 1942, when the Allies faced defeat in almost every theatre of war. Racism fuelled the government's measures against Japanese Canadians, and while small numbers of Germans and Italians were imprisoned—both Canadian nationals and unnaturalized immigrants—illegal actions were not taken to block their return to their prewar communities. The Japanese Canadians were singled out for the harshest prosecutions. Towards the end of the war, Canadian officials even pressured the demoralized Japanese Canadians in their wretched camps to accept dispersal to other parts of the country or face removal to Japan.

Journalists uncovered the story and raised uncomfortable questions about how the nation was fighting tyranny overseas while at the same time bullying the most helpless at home. Surprised by the mounting support for Japanese Canadians, King's cabinet referred the issue to the courts, even as it expedited the deportation of thousands to war-ravaged Japan. Eventually, about 4,000 Japanese Canadians left the country, about 1,300 of whom were under the age of sixteen and almost all of whom were born in Canada. At least three of the exiles were Great War veterans.[11] The humiliated Japanese, on their war-ravaged islands, were bewildered to receive boatloads of Canadians and Japanese nationals on their shores; ironically, they categorized them as "aliens."[12]

After the war, Japanese Canadians sought recompense for the federal government's callous wartime actions. A postwar commission determined compensation of $1.2 million, but the body only considered economic losses suffered from the sale of property by the Custodian of Enemy Property. The figure was considered inadequate by Japanese Canadians because the state had sold the goods at below-market costs and this became the basis for the assessment. There was also to be no recompense for the violation of people's civil rights, although this was perhaps unsurprising. The concept was little recognized at the time and certainly had little resonance with Canadians after a war that had resulted in genocide and mass atrocities overseas. Attitudes hardened also as the 1,500 or so Canadian prisoners of war returned from Japan with stories of torture and neglect far worse than anything faced by Japanese Canadians and Japanese nationals in their camps across the country.

The story of the relocation of Japanese Canadians rapidly sank into obscurity, becoming neglected in history books and buried within the Japanese community that could not publicly address the emotional pain caused by the accusations of disloyalty and the forced relocation.[13] But in 1977, when Japanese Canadians celebrated the centennial of the first Japanese settlers in the country, a public discussion emerged around a photo exhibition in British Columbia that offered a visual record of the wartime forced relocation.[14] The year before, historian Ken Adachi had published

The Enemy That Never Was, which laid bare some of the cruel actions against the Japanese Canadians. Adachi expressed his hope that uncovering the story would "reveal and perhaps exorcise" the ugly past.[15] His history was followed in the early 1980s by several others based on newly opened archival material that laid forth in meticulous detail the government's agenda.[16]

While these histories helped to broaden the analysis beyond the family stories, Joy Kogawa's novel, *Obasan* (1981), humanized the Japanese-Canadian wartime experience for a wider audience. Told from the perspective of a young girl, *Obasan* is the story of the upheaval and persecution suffered by a Japanese-Canadian family, offering sensitive insight into the traumatizing experience of forced relocation and drawing upon themes of remembrance and forgetting, of marginalization and the rediscovery of a painful past.[17]

By 1983, in what became known as the "redress campaign," the National Association of Japanese Canadians (NAJC) emerged as an organized group that pressured the federal government to acknowledge the wartime repression of Japanese Canadians and make financial restitution. That same year, a commission in the United States investigating the internment of Japanese Americans recommended that Washington offer a formal apology and compensation of $20,000 (tax free) per person uprooted.[18] In Canada, Prime Minister Pierre Trudeau responded to the NAJC's appeals for Ottawa to follow the Washington recommendation by claiming it was not the politician's duty to revisit actions made under the law of the land, no matter how unpalatable they may have been. "I do not think it's the purpose of government to right the past," he declared. "It cannot rewrite history. It is our purpose to be just in our time."[19]

Trudeau was not alone in his thinking. The argument that one generation was not responsible for the actions of another resonated with many; once a precedent was set to right the wrongs of history, where would the process stop? What about the Jews aboard the SS *St. Louis* who were turned away from Canada's shores in 1939? What about Ukrainians interned during the Great War or the nineteenth-century Chinese workers exploited during the dangerous work of building the nation's railroads? Were the Canadians of the present, or perhaps even the unborn, responsible for actions carried out in the past?

The Legion and many individual veterans, angry over the government's neglect of the survivors of the Battle of Hong Kong and the prison camps, opposed any official apology or compensation for Japanese Canadians. These veterans felt that Canadian soldiers who had suffered through the horrors of the prison camps deserved financial compensation before monies were given to those forcibly relocated on the home front. The Legion also demanded a formal apology from the Japanese government for the gross mistreatment of the Canadian soldiers, which had included debilitating slave labour. There should be no apology from Ottawa for wartime relocation, argued the Legion, until the same was given by Japan.

Broader societal trends were shaping the interpretation of history in modern Canada. In the 1980s, many countries were struggling with how to deal with historic infringements of human rights perpetrated or tolerated in their name. One way to address this hurt was to offer official state apologies, a widespread phenomenon that lead to the decade being called the "Age of Apology."[20] At the same time, the Canadian Charter of Rights and Freedoms was providing teeth for efforts to force a reappraisal of past injustices. Enshrined as part of the 1982 Constitution Act, the Charter empowered individuals to hold the government and authorities accountable in courts of law for policies and actions that were discriminatory or that infringed on human rights. The NAJC continued to mobilize support for its redress, uncover evidence of racist-driven policies in the nation's archives, and quantify the losses suffered from the seizure and sale of their families' goods, even as it drew upon language of the Charter to illustrate how the rights of Japanese Canadians had been abused.[21]

The Conservative government of Brian Mulroney had made promises during the 1984 federal election to settle the matter with Japanese Canadians. But the government's initial offer of compensation was slight and the NAJC refused it, despite the evidence that the window was closing on the issue, with elderly Japanese Canadians passing away during the process. To apply new pressure, Art Miki, head of the NAJC, commissioned a study by Price Waterhouse, *Economic Losses to Japanese Canadians After 1941*, that tabulated the cost of confiscated property at $443 million in 1986 dollars.[22] Journalists began to pay attention. The call for "justice in our time" was made both within and outside the Japanese-Canadian community, a powerful statement that invoked the wrong-doing and the need to end the long silence.

With the Charter in place, individuals and marginalized groups used the courts to fight present and past acts of discrimination. Meanwhile, the media engaged in widespread discussions about racism and the need for inclusivity. A March 1986 national poll indicated that 63 percent of Canadians supported the redress campaign, and just under half believed it right that individuals receive compensation for their wartime losses. A second poll the next year yielded an even higher rate of approval for a settlement.[23] Many Canadians viewed this as a human rights issue. Others saw providing payment as the right thing to do in a prosperous country like Canada. There were few dissenters of note, and even several provincial Legion branches offered support for the redress.

While there was much talk in the media about the vicious persecution of Japanese Canadians, the discourse lacked insight into the context of Canada fighting in a world war that most at the time saw as an existential struggle for survival. Surprisingly, professional historians shared little knowledge that might have balanced some of presentist claims made in the 1980s that viewed the past through the lens of the Charter. Only York University history professor J.L. Granatstein, the country's leading expert on the Second World War, was willing to comment, writing in the November 1986 issue of *Saturday Night* magazine about the cabinet's wartime decision. He did not deny the racism prevalent in large parts of the country, but he also made it clear that fear of a Japanese invasion had driven many in Canada to behave in extreme ways. Moreover, the cabinet, he noted, had acted without reliable intelligence since the RCMP and other military units had such poor language skills that they could not determine whether there was fifth-column activity.[24] The article enraged many of the activists in the redress movement, and some sought to discredit Granatstein, questioning his motives, impugning his character, and even threatening violence.[25]

On August 10, 1988, the US Senate announced a $1.25 billion compensation package for Japanese Americans that included $20,000 for each individual imprisoned. The foot-dragging in Ottawa ended abruptly. On September 22, 1988, Prime Minister Mulroney rose in the House of Commons to apologize for the forced removal of Japanese Canadians from the coast and to offer a $400 million package—$21,000 to each Japanese Canadian who had been affected. Additional funds were allocated for education and for dissemination of the story. The government's

Prime Minister Brian Mulroney and head of the National Association of Japanese Canadians Art Miki sign the official Japanese Canadian Redress Agreement on September 22, 1988.

formal apology attracted widespread media coverage, with the *Toronto Star* describing it as an act that "cleansed" the past.

From the late 1980s onwards, the forced relocation of Japanese Canadians rapidly became a part of the war's constructed memory. Within a few years, every school history textbook included the narrative of injustice, which, as one historian has noted, was written "in a way consistent with the redress movement's telling of it."[26] This perspective emphasized the government's racist policy of relocation and internment, and underplayed the wartime fear of invasion.[27] The official apology made it difficult to think about the event as anything other than a grossly unfair state persecution of the vulnerable.

With this reclaiming, or cleansing, of the past, the injustice towards Japanese Canadians has become a cautionary tale about the abuse of state power in a time of war. In the late twentieth century, this narrative, in combination with the enduring impact of the Charter in Canadian society and the entrenchment of multi-culturalism as a state-funded policy and symbol, transformed the Japanese Canadian relocation history from a forgotten piece of the past into a dominant strand of memory at the core of the country's Second World War experience. The relocation of these Canadians is sometimes even presented in social discourse and historical discussion as having tainted the entire war effort—the notion being that at the same time that Canada was fighting a war for liberal justice to defeat tyranny and save the oppressed, it was also conducting attacks on civil rights at home. This happened; no one can deny it. And yet there is no equivalency between the two events: on the one hand, one million Canadians fought in uniform to defeat Hitler, and on the other, 23,000 were forcibly relocated during a time of racially driven fear of Japanese invasion.

The forced relocation of Japanese Canadians took on an over-sized role in the narrative of the Second World War. The official Canadian apology and Ottawa's commitment to disseminate the story ensured that significant funds were devoted to rewriting text-books to include the events, as well as establish historic sites and heritage plaques. New generations of Canadians that grew up attuned to the persecution of minorities were continually informed of the wartime forced relocation. This layering of meaning onto a historical event occurs with many incidents, but in this case, the process amplified the story within Canadian history while displacing others. It was important to recognize the harm done to Japanese Canadians during the war, but by the early 1990s, the massive Canadian war effort was hardly recognized. Instead, three narratives dominated the story of Canada's Second World War: the forced relocation of Japanese Canadians, the controversy around conscription in French Canada, and the failed Dieppe Raid.

Many veterans were enraged by Ottawa's formal apology to Japanese Canadians. Doug Fisher, the long-time correspondent for *Legion* magazine—as *The Legionary* was now renamed— was one of them, and he was also a conduit for veterans' letters, which he occasionally published. He wrote after the apology that veterans' correspondence about the issue was "the strongest and most united I have received as a columnist," and that those veterans were very much against the monetary payout.[28] Fisher noted further, "Almost a score of those who regret the apology and award have served in BC during the war years, all giving proof to the extreme seriousness with which the Japanese threat of invasion or raid was taken in 1942–43." There was an intense feeling among the veterans that the admission of guilt of the late 1980s did not reflect the threat and fear that were rife in 1942, and that many of the Japanese Canadians, living in isolated communities, had far deeper connections to the Japanese homeland than was suggested in the activist debate surrounding the apology.[29] As in all controversies, there were diverse voices, and veterans did not all agree. A handful of ex-servicemen wrote to the *Legion* to express their support for the redress, reminding their comrades that the Japanese Canadians who were forcibly relocated from the coast were different from the Japanese soldiers and guards who had tortured the Hong Kong PoWs. But most of the letters were from veterans who were angry about the payout. One of the most common themes of grievance continued to be that the Hong Kong veterans had never received a proper apology from the Japanese government or any adequate compensation for their slave labour. While a formal apology from Japan to Canadian veterans might have alleviated some of the anger, it appears that the veterans' fury was also stoked by the idea that the Necessary War had lost meaning to most Canadians. The high-profile redress campaign brought renewed awareness of the war effort, but it was viewed through the lens of racist governmental policies aimed at a vulnerable group. The visibility and success of the redress campaign became one more sign to veterans that their just war had been twisted into something they neither recognized nor understood.

Canadian PoWs in the Second World War had a very different war experience than most men and women in uniform.[30] There were close to 9,000 prisoners of war in Europe and almost 1,500 survivors from the Hong Kong force. Many European and Far East prisoners felt guilty about being captured in battle, even though most had had no chance to escape, whether they had bailed out of a burning Halifax bomber, scrambled to safety as a corvette sank into the depths, or surrendered on the beaches of Dieppe as the landing craft returned to England. But the survivors of those four pitiless years of captivity in Hong Kong and Japan, from 1941 to 1945, had suffered a unique constellation of maltreatment, malnutrition, disease, beatings, torture, and a shocking level of brutality that left deep physical and mental scars. Through all manner of violence and deprivation, 264 Canadians died in captivity. The death rate of Western Allied prisoners in Japanese camps was 27 percent, whereas 4 percent of prisoners died in German camps.[31] The illegal abuse and deliberate starvation they suffered left the Hong Kong survivors with multiple diseases and permanent ailments.

The atom bombs dropped on Japan in August 1945 had saved the lives of the dying Canadians in the Japanese prison camps. For weeks, their guards had taunted them with the threat that they would be the first to die in the Allied invasion of Japan, but most Canadians realized that they would probably succumb first to malnutrition and

Starving Allied prisoners in the Japanese prisoner-of-war camps.
Thousands died and the survivors carried physical and mental scars.

work exhaustion if the war lasted much longer. After four years of deliberate neglect, the starving men—with their rib cages protruding, their teeth rotting, and their squinting eyes blinded by shortages of essential vitamins—looked like walking skeletons. But when the atom bombs destroyed Nagasaki and Hiroshima, the guards slunk away and the Canadians had a few bewildering days of being on their own. Most could scarcely believe that they had survived.

The withered Canadian prisoners were liberated by Americans who sympathized with their suffering and fed them. After a few days of vomiting from the drastic change in diet, the Canadians made up for four years of starvation by eating ravenously for weeks. Men often put on fifty pounds in the two months before returning to Canada. Although they looked less like cadavers by the time they departed, one American nurse monitoring the Canadians aboard a warship was dismayed at their state of health. All were disease-ridden and physically feeble: she noted, "it was heartbreaking to learn that an elderly-looking, emaciated gentleman before you was a boy in his twenties."[32]

Upon disembarking at Victoria in late 1945, the survivors of the camps were given a month of medical treatment, vitamin supplements, and steady food before returning to their families. But the medical authorities had little experience with tropical diseases, and like most veterans, the Hong Kong prisoners were anxious to get home to their loved ones. Many signed forms declaring that they were free of pain, even as they suffered from dysentery or parasitic worms that were often passed on to wives and girlfriends. When the Hong Kong veterans arrived back in their communities, which were grouped in and around Winnipeg and in Quebec City, their loved ones noticed they were thin but not starved, and with fewer outward scars than anticipated. From the start, it was difficult for the PoWs to convey the horror of the camps.

William Allister, a survivor and one who would be haunted by his experience his whole life, wrote of being grateful to the Americans who helped him and his comrades recover from their half-human existence. But he noted that, in Canada, "There was no counseling, no advice, no awareness that we might act or feel differently. It was sink or swim, you're on your own, boys." And yet, as he admitted, "Like good Canadians we expected nothing, got nothing."[33] This generation that had come up through the Depression already carried its own wounds from want and neglect, and most were not complainers. In turn, Ottawa avoided close examination of the prisoners' experience, even though Hong Kong survivors told authorities that their nerves were shot and that they were fretful, filled with anxiety, and adrift in their homes or communities.

There were a few doctors who were intrigued by the trials of the Hong Kong veterans and by the long-term effects of their incarceration. The survivors were plagued with vitamin deficiency, along with numbness in their limbs, chronic fatigue, gastro-intestinal problems, and failing eyesight. One study in 1947 found that of 553 Winnipeg Grenadiers, 72 percent were infected with parasites, with most men suffering from multiple infestations, such as whipworm, hook worm, and threadworm.[34] Over time, the life expectancy of these men was calculated to be fifteen to twenty years below the national average.

Hong Kong veterans were angry about more than just their permanent injuries. They felt they had been sold out by the government that had shipped the two regiments—Winnipeg Grenadiers and Royal Rifles of Canada—to the doomed colony in 1941. While neither the soldiers nor the Canadian politicians knew that the British has studied the defence of Hong Kong and determined that it could not be held against a sustained Japanese offensive, Ottawa had nonetheless naively sent the Canadians halfway around the world when London called, with almost no appreciation of the threat. It was a terrible error on the part of the King cabinet, although the ministers were pressured by senior Canadian generals who wished to see the army serving in the global war. When the garrison had surrendered, King and his cabinet had covered up their reckless actions, using a wartime public commission to whitewash their reasons for sending the two battalions to Hong Kong. After the war, the government had only half-heartedly prosecuted Japanese war criminals, largely leaving it to other countries to bring the murderers and torturers to justice. About four dozen Japanese soldiers were eventually convicted of crimes against Canadians; prosecuted in Japan, almost all were given prison sentences and freed within a decade.[35] The only death sentence was carried out against the "Kamloops Kid," Kanao Inouye, a Canadian-born Japanese Canadian who sadistically beat, humiliated, and killed several Canadians in the camps.[36] After a lengthy trial, he was hanged for treason in August 1947.

In 1952, the Treaty of San Francisco was signed between the former wartime allies and Japan to end the war. The agreement provided paltry financial compensation for the Hong Kong veterans from a fund created through the sale of seized Japanese assets. The veterans were not consulted in the matter, and they were never informed that their government's acceptance of such a treaty would limit their ability to pursue justice later. Throughout this period, senior officers at the Department of National Defence wanted little to do with the veterans, believing, as one 1950 memo to the minister put it, that such attempts to deal with prisoners—"the debris of past wars"—would divert their efforts from preparing for the next war. It was hoped that the veterans would be satisfied with the monetary payout and go away.[37]

As the war was increasingly left in the past, the Hong Kong veterans found that their experiences—individually and collectively—were far different from those of any other veterans, and that they needed additional care. They banded together for solace and strength, and in 1948 formed the Hong Kong Veterans Association (HKVA), with a membership of about 1,400.[38] The veterans had relied upon one another for survival during the war; now they would do so again in the postwar period.

In the 1950s, these special veterans were the subject of more medical studies, with one report observing, "Almost all suffered some form of nerve damage and debilitating fatigue." And yet Ottawa administrators and bureaucrats often withheld pensions to visibly sick veterans because the men could not prove that their illness was

*This wartime poster implores viewers to remember the garrison
at Hong Kong. The survivors of the battle suffered horrendous
experiences in the prisoner-of-war camps, and were largely forgotten by
Canadian society in the postwar years.*

a result of service.[39] It was cruel and absurd, and dozens of veterans—
many in their late twenties or early thirties—died during the decade
after the war. The HKVA continued to pressure Ottawa for more
generous pensions, often attempting to shame the various governments into admitting that C Force had been sacrificed. In 1958, the
government finally agreed to its responsibilities, and the PoW survivors had an additional fifty cents a day added to their pensions.

Ottawa had been so ungenerous because it viewed the Hong
Kong prisoners as a thorny inconvenience left over from the war,
especially given that Japan rapidly rebuilt and became an economic
powerhouse with which the Canadian government desired a positive

trade relationship. At the same time, Japan refused to acknowledge responsibility for its own aggressive and violent history, being unable or unwilling to come to grips with its wartime atrocities. The culture in Japan, with its stringent sense of honour, made it difficult for political leaders to issue a formal apology. In contrast, West Germany had accepted guilt for its abhorrent wartime actions, had apologized repeatedly, and had paid billions in reparations to other countries. In Ottawa, the government of the day—and the governments of all the days since—refused to jeopardize trade relations with Japan over the old wartime claims and also declined to press on the diplomatic front, ignoring the multiple requests of the Hong Kong veterans for justice and for an official apology.

At the beginning of the 1970s, of the more than one million veterans in Canada, 133,212 were receiving pensions, along with 29,100 dependents.[40] The 1971 overhaul of veterans' pensions was a great victory for the Legion, which had mobilized support and pressured MPs and senators for years. As part of this fight, the Legion had lobbied hard on behalf of the Hong Kong veterans, who received a minimum pension of 50 percent, as well as provisions for the widows and orphans of those who had already died. Five years later, in April 1976, Bill C-92 gave all surviving Hong Kong veterans a minimum of an 80 percent pension, although by then many had died from their permanent wounds. A more generous government would have come to this action decades earlier.

In 1981, Carl Vincent, an archivist at the National Archives in Ottawa, published the first significant Canadian history of the Hong Kong battle based on archival documents since Stacey's official history in 1955. In *No Reason Why*, Vincent offered a scathing account of the Canadian decision to send C Force to Hong Kong—and blamed General Harry Crerar for pushing the cabinet to accept the operation. When recounting the battle, Vincent made a point of describing the resilient defence of the Canadian troops, an important rejoinder to British commander Major-General Christopher Maltby, who had scapegoated the Canadians for his own incompetence. A bitter Maltby had spent his years in the prisoner-of-war camps blaming his own troops for the failed battle, singling out the Canadians as particularly weak. Ottawa had objected strenuously to his report in 1947, and it was only published with many censored sections; later, C.P. Stacey and other historians revealed that when the Japanese recorded "strong opposition," "fierce fighting," and "heavy casualties," they were almost always referring to battles against the Canadians.[41] But there was a sense among the British that the two Canadian battalions had not fought well, adding salt to the wounds of the PoW survivors.[42]

In 1993, the Hong Kong veterans faced another campaign in the war of reputations. In late January, an unexpurgated edition of General Maltby's damning 1947 report was finally released to the public after decades of being buried in the archives. The British general, who died in 1980, had been responsible for the defence of the colony and had been hopelessly outclassed by the Japanese. He had fought as near an incompetent a battle as there was during the war, failing to build up strength where the Japanese were expected to attack, failing to take the high ground, and, in an act of monumental stupidity, failing to guard the primary water tower on the island that was lost early in the battle, and thereby dooming the garrison. In his report, though, he argued that it was the Canadians who had let him down, losing their nerve in battle as a result of poor training and cowardly actions.

Upon the release of Maltby's report, the British press did not fully accept the commander's account, and yet it did adopt his scathing review of the Canadians, with some journalists twisting the dagger in deeper. Canadian veterans lashed out against being branded cowards.[43] Don Nelson, president of the HKVA, labelled it "a lot of B.S," while veteran Robert Manchester called it a "ridiculous" cover-up. John Stroud, also a veteran of the battle and a survivor of the PoW camps, bluntly said, "We saved their [British] asses more than once."[44] A few Canadian journalists thought this might be a good opportunity to talk about the forgotten campaign, and the *Edmonton Journal* suggested they "leave the British to their self-serving revisionism," but most commentators warmed to the idea of bashing the British. Several writers reminded their readers that the Imperials had also condemned the Australians for the fall of Singapore in 1942, when the blame and shame was again theirs.[45] Canadian politicians piled on, scoring easy points against the British—all of them aware, too, that a federal election was soon to be fought. Widening the assault, *The Globe and Mail* columnist Michael Valpy levelled a broadside against all those in command, remarking that it was "a toss-up who posed the greater threat to [Canadian troops]—the British and Canadian generals and politicians who sent them, or the Japanese."[46] Ultimately, senior British politicians apologized a few days after the row, and distanced themselves from the historical debacle that had stirred up such strong feelings in Canada. The Hong Kong veterans were mollified by the overwhelming public support across Canada, but the report had reopened old wounds. They remained dead set on extracting a formal apology from Japan.

—

Hostility to the Japanese ran through the blood of most of the PoW survivors. They did not forget, and most could not forgive. They found no closure since the Japanese refused to apologize for their many wartime atrocities, and they felt abandoned by their own government. It was this potent mix of anger and sense of lingering injustice that had contributed to strife over Ottawa's reparations made to Japanese Canadians. David McIntosh, a Second World War airman, journalist, and long-time champion of veterans, argued that it was shameful for the government to compensate Japanese Canadians while snubbing the Hong Kong veterans who had been treated much worse and suffered far more. Why, he wondered, did the politicians compensate one group while ignoring those in uniform?[47] The answer must surely lie in the fact that elected officials and public servants knew so little about the war and seemed to care so little about those who fought in it.

In the late 1980s, Cliff Chadderton's War Amps worked with the Hong Kong veterans and brought a claim before the United Nations Commission on Human Rights in Geneva to secure compensation.[48] The move embarrassed Mulroney's government, and after years of fractious debate, in December 1998 Prime Minister Jean Chrétien's cabinet decided to pay the surviving 350 veterans and 400 widows $24,000 each in compensation for the pain of slave labour. It justified the expenditure on "humanitarian grounds," but part of the agreement stipulated that it would not ask Japan for a formal apology or payments in future, which frustrated the unfulfilled veterans.[49]

By the 1990s, Japan was the subject of a series of denunciations from China, the Koreas, and many Western nations for its failure to address its reprehensible wartime history. The Japanese government had never formally apologized for the nation's cruel actions against prisoners or for turning Korean and Chinese women and girls into "comfort women"—sex slaves for soldiers.[50] Even though many in Japan regretted the country's ruthless war effort, and a strong antiwar movement existed among both young and old, hardliners who remained in positions of power refused to apologize. For decades, Japanese textbooks downplayed or ignored stories of atrocities perpetrated against civilians. The Second World War, like the illegal and at times genocidal war against China in the early 1930s, was portrayed as a defensive one in Japan—an action forced on the country by its enemies.

Towards the end of the twentieth century, many of Canada's veterans had come to forgive the German people. This was partly because Germany had apologized for its wartime conduct and made reparations, and partly because West Germany had become integral to the North Atlantic Treaty Alliance (NATO) during the Cold War. But Canadian veterans, especially those who fought in the Hong Kong campaign, had a special animosity towards the Japanese. When Governor General Jeanne Sauvé attended the 1989 funeral of Emperor Hirohito, who was Japanese supreme leader during the Second World War, and her successor, Governor General Ray Hnatyshyn, missed the 1990 Remembrance Day ceremony to attend the enthronement of Hirohito's successor, Emperor Akihito, the veterans were incensed.[51] It was proof to many that the heads of state— the governor general is the honorary commander-in-chief of the armed forces—cared more about the Japanese in the present than the veterans who still suffered from past abuses.

In June 1995, the Japanese government offered an apology of sorts for the country's wartime activity, including its invasion of China in the 1930s and its sexual enslavement of women. The apology was much watered down to allow conservatives to sign on, and Prime Minister Tomiichi Murayama said, "In the hope that no such mistake be made in the future, I . . . express here once gain my feelings of deep remorse and state my heartfelt apology. Allow me also to express my feelings of profound mourning for all victims, both at home and abroad, of that history."[52] There was no talk of compensation for the "comfort women" or for Allied prisoners, and commentators noted that the inclusion of "victims of the war at home" weakened the apology, as it was a direct reference to those killed by the American atomic bombs.

As in Germany, after a period of silence and reflection, the Japanese began to share publicly the country's stories of loss and death, both overseas and at home. And as in Germany, the accounts were used by some to show that the Japanese were as much victims as they were perpetrators of violence. Vanquished nations often seek redeeming narratives, but few outside Japan accepted such a reading of the history. In Canada, the Japanese intransigence in refusing to face the past continued to rankle veterans. The *Legion* observed sharply, "There's no consideration in Japan for anything like the complete apology given by the Mulroney government to Japanese and Japanese-Canadians who had been interned during WWII— along with nearly $400 million compensation."[53]

In 1993, the sons and daughters of members of C Force formed a new association, eventually known as the Hong Kong Veterans Commemorative Association (HKVCA). The group worked to care for the remaining veterans and to ensure that the story was known. One of the association's most important acts was the establishment of a memorial on August 15, 2009—the sixty-fourth anniversary of VJ Day. About two dozen of the ninety surviving members of C Force made the trip to Ottawa to unveil the six-metre-long wall, clad in black granite, topped with four stone mountains evoking the Island of Hong Kong and inscribed with the names of 1,976 Canadians who fought in the battle. Paid for by the HKVCA, the memorial struck a chord with some Canadians, many of whom had never heard the grim story. International Trade Minister Stockwell Day, whose grandfather fought in the battle and barely survived his PoW experience only to die shortly after returning to Canada, spoke with much passion, declaring, "These veterans have felt like the forgotten heroes of the Second World War."[54] Phil Doddridge, president of the HKVCA, said at the unveiling of the monument, "Until this stone disintegrates and returns to dust, we will be remembered. May we all from our place in the hereafter be able to look down upon this monument and say, 'My name is written there: I am remembered.'"[55]

A little more than two years later, after much pressure from the international community, Japan's leaders made another formal

The Hong Kong Veterans Commemorative Association erected this memorial in Ottawa on August 15, 2009, to mark the 1,976 Canadians who served in Hong Kong.

apology of sorts—"a statement of regret"—on December 8, 2011. Four of the surviving Canadian Hong Kong veterans travelled to Japan to receive the apology on behalf of their comrades, most of whom were now in the grave. "This important gesture is a crucial step in ongoing reconciliation and a significant milestone in the lives of all prisoners of war," observed Veterans Affairs Minister Steven Blaney. Commenting from Ottawa, Foreign Affairs Minister John Baird felt that the harsh war years had given way to a "mutually beneficial, respectful relationship between Canada and Japan as mature democracies—a legacy of all who served in the Pacific campaigns."[56] The Canadian government thought the matter was finally put to rest.

Veterans saw it differently. Their souls were still seared by the war. George MacDonnell, who was nineteen years old when he was sent to Hong Kong and who later had a successful career as a civil servant in the Ontario government, was not soothed by the apology from Japan, which he felt was inadequate. "This apology means almost nothing to us," he told the CBC, adding, "There may only be 30 of us left. All the rest died on the battlefield, they died of starvation in Japanese camps, or they died since that happened. The Japanese have been denying what happened in Southeast Asia for 70 years now." Hormidas Fredette, another veteran who attended the ceremony, was twenty-three years old when he was taken prisoner in Hong Kong. Sixty-five years later, he still suffered nightmares about the torture, abuse, and inhumanity he endured in captivity. The frail warrior still had fight in him, and he stated bluntly, "I don't accept the apology."[57]

CHAPTER 12

CONTESTING VETERANSHIP

"Today is our chance to save our children [from] this big flame of fire coming toward us in a world war," wrote Peter Gladue from his First Nations reserve, adding, "All Indians of Canada should now look [to the] future if they love their children and their land, to help win this terrible war."[1] Of a population of around 126,000 Status Indians, 4,300 enlisted during the Second World War, along with an unknown number of non-Status Indians, Métis, and Inuit, who were not tracked by the state.[2] Indigenous people who were Status Indians were monitored and controlled by the Department of Indian Affairs, and were considered wards of the state with no voting rights. And yet even as they were subjugated and subordinated by official authorities, many Status Indians felt a strong desire to serve when Canada went to war. Some Indigenous men and women were keen to follow the paths of their fathers and uncles, several thousand of whom had enlisted in the Great War. Others thought that service to king and country in this second global war would lead to better conditions for their people in Canada.[3]

Indigenous veterans described how racial barriers were broken down on the battlefields. The bonds of comradery almost always overcame the ingrained racism of most Canadians, although that did not mean that the armed forces officially embraced diversity in their ranks. However, those in uniform, no matter their origins, relied on each other for survival and forged unique relationships. "We were equals," said Wilfred Westeste of the Bird Tail First Nation, adding that his service in the fighting zone was "the only time in my life I was equal to the white society or anybody else."[4] But it was not lost on Indigenous veterans that, after fighting to rid the world of the Nazi scourge and to free oppressed people, they would still have few rights and face much prejudice when they returned to Canada. Overseas, their service in uniform trumped their Indigenous roots; back home, they met old biases. As one Saskatchewan Indigenous veteran remarked bitterly about his own and others' postwar treatment in Canada, "We were just another Indian."[5]

After the war, the Indian Agents sought to re-exert control over the Indigenous veterans after they demobilized from the armed services. On the reserves, the ex-servicemen were physically isolated and forced to interact with the Department of Veterans Affairs through these government officials. Facing such barriers, many veterans felt that they had been denied rights, monetary compensation, and entry into the Veterans Charter programs. The reality was not easy to uncover, but research into numerous archives reveals that the benefits and programs of the Veterans Charter were generally open to all veterans, including Indigenous Canadians. However, veterans on reserves faced systemic barriers to taking advantage of those offerings.[6]

Like all service personnel demobilizing, Indigenous veterans received payments for new clothes as well as the War Service Gratuity, which was calculated by length of service. But many

Indigenous veterans were not able to access the Veterans Charter programs to aid their reintegration because information was withheld or simply misunderstood by the Indian Agents, who controlled most aspects of their lives. [7] Few veterans seem to have known about opportunities for retraining or going back to school, and if they did, what would they do with such knowledge when there were few jobs on the reserves and no universities? There were other issues. Those living on reserve often lacked access to radios, newspapers, or Legion Halls, where the DVA programs were advertised or discussed. Indigenous veterans could not, for example, take part in land grant programs because, under the terms of the Indian Act, they were not permitted to own land on their reservations. (There was a complicated loan process that passed through several departments and required band approval, but few had basic information about the process, let alone the ability to navigate its bureaucracy.) A handful of Indigenous veterans living off reserve did qualify for land grants, but they were unable to secure the necessary loans to act as collateral. [8] Frustrated veterans usually abandoned their attempts to access the benefits they deserved. [9] According to one veteran, even when Indigenous veterans used some of their accrued wartime money to purchase cattle in the hopes of starting a farm, the animals were branded with the letters "I.D.," signifying "Indian Department." [10] Because of paternal racism and systematic barriers, most Indigenous veterans missed out on the prosperity of the postwar years, left behind while other comrades moved forward in the increasingly affluent Canada.

Even celebrated Indigenous soldiers like Sergeant Tommy Prince found that reintegration and advancement were not easy. Prince was awarded the Military Medal for bravery while serving with the 1st Special Service Force in Italy, and would go on to

Sergeant Tommy Prince, a decorated veteran of the Second World War and the Korean War, served with bravery and distinction. He, like many Indigenous service personnel, were treated as equals overseas, only to return to Canada to face racism.

fight during the Korean War, where he was recognized with the American Silver Star. Yet he still struggled for equality in Canada despite his recognized gallantry. "All my life," Prince said of his motivation to enlist and fight in two wars, "I had wanted to do something to help my people recover their good name. I wanted to show they were as good as any white man."[11] While Prince and others served with distinction, their contributions were largely forgotten after the conflict, with the same inattention occurring in the United States, Australia, and New Zealand, countries that had significant Indigenous populations contributing to the Allied war effort. In Canada, this neglect was perhaps not surprising given that the number of Indigenous members who served was relatively small. There were, for instance, more Jews who served than

Indigenous people.[12] Lacking citizens' rights, unable to vote, living in poverty and isolation, Indigenous people struggled to voice their stories in the aftermath of the war.

By the 1960s, however, there was a resurgence of Indigenous activism in Canada.[13] Indigenous people came together to demand more political power, with Second World War veterans often at the forefront of those movements for greater recognition and rights. In this fight for rights, Indigenous veterans wielded unique influence with the state. They wore their medals proudly and let it be known that they had served the country in a time of need. In 1951, for example, through an amendment to the Indian Act, the ban on Status Indians' access to alcohol was lifted, largely because ex-servicemen and -women had been unfairly barred from the Legion Halls because alcohol was served there. Indigenous veterans invoked their war service to bolster arguments for full citizenship and a voice in the political process, as well as using it to advocate for relief from abject poverty.

But the fight for rights was slow: it was not until 1960 that Indigenous people gained the right to vote in federal elections. Veterans were in the forefront of the movement for change; for example, all the leaders in the Federation of Saskatchewan Indians were Second World War veterans—a sign of their prominent role within various bands but also of their elevated status in the eyes of white society.[14] Steady progress was made in the 1970s and 1980s to raise awareness about the plight of Indigenous people—in particular, their inadequate housing, undrinkable water, and lack of access to social services or employment—although they remained very much on the periphery.[15]

The 1990s was a fraught time in the country, with French- and English-speaking Canadians clashing over language rights and over Quebec's status as a "distinct society." But the decade also saw the rise of a more militant Indigenous movement that had been empowered after the failed constitutional talks of 1987–1992 that had almost entirely ignored Indigenous peoples. During this contentious period, in the late summer of 1990, Indigenous unrest and anger came to a boiling point with the Oka Crisis in Quebec. At that flashpoint on the Kahnawake reserve near Montreal, Mohawks rallied together, constructed barricades, and picked up weapons against a developer trying to build a golf course on contested Mohawk burial grounds. The standoff escalated into violence when the Quebec provincial police, La Sûreté du Québec, moved in. The Canadian forces were called to restore order, and the seventy-eight-day crisis, from July 11 to September 26, 1990, attracted international media attention. Indigenous people across the country offered support to the Mohawk warriors, and Oka became a symbol of unsettled history and unresolved anger that led to the creation of a royal commission to investigate the struggle of Indigenous peoples.[16] It also stimulated researchers to investigate the question of Indigenous veterans' rights, which was part of a larger trend of engaging with Canada's First Peoples.

Early in 1994, the Standing Senate Committee on Aboriginal Peoples invited veterans to speak to the touring group and hired historians to search the archives for evidence on whether Indigenous men and women in uniform had access like other returned service personnel to the various programs under the

The Oka Crisis saw Mohawk warriors facing off against members of the Canadian forces.

Veterans Charter. In its final report, *The Aboriginal Soldier After the Wars*, the committee endorsed the statement that "Aboriginal people from all over Canada—treaty Indians from the Prairies, Indians from remote and urban settings, Metis and Inuit from far-flung locations—went to war to fight for freedom and justice beside all other Canadian soldiers. When they came home . . . nothing had changed for them. Intolerance and injustice persisted."[17] The committee noted that it found no additional deliberate discrimination against Indigenous Second World War veterans as a group, but asserted that there were conflicting responsibilities between the departments of Veterans Affairs and Indian Affairs, and that all veterans on reserves faced obstacles to access the programs. Crucially, "Indian veterans who returned to reserves were confronted with the powers of the Indian agent on a particular reserve who exercised his considerable discretionary power."[18] Senator Leonard Marchand, the first Status Indian elected to Parliament, thought a formal apology was the most important redress needed, remarking, "So many of the veterans feel they don't want to leave the earth feeling that their contribution has gone without recognition."[19]

In 1999, after years of study that concluded the government had an obligation to address the standing grievance of these veterans, a national round table on First Nations issues was established to bring together representatives from government departments, veterans, and members of the Assembly of First Nations. Backed by archival research and veterans' testimonials, the forum's final report, *A Search of Equity*, drew attention to the lack of support for Indigenous veterans and demanded compensation. As part of this program of recognition, the National Aboriginal Veterans Monument was unveiled in Ottawa on June 21, 2001, to mark the military service of Indigenous people and the sacrifice of the more than 500 who died in Canada's wars. The bronze monument depicts a golden eagle, also known as a Thunderbird, which symbolizes the spirit of the Indigenous peoples.[20] Sculptor Lloyd Pinay of the Peepeekisis First Nation in Saskatchewan, whose father was a Second World War veteran, situated four human figures facing the four points of the compass, and below them four spirit guide animals.

In June 2002, the federal government made a formal apology to Indigenous veterans and offered a $39 million compensation package that provided up to $20,000 for each of the surviving 1,800 veterans or spouses. While the memorial and the compensation were welcomed, other emotional wounds lingered—trauma that was entwined with the systematic racism and inequality faced by most Indigenous people. Veteran Russell Modeste testified before the national round table, "I don't expect the government to grant me a fancy living. But certainly treat me the same as you been treating the white guy that has done the same service as I have."[21] The

The Indigenous memorial in Ottawa, unveiled on June 21, 2001,
marks the service of Indigenous people in times of war.

war had lifted Canada out of the poverty of the Depression, and
most Canadians—including those who served in uniform—had
enjoyed the benefits of a wealthier society. Sadly, most Indigenous
veterans were not able to partake in the prosperity.

Not all veterans were treated the same after the war, and a par-
ticular group of service personnel was denied veterans' status.
"The Battle of the Atlantic was not won by the navy or air force.
It was won by the courage, fortitude, and determination of the
British and Allied Merchant Navy."[22] So said Rear Admiral
Leonard Murray, wartime commander-in-chief for the Northwest
Atlantic, in a postwar tribute to the merchant seamen. Of course,

that longest battle of the Second World War was won by the navy warships, the RCAF and RAF air support, the evolving tactics and technology, and the grit of sailors in uniform and in civvies. But the Merchant Navy had been proclaimed the "fourth arm" of the fighting services during the war. Its seamen guided civilian ships through U-boat-infested waters around the world, although their efforts were concentrated in the Atlantic, and they had contributed mightily to the Allied victory by ensuring that Britain was not starved out of the war.

Allied merchant ships made 25,343 runs and carried 164,783,921 tonnes of cargo from North America to Britain, keeping the Allied armies and civilian populations supplied with munitions, food, and all manner of goods.[23] The cost was high. During the war, the Canadian and Allied merchant navies suffered heavy casualties as German U-boats sank more than 21 million gross tonnes of shipping, killing at least 32,000 merchant seamen, including 1,629

A Merchant Navy vessel torpedoed, on fire, and soon to meet its end. The merchant ships carrying war supplies from North America were the primary target for the German U-boats seeking to starve Britain into submission.

Canadians and Newfoundlanders.[24] The mariners—almost all men but occasionally women—were often too young or too old to serve in uniform, or had been rejected for health reasons, but they still wanted to support the war effort. The vulnerable Merchant Navy suffered horrendous casualties during the war, and yet the seamen were not recognized as veterans.

Despite having run the gauntlet of U-boats, the sailors without uniforms were ignored by the government when the war ended. "They are Canada's unsung heroes but they do not want to be sung about," pleaded merchant seaman Walter Shaw of Halifax, Nova Scotia, on October 10, 1945. "All they ask is a fair recognition of the part they played in keeping the country free."[25] That recognition, Shaw hoped, would include access to the Veterans Charter benefits. But the benefits were denied to the mariners, as they were technically not service personnel. This hurt, but most seamen took comfort in Ottawa's promise of postwar jobs. The merchant mariners were not a large group, either, and not sufficiently organized to negotiate in the immediate postwar years. When they did finally organize, their union was infused with Communist ideas, which put them in direct confrontation with politicians in Ottawa. It was a fraught relationship, and within five years, the government cut thousands of mariner jobs, driven to the decision by global economic realities that saw a shift from state-owned ships to private companies, and perhaps by a desire to punish those seamen who had embraced union activism. Merchant seaman Robert Halford stated bluntly that "once the fleet was gone, the wartime merchant sailors vanished from the public consciousness."[26] Most mariners went on with their lives, some feeling cheated, others grateful to be alive, but all knowing that they had served their country with distinction.

MEN *of* VALOR
They fight for you

MERCHANT NAVY——Fourth Arm of the Service.

Outfighting submarines and dive bombers in a three day
battle, Capt. Fred S. Slocombe, M.B.E., and his heroic crew
succeeded in delivering the icebreaker MONTCALM to
Murmansk as a gift from Canada to the U.S.S.R.

*A Canadian wartime poster in the Men of Valor series. This one focuses on the
Merchant Navy, described as the "Fourth Arm of the Service." However, after
the war, the mariners were not treated like veterans and received few benefits.*

In 1945, the Legion paid little attention to the concerns of the
civilian mariners. But within a decade, the organization of veterans
had begun to see the fairness of merchant mariners receiving a type
of federal compensation, although not as full veterans. In June
1957, the Legion recommended to the Department of Veterans
Affairs that those who "served in the Canadian Merchant Navy in
the war zone" be given certain medical and monetary entitlements.
The department refused, responding, "It is evidently the view of
Parliament that these persons in this group are civilians and not
members, and not deemed to be members, of the armed forces."[27]
The Legion pressed the matter over the years, to no avail.[28]

Not only were the merchant mariners ignored by the government, but they also seemed invisible within historical memory: the

few naval histories of the war made little specific mention of the Merchant Navy. However, by the early 1980s, the merchant seamen were attempting to strengthen their voice and their appeal to Ottawa. They were also calling out the Legion—in the pages of *Legion* magazine—for not assisting them. At the 1980 Dominion convention, the Legionnaires had failed to support a resolution demanding that the Civilian War Allowance Act be amended to include Allied merchant seamen, which would have included granting them access to more benefits. George Walters, who served on civilian vessels in the war zone, felt that the Merchant Navy sailors were just as much veterans as any other veterans. Walters chided the Legion members, commenting, "I wonder how many of the delegates were picked out of the drink by these very merchant seamen, and how many of them at the front used the supplies conveyed by these gallant men."[29]

In 1982, surviving mariners formed the Canadian Merchant Navy Association (CMNA), led by Merchant Navy veteran Mervyn Hartley.[30] Four years later, Gordon Olmstead of Nepean, Ontario, established a second organization, the Canadian Merchant Navy Prisoner of War Association, which spoke for Canada's 198 wartime merchant sailors who were captured by the enemy.[31] Two other splinter organizations emerged in the late 1980s, and all four groups of mariners witnessed the success of the Japanese Canadians' redress campaign. Soon, they banded together to fight for recognition of veteran status by petitioning both the Legion and members of Parliament. The mariners' cause was much aided in 1988 when the organizations met with the Legion high command and worked with them to select eighty-six-year-old Hazel

Driscoll of Halifax as the Silver Cross Mother for the National Remembrance Day in 1988. Her son Kenneth, a twenty-one-year-old able seaman, was lost on February 11, 1942, when his tanker, *Victolite*, was torpedoed off the American eastern seaboard. It was the first time the mother of a member of the Merchant Navy was selected as a Silver Cross Mother, and the choice provoked much commentary on Remembrance Day.

In February 1990, a senate subcommittee on Veterans Affairs held meetings to discuss the recognition of merchant seamen as veterans, and mariners Gordon Robertson and Gordon Olmstead testified as representatives of the 12,000 who sailed during the war. In a written brief, they described the Merchant Navy as "a service whose unique contribution was vital to the achievement of final victory; a volunteer force that served Canada and the Allies, faithfully, proudly, and well."[32] Backed by stories and statistics, the two veterans argued that the merchant seamen died in far higher numbers than the professional sailors of the RCN. "The massacre of merchant shipping," Robertson said, "is a matter of record. Strangely, an inference prevails that seamen who enlisted were automatically endowed with superiority over their merchant shipmates who remained and bore the brunt of the casualties in the Battle of the Atlantic." Olmstead was a radio officer on MV *Agnita* when it was sunk on March 22, 1941, and he spent four years as a PoW. He knew from experience that, as he observed, "Merchant seamen prisoners returned without a military halo, and their hardships and sacrifices were deemed unworthy because of it."[33]

In reaction to the hearings, which were well publicized in the media, some veterans refused to embrace the idea that these seamen were equal to those who wore the uniform in the Royal

Canadian Navy. Howard Copeman of the RCAF Prisoners of War Association bluntly stated in the pages of *Legion* in May 1990 that his group, while sympathetic to the mariners, did not support veteran status for the mariners. If everyone who was in danger during the war should be called a veteran, he asked, then wouldn't everyone in eastern Britain be a veteran for having withstood the Blitz or the V-1 rockets raining down? Copeman declared, "There is a distinct difference between those who served as civilian and those who served in the military, who did so on a contractual basis with terms and conditions either clearly specified or fully implied by precedent." He went further, stating that "seamen did not have to act in life-threatening situations and could withdraw their service if they wished." The suggestion that the merchant seamen could have voluntarily ended their service stuck in the craw of many of these men who had risked their lives on the howling seas and as U-boats prowled the waters. The image it conjured seemed almost drawn from a Herbie wartime cartoon—a merchant mariner staring at a surfacing U-boat and telling his captain, "I'd like to withdraw my services now." Copeman was not opposed to monetary compensation, but he was against calling the mariners veterans. Other supporters and the Merchant Navy veterans responded vigorously, fighting it out in the news and in the pages of *Legion*.[34]

From the mid-1980s onwards, the Legion publicly supported making the mariners full veterans, and urged the government to do so rapidly because the mariners, with an average age of sixty-nine, were dying in large numbers.[35] There were also champions of the notion in Parliament. One of the sympathetic MPs, Marc Ferland, said publicly, "I have lived 49 years in this country in freedom because of people like the merchant mariners. I will not take my pension without having done something for them."[36] The merchant mariners had built their case on archival research and first-hand testimonials, but what bolstered their argument was a comparison of the government's responses to the concerns of the merchant seaman to those of Japanese Canadians. Journalist Douglas Fisher commented, "Isn't it ironic that we have had full apologies and generous redress for Japanese and Japanese-Canadians moved from the West Coast in 1942 while the merchant seaman of WWII still await full recognition by their country?"[37]

The Senate's report, *It's Almost Too Late*, authored in 1991 by Normandy veteran Senator Jack Marshall, argued that the seamen should be recognized as veterans, and support for the idea was increasing among MPs, senators, and veterans' organizations.[38] The four merchant seamen groups had come together to form the Merchant Navy Coalition for Equality, which made it easier for them to negotiate and speak with a unified voice. In June 1992, the Mulroney government, in its final days, passed Bill C-84, recognizing the merchant seamen as veterans and making them eligible for a number of programs. The mariners qualified for these new programs by having sailed on one wartime high seas voyage in a foreign-going or home-bound trade vessel, a provision which recognized that many sailors were on non-Canadian ships. The expected cost of granting Merchant Navy veterans this access was $88 million over five years.[39]

The Merchant Navy Book of Remembrance was unveiled in 1994 and was placed within the Memorial Chamber in the Peace Tower on Parliament Hill, assuming its rightful position next to the other books representing the servicemen and -women who fell in defence of Canada. At the unveiling, a government official declared, "The book acknowledges and rectifies the historical bias

Rescued sailors from a sunken ship. The Merchant Navy suffered high casualties during the war, with over 1,600 Canadians and Newfoundlanders killed at sea. And yet they pressed on, undeterred. They would have to wait six decades until they were formally recognized as veterans.

that had long denied the merchant navy its proper place in the history of our citizen-in-arms by adding the approximately 2,000 merchant navy war dead to the roll of those who have given their lives in the cause of Canada."⁴⁰ The fifth book to be added to the altar, it contains the names of merchant seamen from the two world wars, including eight women lost in service. Comprising more than 300 ornate pages, the volume is adorned with hand-drawn maps of Merchant Navy sea routes. The first name in the book is Pauli Adami, a Greek-born seaman who, on August 13, 1915, went down with *Royal Edward*, a Toronto-registered ship. The last name has not yet been added to the book, as more seamen's names are uncovered each year.

In 1993, merchant mariners were invited to take part in the fiftieth anniversary commemorations of the Battle of the Atlantic—the first time that had ever occurred. But other tensions remained: some of the mariners complained that while they were recognized as veterans, they still could not access all veterans' programs. This anger festered for several years within the veterans' community and was made visible to all Canadians in October 1998 when three merchant seamen went to Parliament Hill to publicly starve themselves to death. This threat occurred as Veterans Affairs was leading a large delegation of eighty-three veterans, MPs, and senators to Korea on a commemorative mission that was costing half a million dollars. Matters became frenzied when it was learned that a member of the Bloc Québécois—a party devoted to breaking up Canada for Quebec's independence—was included in the tour.[41] That MP, Maurice Godin, had even dismissed the Canadians during the Second World War as having merely "swept the ice" for the British and Americans, who did the real fighting.[42] The press asked why parliamentarians were on an overseas jaunt with a separatist while mariner veterans who had defended Canada were at home threatening to kill themselves in the name of justice.

"We are the men that saved the world," exclaimed Ossie MacLean during an interview with the CBC conducted on Parliament Hill on October 1, 1998.[43] MacLean, Randolph Hope, and Ward Duke, all merchant mariners in their late seventies or older, had begun their hunger strike two days earlier. The fight was over compensation for the 2,300 ex–merchant seamen still alive; the strikers were seeking a $30,000 lump-sum payment for each mariner, which was meant to compensate for the denied benefits of retraining or free university tuition under the Veterans Charter. Numerous newspaper and media accounts portrayed the mariners sympathetically, noting that they had faced the highest chance of being killed of any Canadian service—and yet they had been abandoned after the war. The hunger strike attracted national interest, and Canadians began to drop off tea and blankets for them. "Governments can't reverse the tide of history, but they can correct oversights," urged one newspaper.[44] The government ultimately caved to the shaming pressure and the public relations disaster. In March 1999, it passed Bill C-61, a financial package with a sliding scale of payments based on months of service, with a maximum of $20,000 for mariners who served more than twenty-four months, and 20 percent more for PoWs. It was a resolution to a fifty-five-year-old fight and a final victory for the merchant mariners who had done so much to keep the Allies in the war against Hitler.

During the late 1980s, the most prominent theme of Canada's Second World War was one of neglect and hurt. The battle of the merchant mariners' for recognition, the struggle of Indigenous veterans for full rights, the seething anger of the Hong Kong veterans, and the Japanese Canadian campaign for redress created and reinforced the notion that Canada had abandoned its own during and after the war. It was difficult to find the idea of the Necessary War within these battles, no matter how important they were for the veterans or civilians affected. These contested and high-profile struggles enriched the complexity of the war story, but amid the strife, the once-dominant narrative of the just and obligatory fight against evil during the Second World War was further diminished.

CHAPTER 13

DENIGRATION

O n Remembrance Day in 1990, about 4,000 people attended the annual ceremony at the national cenotaph in Ottawa. Ninety-two-year-old Silver Cross mother Elsie Pearce, from Trenton, Ontario, lost two sons in the war. Flying Officer Stewart Pearce was killed at the age of nineteen while piloting a Spitfire over the English Channel on December 12, 1942, and her youngest son, Flight Sergeant Jack Pearce, who outlived his older brother, died at age twenty as an RCAF rear-gunner in a Lancaster when it went down over France on July 27, 1944. Elsie outlived her husband, William, a Great War veteran, and given the impact the wars had on her life, she felt compelled to make the trip to Ottawa.

The ceremony had by now settled into a ritualized display of remembrance, with orations, prayers and poppies, silent reflection, and the playing of the "Last Post." At the end of the formal event, the veterans marched in a parade that included modern peacekeepers, Korean War and Second World War veterans, and even a handful of aged warriors from the trenches of the Western Front. Overseas, Canadian forces personnel—eighteen CF-18 fighter jets, three warships, and several medical units—were serving in the Persian Gulf in the allied coalition war against Saddam Hussein in Iraq.

Across the country, events and acts of remembrances were held at the local cenotaphs, as well as in churches, hospitals, retirement residences, schools, and businesses. In Halifax, about 1,200 people gathered for a large military parade led by units at Canadian Forces Base Halifax. The Silver Cross mother in Halifax, ninety-year-old Mary Beaton of Dartmouth, laid a wreath for all the mothers in the province. She had lost her son, eighteen-year-old Able Seaman Joseph Beaton, a member of the Royal Canadian Naval Volunteer Reserve who had served in the Operation Torch landings on a troop ship, *Ettrick*. After disembarking troops in North Africa in November 1942, *Ettrick* was hit by a torpedo near Gibraltar, and Joseph was one of twenty-four lost at sea. His name is commemorated on the Halifax Memorial, but his still-grieving

A Memorial Cross, also known as the Silver Cross, created in 1919 as a sign of personal sacrifice for Canada's mothers and widows. It continues to be given to this day, and has been issued from 2006 to widowers.

mother, fifty-eight years later, recounted how "there was not a thing left of Joseph—not even a piece of paper for me to remember him by." She also remarked on the passing of the veterans and their loved ones, noting, "It seems that every year someone is missing at the service who was here the year before. There are fewer and fewer of us every year."[1]

Fewer and fewer each year, indeed. And although Remembrance Day continued to be marked across the country, there was a sense among concerned veterans that the memory of the war was slipping away as those who served in the Necessary War passed on. The 1980s had been a bleak period for the Second World War generation: their history was little taught in schools, and the most high-profile events were the formal apology to Japanese Canadians and the merchant mariners' fight for veterans' status. In 1990, veteran Strome Galloway lamented in the pages of *Legion* magazine that Canadians knew little about their collective past. "For most Canadians, this country's history—especially military history—is a closed book. This is largely the fault of our education system, which leads us to believe we must only look ahead. The past is meaningless and to learn about it—or from it—is a waste of time."[2] Ella Trow, whose husband, brothers, and friends went into the service, hated the terrible losses in the war, but hated more the fact that so few people in modern Canada even knew it had happened. "Who now remembers or even cares about the truly gallant service men who are left, or about the families of those who did not come back?" she wondered in a 1991 interview.[3] "We are a dying breed," said another veteran at around that same time. "Who," he asked, "will carry our standard on Nov. 11, 25 years from now? Who will assure our comrades' sacrifice are not lost in the cobwebs of time? Our place in history must be left in safe, capable and caring hands."[4] Veterans and those who had been shaped by the Necessary War felt that the conflict's just meaning had been lost over time, and this concern prompted increasing calls for it to be taught more effectively in schools and for broadcasters to provide more programming that would share the story with the majority of Canadians born after victory in 1945.

"No Canadian military history of modern times has produced the furore of the CBC mini-series and book *The Valour and the Horror*, which have caused Senate subcommittee hearings, senior CBC officials to publicly oppose one another, and seemingly endless media coverage and commentary," reported *Saturday Night* magazine in May 1993.[5] The series, consisting of three two-hour episodes created by the National Film Board, was broadcast in January 1992 by CBC during prime time, and more than 4 million Canadians watched the films, roughly 20 percent of the English-language audience. Meanwhile, another 400,000 French-speaking viewers tuned into it on the national French network, Radio-Canada.[6] The series focused on the Battle of Hong Kong in December 1941, the bombing campaign against Germany, and the Canadian defeat at Verrières Ridge in Normandy on July 25, 1944.

Brothers Brian and Terence McKenna, award-winning journalists and filmmakers, were the driving force behind the films. Coming of age in the post-Vietnam period, the McKennas felt that the propaganda about the Second World War had perverted the truth for decades, and they saw it as their mission to expose that truth. The two had written and directed the 1988 documentary *The Killing Ground*, which had explored the Canadian war experience during the Great War. In that film, they portrayed Canadian

Corps commander Sir Arthur Currie as a villain and as little more than a British toady who had callously sent his soldiers to their deaths to please his imperial masters. It was bad, sensationalistic history—Currie was Canada's finest general—but the film had not excited much controversy beyond the veterans' community.[7]

With *The Valour and the Horror*, the McKennas sought to uncover a secret history of the Second World War. While the three events they chose to focus on were not unknown to those who cared to pick up any book related to the Second World War, the general lack of knowledge among Canadians about the war effort made the films appear new and original, and viewers were much taken by the content. The films had high production values, contained little-seen archival footage, and featured several veterans

A Canadian soldier silhouetted on the battlefield at Verrières Ridge. The Canadian defeat at the ridge on July 25, 1944 was the focus of one of the three The Valour and the Horror *documentary films.*

reflecting on the war. The McKennas also employed new storytelling techniques, with actors playing the parts of real-life soldiers and commanders and speaking directly to the camera. This approach added drama and vibrancy, but the McKennas were guilty of inserting fabricated language into the script—a transgression that would later be exposed and criticized.

The story of the Hong Kong battle and the ghastly prisoner-of-war experience in *Savage Christmas: Hong Kong 1941* caused the least controversy. The McKennas effectively portrayed the Canadian government's decision to send troops to that garrison as an act carried out by guileless politicians tricked by the British and pressured by their generals, while the depiction of the treatment of prisoners was true to the harrowing, gut-wrenching experience. One Hong Kong veteran, Roger Cyr, decried on camera the government's move to send "its young men as lambs to the slaughter, in order to meet some sort of political expediency." However, the film about Normandy was much condemned. The McKennas were drawn to the image of defeat, and the focus on Verrières Ridge came at the expense of all the other successful if hard-pounding battles in Normandy and beyond. *Desperate Battle: Normandy 1944* made little mention of the courage, tenacity, and skill the Canadians demonstrated in landing and taking Juno, or of their fierce and successful defence of the beach-head against German counterattacks. The grinding, attritional battles that were to follow were also lightly skipped over, and instead the emphasis was on the low point of the fighting, the attack on Verrières Ridge on July 25, 1944. The countless Canadian actions and sacrifices in Normandy were reduced to a single defeat.

Death by Moonlight: Bomber Command was the most flawed of the three films. In its depiction of the bombing campaign against

German cities, it accused the Allies of slaughtering innocent women and children and of hiding the truth from Canadians. Sir Arthur Harris, the air officer commanding-in-chief of RAF Bomber Command, was played by an actor who chortled about killing German civilians in the cities that he ordered destroyed. Wilkie Wanless, an RCAF air gunner and past president of the Southern Alberta Air Crew Association, told *Western Report* on May 11, 1992, that the film "made us look like a bunch of moronic murderers and nut-cases."[8]

The question of Bomber Command's role in the war was particularly touchy for airmen, as the bombing force's purpose and success had been questioned in the immediate postwar years. Some had condemned the bombers' actions as both morally wrong and operationally ineffective. And yet from mid-1944, the Combined Bomber Offensive had pounded the enemy cities to slow industrial production and punish the Germans. Though the Germans had started the strategy of bombing civilians in the Great War and had continued it in the second conflict, by 1944 the Allied air armadas had overwhelmed the German air force and were smashing cities across Western Europe.[9] But by the final months of the war in 1945, with Germany close to defeat, the bombing was regarded by a few clergymen and members of the public as a case of over-kill. That was hardly true: the German army was still fighting on all fronts and the Nazis had introduced several super-weapons that appeared poised to revive the evil regime.[10] However, the bombing of Dresden in February 1945, with its sickening firestorm sucking in thousands of civilians and reducing them to ashes, was hard to accept, even if it had been demanded by the Soviet forces, who, like other Allies, continued to lose thousands of soldiers every day that the war dragged on.[11]

Wartime poster that declares, "British bombs are dropping on Germany with ever increasing weight." The bombers were one of the few means by which the Allies could strike back at Germany before the invasion on June 6, 1944. Before and after D-Day, the bombers pummelled German wartime industry and sowed terror among civilians.

Churchill was particularly unhelpful in his May 8, 1945, victory speech to the nation and the world, in which he highlighted the resolve and fortitude of the many who contributed to victory on land, at sea, and on the home front. He singled out the work of the fighter squadrons that defended Britain, but made no mention of the airmen in the bombers who took the war to Germany. It hurt the "bomber boys," who felt they had been denied proper recognition for their considerable contributions to victory, especially the many years when they were the Allies' only striking arm.[12] That gnawed away at the airmen, too.

Over the decades following the war, the bombing campaign
and the levelling of German cities was sometimes conflated in
the Canadian imagination with the threat of a Cold War aerial
bombardment—whether by planes or missiles—that promised to
reduce urban citizens to carbonized, shrunken corpses. This modern
fear of mass death reshaped how some viewed the bombing campaign of the Second World War, while others questioned it in the light

A cartoon in the May 1943 issue of Saturday Night *magazine, which depicts
Hitler standing on a mountain of victims from the many cities that Germany
had bombed at the start of the war. He is now wailing that the "bombing of
cities is a crime." There was little sympathy among Canadians during the
war for the German people who supported and contributed to the Nazi
regime, and then suffered under the rain of the bombs.*

of the new international law about the treatment of civilians in a war zone. A handful of commentators have even declared the bombing campaign against German civilians to be as immoral as the Holocaust.[13] Some on the German far right even inflated the 593,000 civilian deaths by bombing (a number that continues to be re-evaluated) to 6 million—a "symbolic total," one German historian wrote, revised to equal "the total number of Jews murdered by the Nazis in the Holocaust."[14] By the end of the twentieth century, more commentators, philosophers, and peace activists began to feel—aided by hindsight, by a misunderstanding of the devastating impact of bombing on the enemy war machine, and by the emergence of harrowing German testimonials about the firestorms—that the Allied bombing campaign had been unnecessary or simply too harsh.[15]

The bomber crews had their own champions—other veterans as well as historians and politicians—but the most vocal was Sir Arthur Harris. The "Bomber," as he was known, had made many claims during the war that the bombers could defeat Germany on their own. Even when that idea was proven untrue—no single combat arm could win the war alone—he refused to be cowed, and for several decades after the war, he stood by the bombing campaign, aiding historians who supported his vision, condemning those who did not. While the stalwart Harris was much admired during the war, his claims were often held against him when the bombers failed to drive Germany to its knees. Over time, Harris became a convenient scapegoat for those who questioned the bombing, even though he was carrying out the policy set by British chief of the air staff Charles Portal and Prime Minister Churchill.[16] Harris died in 1984, belligerent to the end and refusing to denounce the strategy of city bombing. After his death, Bomber Command's effectiveness in carrying out its many missions and the morality of targeting cities was questioned most openly in Germany, but some critics in British society were equally aghast. One 1989 BBC production labelled Harris as the leader of the "bloodthirsty bone-heads and blimps."[17] RCAF veteran Douglas Harvey spoke for many of his comrades in 1981 when he observed, "The contributions made by Canadian bomber crews in World War Two have never been acknowledged and are little known or appreciated."[18] This struggle over the memory of Bomber Command was the context that provoked veterans' furious reaction to *Death by Moonlight*.[19]

The films in *The Valour and the Horror* series were necessarily selective, as all cultural endeavours are, but there were fatal

An RCAF bomber crew during the war in preparation for a night-time sortie. Decades later, the airmen of the bombers often felt that their contributions to victory had been ignored.

omissions. In the bombing campaign episode, for example, it was not made clear that it was the Germans who started the strategy of area bombing urban centres and civilians, and that the entire war was a result of Hitler's mad quest for power. When confronted with such glaring faults, Brian McKenna scoffed, "I assume people come to the film with some knowledge of Hitler and his gang of thugs."[20] Of course, many did not, and as the McKennas were portraying the bombing of cities, they certainly argued—or left it ambivalent enough for viewers to make the connection—that there was little difference between the Allies and the Nazis. There was indeed a difference, and it was shameful not to acknowledge it.

Despite these flaws, the films received many positive reviews, with one journalist calling the series "searingly emotional yet ruthlessly unsentimental." Another declared, "The Valour Deserves a Medal."[21] Many veterans saw it differently. After the first airing, incensed veterans complained that the films denigrated their war experience and those of their comrades. William Cram of Indian Head, Saskatchewan, felt the films were "distorted and malicious fabrications that all WWII ex-servicemen should protest, to ensure all copies are recalled and destroyed," adding, "Most of us lost brothers, comrades and mates to whom we owe a debt beyond repayment. Act now, that they may rest in peace with honour."[22] Some veterans, wives, and children described the series as directly attacking the dead while besmirching the integrity of the living. The three films also offered an unmistakable "presentist" view of history—in effect reading it backwards from the early 1990s, through the lens of the Cold War and the spectre of nuclear warfare, and ascribing modern sensibilities to the total war against Germany. One Canadian airman who flew in Bomber Command nearly wept at the wrong-headed row caused by the McKennas:

"The fools! Have they no understanding of why the war was fought? . . . On that terrible night in Hamburg, once I and the crew I was with got away from the storm, we watched it roar and I was praying for more planes and more bombs. That was the best way I knew to get rid of Hitler and stop the Germans. It may have been beastly but God knows they were to us."[23]

One of the most maddening aspects of the series was that the McKennas chose to centre on defeat rather than victory or a balance between the two. Their focus was Hong Kong and Verrières Ridge rather than the Battle of the Atlantic or the liberation of the Dutch. George Cooper of the Regina Rifles wrote to *Legion* about the courageous defence of Bretteville-l'Orgueilleuse on June 8 and 9, and the awful frontal attack on the Abbaye d'Ardenne a month later. As part of the assault on Caen, the Rifles and other Canadian regiments drove the enemy back and, in the assault on the thirteenth-century monastery, defeated the enemy in a skilled fire and movement advance. Cooper opined, "The price? . . . Costly? No denying it! Necessary? How else does a campaign proceed if the enemy is not engaged?"[24] In this battle, the enemy was dug in behind ancient stone walls and the Reginas had to cross 1.5 kilometres of open ground in full view of the Germans. And somehow they did it. Canadians died, but that did not mean that they had been sacrificed. Too often in the McKenna films, deaths in the war were portrayed as pointless loss.

Director Brian McKenna did not see himself as a muckraker. He testified about being moved by the tremendous courage of the forlorn Black Watch assault on Verrières Ridge, although he condemned the generals who sent the regiment forward. And he was right: it was a badly planned operation. The problem was that McKenna highlighted the attack on Verrières without placing it within the larger, victorious campaign. The defeat at the ridge occurred within three months of steady fighting that saw the Allies drive the ferocious Germans back in bloody campaigns. The Allied planners had thought there was a fifty–fifty chance of the invasion force being annihilated on D-Day; if the invaders survived, the generals hoped that subsequent units arriving on the beaches might defeat the Germans in ninety days. The Allies—Canadians fighting alongside the British and Americans—did it in seventy-seven days, destroying two German armies. But from what the McKennas' films portrayed, one might scarcely have known that the Allies had indeed won the war.

The McKenna brothers refused to cower. Instead, they doubled down, claiming that they had revealed real stories that had lain hidden or had been deliberately obscured by the government for decades. Historians snorted with derision. The McKennas' claims were bogus, and their revelations were marred by numerous errors of fact and dodgy interpretation, especially in the Bomber Command episode.[25] The errors perhaps could have been forgiven, but it was the tone of the series that rankled. Official historian Brereton Greenhous proclaimed of the films, "The McKennas are interested in simplification and sensationalism rather than the truth."[26] The McKennas overstated their claims by erroneously suggesting that Canadians knew little of the horror overseas, especially the bombing campaign and the defeat in Normandy. Somehow, the McKennas argued, Canadians had been tricked by propaganda or by unscrupulous generals and politicians. In the process, the filmmakers diminished the importance of the just and necessary war and those who served in it. But the beleaguered McKennas felt that they had a right to tell the story and that they had told it correctly. "My research is bullet-proof," Brian McKenna asserted boldly.[27] That statement added chum to the water: historians went to town on his script and delighted in highlighting errors of both interpretation and fact.[28] J.L. Granatstein was not wholly critical of the series, although he noted many errors of commission and omission, but in one review he judged the accompanying book by two amateurs to be dreadful, declaring, "The untrained, those who have no conception of history and no expertise, should not be encouraged to write it."[29]

The McKennas believed that the professional military historians in the country were part of the conspiracy of silence, having imbibed the Kool-Aid of glory and sacrifice while also actively blocking others from trying to understand the past. The documentarists claimed, "Not one of them has gone after the nest of incompetence at the top of the Canadian military establishment. The generals have always been protected."[30] Indeed, there had not been much military history published in the country up to the 1980s. But the year before the series was aired, Lieutenant-Colonel John (Jack) A. English's slashing account *The Canadian Army and the Normandy Campaign: A Study of Failure in High Command* (1991) condemned many of the Canadian generals for their poor training of soldiers and inadequate combined-arms fighting in Normandy.[31] English—a respected professional soldier—was surely correct in pointing out the failure of some in command. And yet he was also one of the most vociferous detractors of the McKennas' research, accusing the filmmakers—before the Senate sub-committee later convened to investigate the series—of failing to present the proper historical context for the Normandy battles. Failure and defeat occurs in war, but it is not always accompanied by cover-ups as the McKennas claimed.

———

"The Inaccurate and the Outrageous" was how an April 1992 editorial in *Legion* labelled the films in *The Valour and the Horror*.[32] The Legion's Dominion president, Jack Jolleys, penned a letter to Patrick Watson, chairman of the CBC board, remarking, "The program succeeded in representing members of Canada's armed forces during World War II, and their leaders, as either naïve, bloodthirsty or incompetent. At the same time, Canada's enemies were portrayed as the hapless, innocent victims of an Allied war plan apparently dedicated to the slaughter of as many civilians as possible."[33] Responding to the veterans' vociferous complaints, the Canadian Radio and Television Commission investigated the films in April 1992. Senator Jack Marshall—a long-time veterans champion who had led an inquiry against a previous offending NFB film, *The Kid Who Couldn't Miss* (1983), which accused Great War air ace Billy Bishop of faking his Victoria Cross–winning exploits in June 1917—was pressing hard in the political arena for retaliation on the filmmakers and the CBC.[34] Marshall was supported by Montreal industrialist Hartland Molson, a former RCAF fighter pilot, but most members of Parliament stayed quiet, unsure about how far to wade into the issue. And not all veterans were spitting mad. Columnist Douglas Fisher cited one ex–Normandy veteran who felt it was time for the generals—especially Simonds—to get their comeuppance. It is worth remembering here, and when considering other controversial events, that the veterans are not a single monolithic group, speaking in a unified voice. On the whole, however, veterans and their official bodies, such as the Legion and the War Amps, were deeply upset by the films.

On November 10, 1992, after an internal investigation into *The Valour and the Horror*, the CBC produced a report announcing that "the series as it stands is flawed and fails to measure up to CBC's demanding policies and standards."[35] The films, the report declared, would not be rebroadcast. The CBC judged that the historical claims made in the series lacked contextualizing, and, somewhat bizarrely, that the use of actors to portray various historical figures was confusing because they were not identified as actors. Far more damaging, they noted, was that the actors spoke fabricated words, which was rightly condemned as distorting history.

In the aftermath of the CBC's public *mea culpa*, Senator Jack Marshall organized a Senate subcommittee in late 1992 to investigate the films and the role of the public broadcaster in their creation. The veterans and historians who testified before the senators overwhelmingly condemned the films, and when Brian McKenna finally appeared before the senators, he was treated with open hostility in an undignified harangue.[36] To no one's surprise, the subcommittee eventually concluded that the films were "riddled with inaccuracies and biased perceptions, and suffered from a critical lack of balance."[37] Both the NFB and the CBC were singled out for not rising to their own journalistic standards, although the NFB continued to stand behind the films. There were many others in the media and arts communities who supported the McKennas, including novelist Timothy Findley, historian Michael Bliss, and many journalists. They regarded the veterans' backlash as an attack on free speech—a charge tinged with irony since those veterans were the same men and women who had fought in the war in the name of a fair, just, and free society.

Minister of Veterans Affairs Gerry Merrithew argued strongly in late 1992 for the veterans' cause, asserting, "I have repeatedly said in speeches . . . that only veterans, certainly not young documentary producers, fully understand the confusion of conflict, and it is in the memories and opinions of those who were actually there that will write the story of Canada at war."[38] This perspective signalled a slippery slope, and more than a few historians wondered if Merrithew was suggesting that they should stop studying the war and leave it entirely in the hands of aged veterans. Having emerged as a serious academic field of study in the 1960s, military history was flourishing by the early 1990s, and almost every major book published on the subject during that period was written by a historian who was not a Second World War veteran. And yet much of the pain caused by the film was rooted in the question of who had the right to tell the stories of the past. Veterans did not "own" the war, and certainly others could and should interpret it, if only because the history of the war and its enduring impact extended beyond the experience of the survivors of service. But those same veterans, after decades of neglect, were certainly not going to allow others to paint them as incompetent murderers or foolish victims.

As the Senate sub-committee was convicting the films of bad faith and worse history, the Bomber Harris Trust, which was not affiliated with the Legion, launched a class-action defamation lawsuit over *The Valour and the Horror* and against several individuals and organizations, including the McKennas, noting forty-one errors and distortions in the series.[39] In effect, they were suing for historical tricksterism. The Bomber Harris Trust asked for $500 million, a figure that inspired much ridicule in the media. An Ontario Court justice dismissed the case in January 1994.

In lieu of suing, former RCAF pilot R.L. Harris of White Rock, BC, believed that "a new and more positive approach would be to produce the true story of Canadians' contributions to winning WWII."[40] To right the historical wrong, Richard Nielsen, a former producer for the CBC, began work on a documentary, *No Price Too High*. Terry Copp was the historical consultant, and Barney Danson, a Normandy veteran and former minister of national defence, joined the team to help secure funding and sell it to one of the networks. The film was shown on the Bravo channel on November 11, 1995, but CBC turned it down and did not initially broadcast it on the main network. Danson was able to work his considerable network of connections in the United States to secure its airing on PBS, which embarrassed CBC into broadcasting it and also re-releasing the NFB's *Canada at War* series. *No Price Too High* drew upon eyewitness accounts and archival records to good effect, but its sense of authenticity paled in comparison to the high production values and slick storytelling of *The Valour and the Horror*. Nonetheless, *The Globe and Mail* described *No Price Too High* as "arguably the most comprehensive and genuinely affecting portrait of Canadians at war ever made for television."[41] It was, but only because so little programming of any quality about the war had ever been produced for Canadians.

At this same time, the Directorate of History, the renamed Canadian forces' historical section where Colonel C.P. Stacey had forged his histories, was continuing its work on the Second World War official air war volumes, a project many years in the making. Two lauded books had been published to date—S.F. Wise's *Canadian Airmen and the First World War* (1980) and W.A.B. Douglas's *The Creation of a National Air Force* (1986)—but the great challenge was to conceptualize the mammoth Second World War air operations, which included Fighter, Coastal, Transport, and Bomber Commands. Decades of research finally led to the publication, in 1993, of *The Crucible of War, 1939–1945: The Official History of the Royal Canadian Air Force.*[42]

As the battle raged over *The Valour and the Horror*, a number of veterans publicly called for the official historians to comment on the film's depiction of the bombing campaign. Veteran David McIntosh sniped at the defence historians in the September 1992 issue of *Legion* magazine, denouncing the long delay in publication. Official historian Brereton Greenhous, who was primary editor of the multi-authored history and an accomplished if quarrelsome historian, responded, "If you write your official history too soon, you're asking for trouble. Not because historians are too incompetent but because they were too close to the event." McIntosh scoffed at the response, retorting, "At last we have an excuse, however lame, from the defence department historians for still not producing—47 years after the end of WWII—the official history of the RCAF overseas. They're too close to the event; they wouldn't want to have to interview any actual participants." Of course McIntosh gave no mention to the RCAF shuttering its own historical section after the war. Instead, he added, "If the history directorate had done its job, we might have been spared at least some of the lies, deceit and vilification—not to mention an apology to the Nazis for bombing them—in the CBC/NFB production."[43]

The Crucible of War set off its own firestorm of controversy, as the monumental history emerged in May 1993 during the fierce debate over *The Valour and the Horror*. At some 1,000 pages, it was a dense volume that covered many aspects of the complex air war, which saw squadrons defending Canadian coasts and convoys, hurling back the Luftwaffe over Britain, and then attacking into Europe. It also encompassed the many different types of missions carried out by Bomber Command, including laying mines, destroying transportation, harassing German rocket sites, and smashing cities. Despite its chronicling of the command's many contributions, the book questioned the effectiveness of the bombing campaign. *The Crucible of War* concluded that the sustained bombing assault pulled German resources from the battle front, including 900,000 soldiers engaged in ground defence and 19,713 88mm and 128mm anti-aircraft guns, but that the cost paid by the Allies in air crews and resources was too high.[44]

Brian McKenna immediately claimed that the surprising judgments of the official history—especially the argument that Bomber Command had failed to deliver victory, as Harris had claimed, but also the assertion that the offensive had not done as much damage as was thought at the time—vindicated his film. It did not. However, even by the 1990s, it remained difficult to assess the impact of the bombing, with analysis often including "what if?" speculations about what might have happened without the bombing campaign, especially in the context of its impact on German wartime production and on civilian morale. But later scholarship would more assertively claim that the bombers greatly damaged the war machine and punished the millions of war workers who continued to support the evil Nazi regime.[45]

Many veterans argued that the official history—paid for, ultimately, by tax-payers, as *The Valour and the Horror* had been—appeared to support some of the conclusions of the hated film. However, where *Death by Moonlight* likened the actions of Bomber Command to a secret war crime, the official history refrained from making such erroneous and absurd claims. And still *The Crucible of War* was lumped in with *The Valour and the Horror*, with even J.L. Granatstein remarking, "this account, astonishingly opinionated for official history, too often seems like nothing so much as the TV series with footnotes."[46] Reginald Dixon of Stittsville, Ontario, a combat veteran of the war, was but one ex-serviceman who derided the official historians as "armchair generals," declaring, "Hitler and his cohorts deserved everything they got. Germany invaded and terrorized other countries and initiated the war. The Allies finished it. . . . I have no regrets about my part in killing the enemy because the enemy was doing all it could to kill me."[47]

Efforts to present aspects of the war's history revealed a stark division between veterans and filmmakers, between the Legion and the CBC, and between historians who generally regarded the McKenna series as a travesty and journalists who demanded freedom to express what they saw as obscured truths. These battles of reputation and pride were not easy terrain upon which to find common ground. However, the veterans' anger over the documentaries can be better understood in the context of the decades of neglect they had suffered and the feeling among them that their stories were little known and no longer taught to young people. Not only did *The Valour and the Horror* dwell on defeat and disgrace, but it did so in the face of an increasingly weak understanding of history on the part of the Canadian public. Veterans had been hoping for a renewed interest in their history for years, but these award-winning films were not what they had envisioned. The films and the controversy they generated were a low point in the decades-long evolution of the Necessary War's meaning, especially as the series portrayed soldiers wantonly sacrificed through incompetence in Normandy and Hong Kong, and aircrews engaged in taking the war to defenceless women and children in

German cities. The complexities and nuances of the war were shorn away in the films, leaving only failure and shame. As one combat veteran demanded with incredulity, "What kind of people have snatched the torch we hoped to pass to young Canadians?"[48]

CHAPTER 14

FROM CONTROVERSY TO COMMEMORATION

The Valour and the Horror left deep scars. Canadian veterans had worried for years that the story of the Second World War had faded with the passage of time and the deaths of those who served. Its once almost universally accepted meaning—the Necessary War against Hitler's regime—seemed inexplicably lost. Furthermore, people did not grasp the importance of the war, as history was taught poorly in schools and the Canadians' experience of war was rarely represented in the cultural life of the country. But the McKennas' films were more than a story of forgetting; they were a full-frontal attack on the memory of the war. Neglect had been hard to accept, but a new generation's scorn had first shocked and then infuriated veterans.

The battle over history had wounded the veterans, but a new round of grave injury and insult was to follow. And this time it was self-inflicted. A "swirling controversy" erupted—as *Legion* magazine described it—when the Newton Branch of Surrey, BC, invited veterans to the hall after the Remembrance Day ceremonies on November 11, 1993, but then denied admittance to five Sikh veterans who were wearing traditional headdresses and could not remove them in public for religious reasons.[1] The headdress issue was grounded in the Legion's unique traditions and cultures, which were sometimes different than that of the broader society. One aspect of this culture was the removal of headgear and hats when entering a Legion Hall. This tradition, forged over decades, was infused with the sacred notion of offering a small sign of respect to one's comrades.

Denying Sikh veterans access to a Legion Hall on Remembrance Day led to a hurtful incident that escalated into a national controversy. It pitted the veterans' traditions against those of modern Canada, where the Charter ensured that religious and human rights were respected. That it involved veterans on both sides of the spectrum made it a spectacle. Media outlets reported widely on the issue as it dragged out over many agonizing months.

Some veterans viewed the uproar over the headdresses as the rest of Canada dictating to them how to act. A few offered intemperate—some would say racist—queries: "How can a bunch of immigrants turn our government and our courts upside down and succeed in imposing or forcing their customs and values upon our nation?" asked one veteran from Quebec.[2] William Dennis was another supporter of the ban who felt that the Legion must stand strong and "not bow to political pressure."[3]

Journalists pounced and then pounded the Legion. There were editorials condemning the veterans in newspapers across the country. *Vancouver Sun* columnist Stephen Hume wrote with undisguised venom: "The simple-minded bigots of the Legion insist on the reductionist case that any head covering must be a hat. By this logic, a yarmulke is equivalent to a baseball cap without a brim, a turban just another eccentricity, like a frivolous affection for tweed deerstalkers. . . . It has nothing to do with head coverings, and everything to do with the perceived 'difference' of the people who wear them. . . . The most loathsome part of the Legion argument is the fact that it is so cowardly."[4] Calling veterans cowardly was a broadside attack. He offered more bite and bile: "These must be people who seethe with vile, spite and petty hatreds but are too spineless to make a simple straight-forward statement of their beliefs. Their cowardice and hypocrisy is an insult to the values Canada's war dead fought valiantly to preserve." Many other letter-writers in newspapers across the country demanded a boycott of the poppy and the revoking of the Legion's charity status.

The Legion's Dominion Command knew that the tradition had to end, arguing that it was in the "best interest of comradeship, which is one of the foundations on which the Legion was built."[5] Veterans writing to *Legion* magazine generally agreed, many of them stating that the BC Legion branch had failed its comrades. More than a few veterans raised the question of the Legion members having fought for democracy and freedom of religion, and the sad irony of such a denial of other veterans in a Legion Hall. James Cook of Bancroft, Ontario, felt that "the Royal Canadian Legion must move into the 20th century, survive and defend the needs and rights of veterans and ex-servicemen and women. To do this in what is—and what will continue to be—a cosmopolitan ethnic mix, rules and attitudes must change."[6] Some veterans were so outraged that they dropped their membership. Ernst Frohloff of Hudson, Quebec, was "embarrassed and humiliated," noting that the "media fallout from this decision has been devastating."[7]

The issue, in the end, was muddied, as are all these complex notions of heritage and traditions of an older age rubbing up against the modernity, diversity, and inclusivity of the current age. Is to change and adapt simply to give in to the politicians, the politically correct, and the human rights advocates? Was it right to turn one's back on a symbolic act that represented dead comrades and the fierce bonds of respect between the living? Was this denial of the headdress an attack on freedom of choice? For many veterans, the deciding factor in the end was that this rejection of headdresses was an affront to other Indian veterans. In *Legion* magazine, Dunstan Pasterfield of Arcola, Saskatchewan, recounted how he had served in the Indian Army during the Second World War. "Sikhs died fighting for the cause we were fighting for. All of them wore their turbans in training and in battle. That any of these former comrades should be barred from a Legion lounge because of a misguided idea of tradition is intolerable."[8] Veteranship had to trump tradition, felt Pasterfield, who had been a member of the Legion for more than forty years but was now severing ties.

Depicted as retrograde and racist, the most conservative of the veterans were certainly out of step with the rest of society, although other Canadians had objected to Sikhs in the Royal Canadian Mounted Police wearing headdresses instead of the traditional Stetson hat. The difficult questions of accommodating religion and tradition would rage across society from the late twentieth century and into the twenty-first century, right up to 2019 legislation in Quebec prohibiting people from wearing religious headgear if they work in the public sector. But in reflecting on the veterans' controversy, Douglas Fisher wondered why the media had been so contemptuous, feeling that the "meanness and scorn" was driven by generational anger.[9] "So many columnists, editorial writers, television and radio commentators chose to be nasty about the Legion. . . . Some even mocked those seen as clinging to memories of their personal involvement in WWII and expecting Canada of today to revere their deeds."[10] The headdress controversy was finally rectified, first by letting individual

Legion Halls decide the issue but reminding them to comply with Canadian and provincial human rights' law, and then by rescinding a national bylaw imposing dress regulations. But the hurt caused by framing the veterans as yesterday's men and women remained, as it did among Sikh veterans and their families who had served and sacrificed in the same wars.

When the United Nations gave the world's peacekeepers the Nobel Peace Prize in 1988, Canadians smugly talked of how they deserved a large piece of it. Catching the tenor of the times, *The Globe and Mail* avowed that peacekeeping was "the proudest peacetime tradition of the Canadian military."[11] By the late 1980s, 85,000 men and women had served on peacekeeping missions since 1949, more than any other nation, and peacekeeping had become an emblem of Canada to the world.[12]

A few years later, Ottawa unveiled a peacekeeping monument in Ottawa, opposite the National Gallery, very close to where the National Shrine was to have been built in the 1960s. The competition guidelines made direct reference to inspiration from the 1988 Nobel Peace Prize.[13] The triangular-shaped monument, adorned with peacekeeping figures keeping watch, was less a monument to those killed—although more than 180 service personnel have lost their lives in missions around the world—and more a celebration of the Canadian contribution to world peace. The monument, known as Reconciliation, was unveiled October 8, 1992—even as traditional Pearsonian peacekeeping was dying in overseas killing fields.[14]

When the Cold War ended, a new world order emerged as the West watched the hitherto unthinkable sight of the Soviet

Ottawa built a monument to peacekeepers in October 1992. Long before this, Canadians had embraced the idea of the peacekeeper and heralded it as a symbol of Canada's contribution to world peace.

Union's disintegration. Rampant nationalism flared in many countries as citizens threw off their oppressive Communist leaders. New prophets, strongmen, and warlords emerged to carve up the spoils. Canada was called upon to send peacekeepers to many parts of the world. The problem was that decades of cutbacks to military budgets had left the Canadian forces overextended and unable to recuperate long enough from dangerous missions before being sent to the next one.

The largest peacekeeping operation was in the Balkans, where ancient animosities were unleashed within a ruptured Yugoslavia. The fighting was intranational and fuelled by intense hatred among Croatians, Bosnians, Serbians, and other groups. "Ethnic cleansing" was carried out by all sides, targeting civilians to clear them from vast tracts of land through systematic rape, terror, and murder. Caught in a many-tiered civil war—with military, paramilitary, and death squads roaming widely and shooting freely— the Canadian peacekeepers were vulnerable, especially as their actions were constrained by complex, antiquated, and totally inadequate rules of engagement. They were often instructed to use no force as women and children were raped and massacred around them, while men of all ages, even little boys and hobbling elders, were led off to execution.

After witnessing too much of the horror, the Canadian soldiers began to hit back, especially when fired upon. In the Battle of Medak Pocket, soldiers of the 2nd Battalion, Princess Patricia's Canadian Light Infantry (PPCLI), came under direct Croatian attack on September 15 and 16, 1993, after months of skirmishes, confrontations, ambushes, and roadside bombs. For fifteen hours, a fierce firefight raged until the Croatians finally pulled out, bringing their dead with them. The PPCLI had shown its professionalism by saving the lives of Serbian refugees, but whatever else it had been, that was no peacekeeping mission. In fact, it was one of the largest fights of the Canadian forces since the Korean War. Afterwards, in a shocking display of cowardice, the Canadian government, unsure about how to handle the fallout from a peacekeeping mission-turned-battle, refused to let the Department of National Defence even publicize the event, let alone reward the soldiers with gallantry medals or acknowledge the sacrifice of four wounded Canadians.[15]

As the mass murder in the Balkans was being carried out, a small peacekeeping force commanded by Canadian Major-General Roméo Dallaire was sent to Rwanda. Dallaire, bound by the restrictions of the UN on peacekeepers, watched impotently as a genocide unfolded. Between April 6 and July 16, 1994, an estimated 800,000 Tutsi and moderate Hutu men, women, and children were brutally killed, many hacked to death with machetes by their neighbours. The failure of UN Headquarters in New York to act rapidly had contributed to the catastrophe, and many of the peacekeepers who lived through the genocide were forever traumatized by their own inability to intervene and save the innocent.

But the image of the peacekeeper had already been tarnished in the aftermath of an earlier Somali mission that went terribly wrong. The overstretched Canadian forces had been forced to send paratroopers from the Airborne Regiment to act as peacemakers in a UN mission. Soldiers on the ground were frustrated by the lawless nature of the country, riven by decades of war, a broken society upon which there was no hope of brokering peace. Matters were exacerbated by the low numbers of Canadian service personnel, privates' near-starvation wages, lack of medical support for personnel suffering from PTSD, and a senior command who was later shown to be incompetent or untrustworthy. The Canadian forces' reputation suffered a severe blow when a handful of rogue paratroopers captured and tortured to death a Somali teenager who was caught stealing from the Canadian camp on March 16, 1993.

When the story broke, it appalled Canadians and blotted out years of good work. Even though peacekeepers in Somalia had built infrastructure and distributed food and aid that saved many lives, the only image that resonated was the sight of a few soldiers standing over the battered body of a dead teenager. There was more dismaying news to come. Diligent reporters revealed a systemic cover-up of the murder by senior levels of the Canadian forces. All was laid bare in stark detail in a formal commission of inquiry that lasted almost a year, from late 1995 to fall 1996, with successive senior officers caught in lies and deception.[16] Reported on extensively in television, radio, and print, the Canadian forces was eviscerated in the media for years, with real atrocities and gross failures exposed, but also with minor events magnified in a creeping barrage of criticism.

For several decades, the comforting image of the peacekeeper had prevented many Canadians from engaging meaningfully with the Second World War. Canada revered its peacekeepers, even though, oddly, most Canadians seemed unable to recognize that peacekeepers were soldiers—not separate from them. But the ungovernable and genocidal environments of the Balkans, Rwanda, and Somalia showed that the traditional methods of peacekeeping were dead, even as those blue-helmeted soldiers on the ground did much good, saving lives and bringing aid to the helpless.

Canadians would continue to find solace and meaning in the idea of peacekeeping, even as it became increasingly difficult in the twenty-first century and necessarily more robust in warlike conditions. And yet amid the decline of the martial image, and the chaos within Canadian forces, there was an opportunity for aged veterans and government officers to redeem the story of Canada's long-neglected Second World War.

In the wake of *The Valour and the Horror*, the headdress controversy, and the relentless blows to peacekeeping, Canada had drifted far from the once influential and anchoring idea of the Necessary War. "All across the nation veterans gathered to talk to each other and to seek ways to re-establishing an accurate collective memory of the meaning of the sacrifices of war," recounted historian Terry Copp, writing on the eve on the fiftieth anniversary in 1995. "They discovered the Canadian history texts largely ignored them. In the era of biculturalism and multiculturalism, the new post-colonial history avoided the war effort

overseas, focusing on issues such as conscription and the internment of enemy aliens. When the military was mentioned, it was
to highlight Canadian failures, not achievements."[17] With a
renewed awareness that they must fight for their history, veterans
hoped that the fiftieth anniversary would be an opportunity to
remind amnesiac Canadians of their achievements during the
Second World War.

Anniversaries matter. They trigger memories and attract
media attention. The fortieth anniversary of the D-Day landings
had been a transnational, if politicized, event. However, Canada
had been largely ignored in the commemorations, and US president Ronald Reagan's speech had reminded the world of the crucial role played by the Allies in restoring democracy to Europe,
with the United States in the vanguard.

There had been modest government-led pilgrimages to Vimy for
the seventy-fifth anniversary and to Dieppe for the fiftieth anniversary in 1992, both of which were well covered by the media. Building
on this momentum, Canadian veterans made a more sustained push
for the government to make the fiftieth anniversary of D-Day a pri-
ority. They complained that Canada had been overlooked at the
fortieth anniversary and that Prime Minister Trudeau had been
badly outshone by the other countries' leaders. This time, Canada
should not be sidelined. In July 1993, Duncan Fraser, a retired
Acadia University professor of political science and military studies,
warned the Canadian government that the Americans were poised
to "steal D-Day Anniversary thunder. . . . For decades the Americans
had talked about winning the war and Canada had barely whispered
the truth. . . . One has to wonder about American insensitivity . . .
as one has also to express surprise that Canada has let them get away
with it."[18] There was much fear that the Canadian government

would stand by as the Americans and British again wrote Canada out of Normandy. Veterans shared a persistent sense of gloom that not only did no one remember the role of the men and women who sacrificed so much in the fight against tyranny, but no one cared.

The veterans' fear of being ignored proved unwarranted. In October 1993, the federal government unveiled a new program, Canada Remembers, to mark the coming anniversaries. Administered by Veterans Affairs, Canada Remembers was to be a series of nationwide educational programs to stimulate the teaching of the Second World War. At the same time, the Canadian Mint issued a 1994 commemorative dollar coin that circulated across the country, with the National War Memorial on the face. Another set of six medallions featured details from the Canadian War Museum art collection, depicting the Battle of Britain, Battle of the Atlantic, Far East campaign, Sicily and Italy, Battle of Normandy, and the liberation of the Netherlands. There were special stamps from Canada Post, with four new forty-three-cent stamps issued in November that highlighted house-to-house battles at Ortona, a Canadian warship fighting with a German U-boat in the Atlantic, Bomber Command ground crew loading bombs into a Halifax heavy bomber, and stevedores hauling war supplies onto a ship at a Canadian port. Labatt offered a special D-Day beer, and other companies sought to find connections to the war. Across the country, veterans began to talk more about their experiences. Some even published them for a wide audience, with Company Sergeant-Major Charles Martin's *Battle Diary* becoming one of the finest accounts of the D-Day invasion from a Canadian veteran who had landed on Juno Beach.

Canadians were finally waking up from their great ignorance. Large-scale commemorative activities were planned in Canada, with a focal point in Ottawa. In early 1993, the dilapidated Canadian War Museum (CWM), once the pride of veterans but now run-down through decades of neglect, received $1.7 million to fund exhibitions and displays to depict the Battle of the Atlantic, the Sicily and mainland Italy campaign, and a temporary Battle of Normandy exhibit. A postwar gallery was scheduled to open in 1996 that would explore the Korean War, the Cold War, and the recent Gulf War.

Newspapers ran stories about Canadian veterans and the war, and even reprinted articles from their own papers fifty years earlier. It was surprising for many veterans to see how the D-Day anniversary had channelled interest, although there was a sense that some media organizations, especially the CBC, might be trying to atone for *The Valour and the Horror*. After taking part in days of celebration in Ottawa, W.J.E. Patrick, who served with the Irish Regiment of Canada, wrote an open letter of thanks that was published in the *Ottawa Sun*: "Not since my experiencing of the heartwarming gratitude shown by the people of Holland after their liberation have I seen or accepted such a tremendous, enthusiastic outpouring of appreciation as was shown by the people who lined the route taken by the parade on Monday June 6. The cheering, the clapping, the wide-open smiles and the hand shaking of the people was so honestly spontaneous and generous that it gave me an uplifting of spirit that I have not felt for a very long time." He was surprised by the recognition, and it helped him deal with the nightmares that had plagued him for fifty years. But, he finished, "the memory of so many of my friends in the regiment who suffered and died during the campaign will haunt me forever."[19]

———

The return to the beaches was shaping up to be an epic event, an internationally scaled and staged operation. In the years previous, the British had marked the Battle of Britain and the Blitz, and then the Desert War. Canada had commemorated its own role in the 1943 Battle of the Atlantic, but this had been a fairly limited affair, reflecting the fact that our seafaring nation bordered by three oceans had never been very aware of its maritime history. That same year, an official delegation was sent to Italy, but the soldiers' contribution in that campaign remained relatively unknown, even though the large Allied force had faced twenty-two German divisions in August 1944 that could have been used in the Normandy counterattacks and defence on the Eastern Front.[20]

In June 1994, France hosted the ceremonies on its soil. It had spent decades coming to grips with its defeat in the war, and with the slow and painful revelation that not all French citizens were part of the resistance against the Nazi oppressors. In fact, many collaborated with the Vichy regime.[21] But those revelations, fought over in the public realm, had provided some closure, or at least the ability to acknowledge the war in other ways. And since 1984, the Normandy region had become the central site of memory for the Western allies. The June 1994 ceremony raised the thorny question of whether Germany should be allowed to attend.[22] The once-menacing enemy, totally defeated and left in ruin, was now the economic leader of Europe; what's more, it had undertaken to make official apologies and to make financial restitution to some of its victims. Should German officials be allowed to have an official presence at the commemorations? For years there had been bad blood over the war among the French, British, and German peoples, but it had flared up with the unveiling of the Sir Arthur Harris statue outside the RAF church of

St Clement Danes in the Strand, London. Several German mayors protested the idea of putting up a statue to honour a mass murderer and war criminal—as they characterized Harris—but the British would not be dissuaded. The Queen Mother, who had lived through the war, ignored her advisers who told her to stay away, and unveiled the statue on May 31, 1992. The Bomber War over the Western Front refused to remain quiet, and acts of remembrance and commemoration in one country were often viewed very differently in others.

In early March 1994, British and French representatives told German chancellor Helmut Kohl that he was not welcome at the ceremonies. *The Times* chortled when it declared, "Germany forced to swallow second defeat over D-Day ceremony."[23] German officials wished to use attendance at the D-Day event as an opportunity to be part of a united Europe, employing what scholars call "memorial diplomacy."[24] But ill feelings over the war remained unsettled. As one French official observed, the problem was not so much between "Germany and Europe, but between Germany and its past."[25]

The return to the beaches on June 6, 1994, was an international spectacle of bearing witness, an homage to victory, and a time to shed tears for the loss of comrades. The day commenced with an airborne drop on Normandy, with 1,000 American and 1,400 British and Canadian paratroopers participating in the replication of the invasion fifty years earlier. Thousands of other veterans were piped through the streets of France, past tens of thousands of cheering civilians, many crying and waving photographs of young soldiers. Along the routes where Canadian veterans marched and were driven in vehicles, schoolchildren sang and waved Canadian flags, while others held flowers and little souvenir books. *Vive les Canadiens! Vive les Canadiens! Merci, Canada! Merci!*

The crowds of veterans were joined by Queen Elizabeth, President Bill Clinton, and Prime Minister Jean Chrétien. Clinton was looking to bottle lightning a second time, well aware of how Reagan had won the day ten years earlier. The president spoke aboard USS *George Washington* and later at Pointe du Hoc, where he described the American soldiers on these beaches as "the forces of freedom [that] turned the tide of the twentieth century."[26] The Canadians did not remain on the sidelines, as they had done in 1984. While the main ceremony was held on Omaha Beach, along with a British event at Arromanches, in the Juno sector Prime Minister Jean Chrétien offered stirring words: "There are some who will say these men have nothing in common—not geography, not language, not religion. But they did one thing very much in common. They were all part of a young nation—a new kind of nation— where the ancient hatreds of the past were no match for the promise of the future. They believed they could speak different languages, worship in different ways and live in peace. They died on the shores and in the fields of a Europe consumed by hate and terror."[27]

The Canadian prime minister spoke of unity of purpose and togetherness among the soldiers, no doubt with an eye on the Quebec referendum on sovereignty for the province looming on the horizon. As Quebec separatists called for the dissolution of Canada to form a new country, at Juno Beach the memory of English and French Canadians who had served and died together to restore freedom came alive. It was a powerful symbol of unity, and Bloc Québécois leader Lucien Bouchard only looked petty when he rebuked Chrétien, saying, "It is not for anyone else to say what they thought when they died on those beaches far away from their families."[28] The present was infused by the past, but the past was also being pressed into service for a prime minister engaged in a new campaign.

Two major television networks—CBC and CTV—covered the D-Day events live over several days, with their hosts, Peter Mansbridge and Lloyd Robertson, bringing suitable gravitas to the broadcasts. There was also coverage in French Canada, and Department of National Defence historian Serge Bernier offered commentary about French Canada's contribution to the war effort. Dozens of Canadian journalists joined hundreds of international scribes. Most of the veterans knew they would not be coming back again, and journalists scrambled to interview them. Veterans were reflective about their experiences, talking openly of their anger at the "unfettered madness in the world," as did Geoffrey Corry, who landed with the Canadian Scottish Regiment on D-Day.[29] Others shed tears for the young men who lay buried near the beaches, forever on duty for Canada.

After decades of indifference, Canadians woke up to see their veterans welcomed and celebrated. It was nothing short of shocking. These seemingly living ghosts of the Second World War materialized on television and in print. The veterans broke the silence. And Canadians finally listened.

Canada's history was presented in books, articles, stories, films, newspapers' special sections, and radio and television commentary in the weeks building up to and on D-Day. In London, on June 3, 1994, Queen Elizabeth unveiled the Canada Memorial on ground donated by the Royal Family near Buckingham Palace at Green Park's Canada Gate. It was a monument to the Canadians who served in both world wars, created by artist Pierre Granche of Outremont, Quebec. Polished slabs of red Canadian Shield granite were adorned with bronze maple leaves. Water flows over the inclined rock to create the impression of the maple leaves being carried downstream. The inscription reads: "In looking into the future we honour the past."

"During the early summer, hardly a day went by without news stories or features appearing on television or in the printed media," reported *Legion* magazine.[30] Douglas Fisher was grateful for the interest, but he also observed, "Ours has been a country with a penchant for forgetting or downplaying the roles and worth of our participation in WWII, including the crucial invasion and, eventual, hard-won victory of the Scheldt." In his mind, "we all appreciate that some of the downplay is political and follows from concern over that precious chimera, national unity." [31] For too long Canadians had been silent about the war. The Americans used the war to bind together the disparate peoples, states, and regions, as did the British; Canadians seemed to fear the past and the divisions it might renew. Over time, it was safer to focus on the disasters and defeats and to say sorry than to talk openly of victories, when all in the country did not share in them. Ignoble actions—such as the forced relocation of Japanese Canadians or refusing to allow Jews fleeing Nazi Germany to disembark from MS *St. Louis*—were, paradoxically, easier to discuss. Since the 1960s, some of the Quebec political elite used conscription to highlight the province's oppression by the rest of Canada, albeit at the expense of the tens of thousands of French Canadians who served during the war. While it should have been easy to point out the many Canadian contributions to victory against the fascists, noting both the brave and inglorious events, for decades these acts of service and loss were marginalized at best and, more often, simply ignored. Some of the balance was restored after June 1994, as Canadians witnessed the gratitude of the French people and learned how their aged warriors had fought against the fascists.

The incredible success of "D-Day at fifty" carried forward into the new year and fired the desire by Canadian veterans to mark the end of the war in the Netherlands. There, fifty years earlier, the Canadians had been greeted as liberators who had saved the starving Dutch. While many Canadians had forgotten the powerful link between the Dutch and the Canadians, the return to the Netherlands would become the focal point of the Second World War commemoration in 1995.

The Dutch prepared to welcome the Canadians. Meindert van den Hengel, a seven-year-old boy in 1945 and now the secretary

Dutch children wave Canadian flags to greet those who liberated them fifty years earlier. The May 1995 ceremonies in the Netherlands saw thousands of Canadian veterans feted from cheering crowds, an act of commemoration and celebration not dissimilar to the rapturous reception they received in 1945.

of the "Thank You, Canada" committee, spoke publicly of the war years as a time of occupation, hardship, and starvation. The Canadians had given them back their freedom, and van den Hengel said, "There is no country in the world with which we have such strong bonds as Canada."[32] Veterans Affairs Canada framed the return to the Netherlands as a celebration rather than a commemoration and they had willing partners in the Dutch, with almost every town and city engaging in some sort of grand public party, and all requesting that the thousands of Canadian veterans might parade through them. While June 6, 1994, had been a day with the Americans in full glory, followed by the French and British, and the Canadians finally elbowing their way forward to some recognition, in Holland this was going to be a Canadian show.

An estimated 15,000 Canadian veterans and guests returned to the Netherlands, with commemorations from May 1 to 11, 1995, where they were feted by cheering crowds. At Apeldoorn, 500,000 people lined the streets for a liberation parade, having come from throughout the country. Thousands of Canadian veterans passed through the sea of Dutch, who roared and cried, waved Canadian flags, and sang "O Canada." Some could not help but compare it to fifty years earlier, although those greetings were given by a desperate people who were sick in body and soul after years of subjugation, servitude, and starvation. Now, generations of the Dutch showed an enormous outpouring of gratitude. The parade was planned for two hours; it lasted for eight, as exhilarated Dutch civilians and exhausted veterans sang, cheered, and drank as bottles were passed from the crowd to the thirsty veterans on the march. "I shall never forget the sight of young mothers in their twenties," recounted historian J.L. Granatstein, who served as historical commentator for the CBC, "weeping and cheering simultaneously while holding their babies up to get a sobbing veteran's kiss. Nor will I forget the Dutch mothers telling astonished and typically blasé Canadian reporters that they were doing this because they wanted their children to be able to say that they had been touched by one of the men who liberated the Netherlands a half-century before."[33]

There were other commemorative events, especially a stirring ceremony at Nijmegen, where Prime Minister Chrétien and Princess Margriet attended Groesbeek Canadian War Cemetery, all captured by television cameras, with veterans standing at attention, reflecting on the past, tears wetting their craggy faces. To a man and woman, the Canadians were overwhelmed by the outpouring of gratitude. Allan Notman of the 17th Duke of York's Royal Canadian Hussars talked about how returning to the indebted Dutch had a cathartic effect that helped him heal old wounds: "Once you see the gratitude of the people you saved, you don't feel so mad." His anger came from returning to the graves of his buddies, most in their early twenties, who never had a chance to grow up, and yet, he felt, "they accomplished something."[34] Veteran Gordon Mumford said of the pilgrimage, "I find now—as I get older—that I can cry."[35]

For the Second World War generation, there was no doubt that the war had been the most momentous event that had shaped their lives and that of their country. Yet it was different for someone born one or two generations later, whose life was entwined with multiculturalism, American pop culture, the Charter of Rights and Freedoms, the Quebec question, Western alienation, Maritime economic stagnation, free trade, and fear of the Cold War going nuclear, followed by the shocking end of Communism and with further destabilizing changes that came with globalization. It should not be surprising that the Second World War, which was never heavily heralded in Canada after 1945—with few separate monuments, symbolic acts of remembrance, histories, films, or memoirs by participants—faded far from relevance, unable to be used as a sign of nationhood as was done in the United States and Britain, and only as a warning for future generations.

Despite the solemn commemorations of 1994 and the rapturous celebrations of 1995, few veterans believed that Canadians at home would shift their attitudes from the previous decades of indifference and, at times, hostility. And yet for some who served, they were not yet ready to give up the ghost and shuffle off to the retirement homes. The veterans steeled themselves to fight for their history.

CHAPTER 15

RECLAIMING HISTORY

"How do we take this back home?" asked seventy-year-old Murray Beckett of Rocky Mountain House, Alberta, who served in the Second World War and the Korean War with the Royal Canadian Artillery. He wondered how he could be a hero in the Netherlands and, as he said, a "nobody" at home.[1] Victors overseas; forgotten in Canada. The lack of understanding and recognition by Canadians was widely lamented at the celebrations in May 1995. Even the Dutch remarked upon it. Arnhem mayor Paul Scholten told the delegation, "Canadians are generous at sharing the celebrations and their tragedies. But when it comes to wartime accomplishments, I think you are too modest."[2]

May 1995 was the high-water mark of the fiftieth anniversary of the end of the Second World War and was much more of a celebration than a sacred commemoration. The Dutch and the Canadians had finally found a way to talk about victory. And while Canada had never shown much desire to mark its role in the Pacific campaign, there was a ceremony held at the Canadian War Museum (CWM) on August 12, 1995, and attended by 800 veterans, dignitaries, and interested Canadians.[3] Hong Kong veterans had a significant presence, and were represented by Roger Cyr, president of the Hong Kong Veterans Commemorative Association. The RCAF was also part of the event—with space for the thousands of airmen who served in the Far East, especially in the Burma campaign—along with the navy and specialist units that fought in that theatre of war.

As a signal gun on the roof of the museum fired fifty times—once for each year since the end of the war—one reporter noted that "the veterans stood not so much in celebration as in sombre reflection, with pride—and some bitterness—about the years in between."[4] Minister of Veterans Affair Lawrence MacAulay presented more than 100 Hong Kong veterans with the newly authorized bar to be worn on the ribbon of the Canadian Volunteer Service Medal. A restrained Cyr recounted briefly how the Hong Kong veterans fought for acknowledgment of their unique struggle for many decades, but he also highlighted the importance of remembering the battle and those who served, so that "their names will not be forgotten in the pages of Canada's military history."[5] CWM director Victor Suthren was direct. "You survived an orgy of horror and murder," he said. "We hope that all the recognition you have merited will be yours. We hope that the Japanese will come to see that more needs to be said by them on their role in the war. Then we would be on the road to understanding and perhaps forgiveness."[6]

Building on the importance of the 1994 anniversary, historians sought to reinterpret the Second World War and mark its passage with new books. In 1995, University of Calgary historian David Bercuson published *Maple Leaf Against the Axis: Canada's Second World War*, only the second survey of Canada's war effort in fifty years, which built on W.A.B. Douglas and Brereton Greenhous's

1977 *Out of the Shadows*.[7] In French Canada, Serge Bernier, the director general of the DND's Directorate of History, organized a conference of French-speaking academics in 1994 to explore Quebec's role during the Second World War, and their work was published for a wider audience in 1995.[8] There were other histories, but the most commercially successful book was George G. Blackburn's *The Guns of Normandy* (1995). Blackburn served as an officer with the 4th Field Regiment, Royal Canadian Artillery, and the retired civil servant and playwright offered a highly personal and compelling account of the war in Europe. Focusing on the sharp end of battle, Blackburn recounted harrowing acts of violence he'd witnessed. The book became a national best-seller and was followed by two additional volumes of memoirs.[9] One reviewer said that *The Guns of Normandy* "is no glorious adventure story. Once into the front lines, war is hell."[10]

A forward observation officer who was awarded the Military Cross for gallantry and fought from July 1944 to May 1945, Blackburn had struggled to write the book for decades, finding that each time he tried to recall the war it was "just too anxiety-inducing."[11] In the early 1990s, he had again put pen to paper and wrote in the second person—referring to himself as "you"—and in the present tense, which created a sense of immediacy for the reader, and perhaps distance for himself. But he also told his readers that he wanted his books to address the lack of respect paid to the Canadian forces in Normandy, which had been slighted by such historians as Charles Stacey and his British counterparts. They had, he contended, given the public an "inaccurate, irresponsible conclusion bordering on outright dishonesty . . . regarding the training and fighting qualities of Canadian officers and men of World War II."[12] Stacey's comments had been cautious and his censure limited, but

British and American historians drew upon his work to amplify their criticism of the Canadians in battle. Blackburn also felt compelled to rebut the McKenna brothers' focus on failure, and *The British Columbia Report* claimed that Blackburn's book "does as much as any single volume can to repair the damage done to Canada's military heritage by Brian and Terence McKenna's 1992 hatchet-job documentary *The Valour and the Horror.*"[13]

After years of silence, other veterans had tried to capture the war in their memoirs. The best was Farley Mowat's *And No Birds Sang* (1979), in which the gifted writer revealed the dark narrative of war, with all its fear and hatred, as well as comradery and joy.[14] More accounts followed in the 1980s as veterans retired from working life: some wrote for their families only, or for cathartic release. For decades most had stayed quiet, unable to come to grips with their war. It was too raw, too painful. Many veterans carried the weight of guilt. John Drummond, who served with the Regina Rifle Regiment, recounted his inability to talk about the war. It wasn't until after a life lived, with a family, a job, and then retirement, that the war finally "came to the front again. It was almost like you put the whole thing into a compartment in your brain and it comes out after you're older."[15]

There were also new projects to record the veterans' history. Individuals took tape recorders to fathers, uncles, or neighbours. The Naval Officers Association of Canada started an oral history program in which they captured the wartime experiences of veterans in the multi-volume *Salty Dips* series.[16] Journalist Jean Portugal travelled the country interviewing 750 people who had served during the war. Her findings were published in the eight-volume series *We Were There*, which spanned 1.2 million words. She had been motivated to carry out the project after attending the fortieth D-Day anniversary, where Canada, she felt, had been ignored. "They had all kinds of American units leading the parade, there were French, all kinds of British, Czechs, Poles, you name it," she later recounted. "But there was no place for Canadians."[17]

But more than any other book aimed at general audiences, it was Blackburn's literary success that opened people's eyes. Hundreds of readers wrote directly to Blackburn. Ken Naftel of Ottawa confessed that "many of us never knew our fathers. They came back from the war, but wouldn't talk about it, were distant and often alcoholic. I read this book and said, 'Now I know my father.'"[18]

There was a growing interest in Canada's Second World War, but it was not reflected in the universities. By the 1980s, history professors were moving away from national history to focus their research and lectures on social and cultural history. These new historians sought to reclaim neglected aspects of the past and they had little desire to study military history; indeed, many seemed to regard it as an intellectual plague that would infect the student body and foster militarism. Historian J.L. Granatstein made a study of a number of academic textbooks from the late 1980s and early 1990s, observing that when social historians wrote about Canada's Second World War, they focused almost exclusively on attacks on civil rights and minorities, with minimal attention paid to the overseas forces.[19] The war around the world—and the million Canadians serving in uniform—seemed but a backdrop against which to investigate the state's cruel treatment of its own citizens. Professor Robert Vogel of McGill University took a mordant view of why the study of war and military history had been banished from university classrooms. His acerbic assessment was that studying war had little to do with "finding one's cultural roots, castigating the endless immorality of the effervescent middle classes, illustrating the recently discovered moral superiority of the current generation or raising the consciousness of the present with regards to the past."[20] Naval scholar and RCAF veteran Donald Schurman, in writing about the history profession in 1990, also noted that military history "rarely figures very largely in the typical introductory course in Canadian history."[21]

As these culture wars were playing out in the late 1980s, military history was not entirely banished from the academy; it continued to be taught in isolated pockets, even as it evolved and attracted new scholars. A centre of study emerged at Wilfrid Laurier under Terry Copp, who had been studying, re-evaluating, and publishing on Canada's Second World War since the early 1980s with McGill's Robert Vogel. The first of their multi-volume history of the Canadian Army, *Maple Leaf Route*, was published in 1983, and it analyzed the Normandy campaign; others in the series carried the story forward to the liberation of the Dutch. Copp had started his career as a lauded social historian, and he faced strident opposition from his academic colleagues when he turned to studying military history. However, he later said that he and Vogel were tenured professors who "could ignore the negative reaction of colleagues who shared the view that military history was not a legitimate field in Canadian academia."[22] After talking to veterans and studying the campaigns, Copp returned to the primary sources for a re-evaluation of the Canadians fighting in Northwest Europe, as well as other Allied formations. He combined those findings in the archives with oral histories, aerial photographs of Normandy, and walks on the battlegrounds. After decades of study, Copp emerged as Canada's most prominent historian of the army, with two groundbreaking histories, *Fields of Fire* (2003) and *Cinderella Army* (2006), which showed how the Canadians had been as good as the British and Americans, and at times much better.[23]

As part of this movement to restore a voice to military historians, Copp established an academic publication, which he and managing editor Mike Bechthold called a "journal-in-a-magazine-format," in order to reach a wider audience. *Canadian Military History* (1992) has had broad appeal outside the ivory towers of academia. In its pages, academics, gifted amateurs, and veterans have analyzed everything from combat and battle to the home front, along with the legacy of war and experiences of individuals.

Just as academic and public interest in the Second World War was renewed in the mid-1990s, veterans were dying at a more rapid rate. In 1995, the average age of Second World War veterans was

A Veterans Affairs bilingual poster from the early 1990s imploring Canadians to "Remember." But it was not clear what young people were to remember.

seventy-four, and Legion Halls were shuttering across the country as old age waged a relentless war. While there were 501,690 veterans counted in the country—455,107 male and 46,583 female—in August 1995, *Legion* reported that "the Royal Canadian Legion is in a battle for survival."[24]

The November 11.Remembrance Day ceremonies were still important events for the veterans, and poppies remained an outward symbol worn by millions of Canadians. Veterans also came together during the unity crisis of 1995, when Quebec separatist politicians held a referendum (the second of its kind) to break away from Canada and create a new country. Invoking the sacrifice of old, with English and French serving together, the Legion leaned in heavily to keep Quebec in Canada. The 27,000 members of the Legion's Quebec Command were especially active in promoting unity during the lead-up to the referendum, with talks, paid advertisements, and members working hard to get out the vote.[25] Other Legion commands also devoted time and energy to the fight for Canada, with Lieutenant-Governor Frederick Russell of Newfoundland, a Second World War RCAF pilot, recounting publicly, "It has been said that every Canadian who risked his life to serve his country is still a hero today. Most of us do not care about being heroes, but we all must continue to ensure that the lives of our comrades were not lost for nothing."[26]

The country was nearly lost on October 30, 1995, but slightly more Quebeckers voted to stay than to go, and the close margin was a shock to Canadians. There was a renewed desire to both accommodate Quebec's demands for recognition and make it more difficult to separate. Across the country, Canadians debated about what made us distinct: what was the glue that kept the country from tearing itself apart as many other nations were doing in the 1990s? Some said that the fragmentation of history had allowed shared bonds to erode. Veterans and their supporters had their own take on the near-death of Canada, feeling that the lack of knowledge about Canada's sacrifice in the Second World War was a missed opportunity for Canadians to come together. One Legionnaire, April Bremner of Vancouver, who was not a veteran but who contributed to her local Legion Hall, felt strongly about the need to pass the stories on. "It saddens me to find that so many young Canadians have no concept of the sacrifices made on our behalf by veterans. Those who served in WWI, WWII, and the Korean War should be telling their stories or writing them down for their children and grandchildren. Without this personal touch, young Canadians will think of it as dry history."[27] Time was running out. Invigorated by their rapturous reception in Holland, veterans began to lobby for a permanent museum to document and explain their war experiences for future generations.

The Canadian War Museum (CWM) had been a focal point of remembrance and commemoration in Ottawa during the anniversary years, hosting events for veterans and programs for the city. In May 1995, the museum opened *Victory!*, which presented the hard-fought end of the war, with a focus on the Canadian liberation of the Netherlands. It was attended by Her Royal Highness Princess Margriet of the Netherlands, and it further raised awareness of the Second World War.[28] But those attending the CWM exhibition in the old castle-like building could not help but notice the dark interiors, the threadbare exhibitions, the fluctuating climate control, and the weird groans coming from the cast-iron radiators and old-fashioned pipe coils heated by steam or hot water—all of which made the building unsuitable as a national museum. In fact, years before in 1988, *Legion* had labelled it "shabby and shunned."[29]

For those who had visited the magnificent Imperial War Museum in London or recognized the peerless and prominent place of the Australian War Memorial in Canberra, Australia, the CWM appeared all the more run-down and neglected. Professional academic military historians sneered that the galleries offered a potted history of the past, replete with factual errors, outdated interpretations, and the omission of many meaningful stories. There was little on the home-front experience, and almost none of the new military history, with its emphasis on the social history of service personnel. The exhibitions largely ended in 1945, neglecting the Korean War, the Cold War, and peacekeeping. Second World War veterans were shocked to find that even parts of their war were not presented, with the Italian campaign depicted mostly

The Canadian War Museum in Ottawa housed the country's national collection of military artifacts, art, and other war-related material, but it had long been neglected; by the late 1980s, it was described as "shabby and shunned." Veterans wanted a new museum to present their history.

through an unsatisfying diorama of a Canadian soldier guarding a dejected Italian prisoner. The close to 100,000 Canadian soldiers fighting in Italy—with the battles of Ortona, the smashing of the Hitler Line, and the breaking of the Gothic Line—were reduced to no more than military police. Those who defended the museum talked openly of how the CWM had been starved of resources for decades. More recently, as part of the Canadian Museum of Civilization Corporation, most of the available funding in the 1980s had gone into the new Canadian Museum of Civilization in Gatineau, Quebec, which had building-cost overruns into the many millions and opened in 1989 with few completed exhibitions. With all eyes on architect Douglas Cardinal's swirling stone museum across the Ottawa River, the fusty and musty CWM slipped further into decrepitude.

The Canadian Museum of Civilization reflected museum trends at the time and was occasionally derided as "Disney North" for its focus on entertainment rather than historical interpretation.[30] The main permanent exhibition was Canada Hall, which presented the story of the country's history from early contact to the mid-twentieth century through the lens of social history and a series of reconstructed historical dioramas.[31] It featured almost no political or military history, which was consistent with the lack of interest in national history in the universities that had steadily diminished the value of teaching military, diplomatic, and political history. It was as if those subjects had been cast as irrelevant, old, and unnecessary to understanding the Canadian project. The museum curators assumed that Canada Hall—the primary means by which millions would learn about the past—need barely mention a single prime minister, constitutional evolution, or the two world wars.

Meanwhile, at the Canadian War Museum, Director General Victor Suthren had spent years trying to make bricks with little straw. The creation of the National Gallery had eaten into the CWM's parking lot, so it had no space for visitors, and it had also lost its Trophies Building, where many of the large vehicles had been on display since the museum's opening in 1942.[32] Instead, these tanks, trucks, and artillery pieces were relocated to a decrepit bus warehouse several kilometres from the main building, grandiosely named Vimy House. Visitorship dropped to about 125,000 in the early 1990s, from at least double that at the high-water mark.[33] When there had been funds, Suthren, a student of nineteenth-century naval warfare, put the limited resources into historical re-enactments. In his mind, these living history pageants, with staff or volunteers dressed as period-piece soldiers or sailors, raised the profile of the museum among the general public. But by those who felt the money should be directed towards upgrading the derelict exhibitions, he was mocked, as former CWM curator Hugh Halliday said, as a "Mr. Dressup," whose imaginary battles trivialized history while the real stories were left untold.[34]

In response to the veterans' complaints from the late 1980s, Ottawa established the Task Force on Military History Museum Collections in Canada in April 1991. It included historian Desmond Morton and former chief of the defence staff General Ramsey Withers, and was co-chaired by Denis Vaugeois, a publisher and historian, and G. Hamilton Southam, a Second World War veteran and patron of many cultural institutions. The task force crisscrossed the country, talking and listening to veterans, museum specialists, and historians, and within six months it published its report, which condemned the national museum in Ottawa as an "embarrassment" whose "long history of neglect is regrettable."[35] The report and its undiplomatic language garnered much media attention, and it was widely commented upon that the CWM had been shortchanged of funds for years.[36] The committee recommended a new building be erected near the Aviation Museum to the east of the downtown core and the relationship with the Canadian Museum of Civilization be severed. It also argued that more historians had to be hired to engage in research to upgrade the galleries, which were labelled as "catering only to the interest of a narrow segment of the population." It was necessary to move beyond cases of weapons and uniforms to a deeper engagement with the ways that war had shaped Canada; that, in turn, would stimulate a broader understanding of the country's military history.[37] The Legion welcomed the recommendations, especially after one veteran described the state of the museum as "an insult to the memory of the thousands of Canadians who gave their lives for this country."[38]

The federal government was swimming in debt in the early 1990s and was wary of the Canadian Museum of Civilization's cost overruns. The cabinet had little interest in building a new war museum. And so it fell to Victor Suthern, who set out to rejuvenate and expand the existing museum, hoping to capitalize on the surprise interest in the Second World War in 1994 and the next year. With almost $2 million from the Canadian Museum of Civilization Corporation, whose leaders were stung by the task force's report and its calls to separate the CWM from the larger corporation, the museum staff upgraded the exhibitions, although the existing galleries were too small to engage in substantial additions.[39] Suthren had loftier goals, hoping for a new theatre, a gallery to hang some of the thousands of original artworks from the two world wars, and a post-1945 exhibition space to explore the Cold War and the search for peace.

Another aspect of the museum upgrades concerned the depiction of the Holocaust. With the successful 1993 launch of Washington's Holocaust Museum, which told the story of the Jewish people and others killed in the Holocaust, there was a desire to mark this genocide as an enduring warning.[40] In London, the Imperial War Museum was planning a Holocaust gallery and it was felt that the CWM might follow suit. Internal museum discussions began in late 1996, with Suthren and the head of the Museum of Civilization, George MacDonald, supported by the board of directors led by Adrienne Clarkson, a celebrity broadcaster and future governor general, agreeing to launch a public fundraising campaign to upgrade the museum. It would include revitalized galleries and a new Holocaust exhibition space. Little did the museum's leaders know that the campaign would involve them in a fierce debate about the purpose of a war museum, about whose memories were being preserved, and about anti-Semitism in Canada.

The Holocaust had been a uniquely brutal illustration of the Nazi's horrific ideology. Immediately after the war, few survivors had been able to talk about it, so great had been the ordeal. However, the Adolf Eichmann trial of 1961, brought about by Israeli agents capturing the senior Nazi (who had played a key role in implementing the "final solution") in Argentina, garnered attention around the world.[41] The trial, held in Jerusalem, and his execution on May 31, 1962, were important moments for survivors to talk about the legacy of trauma. There was a new impetus for Jewish people to record the testimonies and eyewitness accounts of those who lived through the Holocaust, and archives of remembrance were created around the world.[42] Further interest was stirred by the 1978

multi-part television series *Holocaust*, which was seen by a staggering number of viewers, estimated at 120 million in Britain, France,
and North America. When it was broadcast the next year in West
Germany, about half the adult population watched it, learning more
about this dark chapter in human history.[43]

From early 1996, the Canadian War Museum's efforts to court
donors extended to targeting Dutch Canadians to raise $2 million
for a Netherlands Memorial Theatre. Its appeal to the Jewish community came with a promise to build a permanent Holocaust exhibition. On February 1, 1997, the *Ottawa Citizen* ran a story about
the museum turning to Jews in what appeared to be a funding
appeal directly related to a promised future exhibition on the
Holocaust. The Canadian Press picked up the story, amplifying the
notion of a quid pro quo deal to a national audience. CWM historian Fred Gaffen and Irving Abella, a York University historian and
specialist on Jewish history in Canada, argued for the need for such
an exhibition. "It has taken time for old biases to fade," said Gaffen,
"and for Canada to become a more tolerant society." A February
6, 1997, *Ottawa Citizen* editorial headlined "Lest We Forget"
argued, "on its own, the creation of the gallery is an important
recognition of a part of our past many Canadians might rather not
acknowledge. And it will go further, challenging Canadians to think
about individual responsibility, looking at other victims of the
Nazis, including gypsies, Slavs and homosexuals, and even touching
on modern examples of genocide, including those in Bosnia and
Rwanda. . . . The gallery's opening would be the right occasion, and
the gallery itself a fitting place for a formal apology for Canada's
history of at least semi-official anti-Semitism."[44] A few days later,
on February 10, Victor Suthren was interviewed by Peter Gzowski
on the CBC's popular radio program *Morningside*, with its reach of

1.2 million listeners. The two discussed the importance of a new Holocaust gallery while also creating an exhibition area within which to highlight other genocides in human history.

Around this time, both CBS's *60 Minutes* and *Dateline NBC* aired stories on "Canada's dark secret": the entry of Nazi war criminals into the country after the war and the haphazard role of federal authorities in prosecuting them. The *Ottawa Citizen* observed that Canada was being portrayed in US news programs as a "haven for Nazis."[45] As Ottawa's indifference to the Nazis living in Canada was revealed, a renewed hunt began to bring war criminals to justice. This scandal bled into the discourse surrounding the CWM's proposed Holocaust gallery in early 1997, and several news stories highlighted the "problem of war criminals," which one journalist contended would have to be addressed at the CWM. Victor Suthren was drawn into the controversy, far from his area of expertise, and he said of the Holocaust, "We can't demonize the German people and say, 'It's only you guys that created an atmosphere of prejudice and hatred,' because it's more a problem of Western society and to a degree, Canada shares in that." Suthren noted that there had been opposition within the war museum in the past to explore these issues, but he replied, "We view this as a large-scale human tragedy" and that the expanded war museum should address the matter.[46]

Some veterans grew concerned about what they viewed as "activist history." They felt that the museum, which had publicly shared its proposals to raise money from Dutch and Jewish Canadians, was turning to special-interest groups and allowing them to "buy" their way into the museum—in effect, giving money to have their stories told. Additional leaked plans also showed that the Holocaust gallery had grown from a modest 2,000 square feet to more than 4,000 square feet, which would have made it larger than the First World War or Second World War galleries.[47] Suthren publicly rejected the quid pro quo allegation, but the issue could not be buried. Equally damaging was the public view expressed by Cliff Chadderton, the CEO of the War Amps, who had emerged as the most recognized warrior of veterans' rights. He complained that the museum was going far beyond its mandate of telling Canada's military history.[48] Other veterans questioned whether the Holocaust was really a part of Canadian military history, suggesting that the gallery belonged in the Museum of Civilization.

Opposition to the Holocaust gallery was muted over the summer of 1997, but it erupted again after a $12 million upgrade

An open grave at Bergen-Belsen. Canadians were involved in liberating Bergen-Belsen, and in the war to free the people of Europe, but some Canadian veterans worried that placing a Holocaust gallery in a refurbished Canadian War Museum would overshadow Canada's military history that spanned hundreds of years.

for the CWM was announced on November 13, 1997, by Adrienne Clarkson, chair of the board of trustees for the Canadian Museum of Civilization Corporation. The new funding would expand the entire exhibition gallery space from 7,545 to 12,800 square feet, create a glass dome to enclose the courtyard in front of the museum, unveil a new Memorial Chamber to mark Canadians killed in time of war, establish an art gallery, and move forward with the Holocaust gallery. "Canadians played a major role in defeating the Nazi regime and ending the Holocaust," said Clarkson. "At the eve of the new millennium, we need to ensure that we continue to learn from the horrors of the past."[49]

Even though many millions of dollars would now fund additional exhibition space devoted to the country's military history, especially in the second half of the twentieth century, the veterans continued to react violently to the idea of the Holocaust gallery. They complained that they had not been consulted, and many feared that the civilian administrators and curators at the museum were undermining their wartime contribution and shifting the museum's focus towards the Holocaust and other genocides.

One day before the official CWM announcement, the War Amps released its comments on "a difficult controversy." Executive director Cliff Chadderton's objections were twofold: that the Holocaust would draw away from exhibitions that "promote Canada's military heritage" and that a Holocaust gallery should not be "part of a War Museum."[50] Chadderton viewed the proposed Holocaust gallery as another way that Canada's military history would again be pushed to the periphery.

Most of the newspapers tread cautiously around the veterans' anger, suggesting that while the country's war history had to be presented, the Holocaust was entwined with Canadian and world history. The *Winnipeg Free Press* felt that it was strange for veterans to object to a Holocaust gallery that included an upgrade to the Second World War exhibition.[51] After all, that was what veterans had been demanding for years. The *Free Press* also believed that "because there are those who would deny the Holocaust, it is important to let future generations know that it really did happen." Situating the story of the Holocaust within the country's war museum was an opportunity to tell that story. "A Holocaust memorial, carefully and intelligently designed, would enrich and strengthen the National War Museum."[52]

Irving Abella wrote an editorial in *The Globe and Mail* on November 22, 1997, condemning the veterans' negative reaction to the Holocaust gallery. "Canadian war veterans are doing themselves an injustice when they reject the construction of a small Holocaust section in a revamped Canadian War Museum in Ottawa. Canadian servicemen and women were instrumental in the fight against Nazism and helped in the liberation of inmates from slave-labour camps and concentration camps."[53] Abella felt that the CWM should certainly focus on Canadian military history but scolded that "those veterans who, for reasons that remain unclear, claim Canada had little or no role in stopping Hitler's tyrannical and murderous campaign against Jews, gypsies and other '*untermenschen*' [inferior people] are not just wrong; they are in fact denying their own military accomplishments." Canadians, he noted, were involved in the liberation, if that is the right word, of some of the death camps, primarily Bergen-Belsen. At the same time, "The Holocaust has become the seminal point from which a new understanding of the devastation of war has emerged." Other Jewish organizations stood behind Abella, and described their hurt at claims that the Holocaust was not part of Canadian history.

George MacDonald, CEO of the Museum of Civilization, wrote a letter to the *Toronto Star* that appeared in the November 28, 1997, edition, saying, "There is a curious perception emerging from recent commentaries that museum officials are quashing proud military traditions and discrediting World War II veterans." That was not the case, he contended, especially since museum staff were expanding coverage of Canadian military history, including that of the Second World War.[54] A new museum wing devoted to the Holocaust would only further enrich the understanding of Canadian service personnel having fought on the side of good. But he also noted that "now and in the future, the Canadian War Museum is, and must be, a national museum for all Canadians."[55] MacDonald was stating in guarded language that the museum did not belong only to the veterans and that it must speak to all Canadians.

The veterans had their own defenders. Journalists David Frum and Peter Worthington, long-time supporters of veterans, both wrote on December 2, 1997, in response to the *Toronto Star* and other stories, that the veterans were being unjustly vilified and abused. The newspaper war was heated. Both Worthington and Frum felt that the Holocaust gallery and the supposed ill treatment of service personnel was "another slap at war veterans" and a continuation of the assault by misguided or malicious museum staff who were, they believed, intellectually aligned with the McKenna brothers.

By the end of 1997, both the CWM and the Museum of Civilization were in full damage control. MacDonald fired Suthren over his handling of the issue, but the museum clung precariously to its position and continued to speak publicly of the large-scale expansion that would include the Holocaust gallery.[56] The fierce public battle continued, as supporters railed at how the gallery was necessary to combat systemic racism, while opponents argued that the focus on the Holocaust would blot out Canada's wartime contributions, as well as a Canadian war history spanning several centuries. Some of the debate was tinged by anti-Semitism, with accusations by some that Jewish people were trying to impose their history, through the Holocaust, on the memory of the Second World War.

Frustrated veterans turned to allies in the Senate. In early February 1998, the Senate sub-committee on veterans' affairs held public meetings over several days to explore the issue. It was clear from the opening remarks that the senators were sympathetic to the veterans' discomfort with the Holocaust gallery, with Senator Orville Phillips claiming publicly that "many veterans are concerned that the Canadian War Museum has strayed from its original goals and objectives: to preserve and promote our shared history of Canada at war and to commemorate the ultimate sacrifice made by many men and women."[57] Around fifty individual witnesses and organizations testified before the committee and almost all were against the creation of a separate Holocaust gallery, arguing that it would overpower the story of Canada's military history, which was more comprehensive than simply the Second World War.[58] The representative of the Sir Arthur Pearson Association of War Blinded testified, "We have difficulty with the suggestion that the Holocaust was central to the Second World War. The membership of the Sir Arthur Pearson Association, all war-blinded persons, saw a great deal of war until they lost their sight, but they wish to make it clear that they knew little or nothing about the Holocaust." Other groups, such as the Canadian Peacekeeping Veterans Association and the Federation of Military and United Services Institutes of Canada, were firmly against the Holocaust gallery, on the grounds that the museum had to cover more than just the Second World War, and that the entire peacekeeping story was absent.

In its final May 1998 report, "Guarding History," the Senate committee concluded that the Canadian effort during the Second World War was separate from the Holocaust. [59] It sided with the vocal veterans that this was an unfortunate avenue of engagement for the museum that would only further diminish Canada's military history. Throughout the hearings, there was, observed CWM historian Cameron Pulsifer, a widely held view among veterans that the museum bureaucrats were "seeking to impose sanitized, politically correct exhibits on the CWM, intended to deflect attention away from the accomplishments of Canadians in battle."[60] A few days after the Senate hearings, and several months before the report, the museum board announced that the expansion had been put on hold. Behind the scenes, it had come to the inescapable conclusion

"It's Our War" declares this Second World War poster, telling all Canadians to support the war effort. More than fifty years later, some veterans questioned who should tell the story of "our war" and what story should be presented, and they wondered where Canadians would learn about it.

that the Holocaust gallery was political dynamite, pitting veterans against the museum and veterans against Jewish groups. Most of the $12 million was withdrawn from the project and the existing CWM limped forward, although now very much in the public eye. Adrienne Clarkson said of the museum's retreat: "I sympathize totally with the veterans who feel they don't want to be forgotten," she said. "They will not be forgotten, that is our commitment."[61]

The maelstrom of debate that centred on the museum's attempt to upgrade its exhibitions and add different facets to the galleries was a sign of the veterans demanding greater control over their history. *The Valour and the Horror* had stolen a march on creating a version of the past that offended the veterans, but the successful ceremonies and pilgrimages to mark important anniversaries had sparked a surprising interest in veterans and Canada's war history. With veterans dying in large numbers from old age, there had been a compelling wish to build a proper museum to tell their stories. But now the plan lay in ruins, largely at the hands of veterans. And yet, as the smoke settled on the controversy, talk in the veterans' community of a new war museum rekindled, although few could imagine Ottawa stepping up quickly to meet the demand after the painfully public war of words. Bill Vradenburg, a veteran who was a guide at the CWM, thought the government was waiting for him and his colleagues to die out. "Our military history should be taught standing proudly, but go into the schools and you will be appalled at the abysmal lack of knowledge about the sacrifices so many people made. I'm too old to make enough noise to make a difference, but I will say this: The disregard of our veterans is disgraceful—and damn near sacrilegious."[62]

CHAPTER 16

SITES OF MEMORY

C anada's national monument on Vimy Ridge has stood since its unveiling in 1936 as a recognizable memorial to the country's dead and a symbol of a hard-fought victory by Canadian soldiers. With its still-shattered landscape, preserved trenches, and underground tunnels, Vimy is one of the few battlescapes left mostly intact on the Western Front. For decades, it has been a site of mourning, memory, and sojourning, although it, too, rose and fell within Canadian consciousness. But even from the 1950s to the 1980s, when few visited Vimy, it has always been there, waiting for Canadians to return. Vimy remains a site of martial pride and a place to bear witness to all that the Great War contradictorily represents: deep sorrow and sweeping pride, disunity and the path to nationhood. The monument is also Canada's ambassador in Europe, reminding the Western Europeans, Britain, and our other allies of a time when half a million Canadians left their homes to cross the Atlantic to fight in a cause of liberal justice, standing shoulder to shoulder with our allies, dying together as they drove Germany out of Belgium and France.

By the 1990s, Vimy was drawing 750,000 visitors a year, almost all French and British. They came to Canada's battlesite to learn of

*Canada's national monument overseas at Vimy Ridge in France is a
towering, majestic memorial to the Great War fallen. It is also a silent
ambassador to Europeans that speaks louder than any politician to
Canada's service and sacrifice. Why did successive federal governments
never deem it necessary to build a similar memorial to Canada's service,
contributions, and legacy of the Second World War?*

our history and contributions. This was the country that rarely
talked about its success, other than in the hockey arena, and many
visitors must have wondered where the equivalent Second World
War memorial was to Canada's enormous contributions in that terrible but necessary war. If they did not know about Canada's even
greater wartime contribution from 1939 to 1945, with another generation shedding blood to liberate Europeans, it was not their fault,
since Canadians had done a terrible job in telling their own story.

Attempts had been made in the past to build a Second World War
national overseas memorial of some sort, with the Canadian

Legion suggesting Dieppe in the 1950s, but this idea found little purchase with various governments. One of the challenges acknowledged by all who desired an overseas memorial was where to put it. The Great War was defined by the battles on the Western Front, with key engagements at Ypres, Vimy, and Amiens. Vimy was chosen for several reasons, but primarily because it was the first time the four divisions of the Canadian Corps fought together. It was also the first clear-cut victory, a place where the Canadians succeeded and where the French and British had not; as well, the ridge and surrounding area were largely uninhabitable and offered a commanding view of the terrain. But where would a Second World War monument be erected? If Dieppe were chosen, the 100,000 Canadians who served in the Italian campaign or the 10,000 or so in the Far East would not be properly included. What about those involved in the liberation of the Dutch or the fight into Germany; or the war at sea around the world, or the bombing of German cities and infrastructure? Despite the importance of those far-flung battlefields, the answer seemed clear after the fortieth and fiftieth anniversaries in Normandy. Juno Beach had been the nexus for the Canadians, the point where on June 6, 1944, Canadian army, navy, and air force units had fought together as part of the Great Crusade to liberate Europe. It was a place where Canadians stood as equals with the Americans and British. And yet in a shocking display of neglect of history and Canada's self-interest, various federal governments expressed little enthusiasm for building a monument there to that generation of warriors.

The Americans had more foresight. Since 1923, the American Battle Monuments Commission (ABMC) has been erecting monuments and cemeteries on overseas battlefields and in the United States. While the ABMC marks many wars, it had a large presence in Normandy, especially at the American invasion beaches: Point du Hoc, Utah Beach American Memorial, and the Normandy American Cemetery.[1] A few memorials to the Canadian liberators were erected in France, but they tended to mark the liberation of a village or town by a specific Canadian unit. In Belgium, the Netherlands, and Germany, there were almost none.[2]

In 1992, the grand museum in Caen, Le Mémorial, opened to tell the story of the clash in Normandy. Caen had been a primary battleground, and much of the city was destroyed in the month-long campaign after the D-Day landings as the Germans used it as a fortress in their defensive lines. Finally, on July 8, the Canadians and British surged forward to capture it in fierce fighting that extended over several days. And yet, bewilderingly, the Canadian contribution to Allied victory was almost entirely absent from the museum, and no Canadians attended the opening. In contrast, the Americans were an oversized presence. At Caen, a large and elaborate memorial garden was erected to mark the American contributions to victory, even though they had landed and fought more than fifty kilometres to the southwest. The French authorities were uncomfortable with the large shadow cast by the Americans—and with the Canadian absence—and they turned to Ottawa to inquire if the federal government might like to participate in a commemorative project to honour its soldiers. But Ottawa declined, once again failing to raise the profile of the Canadians who fought in Normandy.

As word of this neglect emerged in the media, Gordon Hamilton Southam, a Second World War veteran, diplomat, and founder of the National Gallery, was motivated to action. He and several other veterans created the Canadian Battle of Normandy Foundation (CBNF) in 1992. Responding to the lack of Canadian presence in Normandy, and then fuelled by the anger over *The*

Valour and the Horror, the foundation set out to trumpet the Canadian contributions to the Allied victory.

The CBNF, later known as the Canadian Battlefields Foundation (CBF), raised money and created partnerships, especially with Terry Copp, a professor of military history at Wilfrid Laurier University, who published the first Canadian battlefield guide of Normandy in 1994. With it, the history of the Canadian battles could be read while standing on the land the soldiers had fought on fifty years earlier. Battlefield tours were also offered to Canadian university students, with the first run in 1995 by Copp and Serge Durflinger, later an historian at the Canadian War Museum, professor at University of Ottawa, and author of several books on Canada's Second World War. The tours continue to this day and have been an important teaching tool for young scholars, exposing them to the rich and emotional experience of learning on the battlefields, where they debate tactical decisions and the cost of fighting in Normandy, and, more recently, in Italy. Mike Bechthold, a student participant on the first CBNF tour in 1995 and a future historian, once observed a young student at the foot of her grandfather's headstone in Italy: "It was a very powerful and moving moment. Though she'd never met him, you could tell her affection for him ran deep."[3]

The Canadian Battlefields Foundation also raised funds for a modest memorial at Caen. Unveiled in May 1995, the Canadian Memorial Garden received mixed reviews, with some comparing it unfavourably to the Vimy Memorial. It also lacked the raw immediacy of Beaumont Hamel, a haunting battlefield still scarred with trenches and broken ground where the Newfoundland Regiment had been destroyed on the first day of the Battle of the Somme, July 1, 1916. And yet Canada's memorial garden was never so ambitious—although it might have been if Ottawa had been more interested in funding it.⁴ A grove of trees leads to water running over sixteen black stones inscribed in Latin: "No day will erase your generation from our memory." The running water is part of the large garden that stretches 38 metres wide, accessed by a winding, narrow path leading up to a terrace. There, another bilingual inscription reads: "Liberation Comes from the Sea," accompanied by a list of more than a hundred Norman towns and villages freed by the Canadians.

Canada has slowly reclaimed aspects of its history in Normandy, but there is a marked absence of even small plaques and memorials on other battlefields.⁵ The difficult clearing of the Channel ports—a task that Field Marshal Bernard Montgomery gave to the Canadians as he sought the glory of Operation Market Garden and a rapid victory in September 1944—was an accomplishment little noticed and even less present in the social memory of Canadians. The crucial battle for the Scheldt, which took place from early October to November 8, saw fighting of the worst kind, through thigh-deep mud and water reminiscent of Passchendaele a generation earlier, and is almost entirely unmarked by the Canadian government. So, too, is First Canadian Army's part in the final campaigns into Germany.⁶

All the founding veterans of the CBF are now dead, but their work continues to raise awareness of the memory of the war. Without attention and persistence, history will fade and flicker away. There must be guardians of memory who struggle, build, and sacrifice to keep the memory alive.

Aside from a few gardens and plaques, Canada had mostly written itself out of the Normandy campaign through its short-sighted neglect to build monuments or other sites of memory for the more than one million visitors a year who travelled to the Normandy region. But there was a darker place of bereavement beyond Juno Beach, which emerged to greater prominence towards the end of the century. The Abbaye d'Ardenne, with its vaulted dome, clean gothic lines, and a history stretching over 800 years, was a place of foreboding. The weight of the executions of Canadian soldiers in early June 1944 by Kurt Meyer's Nazi soldiers hangs as a heavy presence.

Small groups of Canadians had visited the abbey for many years, but it was in private hands and, before Copp's 1994 guidebook remedied the situation, infrequently marked on maps or tour guides. The murder of the Canadian prisoners by Meyer's 12th SS Division had been allowed to fade from memory—and over time, the Abbaye d'Ardenne was largely forgotten by Canadians too. But when Canadians found their way to the abbey, the owners, the Vicos brothers, offered tours and talks. Jean-Marie, Michael, and Jacques all carried a strong sense of debt to their liberators, as their family had been a part of the French Resistance and had seen the Gestapo murder friends. The Vicos always went out of their way to welcome the handful of Canadian tourists or veterans who travelled to the site each year.

In 1984, Normandy veteran Stanley Hughes visited the abbey where he, as a twenty-two-year-old private with the North Nova Scotia Highlanders, had been interrogated after his capture on June 7, forty years earlier. He had watched as two comrades next to him were selected, taken away, and murdered. Hughes was spared and sent to a PoW camp. "You say to yourself, 'Why them? Why not me?'" And yet Hughes, haunted by what had happened there, felt compelled to come back, no matter how painful it was. "I was looking for something, I guess, something of myself that I left here."[7]

*The dark memorial at the Abbaye d'Ardenne recognizes the execution of
Canadian soldiers during the opening phase of the Battle of Normandy.*

Colonel Ian Campbell, a commanding officer of the 4th
Canadian Service Battalion in Germany, explored the abbey in
1979 and was moved to action when he found no official
Canadian memorial there. Even the names of the Canadians were
not recorded. After nearly two decades of research, Campbell
published *Murder at the Abbaye* (1996), seeking to reclaim his
forgotten countrymen from Nazi victims to the soldiers they once
were. Campbell tracked down the families of those killed and
was able to publish their personal letters and archival material.
In an act of retrieving a difficult history, Campbell wrote, "These
twenty men, who went away to that war over half a century ago,
were very real people. They were extraordinarily ordinary and
totally unremarkable men. . . . Their deaths were tragic, but to
forget them, or to remember them only as faceless statistics, is
more tragic still."[8]

The Abbaye d'Ardenne is a place that stirs emotions. It is a memorial, but one that gathers its meaning from atrocity. Those who attend feel a strong presence of loss. It is a reminder of the evil that the Canadians fought against during the war, although that larger idea is not easy to grasp within the cool shade and gently swaying trees. Many memorials bring closure, but this is a site of memory that remains an open wound. And yet it beckons Canadians. Since the 1990s, annual anniversary ceremonies have been held in that poignant place, supported by the Canadian Battlefields Foundation and Veterans Affairs Canada. "There is a curtain of sadness that pervades the garden, a physical feeling almost," said Jan Goertzen, a student on one of the CBF tours. "It's quiet and cool and shaded, but it is not a comfortable place. It's as if, and excuse the imagination, we can only see one face of the garden and the Canadian soldiers' souls inhabit another plane. We can feel them, but not see them."[9] And another student, who was around the age of most of the executed Canadian soldiers, remarked, "No one had to tell us to stand mute. The garden speaks volumes of silence."[10]

The 1980s saw a significant change in how history and heritage were studied in Canada and around the world. Some scholars have called this "the memory turn" or "the memory boom," and it led to a renewed interest in the past, specifically in the world wars. At the same time, the history was often contested and challenged by different groups, with neglected stories intersecting with national politics and identity in the present. In Canada, the Japanese-Canadian redress movement and the merchant mariners' fight for veteran status were most prominent, and this politicized engagement with the legacy of the war raised the profile of these two groups and their contested history. It was important to uncover injustice, but in Canada this led to the further displacement of the idea of Canada's Necessary War. Instead of grappling with difficult events of the past, Canada seemed only willing to engage in hand-wringing, teeth-gnashing and apology. Canadians struggled to make meaning of the country's wartime actions and consequences, even as other nations turned to the war as a touchstone of culture, heritage, and history.

The Americans had always been very good at telling their war history, but in 1998 Steven Spielberg's *Saving Private Ryan* revolutionized war films. Several popular Second World War films were released in the 1990s—in particular *Memphis Belle* (1990), *Stalingrad* (1993), and the epic Holocaust movie *Schindler's List* (1993)—but Spielberg and actor Tom Hanks, with historian Stephen Ambrose as consultant, turned their sights on D-Day and the Normandy battles. With its shaky, blood-splattered camerawork and a cacophony of battle sounds, the film captured the raw destruction and gut-wrenching courage of the Americans at Omaha Beach on June 6, 1944. The first twenty-seven minutes of *Saving Private Ryan* are arguably among the greatest scenes in cinema history, and the blockbuster film, which won critical and commercial success, shared the trauma and bravery of the Second World War with a whole new generation. The movie unleashed a floodgate of emotions in veterans, some of whom finally found the words to talk about their own long-buried war experiences. And many younger people listened.

Just as in *The Longest Day* (1962), the Americans in *Saving Private Ryan* were again rescuing Europe from fascism. This was American exceptionalism at its best and a victory with purpose.[11] As one American veteran said, "It is a story of courage, bravery, and heroism. It is a story about soldiers. It is a story about America."[12] America, indeed. It would be absurd to criticize Spielberg or Hanks for not offering a documentary-like balanced coverage of the Americans, British, and Canadians on D-Day, but the triumph of *Saving Private Ryan* again stirred the realization among Canadian veterans that they had been written out of history.

The impact of *Saving Private Ryan* was another stark example of how the country's cultural producers had done a poor job of telling the Canadian war story. The CBC and NFB, funded annually with hundreds of millions of taxpayers' dollars, seemed particularly culpable. When Canadians did talk about the war, it was about defeat and disgrace, with Dieppe and the relocation of Japanese Canadians often taught as a warning—a lesson about how the British did us in, and about how war leads to the diminishment of civil liberties. One reviewer of *Saving Private Ryan* in *The Globe and Mail* snickered about the propensity of Canadians to talk of ignominy instead of heroics: "The unschooled may emerge from *Private Ryan* asking what Canadians were doing on June 6 while the American soldiers were pushing ashore through a barrage of Nazi shells, mines and bullets." While thousands of Canadians were fighting on the beaches, in the air, and at sea, our national broadcaster and filmmakers had all but ignored these deeds during the previous half-century. The reviewer, Steve Weatherbe, was scathing about the neglect by Canadian onscreen storytellers: "Our pop-culture elite at the CBC, the National Film Board, and the private production houses have been obsessively exposing Canadian war efforts as unmitigated disasters and frauds. A quick survey of Canadian film and TV treatments of the Second World War suggests that if we'd made *Saving Private Ryan*, the Allies never would have gotten off the beach."[13] If

Canadians did not know about the role of their grandfathers and grandmothers during the Second World War, it was not the fault of the Americans or the British. Canada was to blame.

While Canadians watched and appreciated *Saving Private Ryan* and other series, like the brilliant HBO-produced *Band of Brothers* (2001), more than a few groaned about why Canadians failed to tell their own stories. Where was the CBC? While its radio programs were acknowledged as some of the best in the world, most of the television series stayed far away from the country's rich, complex, and contested history. The exception to the rule was the seventeen-part series *Canada: A People's History* (2001). With a budget of over $25 million, it told the country's history vividly and passionately, with key stories illuminating the evolution of the nation-project. It was seen by millions, won awards, and was a valuable resource in classrooms. And it afforded suitable space to the world wars within the unfolding narrative of the nation. Predictably, academic historians condemned it for ignoring minority groups, regions, and questions of diversity. Some of the criticism was merited, and there was an obvious concentration on Quebec and Ontario in the post-Confederation episodes, but the academics offered few suggestions about what might have been cut to make way for everything that they thought should have been included.[14] History on television is no easy task, but *Canada: A People's History* was a good program, and the CBC should have been emboldened by its television triumph to engage in more attempts to tell Canadians about their history.[15] Its success showed that Canadians were hungry for their history, and yet, disgracefully, there has never been a dedicated CBC series to explore Canada's contribution during the Second World War. Surely that is an epic story that would stir greater understanding and compassion among Canadians for their own history and veterans, and one that might have forced politicians to think more deeply about how Canada needed to step up to tell its stories. In this vein, historian David Bercuson lamented in 2001 that with *Band of Brothers* being so brilliant, "the Canadian public, and more important, Canadian youth, is getting the message that the Americans won the Second World War." As he rightly noted, we seem unable to tell our own stories. "The problem lies not there but here. We literally do nothing."[16]

The post-1945 belief that the memory of the war was best preserved by functional structures rather than sacred stone monuments left the commemorative landscape bereft of sites by the end of the twentieth century. Over four decades, most of the libraries, arenas, and named spaces had either been replaced with more modern structures or their meaning long forgotten. The lack of the sacred had led to silence. However, in the aftermath of *The Valour and the Horror*, the fiftieth anniversary celebrations, and the awareness that Canada had allowed the Americans to claim the glory of liberating Europe, there was a renewed drive for an overseas monument. And if it was to be built before all the veterans passed away, it would have to be done by the veterans themselves.

D-Day gunner Garth Webb, who served with the 14th Field Regiment, Royal Canadian Artillery, set out to build a museum to the Canadians in Normandy. He was not impressed with the Canadian Memorial Garden erected at Caen, finding it too abstract and not sufficient for telling new generations about Canada's wartime efforts. Having made significant money in real estate in Toronto, Webb planned to build a memorial and museum at Courseulles-sur-Mer, where the Royal Winnipeg Rifles came ashore on D-Day. He began to spread the word and raise funds, even as the Canadian government declined to get involved. Undeterred, Webb and his small team reached out to Canadians directly and asked them to contribute. "The responses in the mail made me cry," recounted Lise Cooper, who had knitted socks for overseas soldiers during the war and was a crucial team member. "We'd receive a $10 cheque from someone in Newfoundland or B.C. and a note saying: 'I lost my brother there' or 'Bless you for doing this. It's something that should have been done ages ago.'"[17]

The donations came from across Canada and around the world, but it was well short of the $10 million needed for the centre. Webb turned to Walmart, the American superstore that had recently entered Canada by buying up the Woolco chain. Some Canadians disliked Walmart because of its American origins, its low wages for workers, and its pattern of driving out smaller competitors. Walmart, eager to win the hearts and minds of its customers, agreed to put special containers in its stores that encouraged shoppers to donate their coins and bills towards the Juno Beach Centre. The goodwill gesture initially raised $1.8 million for the project, with additional funds in subsequent years.[18]

Canadians were more attuned to Canada's wartime experiences overseas after the fiftieth anniversary commemorations, as evidenced by the emotional impact of a Bell Canada commercial that aired in the late 1990s. It featured a backpacking young man calling his grandfather, a veteran, in Canada, using a clunky portable phone from Dieppe. The strong sentiments between the youthful grandson and his granddad, who is overcome by the act of remembrance, struck a chord with viewers, and the TV ad became one of the most memorable of the decade. Webb continued to raise money by tapping into this strong emotional appeal that time was running out and the younger generations owed something to those who had sacrificed in the war.

Ottawa realized late in the game that it should not allow a private citizen to have control of Canada's commemorative face at Juno, but the bureaucrats had little leverage over Webb, who had already raised more than $5 million by 2001.[19] Stubborn and pugnacious, Webb was certain that working with civil servants would only interfere with his vision and delay the project. "We're not going to be here forever and we want this thing open," said Webb.[20] When Canadian historians became concerned that the museum might be built with no one other than Webb and his supporters having any say over the content, there was an attempt to offer curatorial services.[21] Webb refused and continued to act with vigour, eventually securing several million in financing from the regional governments in France and from Ottawa, and without diluting his vision underlying the project.

The Juno Beach Centre (JBC) opened on June 6, 2003, with much television coverage and 4,000 attendees, including Prime Minister Jean Chrétien and an estimated 1,000 Canadian veterans proudly wearing their medals. The veterans all paid their way; some joked they had come for free the first time in 1944. Widows came alone to stand on a beach that had always been a part of their lives, and children of veterans made the trip to spread a father's ashes. Chrétien spoke well of the "indomitable bravery and determination" of the veterans, but his words must have stung when he talked about the veterans who took it upon themselves to build the memorial because they "realized that while the acts of valour witnessed on this beach changed the course of history, there was no tangible evidence of what happened that day."[22]

The absence of any memorial had indeed left Canada without a visible reminder of the events half a century earlier, but successive federal governments stretching back to 1945 had stubbornly chosen not to tell the story of Canadians at Juno.

A crowd of veterans and civilians watched as tens of thousands of poppies, one for each of Canada's Second World War dead, drifted down and across the new building, an evocative and symbolic structure in the shape of a pentagon. Designed by Canadian architect Brian Chamberlain, the building's five-sided shape draws inspiration from the maple leaf and evokes the five beaches upon which the Allies landed. Wrapped in an outer shell of titanium, the concrete and steel structure has the look of a bunker. At the opening, veteran Bruce Melanson, who sat on the JBC board, mused sorrowfully that as "Gratifying as it is to see the centre up and running," he and his friends were "troubled that it took so much time, and so much arm twisting, to recognize Canada's role in the liberation of Europe—a role that took 45,000 lives from the more than one million who served." The JBC would help to present the history, but with large numbers of veterans dying from old age, said Melanson, "those who remain are trying to hold back a creeping tide of indifference."[23]

The Juno Beach Centre, opened in June 2003, finally gave Canada a physical presence at Juno. It would not have been built without veterans.

The Juno Beach Centre was a new outpost of commemoration in Normandy, a place where, eventually, hundreds of thousands of visitors would go to learn about Canada's role in the Second World War. But the museum initially featured wretchedly bad history texts that were riven with errors of interpretation and fact. While there were impressive installations—a darkened space that acted as a landing craft from which visitors emerged was particularly effective—the historical commentary was amateurish. In fact, one room devoted to prewar Canada appeared, according to two learned observers, "to have been developed by a left-wing Quebec nationalist determined to portray the country that went to war in 1939 in the most negative light possible."[24] Historian J.L. Granatstein, writing in the *National Post*, observed that "what little military history there is contains numerous errors."[25] It took at least a decade before the history presented was updated with more accurate interpretations, but most visitors seemed not to have noticed. After years of neglect, they could not tell historical truth from errors of interpretation or overreach.

Despite its interpretative shortcomings, the JBC pleased visitors who finally had a pilgrimage site. "Today, our vets and the Canadians who died in the war have a fitting memorial to recognize and preserve the memory of their great courage and effort," wrote Haligonian Diane Kenny, the proud daughter of an eighty-year-old Second World War veteran.[26] The Canadian liberation had never been forgotten by the grateful locals in France, but finally the Juno Beach Centre gave Canada a brick-and-mortar presence.[27] And yet the JBC would not have happened without veterans like Webb, who passed away in 2012. He and his comrades had fought for their history.

———

The Juno Beach Centre has gathered in importance since its unveiling, and Normandy has displaced Dieppe as the primary Second World War site of memory. Anniversary commemorations have been held at this Canadian enclave, including the large ceremonies in 2004 to mark the sixtieth anniversary (and the first time the Germans and Russians were officially invited to send delegations), the seventieth anniversary in 2014, and the seventy-fifth in 2019. The JBC has become a place to remind the world that Canada fought alongside Britain and the United States at the sharp end of the liberation of the oppressed people of Europe. Ottawa, too, has finally understood the value of marking such events; now, through government programs like Canada Remembers and the ongoing work of the CBF, young people are sent to attend these events, with the goal of passing the torch from one generation to the next. However, more work remains to be done: a survey around the time of the JBC opening indicated that only a third of adult Canadians knew that D-Day signalled the invasion of France, with many thinking erroneously that it had something to do with the bombing of Pearl Harbor.[28] With this significant lack of knowledge and

The Juno Beach Centre has become a focal point of remembrance for Canada and has been a site for veterans to return to the old battlefield.

the ongoing domination of American history, veterans wanted a proper museum in Canada that was more easily accessible to all Canadians, a museum that would teach, educate, and keep their memories alive. Once again, they would have to fight to get one.

CHAPTER 17

MUSEUM OR MEMORIAL?

"**I**f there's going to be a new National War Museum, there's going to have be an attack," wrote Dave Brown, a journalist and long-time supporter of veterans, in October 1999. "Those who advocated preservation of Canada's proud military history are failing miserably in their polite, but useless, requests for cooperation from politicians."[1] In his mind, and the minds of many veterans, the politicians were deliberately procrastinating. Only an all-out battle brought on by the veterans would result in a new museum.

The increasingly urgent calls for a new museum came after years of condemnation of the existing Canadian War Museum from every quarter. Veterans, teachers, and academics complained that it was old, outdated, and inadequate. The special committee of experts in 1991 had labelled the museum a national embarrassment. Journalists railed about how the covenant with those who gave their lives for the country had been broken by successive governments that refused to properly chronicle the country's war history. "In exchange for risking everything," raged the *Ottawa Citizen* in October 1998, "Canada promised its soldiers they would never be forgotten. Whether it is called a bond, an oath or a pact, it was a moral contract between Canada and her dead."[2]

In the aftermath of the Holocaust gallery debacle, veteran and former minister of national defence Barney Danson was appointed to the board of trustees of the Canadian Museum of Civilization Corporation and became chair of the newly constituted CWM advisory committee. Danson had enough influence to directly call Prime Minister Jean Chrétien, with whom he had served in cabinet decades earlier, to argue the case of the museum.[3] Chrétien had no special connection to the Second World War, but he had been moved by his experience at the fiftieth anniversary commemorations. The prime minister's well-tuned political antenna also sensed that Canadians' appreciation of military history had changed significantly in just a few years, with the armed forces battered by the grim failures in Somalia and Rwanda and then redeemed in some eyes with the great outpouring of attention to the Second World War.

But the war museum needed many champions. After former director Victor Suthren's firing over the Holocaust gallery, Danson recruited J.L. Granatstein, a former officer in the Canadian forces, retired history professor from York University, and prolific author. No one expected the outspoken Granatstein to be a safe, cultural bureaucrat when he was appointed director-general and CEO of the CWM in February 1998, but more than a few were surprised when he described it publicly as "stodgy, boring and dull. Its exhibits are tacky. As a museum, it's just appalling."[4] Others had said far worse, and Granatstein was right about how the CWM failed as a modern institution: its exhibitions were outdated, it lacked educational facilities, and it had suffered dwindling visitorship.

Granatstein's appointment was a sign to the veterans that a prominent Canadian would lead the fight to rejuvenate Canada's military history museum. He had also been in the news for his national best-seller *Who Killed Canadian History?* (1998), which

Normandy veteran Lieutenant Barney Danson, pictured here during the war, suffered a traumatic wound to his eye in combat and lost most of his friends killed in combat. He carried physical and mental scars, but he had a successful postwar career, eventually serving as minister of national defence. Danson played a key role in gathering political support for a new Canadian war museum.

argued that historians in the universities were failing the country in their skewed reading of the past.⁵ *Ottawa Sun* journalist Linda Williamson suggested that Granatstein would play "a small part in reversing the past several decades in which Canada's history— particularly our war history—was simply not taught to kids."⁶ Granatstein indeed planned to tell those stories of war and conflict but felt it would be a difficult road ahead for Canadians who had imbibed the myth that they lived in a nation of peace without a war history. "It's going to take a long time," said Granatstein, "to undo the damage of a generation."⁷

In November 1998, the federal government announced that a new war museum would be built near the Aviation Museum along the Ottawa River, on thirty-five acres of National Defence land. Although its location was outside the downtown core, the new project generated much excitement, as the government had promised a $58 million contribution. The Museum of Civilization, the parent corporation of the CWM, would put forth $7 million, but the CWM had to raise $15 million.[8] Granatstein spoke publicly about how the new museum would be more than tanks and guns, with the war at the front and at home presented using contemporary museological approaches. The goal was to show how centuries of war had contributed to shaping the country, from its origins to the modern period.

The initial government statement was followed by months of silence from Ottawa and mounting frustration among concerned Canadians because the Chrétien cabinet refused to release the $58 million.[9] It was a bewildering delay and it held up the crucial fundraising campaign led by General Paul Manson, former chief of the defence staff. Journalists and editors sympathetic to the veterans turned the vise to hold the government accountable. "'We shall remember them.' We say so every Nov. 11. In 1949, it seemed superfluous. In 1999, it sounds hollow." So scolded an *Ottawa Citizen* editorial in the lead-up to the Remembrance Day at the end of the century, directing the angry words at Chrétien's cabinet. The government had put up the land for the new CWM, but the Department of Canadian Heritage had withheld the $58 million for months. No one could make sense of it. The *Citizen* conjectured that the department's senior civil servants were inherently against the idea of a war museum, delaying the project in the hope that support might shift. Indeed, time seemed to be running out, and there was an urgency as veterans were dying in great numbers. The *Citizen* pleaded that "the schools have forgotten and the

CBC's idea of remembering is *The Valour and the Horror*."[10] There was a duty to remember and to teach.

To excite Canadians about the new museum-in-waiting and to help fundraising, Granatstein's staff curated an art exhibition, *Canvas of War: Masterpieces from the Canadian War Museum*. Drawing upon the priceless CWM art collection of 13,000 works, curator Laura Brandon showcased the art from both world wars. When the exhibition opened in February 2000 at the Museum of Civilization, more than a quarter-million visitors paid to see the blockbuster before the show travelled across the country and was seen by another quarter-million.[11] Most of the war art had been in storage and inaccessible for decades since the National Gallery did not want it and transferred most of the collection to the CWM in 1971.[12] While there had been occasional exhibitions at the CWM, but they had only short runs because the temperature fluctuations in the inadequate museum damaged the art. The success of *Canvas of War* revealed a pent-up desire of many Canadians to better understand their military history.

A second substantial event occurred in May 2000 with the return of Canada's Unknown Soldier from an overseas cemetery. After the Great War, Canada joined with Britain and the other dominions to select one nameless soldier from the immense graveyards of dead and to inter him in Westminster. The sacred tomb of the Unknown Soldier was a symbol of grief and loss, and millions had visited it during the twentieth century to pay their respects and perhaps to imagine that there lay a father or son resting among the great British poets, writers, and royalty.

But in 1993, Australia repatriated one of its fallen to Canberra, interring him at the Australian War Memorial.[13] The Royal Canadian Legion urged Ottawa to follow suit, which it undertook

The return of Canada's Unknown Soldier in May 2000 stimulated a new discussion around Canada's military history.

as a millennial project. The removal of the unknown Canadian from Cabaret-Rouge British Cemetery was a sacred act of remembrance and reclamation: after a ceremony at the Vimy memorial, the soldier was returned to Canada and laid in a granite sarcophagus at the national monument in Ottawa in a nationally broadcast ceremony on May 28, 2000. Governor General Adrienne Clarkson gave a moving eulogy: "Over two thousand years ago, Herodotus wrote: 'In peace, sons bury their fathers; in war, fathers bury their sons.' Today, we are gathered together as one, to bury someone's son. The only certainty about him is that he was young. If death is a debt we all must pay, he paid before he owed it."[14] The addition of the Unknown Soldier changed the nature of the National War Memorial, and Barney Danson spoke of how it was now "more than a memorial, it is a shrine. There is a human element to it."[15]

The return of the Unknown Soldier to Canada seemed to fan the flames of sacred commemoration. In English and French Canada, attendance at Remembrance Day ceremonies grew in size across the country. Many of those who came were the same baby boomers who had rebelled against their parents' Second World War experiences, people who had been involved in protesting war and nuclear annihilation since the 1960s. Now, as they aged, and as their parents passed away, they adopted a new perspective on what that older generation had done to shape the world that they had inherited.

While the CWM staff mapped out the intellectual content of the new museum, there was still no public announcement of government funding. To stir up interest—and perhaps trouble— Granatstein publicly mused to a journalist in February 2000 about selling one of the museum's star artifacts, Adolf Hitler's bulletproof Mercedes limousine. The car had been brought back to North America by an American padre, where it was initially thought to belong to Hermann Göring. It found its way to the CWM in 1970, when its true connection to the Führer was revealed.[16] The sleek black limousine had always been among the museum's most controversial artifacts, regarded as an ominous presence by some, fascinating to others. The estimated $20 million from the sale could be put towards a new museum, Granatstein suggested.

When news of the proposed sale broke, the idea was widely rebuked. One worried Canadian wrote, "I would much rather have it stay in the museum, with government sponsorship, than sold to a neo-Nazi group." Another person observed, "Hitler was an ugly figure but an important one. The car represents why so many Canadians went to war."[17] Even Granatstein was "amazed at the response," especially as many commented in the media that the drastic action would not be necessary if the government lived

up to its promise of funding.[18] There was power in that dark artifact, and it embodied both the beguiling appeal of Nazi imagery
and all that Canadians abhorred in the fight to end that heinous
regime. John English, a respected historian and chairman of the
board of trustees of the Canadian Museum of Civilization, felt that
the robust public reaction suggested that Canadians were concerned
with the fate of the museum, its artifacts, and their history.[19]

The CWM kept Hitler's car and the Chrétien government
released the $58 million a month later. The museum was to be built
on the site of the now-closed Rockcliffe air base, on an escarpment
rising from the Ottawa River. It was in close proximity to the
National Aviation Museum and it was also only a few kilometres
from Beechwood Cemetery, Canada's official military burial
ground, where Generals Crerar and McNaughton and several thousand veterans lay buried. Ottawa resident David Anido shared his

The Hitler car at the Canadian War Museum is a dark artifact that speaks to
the evil of the Nazis. When the museum suggested it might be sold to raise
money for a new building, the federal government finally released crucial funds.

thoughts in the *Ottawa Citizen* that Rockcliffe would be a good site for a Canadian War Museum, which, "like the Australian War Museum in Canberra, needs a location that will remind people of the trials that helped build a nation, and reinforce a culture that needs all too often to be reminded of its greatness."[20]

Barney Danson had played a key role in advocating for releasing the funds, with one journalist describing how the seventy-nine-year-old former Liberal cabinet minister used all "his considerable political guile and powers of persuasion" to convince the new Liberal cabinet to open the coffers.[21] Danson had fought with the Queen's Own Rifles in the later battles of Normandy, where most of his best mates were killed, and his service ended when he was blinded in combat. "This is not about veterans," he said with great emotion when Minister of Canadian Heritage Sheila Copps announced the funding, "it is about those who never got to be veterans. It's about the beautiful young men we served with who earned the medals we wear, but never got to wear them themselves."[22] Now the Friends of the CWM began the heavy lifting to raise millions. Veterans as a group contributed significant funds to the building, often in small denominations as befitting those living on pensions, but the Royal Canadian Legion donated $500,000 to kick off the Passing the Torch goal of $15 million.

Granatstein's two-year term expired in June 2000, and he was lauded by journalists for having "rekindled public interest in the museum, strengthened its research capabilities, and been a tireless, outspoken proponent of new facilities to replace the inadequate buildings."[23] Granatstein handed the building of the museum to Joe Geurts, an experienced cultural administrator.[24] Planning for the museum exhibitions continued, but there was soon another shock for veterans. In May 2001, the government moved the museum to LeBreton Flats, with funding almost doubled to $100 million. The new museum would be the focal point of a redevelopment in a large space to the west of the downtown core that had been the former site of lumber companies and workers' houses. They had been torn down in the 1960s to make way for a new National Arts Centre, but when that building was moved closer to Parliament, the area remained empty.

Some veterans reacted to the move with dismay. Even though the LeBreton site was a better draw for tourists and created a potential link between the museum and the Parliament Buildings along a ceremonial route, War Amps CEO Cliff Chadderton claimed that the veterans were victims of "a grandiose snow job."[25] The surprise move was hard for veterans to accept because they were not consulted and they were intensely wary of the government and museum administrators after the Holocaust gallery debacle.[26] The move was also expected to delay the project and now time was also an enemy, with the dominion president of the Royal Canadian Legion, William Barclay, lamenting that with each passing year of delay, an estimated 25,000 veterans would die from old age.[27] But there was no conspiracy and the project continued to move ahead, with Chadderton and other veterans eventually giving it their blessing.[28]

A star architect—seventy-two-year-old Japanese-Canadian Raymond Moriyama—was selected to design the museum in a joint venture with fellow architect Alexander Rankin and large teams from their respective firms. Moriyama had created the Bata Shoe Museum in Toronto and had his own link to the Second World War, when his family was forcibly relocated from the coast. Moriyama's grand vision for the building was one of regeneration after war, with landscapes and societies emerging out of the ashes of the conflict. He said, "Nature may be ravished by human acts of war, but inevitably it hybridizes, regenerates and prevails."[29] The concept was embodied in a structure with a large prow-like feature; it seemed to emerge from the landscape and point toward the Peace Tower, one kilometre to the east.

With its disjointed, jutting, and jagged concrete, its subtle interplay of copper and glass, its narrow-slit windows evoking a bunker's firing apertures, the building drew inspiration from war's chaos. But the museum's innards—what visitors encountered and experienced—would be fashioned by a relatively small team of historians writing the storyline and deciding the messages to be conveyed to visitors. Later, artifact specialists, educational professionals, interpretative planners, and designers would come together to create and populate the large exhibition space. The key message of the museum was how war had changed Canada, from Indigenous conflict to the present nuclear age, with the historians acting as curators. Roger Sarty, and, towards the end of the project, Dean Oliver, led the team, which included Martin Auger, Laura Brandon, Tim Cook, Serge Durflinger, and Peter MacLeod. All were holders of history doctorates and none were veterans. The historians forged the intellectual storyline that underpinned the exhibitions, attempting to situate and explore the story of Canada's wars at the strategic, national, unit, and personal level. This was unabashedly national history, and far different from what was taught in most universities at that time. But always, the greatest emphasis was on ordinary Canadians struggling in extraordinary circumstances. Sarty, a former official historian and international expert in naval warfare, spoke of the impact of "emotive messaging" and the importance of relying on the eyewitnesses to history and their artifacts to guide the story. The exhibitions would not shy away from the grit and determination of Canadians in battle, along with the heroics and horror of combat. "War is about killing people and breaking things," Sarty said during the early planning of the exhibitions in a public interview. "We can't escape that fact."[30]

From the project's inception, there was much discussion about whether the new CWM was a museum or a memorial. The Australian War Memorial, with the country's Unknown Soldier interred there since 1993, is a sacred space of reverence. More than 100,000 names of fallen service personnel are inscribed on the walls. While a memorial can also be a place to talk about history, it is primarily designed for contemplation and remembrance. In Canada, the museum's staff and administrators felt that a museum of history had to be free to engage in difficult history. The new museum should present the glory, service, sacrifice, and heroics in war alongside fear, brutality, cowardice, and dissent. The two ideas—of a museum and a memorial—are not automatically at odds, but there can be challenges in twinning such concepts in a single structure.

Separating the two functions was not made easier when Moriyama designed a memorial space in the heart of the building. Adjacent to the low-roofed lobby, Moriyama placed a memorial chamber where the headstone of Canada's Unknown Soldier is mounted on the wall in a concrete cube. On November 11, sunlight passes through an opening in the high-walled concrete to alight on the headstone. At the first Remembrance Day after the museum's opening in 2005, and every year after, visitors lined up to bear witness and often left their poppies on the headstone. There are other commemorative aspects, not the least being "Lest We Forget" in Morse code through a series of windows along the south side of the building.

———

The Memorial Chamber of the Canadian War Museum where,
on November 11, the light shines through the aperture and illuminates
the headstone of Canada's Unknown Soldier.

The new Canadian War Museum opened on time: May 8, 2005, the sixtieth anniversary of the end of the Second World War. There were ceremonies overseas and across the country, but most eyes were on Ottawa. It was a gorgeous, absurdly hot day, and the capital had created a festival to celebrate the end of the war and the beginning of a new museum. Several thousand veterans and their families were honoured at the National War Memorial for a ceremony and then marched or were driven down Wellington Street, passing the Supreme Court and the National Archives before arriving at the new Canadian War Museum. While the museum was devoted to exploring, educating, and sharing the stories of Canada's entire span of military history, the presence of a large number of Second World War veterans ensured that on this day there was a focus on the Necessary War.

Thousands of Canadians and veterans passed into the climate-controlled building, studying the slanting walls of unfinished

Canadian veterans marching to the new Canadian War Museum
on opening day, May 8, 2005.

concrete, visiting the large theatre and research centre, and then entering the permanent gallery exhibitions that presented Canada's rich military history. Weapons and military technology, set amid reconstructions of shattered landscapes, were displayed next to and often entwined with stories of courage, perseverance, and tenacity. Several thousand artifacts formed the core of the exhibitions, ranging from Hitler's limousine to Brock's tunic from the War of 1812 with its musket-ball hole through the lapel. There were tanks like the Russian T-72 and smaller, intimate relics, like a teddy bear given by a young girl to her father, Lieutenant Lawrence Rogers, who went off with the Canadian Expeditionary Force and never returned. Some 315,000 words of bilingual text told the history, along with high-impact large-scale reconstructions depicting the Battle of Ortona, the mud of Passchendaele, and the grimy trenches of the Western Front. The war art by Arthur Lismer, Frederick Varley, Alex Comfort, and others was finally able to be displayed, and it was incorporated into the storytelling throughout the exhibitions as well as in stand-alone clusters.

It is a "sacred place," wrote one journalist.[31] Both the building and the exhibitions were lauded, with nearly universally positive coverage in the media. The museum's "purpose isn't to glorify war but to serve as a reminder of its stark realities and as a tribute to those who fought and fell," argued an editorial in the *Ottawa Sun*.[32] Carefully crafted exhibitions on the Merchant Navy, the Hong Kong veterans' experience, and the forced relocation of Japanese Canadians ensured that those groups did not feel marginalized. The museum was praised for exposing hard truths and not sanitizing combat, but it was noted by a few that there was only a small Holocaust display space, albeit accompanied by an eyewitness account by a Canadian serviceman: "This is why we're fighting World War II."[33]

Decorated pilot Charley Fox—who was eighty-five years old and reputed to be the man who in an aerial sweep riddled Field Marshal Erwin Rommel's car in Normandy and severely wounded him—spoke about the importance of a museum for preserving the history for all Canadians. "We have to realize that our time is finished," said Fox. "Our stories need to be told, passed on to the students so they become the torchbearers of the future."[34] The stories were indeed told and at the opening, and in the weeks, months, and years to follow, the aging veterans would visit the museum, including many who volunteered and acted as eyewitnesses to history, while others were accompanied by their extended families. One of the first to walk through the exhibitions, Bruce Coulson, a veteran of the Italian campaign, made the trip from Charlottetown, PEI. "It's very well done. I think this is very important to Canada. It will help the younger generation to remember, like they do in Holland."[35]

The museum, the *Montreal Gazette* enthused, would lead to a "reawakening of interest in history."[36] And while the more than half a million visitors in the first year were a sign of the museum's new role as a cultural institution, there was a slow-burning controversy over the presentation of the Allied bombing campaign. In the Second World War gallery, the space devoted to exploring the bombing campaign was a rich area of artifacts and stories, of archival film footage of bombers striking cities and German defences. It presented the terrifying experience of aircrews in their nightly sorties and the high cost of lives expended in the bombing of enemy positions, all of which was supported by contextualizing text and panels that highlighted the impact of bombing. One passage read, for example, "Attacks on industrial centres, military installations and cities devastated vast areas and killed hundreds of thousands. They also diverted German resources from other fronts and damaged essential elements of the German war effort."

However, there was also a concluding panel in the Bomber Command section entitled "Enduring Controversy." The panel would become the focus of intense argument. It read in full:

> The value and morality of the strategic bomber offensive against Germany remains bitterly contested. Bomber Command's aim was to crush civilian morale and force Germany to surrender by destroying its cities and industrial installations. Although Bomber Command and American attacks left 600,000 Germans dead and more than five million homeless, the raids resulted in only small reductions in German war production until late in the war.

These sixty-six words, of more than several hundred thousand in the museum, angered some veterans.[37] They zeroed in on two issues raised in the text, which had been disputed and debated by historians, philosophers, veterans, and many others who had studied the war over the previous half-century: the morality of bombing civilians in cities and the effectiveness of the bombing campaign. The panel described the debate in a way as to leave the questions open-ended, and perhaps to generate discussion on an issue with no clear answer. But the conversation rapidly turned to rage.

In the months after the opening, individuals or small groups of veterans wondered why the museum was drawing attention to the bombing controversy. Simply raising the issue that there were disagreements surrounding strategic bombing was disrespectful to comrades who had served in the air war, said a handful of vocal veterans. The Smithsonian had experienced a similar high-profile battle from 1994 to 1995 over the interpretation of the role of the B-29 Superfortress *Enola Gay*, the American bomber that dropped the atomic bomb on Hiroshima. With the museum planning for an exhibition that explored the end of the war in Japan with the atomic bombs and the origins of the Cold War, veterans used their influence with politicians and the media, and their own considerable role in American society, to hound the museum to modify its exhibition. They were driven, it seemed, by their angst over showing the effects of the atomic bomb on Japanese civilians. In the end, after much public controversy, the exhibition was scaled back and reduced to a homage to the *Enola Gay* and its aircrew, in what some called "patriotic correctness."[38]

For those unaware of the Smithsonian controversy ten years earlier or of the Canadian veterans' long and testy engagement over the issue of strategic bombing, particularly with *The Valour and the Horror* series, their negative reaction to the CWM's "Enduring Controversy" panel seemed rather mystifying, or at least thin-skinned. But the issue did not go away, and it grew to a steady chorus, gathering in intensity as more veterans became aware of the issue. Or perhaps cacophony is a better word, as there was no single group of veterans and no universal approach about how to solve the issue. Some veterans demanded the text panel be excised completely; others insisted on a rewrite; others, still, wanted the offending historians removed in a purge. After consultations between museum executives and veterans over several months in 2006, changes were made to the introductory panel to provide more context around the bomber campaign that emphasized that Germany started bombing civilians first, and more explanation was given about how bombing tied down and wore down enemy resources. In one area, where there was an image of dead German civilians, a series of quotations was added to the panel to provide a voice to the Allied airmen. However, those measures did not soothe the angriest veterans, and the *Legion* magazine even suggested boycotting the museum. "I'm offended and damned angry," wrote Frank Laverty, a navy veteran who saw his own service implicated in the "attack" on his Bomber Command comrades.[39] While the museum acknowledged that the veterans should be a part of the conversation, it did not offer them the editing pen to do as they saw fit. How could it? It was not a museum solely for veterans and if such monitoring occurred, where would it stop? Japanese Canadians, Ukrainian Canadians, and champions of various services or units would all certainly demand an opportunity to recast "their" panels as they saw fit. No museum of national history could operate in such a manner.

The media latched on to the aged warriors' anger. A Bomber Command veteran raged in the news that the panel "said that we were responsible for 600,000 dead. I took offence that we were just helter-skelter bombers. We always had justified targets."[40] The panel had indeed noted the impact of the bombers, but no one flying over the cities and the firestorms that consumed entire neighbourhoods could have imagined that they were only hitting factories. And while scholars over the decades have sought to analyze the effectiveness of the bombing campaign, with many conflicting assessments, the archives of strategic and operational reports make it irrefutably clear that civilians were deliberately targeted by the Germans first and then by the Allies.[41]

Newspapers, after heaping praise on the museum when it opened, reported on the story with much vigour and no little glee. Not all articles and editorials were against the museum; one from the *Ottawa Citizen* on September 29, 2006, argued that "by making visitors think about war in all its complexity, including the fundamental moral questions of what limits 'our' warriors must respect in fighting for us, and whether there's such a thing as an honourable enemy, the Canadian War Museum is fulfilling its mandate. Canada's brave veterans deserve such detailed reflection, which honours them and their fallen comrades' memories more than any hollow tribute ever could."[42] But there were far more negative letters, such as the September 29, 2006, missive from Retired Lieutenant-General Bill Carr: "The veterans have earned the right to be heard. They are totally justified to complain about the unfair and moralistic position being taken by Canadian War Museum staff. They were there. These critics were not."[43]

This controversy had moved far beyond the field of measured debate over history into the unpredictable arena of emotions. For

A Halifax bomber from 405 Squadron, Royal Canadian Air Force, preparing to bomb targets in Europe.

the veterans, even those who had not flown in Bomber Command, there was a sense that this memorial to history—the long-awaited museum—was being besmirched by this single panel. Veterans invoked the legitimacy of their voices over that of experts. "What were the credentials of the historians?" questioned one writer. "Had they flown in the war?[44] Museum staff were labelled as shameless "revisionists," a term that no one defined but clearly meant unqualified civilians twisting real history to condemn heroes.[45] "For people like me who flew in Bomber Command during the war it's a real insult," said Bob Dale, an eighty-six-year-old former squadron leader who survived three tours of duty. "It's a snub to the 50,000 aircrew who were killed, including 10,000 Canadians."[46] This powerful argument centred on what was owed to the dead, who should speak for them, and who owned the history.

During this time, the Canadian forces were engaged in combat in Afghanistan—with Special Operations Forces in that country since late 2001 and other units serving in complex military operations beginning the next year. By mid-2006, the fighting against the Taliban had increased in intensity into combat operations.[47]

Afghanistan was front-page news, including the gut-wrenching coverage of the ramp ceremonies at Canadian Forces Base Trenton in Ontario that saw the bodies of slain Canadians arrive home and be transported in a convoy along the soon-to-be named Highway of Heroes. There was much coverage of the grief among the next of kin.[48] Canadians were more attuned to thinking about war and its high costs.

As this was happening, the Bomber Command story raged on, with a buzz saw of criticism cutting through the museum. A November 2006 *National Post* online survey found that 90 percent of respondents thought the CWM's text panel was "unfair."[49] Historical experts were called in to examine the exhibition, and while they generally supported the curators' interpretation, their final reports had little impact on the growing outrage.[50] "The turning point" in the affair, observed Museum of Civilization CEO Victor Rabinovitch, was when a subcommittee of the Senate Veterans Affairs Committee was convened in May 2007 to listen to arguments from veterans' groups, the museum corporation, and experts in history and museums. The veterans, some more than ninety years old, were often unable to specify their disagreement with the historical interpretation, but it was clear that they were offended by what they viewed as a disrespectful tone. An air force veteran from a different generation, General Paul Manson, who spearheaded the museum's fundraising campaign, was an influential witness who demanded that the panel be changed. In January 2007, he penned a syndicated op-ed piece articulating the veterans' anger, noting that "although the War Museum's public image has been hurt by the bomber panel episode, it is not too late to do the right thing.[51] In the end, the Senate committee reported in June 2007 that while the history might be factually correct, the CWM needed to find a way to resolve the "sense of insult" to the veterans, for the good of those who served, the museum, and the public.[52]

Museum officials sat down with veterans' groups and by August 2007, a revised 202-word panel was installed—about twice as long as the museum's main text panels—which told the story of bombing in greater detail and emphasized its impact in contributing to the Allied victory.[53] The text panel went up and sucked the oxygen out of the story. Veterans' groups were content, the Royal Canadian Legion supported the alteration, and the media coverage withered away. The controversy ended, at least for the moment, although this fierce debate over the interpreted history became one more way station in the long arc of an enduring controversy that stretches back to the war years.

Since 2005, the museum's exhibitions have steadily drawn over half a million visitors a year and received much critical acclaim. More than fifteen years later, the vast majority of visitors have expressed very high satisfaction with their museum experience. While the Bomber Command controversy frayed relations between some veterans and the museum, it was but a tiny part of the museum's overall presentation of history that spanned hundreds of years of military history. Aware of the damage of the controversy to the museum administrators and staff, which included Joe Geurts being forced out of the job as head of CWM, the new director general, Mark O'Neill, set to repairing the relationship with veterans and the Friends of the Canadian War Museum, which continues to advocate and raise funds on behalf of the museum.

While the panel was changed, the museum does not only offer heroic history with the difficult parts erased. Films, works of art,

The stunning Canadian War Museum presents the complex history of Canada's wars and conflicts, from Indigenous people to the present. Its opening in May 2005 presented the country's military history for all Canadians.

photographs, artifacts, and dioramas speak to suffering, strife, death, and grief. There are also stories of eye-watering courage and heartrending self-sacrifice. These are combined with the dark presentation of the trampling of civil liberties in times of war, be it the internment of Germans and Ukrainians in the Great War, the forced relocation of Japanese Canadians, or the October Crisis of 1970, albeit contextualized within the broader war efforts or periods of strife. Throughout the museum, the veterans' experiences infuse the exhibitions, as the museum endeavours to depict conflict, war, and the search for peace.

The clash over Bomber Command revealed how historical interpretation could dredge up dormant pain. In the case of the CWM panel, it was almost entirely a secondary conflagration caused by the embers of *The Valour and the Horror*. At the same time, the contested meaning of the bombing campaign emerged partly because veterans felt that they held a big stake in the much-anticipated new museum. Indeed, the veterans did have an emotional grounding in the museum's history, but not a veto. It was intended to be a museum for all Canadians and not a memorial just for veterans. Within its walls, the hard truths of war must be raised and addressed. The rewritten panel did little damage to the message, and yet this intense battle that raged for two years spoke to the challenges of talking about Canada's military history, especially after decades of neglect. It revealed the fault lines of the past and how they continue to divide in the present. The museum was to be the veterans' legacy project for Canadians. In many ways it is: situated in the heart of Ottawa and bringing history to millions. But the museum is also a site of unsettled stories that continue to shape memory, commemoration, pride, sorrow, and the ongoing fight for history.

CONCLUSION

A WAR REMEMBERED

D. 83009 Private Gordon Hutton

The Black Watch, Royal Highland Regiment of Canada

28th July 1944

Age 19

NOT ONLY TODAY

BUT EVERY DAY

IN SILENCE WE REMEMBER.

Private Gordon Hutton of Verdun, Quebec, is but one of the tens of thousands of Canadians who lie buried on foreign soil, having given their lives in the Necessary War. Their families and many others across Canada still carry deep grief over the loss of these men and women. It is a wound that has moved through generations. Some felt a profound sense of absence: children who aged never knowing their fathers; widows who mourned and tried to move on. Families were missing cousins and uncles, young men who never had a chance to grow up. Parents had to find ways to keep going after the unnatural act of outliving their children. In

Private Gordon Hutton never had a chance to grow up and contribute to the postwar prosperous Canada that emerged from the Necessary War.

the years and decades that unspooled from the 1945 victory, trips would be arranged to gravesites in France, the Netherlands, Italy, or to the other battlefields around the world. There, the weight of history can be crushing, as people gather in peaceful spots of what were once shocking sites of violence. Order has been brought to disorder; the lost have been found. Pride and sorrow infuse these sacred places that are forever a part of history and of Canada.

Closer to home, the Peace Tower in Ottawa, with the Books of Remembrance, draws Canadians to it. Private Stuart Shantz enlisted in July 1940 and fought with the Toronto Scottish Regiment. He was killed in the Battle of Verrières Ridge, south of Caen, on July 25, 1944, and was buried at Bény-sur-Mer Canadian War Cemetery. His family had never been able to visit his grave, but Stuart's name is written in the Second World War Book of Remembrance in the Memorial Chamber—as are more than 44,000 others. In 2008, on September 23, the day that Stuart's page would be on display, his cousin Wayne Shantz made the trip to pay his respects; the two had grown up in the same area, Punkeydoodles Corners, a farming community to the west of Kitchener, Ontario. It was a day of "overwhelming emotion," and the officials allowed Wayne and his wife, Ann, to remain after others left. They watched as officials at 11 A.M. began the process of unlocking the cases to the seven Books of Remembrance, turning the page of each with solemn care, and then saluting.[1] The Shantz family bore witness to this moving act of remembrance, reflecting on a cousin lost to his family, his community, and his country. And yet he was not forgotten. In silence, they remembered.

———

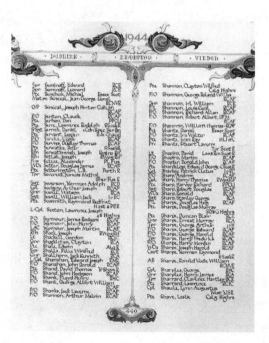

The page from Canada's Second World War Book of
Remembrance listing Private Stuart Shantz.

Since the early twenty-first century, Canadians across the country have paid more attention to marking the Second World War. While it remains overshadowed by the Great War in the memorial landscape, the Second World War's impact on Canadian and world history cannot be denied. And yet even the name of the First World War seems to offer some qualitative difference. It was known by contemporaries as the Great War, and many have returned to calling it that. The war was indeed monstrously great. Somewhat ironically, the stakes in the Second World War were even greater than the first one, and it was a true war for civilization. The phrase used during the Great War and imprinted on the British Empire's service medals was "The Great War for Civilisation, 1914–1919." But in the realm of signs and symbols, the Great War continues to dominate. A painting at the Canadian War Museum, *Sacrifice* (c. 1918) by Charles Sims, depicts the Crucifixion, a representation of the soldiers who died for us during the Great War. That is how many Canadians viewed that struggle, both during the war and in the decade after, when most of the memorials were constructed, and when the reverential language surrounding the war's fallen was firmly established in social memory.

The theme of sacrifice fit less easily a generation later, where the war was regarded as a great crusade against evil, a necessary war that had to be won, no matter the cost. Furthermore, the act of commemoration tends to focus on grief. This is one important way that Canadians framed the Great War (along with the notion of a new Canada birthed in the struggle), but it is not how Canadians initially understood the Second World War, which, at its heart, is about a victory. Nor can a country be born twice. The challenge seems to lie in the fact that it is not easy to celebrate victory in war without appearing militaristic or vainglorious. The language of commemoration is also not well suited to talking about victory in a meaningful way, and so we turn to victims, loss, and sacrifice.

This book has tried to show how the meaning of the Second World War was difficult to articulate, and why it lacked some of the emotional resonance of the Great War. There were other factors too: the changing nature of Canada in the postwar years, the haphazard way we told our stories, our fear of dredging up history that might divide, the adoption of new identity-shaping symbols, and the many battles by groups over the meaning of the war through redress, apology campaigns, or seeking veterans' status. While it was only natural that with time the war would drift from the nation's consciousness, the lack of a centralizing Vimy-like battle in Canada's global war effort also hurt the means by which memory was constructed throughout the second half of the century. By the early 1990s, the Necessary War was forgotten by many or so badly misinterpreted as a conflict defined by defeat and disgrace that it was a suitable topic for denigration. Of course, not everyone banished the war to oblivion, with many Canadians caring about a veteran in the family, uncovering the history of the war on their own, or even becoming excited about the topic through dedicated teachers. But for decades the war was rarely invoked in the country's social memory. That is why the high-profile commemoration in Normandy in 1994 and the hugely welcoming celebration in the Netherlands the next year were so surprising, as was the subsequent emergence of a new desire to tell the Canadian story. Since those anniversary ceremonies, Canadians have experienced a significant transformation in how we embraced the war's many meanings.

And just as the 1960s was a period where Canadians were stridently against war, including the Second World War, the stirring of memory in the 1990s followed broad societal trends, as the Second World War generation began to die. At the same time, the near-destruction of the country in the 1995 Quebec referendum spurred a greater interest in history as a way to explore Canadians' shared past. In the twenty-first century, with the 9/11 catastrophe and the War on Terror that followed, there was new interest in Canada's historic and current participation in war and conflict. Traditional peacekeeping died in the 1990s, and armed peacemaking was the only way forward in the lawless and dangerous Afghanistan. Canada's substantial role in the war in Afghanistan—with 40,000 personnel serving there from late 2001, almost 160 killed, and many more wounded in body and spirit, with dozens taking their own lives in the years that followed their service—had a significant impact on Canada. While the Afghanistan mission divided Canadians over its goals and methods, its cost in blood and treasure, Canadians also came together to support the service personnel and veterans in ways not seen for decades. There were new commemorative acts, like the ramp ceremonies to honour and bring home the dead, the naming of the Highway of Heroes, Red Fridays to show support, and a campaign by the federal government to reshape national icons and symbols, emphasizing the warrior over the peacekeeper. Canada's war in Afghanistan brought a greater awareness to Canadians of their own war history and the realization that the country's contributions during the Second World War had been neglected for too long.

This is the first book to offer a sustained examination of Canada's conflicted and contested memory of the Second World War. It will not be the last. Others will test the assertions and perhaps delve deeper into issues through the lens of gender, ethnicity, or region. Every study of war in Canada has to address the different ways that meaning is constructed by English and French Canada, including the reasons why the Second World War was less damaging to national unity than the First World War, and yet how the period of 1939 to 1945 still became a dislocating historical event. It is likely that the unsettled memory of the Afghanistan War or other conflicts not yet fought will further influence how previous wars are understood. The unearthing of the past—and the re-sculpturing of it—will continue in the next generation and those that follow. But at this stage in our history, at the seventy-fifth anniversary of victory in 1945, this is a good time to take stock of the mapping of memory onto the past.

And it is clear that Canada's Second World War for decades suffered from a lack of separate recognition in the commemorative landscape. Vimy and Beaumont Hamel overseas are evocative sites of remembrance that show Europeans that Canadians crossed the Atlantic to serve, fight, and die alongside British, French, and Belgian soldiers.[2] For decades, Canadian officials chose not to mark the Second World War. It was not until veterans took it into their own hands at Juno Beach that Canada now has a museum through which to tell its stories, engage in active remembrance, and make meaningful memories. However, there is much that still needs to be done, both in Canada and abroad. One example must suffice: a 2012 British survey of more than 1,000 children aged eleven to eighteen were asked about Britain's allies in the Second World War. They gave as their response: the United States (66 percent), France (44 percent), Russia/Soviet Union (13 percent), Australia and New Zealand (9 percent), Italy (7 percent), China (2 percent), Germany (2 percent), and Japan (1 percent). Seven percent chose another country, while 21 percent could not name one ally, which is perhaps better than the 3 percent who chose Germany and Japan.[3] Not a single child picked Canada—in other words, total absence in Britain's young people's social memory.

While sustaining the remembrance of the Second World War continues to require curation and care, there is not a total gap in Canada's social memory. Thousands of local memorials remain across the country, most containing the names of the Second World War fallen, alongside those from the Great War and the Korean War. They act as a poignant legacy at the community level of how the war reached into cities, towns, and villages. While the National Shrine project was buried by the mid-1960s, Canadians have also come to accept the National War Memorial in Ottawa as the one monument that stands for all wars and all service personnel, although one wonders at where the Second World War would sit in the country's historical imagination had the shrine been built. There are other sites of commemoration, such as the naval memorials like corvette HMCS *Sackville* and destroyer HMCS *Haida*. Regions have sites of memory, like the Halifax Memorial or Winnipeg's monument to women who served in uniform, while Ottawa marks those who fell in the air-training program and in Hong Kong and honours Indigenous Canadians who served in wars and areas of conflict. Merchant Navy Day and Battle of the Atlantic Day are marked by some. And so the Second World War is not absent from the memorial landscape, but it continues to pale in comparison to the Great War.

The link with the Dutch remains vibrant, with the living memorial of the Tulip Festival still going strong and the occasional sculpture to mark the liberation. It can be difficult for Canadians to understand the meaning of the 1945 liberation, but to walk among

the Dutch even to this day is to be reminded that previous generations gave an oppressed people back their lives and restored their
country. Dutch children are still taught about the liberators, and for

Canadian veterans greeted by the Dutch in the Netherlands.

decades they learned the Canadian national anthem as part of the
school curriculum. Gert van Holt, a Dutch girl who lived through
the war and liberation, remarked of the bond in 2005: "I think no
two countries share the magnificent love that is so evident between
Canada and the Netherlands. It is because after five years of occupation, the Canadian soldiers gave back our liberty, our freedom, and
the bonds were stronger because the Canadian soldier stayed in the
Netherlands after the war."[4] The restoration of freedom to the
Dutch will not soon be forgotten in the Netherlands.

And yet Canada remains without a major, unifying Second
World War memorial. The United States, so proud of its role during
the war, only built its national memorial in Washington in 2004.[5] Is
it too late for Canadians to do the same? This book has revealed

that in the struggle for history, memorials matter. If you build it, they will come; if you do not, future generations will wander, lost.

American historian John Bodnar has noted that over time, the darker legacies of the war in the United States dropped away or were pushed to the periphery as the war was used to illustrate American exceptionalism, with little room for dissent.[6] In Canada, up until the early 1990s, the opposite was in effect: the dark stories worked their way to the surface, becoming more dominant over time. One need only think of the focus, even fixation, on Dieppe rather than on D-Day, the Italian campaign, or the Battle of the Atlantic. From the 1980s, the apology campaign of the Japanese Canadians was one of the most prominent historical examples of that reshaping of memory. It became a symbol of a wartime attack on civil liberties, driven by racism, even as Canadians were fighting and dying on behalf of oppressed people overseas. The redress campaign had a profound impact on the constructed memory of Canada's Second World War, and it also led other marginalized groups to band together to fight for recognition. They were successful in many cases, and their historical struggles resulted in formal apologies and monetary compensation for Ukrainians interned in the Great War; Chinese workers forced to endure racism and pay a head tax starting in the late nineteenth century; and an apology in November 2018 to Jewish people for the turning back of MS St. Louis in 1939. In the latter case, Canadian authorities consigned 254 of the more than 900 Jews onboard to their deaths when Western Europe was overrun by German forces.[7] With so many apology campaigns for all manner of historical actions, they have begun to be viewed with cynicism by some Canadians who think governments express their regret for past events solely in order to curry favour with blocs of the voting public. But a formal apology does have an impact on groups, and the lack of one can leave scars, as it did to the Hong Kong veterans who waited for so long.

These campaigns also have an effect on what parts of history are remembered and taught. The fight for redress almost always ensures that the subject is included as a prominent aspect of the country's history, usually after decades of being silenced. The mobilization involves supporting books and articles, the gathering of eyewitness accounts from the aged, and the construction of memorials, all created to bring awareness and to right a wrong. These apology campaigns often use history as another tool to achieve a goal. This isn't always bad, of course, but it is a different motivation driving the understanding of the past. While historical wrongs like the Japanese forced relocation had to be addressed, the activist history that underpinned the argument for redress is not the best foundation for future historical understanding.

History can be dangerous. Governments are often afraid of it and the passions that it stirs up. Politicians prefer heritage, a much more anodyne reading of what came before, and more celebratory than critical. But as this book suggests, we must continue to ask hard questions of the past. It is professional historians who tend to do the heavy lifting in the archives to reclaim what has been forgotten, even if their narrowly specialized and little-read articles and scholarly books rarely reach the general public. And yet the study of military history in Canada has expanded since the 1990s, with more sophisticated analysis and new research underway.

Despite these encouraging signs of engaging with the past, a significant challenge remains. The history battles continue in the ivory towers of universities, with many professors carrying fierce if misplaced convictions that learning about war is bad, mad, and leads to militarism (even as the few courses offered are almost always filled to capacity). It is an absurd prejudice from scholars who are supposed to be open-minded, and one akin to saying that an oncologist who studies cancer "likes" it, and that the search for the cure will somehow stimulate more public favour with the disease. There is also neglect and absence. The CBC continues to ignore the Second World War as a defining event in Canadian history. It must be said that where CBC does fulfill its mandate (along with the other two national networks, CTV and Global) is in its commitment in recent years to marking and broadcasting the anniversaries of D-Day, VE Day, and Remembrance Day.

While it is no easy thing to make a commercial film in Canada, in the country's theatres, from 1945 to the present, it has been British and American war films that Canadians consumed. With Canada's relatively small market, perhaps this has been unavoidable, although in recent years there have been a handful of small-scale docudramas: *Storming Juno* (2010) directed by Tim Wolochatiuk and before that *Dieppe* (1993) by director John N. Smith. They had little impact on the country's social memory. Corus Entertainment's History channel was a more important venue for filmmakers in the first decade after its launch in 1997 as History Television, and while its programming has moved sharply from historical documentaries to reality-TV shows, there is still some room to present Canadian history, and especially Second World War history, which appears to resonate with viewers. Before this, the War Amps of Canada had produced about thirty documentaries in the *Never Again!* series that were broadcast on community television channels, distributed to schools and libraries in VHS tapes from 1985, and which now live on in digital format. The CEO, Cliff

Chadderton, who passed away in 2013 after a lifetime of service to veterans, had felt that the programs were necessary to "dispel the myths of Hollywood films that glorify war, while paying tribute to those who served."[8] Library and Archives Canada has also steadily digitized its vast collection of war records, everything from the Canadian Army Newsreels and archival photographs to the personnel files of Canadians killed during the war. These vectors of memory—which support public discussion and debate—have revealed a renewed desire to tell our story, to explore the past, and to reclaim and recast old memories in a new Canada.

As we move into the twilight time of the Second World War veterans, we must do two things. Collectively, we must listen and we must record. For a long time, veterans were not able to talk about their war experiences. Nobody seemed to care. No one would understand. Many also suppressed their feelings, finding them too raw to explore. Lionel Gauthier of Timmins, Ontario, who fought with the

Jerry Bowen, a veteran of the Second World War and the Korean War,
sharing his stories with young people at the Canadian War Museum.

Queen's Own Rifles, recounted late in life, "I was afraid of all these emotions. It's not good for my heart to feel these things. I try, I try to control it."[9] Others were dealing with the war's lasting wounds—to the body and the mind. While many service personnel had good wars, never confronting the enemy, others were put in impossible conditions of kill or be killed. Each survivor dealt with the war differently. Some were ruined for life; most pushed through what we now call post-traumatic stress injuries. Physical wounds healed with scars, and sometimes the same occurred with the mental ones. But many service personnel found the war never left them, lingering until it crept forward from the depths, biting and scratching.

By the early 1980s, after decades of silence, more and more veterans began to share their experiences. They gave voice to the persistent hurt. Others put pen to paper and tried to write the war out of their systems. As veterans retired from their jobs and reflected on their lives, all the while watching their old comrades succumb to age, many were compelled to capture the memories. Families began to record a father's or grandmother's recollections. There were formal programs like the Dominion Institute–Historica's The Memory Project Digital Archive, launched in June 2003, when Director Rudyard Griffiths talked of the necessity of archiving these "incredible stories."[10] From the 1980s, veterans also began to visit schools in larger numbers to speak to young people and to answer questions. These living memorials were much cherished by students, who were often quite astonished to find in front of them men and women who not only talked of history but had made it. Perhaps these young people from the 1980s were part of the surge of Canadians from the mid-1990s who sought to better understand their country's history and the role played by veterans in shaping it.

"You are the living witnesses of a horror we want to draw on," said Prime Minister Paul Martin to an audience of civilians and veterans during D-Day's sixtieth anniversary. "But you are also the guarantors of our memory."[11] Veterans are indeed the owners of these memories, but they have known for decades that they must pass on their private stories to all Canadians so that succeeding generations embrace the value of remembrance and commemoration. Many Canadians must be taught; others have the history running through their blood. Families of veterans are an influential group intent on keeping these memories alive, and there are millions across the country. For many Canadians, the war is an intimate event, one that grounds them in their community and tells them something about their distant family. They learn about a time when their ancestors underwent a period of tremendous anguish and loss, yet stood together with other Canadians for the ideals in which they believed. Reflecting back on the war in 2005, Andy Anderson, who served in Northwest Europe with 1st Canadian Parachute Battalion, still felt that "we had a duty that had to be done and we did it."[12]

The meaning behind that duty became blurred over time, and as layer upon layer of memory was superimposed onto the past, it took longer for millions of Canadians to discover their own family history. But many have, or eventually will do so, realizing that the great-great-grandfather in the photograph was once an infantryman at Ortona, or that the nurse's badge rattling around in an old drawer, passed down from generation to generation, links to a woman who served her country and the wounded from the front. But it is not just about direct descendants. All Canadians would do well to remember the Necessary War and the part played by Canadians. It was a time when Canadians strained to fight in a war that had to be won. At the unveiling of the Juno Beach

Centre in 2003, a young serving member of the Canadian forces, Private Darcy Rae, watching the ceremony from Edmonton, was interviewed. He choked up when he saw the aged veterans at Juno weep in joy and sorrow: "It makes me extremely humble. It's hard to talk about it. These men have seen things we, and most Canadians, have never seen and no one may ever see again."[13]

The Fight for History has shown how several generations of Canadians have engaged with a monumental event in the country's history. The Second World War forever transformed the nation. It left a powerful legacy, not the least being the creation of another generation of veterans as an identifiable group of Canadians and their work in fostering a more generous state. As individuals and as a group, veterans contributed to shaping the memory of the war over time, but they were not alone, and sometimes were not even the most significant agents of change. During the lean years when Canadians pushed their war history aside to embrace new symbols of their changing country, often it was veterans and their loved ones who kept the flame burning. And yet the war's veterans have largely passed away, and their children are aged now. One of the great worries of the veterans was what would happen to that torch of memory. Will future generations care for it, or will it be snuffed out? One can abhor war—as all should—and still acknowledge that this generation fought in a necessary war against evil and that their service must be remembered. During the war years, many left behind their loved ones and set off on a path to danger. They went, knowing they would suffer hardship and strain, and perhaps make the ultimate sacrifice. They nonetheless stepped forward when Canada and the Western world called to them. Seventy-five years

Young Canadians at the Menin Gate in Ypres, Belgium, marking the sacrifice of Canadians. They and other young people have been thrown the torch of remembrance. How will we support them in understanding Canada's history?

later, they should be remembered as the ordinary men and women who found the courage to do frightening things, pushing themselves beyond their limits, aware that to lose or even draw with the Nazis would leave the world a much darker place.

Having fought to liberate the oppressed, the veterans saw their contributions largely forgotten. In much of the succeeding seventy-five years, the fight was to reclaim this history. It was long and hard, and the battle was sometimes infused with bitterness and anger. And yet, as in the war, they fought another necessary war—a decades-long struggle to ensure that their fallen comrades were not forgotten. Now that they are at the end of their journeys, who will continue to make the effort to ensure the history is not banished to irrelevance?

In the fight for our history, this book has shown the necessity of guardians of the past. Cultivating meaningful memory, engaging in acts of remembrance, ensuring that events, deeds, and individuals are not forgotten—all of this takes work. The dykes of memory are always crumbling and there are too few involved in the spadework to shore them up. The work is hard and not always appreciated in broader society, and yet amateur and professional historians are still doing their bit: researching, writing, and telling stories. Often they uncover acts of heroism, self-sacrifice, and courage that go hand in hand with hurt, loss, and trauma. This search is enriched by partnerships with curators in museums and archivists in the memory houses of the nation. It is done at the national, community, family, and personal level. It involves high school teachers and their students. Journalists, filmmakers, authors, and painters can all reach different audiences and play their role in uncovering the past and in presenting new interpretations. If there is one unifying thread in this ongoing fight, it is that there was no single narrative of the war, and nor should anyone want to reduce it to only one. History is messy, tangled, and complex; it is unsettled and contradictory. It takes effort to understand, and its meaning changes from generation to generation. But we must push back against apathy and indifference. We must tell our stories, truthfully and bravely. For if we do not embrace our history, no one else will.

While Canada neglected the Second World War for many decades, it never entirely disappeared. It has been waiting for us to return to it. The war ended in victory in 1945; but the fight for history has raged for seventy-five years. And it is not yet over.

ENDNOTES

INTRODUCTION

1 C.P. Stacey, "The Life and Hard Times of an Official Historian," *Canadian Historical Review* LI.1 (1970) 29. For Claxton, see David Bercuson, *True Patriot: The Life of Brooke Claxton, 1898–1960* (Toronto: University of Toronto Press, 1993).

2 Tim Cook, *Clio's Warriors: Canadian Historians and the Writing of the World Wars* (Vancouver: University of British Columbia Press, 2006) 3.

3 On social memory, see David Lowenthal, *The Past Is a Foreign Country* (Cambridge: Cambridge University Press, 1990); Richard Ned Lebow, Wulf Kansteiner, and Claudio Fogu (eds.), *The Politics of Memory in Postwar Europe* (Durham: Duke University Press, 2006); Jay Winter, *Sites of Memory, Sites of Mourning: The Great War in European Cultural History* (Cambridge: Cambridge University Press, 1995); Michael Kammen, *Mystic Chords of Memory: The Transformation of Tradition in American Culture* (New York: Alfred A. Knopf, 1991); and Nancy Wood, *Vectors of Memory: Legacies of Trauma in Postwar Europe* (New York: Berg Publishers, 1999).

4 Viet Thanh Nguyen, "Remembering War, Dreaming Peace: On Cosmopolitanism, Compassion, and Literature," *The Japanese Journal of American Studies* 20 (2009) 149.

5 John Bodnar, *The "Good War" in American Memory* (Baltimore: Johns Hopkins University Press, 2010); Kenneth D. Rose, *Myth and the Greatest Generation: A Social History of Americans in World War II* (New York: Routledge, 2008); G. Kurt Piehler, *Remembering War the American Way* (Washington: Smithsonian Institution Press, 1995); and Edward T. Linenthal and Tom Engelhardt (eds.), *History Wars: The Enola Gay and Other Battles for the American Past* (New York: Henry Holt, 1996).

6   David F. Crew, *Bodies and Ruins: Imagining the Bombing of Germany, 1945 to the Present* (Ann Arbor: University of Michigan Press, 2017); Bill Niven, *Facing the Nazi Past: United Germany and the Legacy of the Third Reich* (London and New York: Routledge, 2001); Geoff Eley (ed.), *The "Goldhagen Effect": History, Memory, Nazism—Facing the German Past* (Ann Arbor: University of Michigan Press, 2000); Pieter Lagrou, *The Legacy of Nazi Occupation: Patriotic Memory and National Recovery in Western Europe, 1945–1965* (Cambridge: Cambridge University Press, 2000); and Wolfgang Schivelbusch, *The Culture of Defeat: On National Trauma, Mourning, and Recovery* (London: Granta Books, 2004).

7   On British memory, Mark Connelly, *We Can Take It! Britain and the Memory of the Second World War* (London: Pearson Education Limited, 2004); Lucy Noakes and Juliette Pattinson (eds.), *British Cultural Memory and the Second World War* (London: Continuum, 2013); Paul Addison and Jeremy A. Crang (eds.), *The Burning Blue: A New History of the Battle of Britain* (London: Pimlico, 2000); and Graham Dawson and B. West, "Our Finest Hour? The Popular Memory of World War Two and the Struggle over National Identity," in G. Hurd (ed.), *National Fictions: World War II in British Films and Television* (London: BFI Books, 1984).

8   Henry Rousso, *The Vichy Syndrome: History and Memory in France since 1944*, trans. Arthur Goldhammer (Cambridge: Harvard University Press, 1991); and Pierre Laborie, *Le Chagrin et le venin: La France sous l'Occupation, mémoire et idées reçues* (Paris: Bayard, 2011).

9   Richard Ned Lebow, "The Memory of Politics in Postwar Europe," in Lebow et al. (eds.), *The Politics of Memory in Postwar Europe*, 33–4.

10 Olga Kucherenko, "Their Overdue Landing: A View from the Eastern Front," in Michael Dolski, Sam Edwards, and John Buckley (eds.), *D-Day in History and Memory: The Normandy Landings in International Remembrance and Commemoration* (Denton: University of North Texas Press, 2014) 221–256.

11 Jonathan Vance, *Death So Noble: Memory, Meaning, and the First World War* (Vancouver: University of British Columbia Press, 1997); Alan Bowker, *A Time Such as There Never Was Before: Canada After the Great War* (Toronto: Dundurn Press, 2014); and Tim Cook, "A Many-Layered Legacy," *Canada's History* 98.5 (October–November 2018) 12–28.

12 Tim Cook, *Vimy: The Battle and the Legend* (Toronto: Allen Lane, 2017).

13 See Amanda Betts (ed.), *In Flanders Fields: 100 Years: Writings on War, Loss and Remembrance* (Toronto: Knopf Canada, 2015).

14 Tim Cook, *The Necessary War: Canadians Fighting the Second World War, 1939–1943* (Toronto: Allen Lane, 2014); and *Fight to the Finish: Canadians in the Second World War, 1944–1945* (Toronto: Allen Lane, 2015).

ENDNOTES

CHAPTER 1

1   Peter Neary, *On to Civvy Street: Canada's Rehabilitation Program for Veterans of the Second World War* (Montreal and Kingston: McGill-Queen's University Press, 2011) 61.

2   C.P. Stacey, *Arms, Men and Governments: The War Policies of Canada, 1939–1945* (Ottawa: Queen's Printer, 1970) 590.

3   Jonathan F. Vance, *Maple Leaf Empire: Britain, Canada, and the Two World Wars* (Don Mills: Oxford University Press, 2011) 150.

4   Tami Davis Biddle, "On the Crest of Fear: V-Weapons, the Battle of the Bulge, and the Last Stages of World War II in Europe," *Journal of Military History* 83.1 (January 2019) 157–94.

5   Paul Dickson, *A Thoroughly Canadian General: A Biography of General H.D.G. Crerar* (Toronto: University of Toronto Press, 2007) 425.

6   J.L. Granatstein, *The Best Little Army in the World: The Canadians in Northwest Europe, 1944-1945* (Toronto: HarperCollins, 2015) 225.

7   James Alan Roberts, *The Canadian Summer: Memoirs of James Alan Roberts* (Toronto: University of Toronto Press, 1981) 125.

8   Rod Mickleburgh, *Rare Courage: Veterans of the Second World War Remember* (Toronto: McClelland & Stewart, 2005) 47.

9   "One Day in May," *Legion* (May 1995) 27.

10 Mark Celinscak, *Distance from the Belsen Heap: Allied Forces and the Liberation of a Nazi Concentration Camp* (Toronto: University of Toronto Press, 2015) 50.

11 Celinscak, *Distance from the Belsen Heap*, 107.

12 Leo Heaps, *Escape from Arnhem: A Canadian among the Lost Paratroops* (Toronto: Macmillan, 1945) 155–56.

13 Laura Brandon, "Reflections on the Holocaust: The Holocaust Art of Aba Bayefsky," *Canadian Military History* 6.2 (Autumn 1997) 67.

14 Glen Hancock, *Charley Goes to War: A Memoir* (Kentville: Gaspereau Press, 2004) 282.

15 Celinscak, *Distance from the Belsen Heap*, 44.

16 Henri A. van der Zee, *The Hunger Winter: Occupied Holland, 1944–5* (London: Jill Norman, 1982) 304–6.

17 Mickleburgh, *Rare Courage*, 177.

18 David Kaufman and Michiel Horn, *A Liberation Album: Canadians in the Netherlands, 1944–1945* (Toronto: McGraw-Hill Ryerson, 1980) 53.

19 van der Zee, *The Hunger Winter*, 304.

20 Lance Goddard, *Canada and the Liberation of the Netherlands, May 1945* (Toronto: Dundurn Press, 2005) 163.

21 Kaufman and Horn, *A Liberation Album*, 59.

22 Kaufman and Horn, *A Liberation Album*, 91.

23 Kaufman and Horn, *A Liberation Album*, 105.

24 Goddard, *Canada and the Liberation of the Netherlands, May 1945*, 214.

25 Goddard, *Canada and the Liberation of the Netherlands, May 1945*, 187.

26 Kaufman and Horn, *A Liberation Album*, 72.

27 Jeffrey A. Keshen, *Saints, Sinners, and Soldiers: Canada's Second World War* (Vancouver: University of British Columbia Press, 2004) 253-5; also see Michiel Horn, "More than Cigarettes, Sex and Chocolate: The Canadian Army in the Netherlands, 1944–1945," *Journal of Canadian Studies* 16.3&4 (1981) 156–73.

28 Pat Sullivan, "Unknown Soldiers," *Legion* (September 1983) 28.

29 Jacqueline Chartier, "Canada's Forgotten War Babies," *Esprit de Corps* 12.4 (April 2005).

30 Kaufman and Horn, *A Liberation Album*, 164.

CHAPTER 2

 1 Les Wagar, "One Man's Canada," *Legion* (April 1992) 10 (reprint).

 2 J.W. Pickersgill, *The Mackenzie King Record Volume 1, 1939/1944* (Toronto: University of Toronto Press, 1960–70) 591.

 3 W.S. Woods, "Veterans' Affairs and the Troops," *The Legionary* (September 1945) 10.

 4 See Historical Section, Report No. 177, Canadian Military Headquarters, declassified report. Also see Alan Allport, *Demobbed: Coming Home after World War Two* (New Haven: Yale University Press, 2009); Ben Shephard, *The Long Road Home: The Aftermath of the Second World War* (London: The Bodley Head, 2010); and Peter Neary, *On to Civvy Street: Canada's Rehabilitation Program for Veterans of the Second World War* (Montreal and Kingston: McGill-Queen's University Press, 2011).

 5 D.M. Giangreco, *Hell to Pay: Operation Downfall and the Invasion of Japan, 1945–1947* (Annapolis: Naval Institute Press, 2009).

 6 Gordon Brown and Terry Copp, *Look to Your Front . . . Reginal Rifles: A Regiment at War, 1944–1945* (Waterloo: Laurier Centre for Military, Strategic, and Disarmament Studies, 2001) 208.

 7 John Costello, *Virtue Under Fire: How World War II Changed Our Social and Sexual Attitudes* (Boston: Little, Brown & Company, 1985).

 8 Neary, *On to Civvy Street*, 172.

 9 "First Husband Returns," *Charlottetown Guardian*, 22 June 1945.

10 "Young War Widow Should Marry Again," *Windsor Star*, 17 April 1947.

11 Magda Fahrni, *Household Politics: Montreal Families and Postwar Reconstruction* (Toronto: University of Toronto Press, 2005); and Magda Fahrni, "The Romance of Reunion: Montreal War Veterans Return to Family Life, 1944–49," *Journal of the Canadian Historical Association* 9.1 (1998) 187–208.

12 Andrew Iarocci and Jeffrey A. Keshen, *A Nation in Conflict: Canada and the Two World Wars* (Toronto: University of Toronto Press, 2015) 207.

13 R. Scott Sheffield and Noah Riseman, *Indigenous Peoples and the Second World War: The Politics, Experiences and Legacies of War in the US, Canada, Australia and New Zealand* (Cambridge: Cambridge University Press, 2019) 125.

14 "Understanding the Veteran," *The Legionary* (April 1946) 46. For other challenges, see Thomas Childers, *Soldier form the War Returning: The Greatest Generation's Troubled Homecoming from World War II* (Boston: Houghton Mifflin Harcourt, 2009).

15 Doug Owram, *Born at the Right Time: A History of the Baby Boom Generation* (Toronto: University of Toronto Press, 1996).

16 Jeffrey A. Keshen, *Saints, Sinners, and Soldiers: Canada's Second World War* (Vancouver: University of British Columbia Press, 2004) 182–186.

17 Desmond Morton and J.L. Granatstein, *Victory 1945: Canadians from War to Peace* (Toronto: HarperCollins, 1995) 171.

18 Rod Mickleburgh, *Rare Courage: Veterans of the Second World War Remember* (Toronto: McClelland & Stewart, 2005) 48.

19 Robert Bothwell, *The Penguin History of Canada* (Toronto: Penguin Canada, 2006) 350.

20 Morton and Granatstein, *Victory 1945*, 86.

21 Barry Broadfoot, *The Veterans' Years: Coming Home from the War* (Vancouver: Douglas & McIntyre, 1985) 15.

22 "Veterans Replacing Temporary Employees," *The Legionary* (May 1946) 19.

23 "Veterans Got 82% of Male Jobs in Civil Service During 1946," *The Legionary* (March 1947) 13.

24 See Desmond Morton, "The Canadian Veterans' Heritage from the Great War," in Peter Neary and J.L. Granatstein (eds.), *The Veterans Charter and Post-World War II Canada* (Montreal and Kingston: McGill-Queen's University Press, 1999) 15–31

25 Neary, *On to Civvy Street*, 23.

26 Clifford H. Bowering, *Service: The Story of the Canadian Legion, 1925–1960* (Ottawa: Dominion Command, Canadian Legion, 1960) 154.

27 Walter S. Woods, *Rehabilitation: A Combined Operation* (Ottawa: Edmond Cloutier, 1953) 60.

28 "More than 46,000 Veterans [. . .]" *The Legionary* (December 1946) 41.

29 Neary, *On to Civvy Street*, 117.

30 "Education First," *The Legionary* (October 1945) 16; Ian Mackenzie, "Canada's Rehabilitation Program," *The Legionary* (March 1946) 8; and Peter Neary, "Canadian Universities and Canadian Veterans of World War II," in Neary and Granatstein (eds.), *The Veterans Charter*, 122.

31 Broadfoot, *The Veterans' Years*, 8.

32 See, for example, Dr. H.L. Stewart, "Post-War Education," *The Legionary* (February 1946) 17.

33 For statistics, see David Kaufman and Michiel Horn, *A Liberation Album: Canadians in the Netherlands, 1944–1945* (Toronto: McGraw-Hill Ryerson, 1980) 142.

34 Jean Bruce, *After the War* (Markham: Fitzhenry & Whiteside, 1982) 25.

35 See Linda Granfield, *Brass Buttons and Silver Horseshoes: Stories from Canada's War Brides* (Toronto: McClelland & Stewart, 2002); Olga Rains, Lloyd Rains, and Melynda Jarrett, *Voices of the Left Behind: Project Roots and the Canadian War Children of World War II* (Toronto: Dundurn Press, 2006); and Melynda Jarratt, *War Brides: The Stories of the Women Who Left Everything Behind to Follow the Men They Loved* (Toronto: Dundurn Press, 2009).

36 "Rehabilitation Committee Report," *The Legionary* (June 1946) 19.

37 "Legion Council Submits Brief," *The Legionary* (December 1946) 11.

38 "Legion Leader's Stirring Address," *The Legionary* (August 1946) 8.

39 Shirley Tillotson, *Give and Take: The Citizen-Taxpayer and the Rise of Canadian Democracy* (Vancouver: University of British Columbia Press, 2017).

40 Taylor Hollander, *Power, Politics, and Principles: Mackenzie King and Labour, 1935–1948* (Toronto: University of Toronto Press, 2018).

41 See J.L. Granatstein, *How Britain's Weakness Forced Canada into the Arms of the United States* (Toronto: University of Toronto Press, 1989).

42 Morton and Granatstein, *Victory 1945*, 182.

43 Hector Mackenzie, "Transatlantic Generosity: Canada's 'Billion Dollar Gift' to the United Kingdom in the Second World War," *International History Review* 34.2 (2012) 293–314; and Hector Mackenzie, "Sinews of War and Peace: The Politics of Economic Aid to Britain, 1939–1945," *International Journal* 54.4 (1999) 648–670.

44 "DVA Patients Have Almost Doubled," *The Legionary* (December 1946) 48.

45 Major E.A. Dunlop, "Disability Philosophy," *The Legionary* (February 1946) 16.

46 Serge Marc Durflinger, *Veterans with a Vision: Canada's War Blinded in Peace and War* (Vancouver: University of British Columbia Press, 2010).

47 "The House Where Dead Men Walk," *The Globe and Mail*, 18 June 1946. Also see Terry Copp, "From Neurasthenia to Post-Traumatic Stress Disorder:

Canadian Veterans and the Problem of Persistent Emotional Disabilities," in Neary and Granatstein (eds.), *The Veterans Charter*, 149–159.

48 "Veteran Suicides After Wounding Wife with Gun," *The Globe and Mail*, 18 February 1946.

49 Iarocci and Keshen, *A Nation in Conflict*, 207.

50 Cited in "Returned Man's Mind," *The Legionary* (October 1945) 18.

51 May Croft-Preston, letter, *The Legionary* (March 1946) 29.

52 Cited in Douglas Fisher, "Between the Lines," *Legion* (March 1991) 4.

CHAPTER 3

1 Tim Cook and William Stewart, "War Losses: (Canada)," 1914-1918, International Encyclopedia of the First World War.

2 David Crane, *Empires of the Dead: How One Man's Vision Led to the Creation of WWI's War Graves* (London: William Collins, 2013) 141; Fabian Ware, *The Immortal Heritage: An Account of the Work and Policy of the Imperial War Graves Commission During Twenty Years, 1917–1937* (Cambridge: The University Press, 1937); and Lisa M. Budreau, *Bodies of War: World War I and the Politics of Commemoration in America, 1919–1933* (New York: New York University Press, 2010).

3 See Robert Shipley, *To Mark Our Place: A History of Canadian War Memorials* (Toronto: NC Press Limited, 1987); and Jonathan Vance, "Remembering Armageddon," in David MacKenzie (ed.), *Canada and the First World War: Essays in Honour of Robert Craig Brown* (University of Toronto Press, 2005) 461–77.

4 Jonathan Vance, *Death So Noble: Memory, Meaning, and the First World War* (Vancouver: University of British Columbia Press, 1997); Edward Peter Soye, "Canadian War Trophies: Arthur Doughty and German Aircraft Allocated to Canada after the First World War" (Master's thesis: Royal Military College of Canada, 2009); and Alan Young, "We Throw the Torch: Canadian Memorials of the Great War and the Mythology of Historical Sacrifice," *Journal of Canadian Studies* (1989–90) 5–28.

5 See Tim Cook, *Vimy: The Battle and the Legend* (Toronto: Allen Lane, 2017); and Katrina D. Bormanis, "The Monumental Landscape: Canadian, Newfoundland, and Australian Great War Capital and Battlefield Memorials and the Topography of National Remembrance" (Ph.D. dissertation: Concordia University, 2010).

6 Wes Gustavson, "'Fairly Well Known and Need Not Be Discussed': Colonel A.F. Duguid and the Canadian Official History of the First World War," *Canadian Military History* 10.2 (Spring 2001) 41–54.

7 W.A.B. Douglas et al., *No Higher Purpose: The Official Operational History of the Royal Canadian Navy in the Second World War, 1939–1943, Volume 2, Part 1* (St. Catharines: Vanwell Pub., 2002) 634; C.P. Stacey, *Arms, Men and Governments: The War Policies of Canada, 1939–1945* (Ottawa: Queen's Printer, 1970) 66.

8 Max Hastings, *All Hell Let Loose: The World at War (1939–45)* (London: HarperPress, 2012) 669; and Jurgen Forster, "From 'Blitzkrieg' to 'Total War': Germany's War in Europe," in Roger Chickering, Stig Förster, and Bernd Greiner (eds.), *A World at Total War: Global Conflict and the Politics of Destruction, 1937–1945* (Cambridge: Cambridge University Press, 2005) 102.

9 Rana Mitter, *Forgotten Ally: China's World War II, 1937–1945* (New York: Houghton Mifflin Harcourt, 2013) 378.

10 Suzanne Evans, *Mothers of Heroes, Mothers of Martyrs: World War I and the Politics of Grief* (Montreal and Kingston: McGill-Queen's University Press, 2007); and for death policy, see Serge Durflinger, "'I Regret to Inform You': Next-of-Kin Notification and Official Condolences: The Case of Flight Lieutenant George J. Chequer, RCAF," *Canadian Military History* 9.4 (2000) 44–55.

11 H.F. Wood and John Swettenham, *Silent Witnesses* (Toronto: Hakkert, 1974) 8.

12 Douglas How, "Canada's War Dead to Remain on Battlefield," *Charlottetown Guardian*, 4 October 1945.

13 "Chapel to Honor Soldier, Though Ashes Return Overseas," *The Globe and Mail*, 8 March 1946.

14 "Burial of Unknown Soldier," *The Legionary* (June 1946) 57.

15 G.W.L. Nicholson, *"We Will Remember": Overseas Memorials to Canada's War Dead* (Ottawa: Minister of Veterans Affairs for Canada, 1973) 90.

16 "British Officer Outlines [. . .] in Search for Missing Fliers," *Crossfield Chronicle*, 31 January 1947.

17 "Silent Cities," *The Legionary* (November 1946) 7.

18 "Caring for Graves," *Gleichen Call*, 26 September 1945.

19 "Gardens of the Dead," *Charlottetown Guardian*, 9 November 1945.

20 "Silent Cities," *The Legionary*, 7.

21 Jean-François Born, "'Truly they died that we might be free': Remembering the Westlake Brothers," *Canadian Military History*, 20.3 (2011) 19–29.

22 J.L. Granatstein, "The Roads to Victory," *Legion* (1 May 2010); and Douglas How, "Canadian Dead Will Be Removed from Germany," *The Globe and Mail*, 30 October 1945.

23 Mark Sweeney, "'Representing Canadian Interests in All Matters Relative to Canadian War Dead': Lt. Col. J.A. Bailie and the Recovery, Concentration and

Burial of the 'C' Force Casualties in Japan and Hong Kong," *Canadian Military History* 27.1 (2018) 1–28.

24   Lotta Dempsey, "Person to Person," *The Globe and Mail*, 11 November 1955.

25   "Ontario Ships 8,900 Trees to Europe," *Didsbury Pioneer*, 24 May 1950.

26   Wood and Swettenham, *Silent Witnesses*, 17.

27   Philip Longworth, *The Unending Vigil: A History of the Commonwealth War Graves Commission, 1917–1984* (London: Leo Cooper, 1985) 200.

28   Eric McGeer, *Words of Valediction and Remembrance: Canadian Epitaphs of the Second World War* (St. Catharines: Vanwell Press, 2008) 12.

29   Wood and Swettenham, *Silent Witnesses*, 18.

30   MHRC, Order of the Ceremony at the Unveiling of The Halifax Memorial (pamphlet: 12 November 1967).

31   "Useful Memorials Planned After the War," *Calgary Herald*, 12 January 1945; and "Future War Memorials to Be Utilitarian," *Calgary Herald*, 17 March 1945.

32   Denise Thomson, "National Sorrow, National Pride: Commemoration of War in Canada, 1918–1945," *Journal of Canadian Studies* 30.4 (Winter 1995–96) 5–27; and "Useful Memorials Planned After the War," *Calgary Herald*, 12 January 1945. There was a similar debate in the United States; see John E. Bodnar, *The "Good War" in American Memory* (Baltimore: The Johns Hopkins University Press, 2010) 97–8.

33   "Saskatchewan Remembers," *The Legionary* (April 1956) 31.

34   "Opinions of the Legion on War Memorials," *Charlottetown Guardian*, 16 February 1945.

35   "Our National War Memorial," *The Legionary* (October 1945) 27.

36   Robert W. Thom, "Spiritual Values Should Prevail," *The Globe and Mail*, 11 July 1945.

37   Reprinted in "Too Utilitarian," *Regina Leader-Post*, 24 January 1946.

38   "Plan Service to Honor War Dead," *The Globe and Mail*, 19 July 1944.

39   "Useful Memorials Planned After the War," *Calgary Herald*, 12 January 1945

40   "A Living Memorial," *Charlottetown Guardian*, 16 October 1945.

41   "New Schoolroom Is War Memorial," *The Globe and Mail*, 15 October 1948, 8.

42   Jonathan Vance, "An Open Door to a Better Future: The Memory of Canada's Second World War," in Geoffrey Hayes, Mike Bechthold, and Matt Symes (eds.), *Canada and the Second World War: Essays in Honour of Terry Copp* (Waterloo: Wilfred Laurier University Press, 2012) 475.

43   Robert W. Thom, "Spiritual Values Should Prevail," *The Globe and Mail*, 11 July 1945.

44   James Hale, "Resolution Follows Long Battle over Memorial," *Legion* (February 1981) 32.

45 "Memorial Gets a Face-Lift," *Legion* (November 1993) 34.

46 Library and Archives Canada (LAC), William Lyon Mackenzie King diary, 24 April 1928; and D.L.A. Gordon, "William Lyon Mackenzie King, Town Planning Advocate," *Planning Perspectives* 17 (2002) 97–122.

47 David L.A. Gordon and Brian Osborne, "Constructing National Identity in Canada's Capital, 1900–2000: Confederation Square and the National War Memorial," *Journal of Historical Geography* 30.4 (2004) 633.

48 "Our National War Memorial," *The Legionary* (October 1945) 27.

49 "Our National War Memorial," *The Legionary*, 27.

50 Gordon and Osborne, "Constructing National Identity in Canada's Capital, 1900–2000," 633; Joseph Bovenzi, "'An Enduring Vision': The Federal Plan Commission, Edward H. Bennett and the Creation of Canada's Capital," (Master's thesis: Queen's University, 2005) 215; Alain Miguelez, *Transforming Ottawa: Canada's Capital in the Eyes of Jacques Gréber* (Ottawa: Old Ottawa Press, 2015) 54 and 58; and Hansard debates (21 April 1944) 2237–8.

51 J.A. Hume, "Advocates Memorial," *Ottawa Citizen*, 6 April 1945.

52 "A Poor Memorial," *Edmonton Journal*, 4 September 1945.

53 "A Cenotaph on the Hill," *Ottawa Citizen*, 11 October 1945.

54 "A Cenotaph on the Hill," *Ottawa Citizen* reprinted in *The Legionary* (March 1946) 21.

55 "A Cenotaph on the Hill," *Ottawa Citizen* reprinted in *The Legionary*, 21.

CHAPTER 4

1 The Canadian Legion of the British Empire Service League, "The Legion's Call for Total War: Presented to the Prime Minister of Canada" (Ottawa: The Legion, 1941); and "The Legion's Call for Total Victory," *The Legionary* (December 1945) inset page.

2 "Winning the Peace," *The Legionary* (September 1945) 23.

3 Dave Mcintosh, "War Veterans," *The Canadian Encyclopedia*.

4 See Tim Cook, *The Secret History of Soldiers: How Canadians Survived the Great War* (Toronto: Allen Lane, 2018) 322–48.

5 Douglas Smith, "Where Do We Go From Here?" *The Legionary* (July 1946) 15.

6 "A Bouquet," *The Legionary* (September 1945) 29; "Circulation," *The Legionary* (March 1947) 5; and Captain J. Harper Prowse, "The Road Ahead," *The Legionary* (September 1945) 8.

7 Smith, "Where Do We Go From Here?" 16.

8 Jonathan F. Vance, *Maple Leaf Empire: Britain, Canada, and the Two World Wars* (Don Mills: Oxford University Press, 2011) 200.

ENDNOTES

9 Bill McNeil, *Voices of a War Remembered: An Oral History of Canadians in World War II* (Toronto: Doubleday Canada, 1991) 241.

10 Donald Pearce, *Journal of a War: North-West Europe, 1944–1945* (Toronto: Macmillan, 1965) Introduction.

11 "Dominion-Wide Survey of Canada's War Veterans," *The Legionary* (January 1947) 40.

12 Patrick Dare, "Crowds Flock to Museum Opening," *Calgary Herald*, 8 May 2005.

13 Daniel Byers, *Zombie Army: The Canadian Army and Conscription in the Second World War* (Vancouver: University of British Columbia Press, 2016) 156.

14 See J.L. Granatstein and J.M. Hitsman, *Broken Promises: A History of Conscription in Canada* (Toronto: Oxford University Press, 1977); and Mélanie Morin-Pelletier, "'J'ai combattu le bon combat, j'ai achevé ma course, j'ai gardé la foi': Récit de guerre d'un conscript néo-brunswickois, 1943–1945," *Canadian Military History* 22.4 (2013) 45–58.

15 Byers, *Zombie Army*, 6.

16 "Salute to Crerar," *The Legionary* (September 1945) 4.

17 See Editor's note, *The Legionary* (February 1946) 32; and "New Discharge Button," *The Legionary* (February 1946) 37.

18 "The Quebec Convention," *The Legionary* (June 1946) 9–10.

19 "The Quebec Convention," 9–10.

20 "The Silver Jubilee Convention," *The Legionary* (October 1950) 15; and Richard Cleroux, "Quebec: A Very Different Command," *Legion* (July 1976) 8.

21 Smith, "Where Do We Go from Here?" 16.

22 Cliff Chadderton, "Our Heritage," *The Legionary* (December 1946) 17.

23 "The Helping Hand," *The Legionary* (March 1947) 20.

24 G.F. Young, letter, *The Legionary* (October 1945) 33.

25 See Amanda Betts (ed.), *In Flanders Fields: 100 Years: Writing on War, Loss and Remembrance* (Toronto: Alfred A. Knopf Canada, 2015); and Natascha Morrison, "Looking Backwards, Looking Forwards: Remembrance Day in Canada, 1919–2008" (Master's thesis: Carleton University, 2010).

26 "Report of the Poppy Committee," *The Legionary* (June 1946) 36.

27 "Poppy Day, 1946," *The Legionary* (October 1946) 23.

28 W.F. Ferris, letter, *The Legionary* (July 1946) 31.

29 Gordon Brown and Terry Copp, *Look to Your Front . . . Regina Rifles: A Regiment at War, 1944–1945* (Waterloo: Laurier Centre for Military, Strategic, and Disarmament Studies, 2001) 207.

30 Editorial, *Charlottetown Guardian*, 8 May 1945.

31 "A Canadian Epic," *The Legionary* (December 1945) 16.

32 "A Canadian Epic," *The Legionary*, 16.

33 Cited in *The Globe and Mail*, 22 July 1946.

34 Peter Simonds, *Maple Leaf Up, Maple Leaf Down* (New York: Island Press, 1946) 1, 2, 20, 29.

35 Bill McAndrew, Donald E. Graves, and Michael Whitby, *Normandy, 1944: The Canadian Summer* (Montreal: Éditions Art Global and Ottawa: Department of National Defence, 1994) 82.

36 On the challenge of writing, Samuel Hynes, *The Soldiers' Tale: Bearing Witness to Modern War* (New York: Penguin Books, 1998); and Ted Barris, *Breaking the Silence: Veterans' Untold Stories from the Great War to Afghanistan* (Toronto: Thomas Allen Publishers, 2009).

37 Mark Celinscak, *Distance from the Belsen Heap: Allied Forces and the Liberation of a Nazi Concentration Camp* (Toronto: University of Toronto Press, 2015) 3.

38 For the appeal of the anti-hero, see Tim Cook, "Anti-heroes of the Canadian Expeditionary Force," *Journal of the Canadian Historical Association* 19.1 (2008) 171–193.

39 Tim Cook, *Clio's Warriors: Canadian Historians and the Writing of the World Wars* (Vancouver: University of British Columbia Press, 2006), 4; also see S.F. Wise, "Canadian Official Military History: The End of an Era?," in Jeffrey Grey (ed.), *The Last Word?: Essays on Official History in the United States and British Commonwealth* (Westport: Greenwood Publishing Group, 2003).

40 Wes Gustavson, "'Fairly Well Known and Need Not Be Discussed': Colonel A.F. Duguid and the Canadian Official History of the First World War," *Canadian Military History* 10.2 (Spring 2001) 41–54.

41 For Stacey's wartime career, see C.P. Stacey, *A Date with History: Memoirs of a Canadian Historian* (Ottawa: Deneau Publishers, 1983).

42 Cook, *Clio's Warriors*, 134.

43 Library and Archives Canada (LAC), RG 24, 1983-84/167, box 498, file 1700-N/HIST (pt.1), Tucker to DNPI, 22 May 1946; Directorate of History and Heritage (DHH), URF, box 1, file 1-0, pt. II, Meeting of Service Historians, 2 April 1947.

44 C.P. Stacey, "The Life and Hard Times of an Official Historian," *Canadian Historical Review* LI.1 (1970) 33.

45 Stacey, "The Life and Hard Times . . .," 32–3.

46 LAC, RG 24, v. 12752, 24/LIAISON/1, Memorandum [written by Stacey], 2 February 1944; Ibid., Memorandum [written by Stacey], 17 August 1944; University of Toronto Archives (UTA), Stacey's personal diaries, 15 January 1948 and 23 January 1948.

47 John Hundevad, *The Legionary* (May 1948).

48 LAC, RG 24, v. 20270, Colonel C.P. Stacey, "The Nature of an Official History," unpublished [1946] 10.

49 LAC, RG 24, v. 12752, 24/LIAISON/1/2, Liaison Visit—Historical Division, W.D.S.S. Washington, memo by Stacey, 11 June 1946.

50 "What Is Military History?" *History Today* 34 (December 1984) 7.

51 On Currie's battle, see Tim Cook, *The Madman and the Butcher: The Sensational Wars of Sam Hughes and General Arthur Currie* (Toronto: Allen Lane, 2010).

52 Paul Douglas Dickson, *A Thoroughly Canadian General: A Biography of General H.D.G. Crerar* (Toronto: University of Toronto Press, 2007) 442. Also see Doug Delaney, *Corps Commanders: Five British and Canadian Generals at War, 1939–1945* (Vancouver: University of British Columbia Press, 2011).

53 Dickson, *A Thoroughly Canadian General*, 459.

54 McNeil, *Voices of a War Remembered*, 259.

55 Chris Vokes, *Vokes: My Story* (Ottawa: Gallery Books, 1985); E.L.M. Burns, *General Mud: Memoirs of Two World Wars* (Toronto : Clarke, Irwin, 1970); George Kitching, *Mud and Green Fields: The Memoirs of Major General George Kitching* (Langley: Battleline Books, 1986); and J.A. Roberts, *The Canadian Summer: The Memoirs of James Alan Roberts* (Toronto: University of Toronto Press, 1981).

56 Nigel Hamilton, *Monty: The Field Marshal, 1944-1976* (London: Hamish Hamilton, 1986) 862.

57 "Monty's Visit," *The Legionary* (December 1945) 27.

58 On his wartime leadership style, see Tim Cook, *Warlords: Borden, Mackenzie King, and Canada's World Wars* (Toronto: Allen Lane, 2012).

59 J.L. Granatstein, *Canada's War: The Politics of the Mackenzie King Government, 1939-1945* (Toronto: University of Toronto Press, 1975).

60 See David Reynolds, *In Command of History: Churchill Fighting and Writing the Second World War* (London: Penguin Books, 2005); and Christopher Dummitt, *Unbuttoned: A History of Mackenzie King's Secret Life* (Montreal and Kingston: McGill-Queen's University Press, 2017).

61 Kerstin von Lingen, *Kesselring's Last Battle: War Crimes Trials and Cold War Politics, 1945–1960* (Lawrence: University Press of Kansas, 2009).

62 Ronald Smelser and Edward Davies, *The Myth of the Eastern Front: The Nazi-Soviet War in American Popular Culture* (Cambridge: Cambridge University Press, 2008); and Donald McKale, *Nazis After Hitler: How Perpetrators of the Holocaust Cheated Justice and Truth* (Lanham: Rowman & Littlefield Publishers, 2012).

CHAPTER 5

1 Michael E. Sullivan, "Combat Motivation and the Roots of Fanaticism: The 12th SS Panzer Division Hitlerjugend in Normandy," *Canadian Military History* 10.3 (Summer 2001) 43–56; and Craig H.W. Luther, *Blood and Honor: The 12th SS Panzer Division "Hitler Youth," 1939–1945* (San Jose: R. James Bender Publishing, 1998).

2 Marc Milner, *Stopping the Panzers: The Untold Story of D-Day* (Kansas: University of Kansas Press, 2014).

3 National Archives Washington (NARA), RG 242, BDC A3433, roll SSO-313A, file "Meyer, Kurt," performance review, 30 October 1940, cited in P. Whitney Lackenbauer and Chris M.V. Madsen, *Kurt Meyer on Trial: A Documentary Record* (Kingston: Canadian Defence Academy Press, 2007) 5.

4 NARA, RG 242, BDC A3433, roll SSO-313A, file "Meyer, Kurt," performance review, 29 April 1943, cited in Lackenbauer and Madsen, *Kurt Meyer on Trial*, 6.

5 Howard Margolian, *Conduct Unbecoming: The Story of the Murder of Canadian Prisoners of War in Normandy* (Toronto: University of Toronto Press, 1998) 123.

6 Library and Archives Canada (LAC), RG 24, v. 5300, SHAEF report.

7 LAC, RG 24, v. 2881, file HAQ 8959-9/1, "Supplementary Report of the Supreme Headquarters Allied Expeditionary Forces Court of Inquiry re Shooting of Allied Prisoners of War," April 1945.

8 For some of these issues, see Tomaz Jardim, *The Mauthausen Trial: American Military Justice in Germany* (Cambridge: Harvard University Press, 2012).

9 Also see Special Interrogation Report, "Brigadeführer Kurt Meyer, Commander 12th SS Panzer Division 'Hitler Jugend'" (6 June–25 August 1944), *Canadian Military History* 11.4 (Autumn 2002) 59–70.

10 See Richard L. Lael, *The Yamashita Precedent: War Crimes and Command Responsibility* (Wilmington: Scholarly Resources, 1982); and Lawrence Taylor, *A Trial of Generals: Homma, Yamashita, Macarthur* (Indiana: Icarus Press, 1981).

11 LAC, RG 24, v. 12837, file 67/CNO/12 SS/1, Jesionek statement, 22 April 1945; and Bruce J.S. Macdonald, *The Trial of Kurt Meyer* (Toronto: Clarke, Irwin, and Co., 1954) 58–63.

12 Macdonald, *The Trial of Kurt Meyer*, 195.

13 Ralph Allen, "Canadian Troops Shot With Their Hands Up, Military Court Told," *The Globe and Mail*, 12 December 1945.

14 Ralph Allen, "Lonely Walk of Canadians to Death Told," *The Globe and Mail*, 15 December 1945.

15 Ross Munro, "He Saw Prisoners Shot: Canadian Wounded by SS," *The Maple Leaf*–UK Edition, 13 December 1945.

16 Tony Foster, *Meeting of Generals* (Toronto: Methuen, 1986) xxiii, 350.

17 Macdonald, *The Trial of Kurt Meyer*, 195.

18 Directorate of History and Heritage (DHH), file 112.3H1.003, D2, Vokes to Ian Campbell, 15 May 1981.

19 Lackenbauer and Madsen, *Kurt Meyer on Trial*, 19; and Major General Chris Vokes with John P. Maclean, *Vokes: My Story* (Ottawa: Gallery Books, 1985) 205–8. Also see LAC, RG 24, v. 12843, remarks by confirming officers, 21 January 1946 [a memo by Vokes on the reasons for commuting the sentence.]; and Foster, *Meeting of Generals*, 350.

20 *Toronto Telegram*, 15 January 1946.

21 "Rabbi Deplores Nazi's Sentence," *Toronto Star*, 17 January 1946. For other reactions, see Directorate of History and Heritage (DHH), 159.95 (D1).

22 Lackenbauer and Madsen, *Kurt Meyer on Trial*, 19; and Lisa Goodyear, "In the Name of Justice or Finding a Place: Canadian War Crimes Prosecutions at the end of the Second World War" (Master's thesis: Royal Military College of Canada, 2002) 66.

23 Ralph Allen, "Was Kurt Meyer Guilty?" *Maclean's*, 1 February 1950.

24 "Meyer Can't Kick at Civil Prison," clipping, in LAC, RG 73, v. 9, file 2265, no. 4.

25 See *Maclean's*, P.M. Wass and Mary Gates, 15 March 1950.

26 On the challenge of German East and West relations, see Pertti Ahonen, *After the Expulsion: Western Germany and Eastern Europe, 1945–1990* (Oxford and New York: Oxford University Press, 2003).

27 David Bercuson, "The Return of the Canadians to Europe: Britannia Rules the Rhine," in M.O. MacMillan and D.S. Sorenson (eds.), *Canada and NATO: Uneasy Past, Uncertain Future* (Waterloo: University of Waterloo Press, 1990) 15–26.

28 L.B. Pearson, *Mike: The Memoirs of the Right Honourable Lester B. Pearson, vol. 2: 1948–1957,* eds. John A. Munro and Alex I. Inglis (Toronto: University of Toronto Press, 1973) 85.

29 "Delayed Action," *Time*, 26 February 1951. Also see clippings in LAC, RG 73, v. 9, file 2265, no. 2.

30 Patrick Brode, *Casual Slaughters and Accidental Judgments Canadian War Crimes Prosecutions, 1944–1948* (Toronto: University of Toronto Press, 1997) vii.

31 LAC, RG 2, v.2751, Cabinet Defence Committee documents, minutes of meeting, 12 September 1951.

32 *The Globe and Mail*, 22 October 1951.

33 Ray Gardner, "Wanted for Murder" (pamphlet: 1951).

34 Douglas How, "Gen. Meyer Out on Pass from Prison," *The Globe and Mail*, 26 November 1951.

35 Directorate of History and Heritage (DHH), 159.95 (D1), "References in Hansard."

36 See Lackenbauer and Madsen, F1-5.

37 LAC, RG 2, v. 2653, German war criminals, 13 August 1953.

38 Order-in-Council P.C. 1954/75; LAC, RG 25, v. 4229, German war criminals, 17 March 1952.

39 *Toronto Evening Telegram*, 16 January 1954.

40 *British Colonist*, 19 January 1954. Also see Directorate of History and Heritage (DHH), 159.95 (D1), "References in Hansard."

41 "Keep Moving—Don't Block the Exit," *Calgary Herald*, 28 January 1954.

42 Mark Reynolds, "The Kurt Meyer Conundrum," *The Beaver* (April/May 2003) 19.

43 Macdonald, *The Trial of Kurt Meyer*, 204–5; Sam H.S. Hughes, review, *Canadian Historical Review* 36.1 (March 1955) 164–5.

44 George H. Stein, *The Waffen SS: Hitler's Elite Guard at War, 1939–1945* (London: Cornell University Press, 1966) 252–8.

45 Kurt Meyer, *Grenadiere* (Munich: Schild, 1957); and Kurt Meyer, *Grenadiers*, trans. Michaele Mende (Winnipeg: F.F. Fedorowicz, 1994).

46 "The Veteran More Than Holds His Own," *The Legionary* (November 1946) 39.

47 Serge Marc Durflinger, *Veterans with a Vision: Canada's War Blinded in Peace and War* (Vancouver: University of British Columbia Press, 2010) 222.

48 Norman Shannon, "Is the Legion a Victim of Success?" *The Legionary* (March 1956) 23.

49 Barry Broadfoot, *The Veterans' Years: Coming Home from the War* (Vancouver: Douglas & McIntyre, 1985) 11.

50 Doug Smith, "On Fast Workers and War Brides," *The Legionary* (January 1962) 34.

51 James Hale, *Branching Out: The Story of the Canadian Legion* (Ottawa: Royal Canadian Legion, 1995) 94. Also see Harold Baldwin, "Youth Will Be Served," *The Legionary* (March 1946) 15.

52 "The Dominion," *The Legionary* (December 1957) 20.

53 Douglas Fisher, "The Observation Post," *The Legionary* (October 1950) 56.

54 "Canada Must Live," *The Legionary* (March 1947) 27.

55 See David J. Bercuson, *Blood on the Hills: The Canadian Army in the Korean War* (Toronto: University of Toronto Press, 1999); and "1957 in Retrospect," *The Legionary* (January 1958) 12.

56 Leslie Morrison, "No Greater Joy," *The Legionary* (October 1957) 10–11.

57 "Benefits Extended," *Legion* (January 1970) 42.

58 John O. Anderson, "Quo Vadimus?" *The Legionary* (October 1955) 14–15.

59 Norman Shannon, "The Valiant Lady of Vibank," *The Legionary* (December 1955) 10–11.

60 "The Meaning of Remembrance," *The Legionary* (October 1956) 11–12.

61 "Canada Pays Tribute to War Dead," *Edmonton Journal*, 12 November 1957.

62 "The Meaning of Remembrance," *The Legionary* (October 1956) 11–12.

63 Reprinted in *The Legionary* (December 1960) 17.

64 Norman Shannon, "The Legion, 1925–1960," *The Legionary* (August 1960) 10–15.

65 R.B. Shaw, "Revitalize the Legion!" *The Legionary* (June 1960) 15.

CHAPTER 6

1 Charles Lynch, "Tenth Anniversary: D-Day Veterans Revisit Normandy Battle Sites," *The Globe and Mail*, 5 June 1954.

2 "World War II Book of Remembrance," *The Legionary* (January 1957) 10.

3 "World War II Book of Remembrance Unveiled by the Governor-General," *The Legionary* (December 1957) 7.

4 "World War II Book of Remembrance Unveiled by the Governor-General," *The Legionary,* 7.

5 "Some Further Thoughts on A National Cenotaph," *The Legionary* (March 1956) 4.

6 "A National Cenotaph," *The Legionary* (December 1955) 12

7 Cabinet Conclusion Document, "National Memorial Building," item number 16472, 4 November 1957; "Site Near Parliament Hill Chosen for New Cenotaph," *The Globe and Mail*, 1 May 1956; and *Hansard*, 30 April 1956.

8 *Hansard*, 30 April 1956, accessed online; and "National Cenotaph and Remembrance Shrine to Be Erected in Nation's Capital," *The Legionary* (June 1956) 12.

9 *Hansard*, 17 February 1960.

10 The Ottawa Bureau, "Towering War Memorial Planned," *The Globe and Mail*, 20 February 1963.

11 "High Principles," *The Legionary* (May 1962) 8.

12 Douglas Fisher, "Between Ourselves," *Legion* (November 1975) 2A.

13 See John Ross Matheson, *Canada's Flag: A Search for a Country* (Boston: G.K. Hall, 1980).

14 "The 20th Dominion Convention," *The Legionary* (July 1964) 7.

15 Lester B. Pearson, "Address by the Prime Minister," *The Legionary* (July 1964) 44.

16 Rick Archbold, *I Stand for Canada: The Story of the Maple Leaf Flag* (Toronto: Macfarlane Walter & Ross, 2002) 3.

17 Christian P. Champion, *The Strange Demise of British Canada: The Liberals and Canadian Nationalism, 1964–68* (Montreal and Kingston: McGill-Queen's University Press, 2010); and José E. Igartua, *The Other Quiet Revolution:*

National Identities in English Canada, 1945–71 (Vancouver: University of British Columbia Press, 2006).

18 Archbold, *I Stand for Canada*, 24.

19 "An Epic Speech," *The Legionary* (November 1964) 32.

20 "$1,500,000 Job," *The Globe and Mail*, 6 August 1963, 1.

21 "Shrine Delights Legion," *Ottawa Citizen*, 8 August 1963. Also see Malcolm Ferguson, "Canada's Response: The Making and Remaking of the National War Memorial" (Master's thesis: Carleton University, 2012); and John Hundevad, "Plans for National Memorial to All Canada's Fallen Are Announced," *The Legionary* (April 1963) 13–4.

22 Library and Archives Canada (LAC), Lester B. Pearson papers, MG26 N3, Vol. 39, G.F. Maclaren to Lester B. Pearson, 6 September 1963.

23 Doris Anderson, "A Birthday Present We Don't Need," *Chatelaine*, October 1963, 3.

24 Doris Anderson, "A Birthday Present We Don't Need," 3.

25 LAC, Lester B. Pearson papers, MG26 N3, Vol. 39, C. Carter to Lester B. Pearson, 21 October 1963.

26 Arnold Edinborough, "Let Canada Be the Memorial," *Saturday Night*, December 1963, 8.

27 "Should Ottawa Build a New War Memorial?" *Montreal Gazette*, 15 August 1963.

28 Oakley Dalgleish, "In Memoriam," *The Globe and Mail*, 23 February 1963.

29 "War Memorial," *Calgary Herald*, 7 September 1963.

30 James Hale, "Resolution Follows Long Battle over Memorial," *Legion* (February 1981) 32.

31 *Hansard*, 28 October 1963, 4078.

32 LAC, Lester B. Pearson papers, MG26 N3, Vol. 39, Lloyd Francis to Lester B. Pearson, 10 September 1963.

33 LAC, Lester B. Pearson papers, MG26 N3, Vol. 39, J.S. Hodgson to Roger Teillet, 19 August 1963.

34 Norman Campbell, "Parliament," *Ottawa Citizen*, 22 February 1964; Richard Jackson, "Hill Talk," *The Ottawa Journal*, 7 March 1964; and J.A. Hume, "$17 Million War Memorial Program," *Ottawa Citizen*, 4 December 1965.

35 "Legion's Brief to Cabinet," *The Legionary* (December 1964) 11.

36 "Dominion President's Report," *The Legionary* (July 1964) 38.

37 Sarah Jennings, *Art and Politics: The History of the National Arts Centre* (Toronto: Dundurn Press, 2009) 10.

38 Jonathan F. Vance, *A History of Canadian Culture* (Toronto: Oxford University Press, 2009) 380.

39 *Hansard*, 15 January 1964, 826.

ENDNOTES

CHAPTER 7

1 University of Toronto Archives, C.P. Stacey's diary, 26 February 1954, 2 March 1954; and C.P. Stacey, *A Date with History: Memoirs of a Canadian Historian* (Ottawa: Deneau, 1983) 153.

2 C.P. Stacey, *Six Years of War: The Army in Canada, Britain and the Pacific (The Official History of the Canadian Army in the Second World War), vol. 1* (Ottawa: Minister of National Defence, 1955) 397–404.

3 Forrest C. Pogue review in the *Journal of Modern History* (June 1957).

4 Directorate of History and Heritage (DHH), Unprocessed material, box 1, file 1-0-1-1, Nicholson to Stacey, 18 March 1960.

5 C.P. Stacey, *The Victory Campaign: The Operations in North-West Europe, 1944–1945 (The Official History of the Canadian Army in the Second World War), vol. 3* (Ottawa: Queen's Own Printer, 1960).

6 DHH, Unprocessed material, box 8, file 1-15-0, Stacey, "Removal of Commanding Officers in Normandy," 28 January 1959; and Tim Cook, *Clio's Warriors: Canadian Historians and the Writing of the World Wars* (Vancouver: University of British Columbia Press, 2006), 192–4.

7 Stacey, *The Victory Campaign*, 275.

8 C.P. Stacey, "The Life and Hard Times of an Official Historian," *Canadian Historical Review* 51.1 (1970) 45–6; and Stacey, *The Victory Campaign*, 275.

9 Cited in Jeffrey Grey, *A Commonwealth of Histories: The Official Histories of the Second World War in the United States, Britain and the Commonwealth, Trevor Reese Memorial Lecture 1998*, (London: Sir Robert Menzies Centre for Australian Studies, 1998) 7.

10 *The Globe and Mail*, 27 September 1958, 16.

11 *The Globe and Mail*, 27 September 1958, 16.

12 Both citations from Zachary Abram, "The Knights of Faith: The Soldier in Canadian War Fiction" (Ph.D. dissertation: University of Ottawa, 2016) 131–2.

13 Interview, 19 June 2019.

14 Interview, 7 July 2019.

15 See Thomas Doherty, *Projections of War: Hollywood, American Culture and World War II* (New York: Columbia University Press, 1993); and Gregory D. Black, *Hollywood Goes to War: How Politics, Profits, and Propaganda Shaped World War II* (Berkeley: University of California Press, 1987).

16 Nicholas Pronay, "The British Post-Bellum Cinema: A Survey of the Films Relating to World War II Made in Britain between 1945 and 1960," *Historical Journal of Film, Radio and Television* 8.1 (1988) 5; and Robert Murphy, *British Cinema and the Second World War* (London: Continuum, 2000) 235.

17 See Sarah Klotz, "Shooting the War: The Canadian Army Film Unit in the Second World War," *Canadian Military History* 14.3 (2005) 21-38.

18 Dominique Bregent-Heald, "Big Spy Country: Film and the U.S.-Canada Border-lands during the Second World War," *49ᵗʰ Parallel* 29 (Summer 2012) 1–20.

19 Hugh Halliday, "Airman on Set," *Legion* (7 September 2017).

20 *Toronto Daily Star*, 12 February 1942.

21 Paul Litt, *The Muses, The Masses, and the Massey Commission* (Toronto: University of Toronto Press, 1992).

22 Cornelius Ryan, *The Longest Day* (New York: Simon and Schuster, 1959) Foreword.

23 See Robert Brent Toplin, "Hollywood's D-Day from the Perspective of the 1960s and 1990s: *The Longest Day* and *Saving Private Ryan*," in Peter C. Rollins and John E. O'Connor (eds.), *Why We Fought: America's Wars in Film and History* (Lexington: The University Press of Kentucky, 2008) 303–14.

24 Gordon Stoneham, "At the Movies," *Ottawa Citizen*, 9 February 1963.

25 Bob Shiels, "The Longest Day," *Calgary Herald*, 1 March 1963; and Michael R. Dolski, "'Portal of Liberation': D-Day Myth as American Self-Affirmation" in Michael Dolski, Sam Edwards, and John Buckley (eds.), *D-Day in History and Memory: The Normandy Landings in International Remembrance and Commemoration* (Denton: University of North Texas Press, 2014) 57.

26 Frank Morriss, "*Longest Day* Is Memorable Movie," *The Globe and Mail*, 20 December 1962, 13; also see Jim Coleman, "On Zanuck's *Longest Day*," *Edmonton Journal*, 21 December 1962.

27 "People," *Ottawa Citizen*, 6 February 1963; and Al Watson, letter, *Ottawa Citizen*, 5 March 1963.

28 Terry Copp and Matt Symes, "Canada's D-Day: Politics, Media, and the Fluidity of Memory," in Michael Dolski, Sam Edwards, and John Buckley (eds.), *D-Day in History and Memory: The Normandy Landings in International Remembrance and Commemoration* (Denton: University of North Texas Press, 2014) 140.

29 The National Film Board of Canada, *Donald Brittain: Never The Ordinary Way* (Winnipeg and Vancouver: NFB Canada, 1991) 15–16; and "World War II Flashback," *Edmonton Journal*, 7 April 1962.

30 "Sights, Sounds of Canada at War," *Ottawa Citizen*, 24 March 1962; and "'Canada at War': Series to Be Shown on T.V. by C.B.C.," *The Legionary* (March 1962) 16.

31 "13-Week Series: Canada's War Memories Evoked," *The Globe and Mail*, 23 March 1962; and "'Canada at War,'" *The Legionary*, 16.

32 "CBC-TV Now Reviews Canada's War Role," *The Globe and Mail*, 5 April 1962.

33 "CBC-TV Now Reviews Canada's War Role," *The Globe and Mail,* 5 April 1962.

34 "Bob Shiels on Television," *Calgary Herald,* 14 April 1962.

35 Phil Lee, "T.V. with Lee," *Times Colonist,* 13 April 1962.

36 "The Week's Highlights: Wacky World of Jerry Lewis Is Visited," *The Globe and Mail,* 25 May 1962.

37 This point is made in Ted Barris, *The Great Escape: The Untold Story* (Toronto: Dundurn Press, 2013).

38 A.R. Trimble, letter, *Legion* (October 1969) 7.

CHAPTER 8

1 Scott Young, "Legislation to Remember?" *The Globe and Mail,* 15 August 1968.

2 "Let's Stop Tampering with November 11th," *The Fragment* (December 1968) 4.

3 "This Bill Must Not Pass!," *Legion* (January 1970) 7; and Barney Danson with Curtis Fahey, *Not Bad for a Sergeant: The Memoirs of Barney Danson* (Toronto: Dundurn Press, 2002) 102–4.

4 Interview with Dr. Alan Bowker, 16 April 2019.

5 "Let's Stop Tampering with November 11th," *The Fragment* 4.

6 Robert Shipley, *To Mark Our Place: A History of Canadian War Memorials* (Toronto: NC Press Limited, 1987) 14.

7 "The 1960 Poppy Campaign," *The Legionary* (June 1961) 31–2.

8 "Honour the Dead: Remember the Living," *The Legionary* (October 1961) 9.

9 Clifford H. Bowering, *Service: The Story of the Canadian Legion, 1925–1960* (Ottawa: Dominion Command, Canadian Legion, 1960) 195.

10 R.G. Lovell, "Our Heritage: Lest We Forget," *The Legionary* (September 1964) 32.

11 Lovell, "Our Heritage: Lest We Forget," *The Legionary* 32.

12 A.W. Harrison, letter, *The Legionary* (October 1964) 5.

13 "Canadians Write Dutch Families Caring of Graves," *Wainwright Star,* 16 May 1947.

14 "Dutch 'Adopt' Canadian Graves," *The Legionary* (March 1947) 11.

15 Bruck West, "Letter to a Canadian Mother," *The Globe and Mail,* 14 April 1949.

16 Karin Roos, letter, *The Legionary* (March 1961) 5.

17 "Graves of Canadians Shaped in Maple Leaf," *The Globe and Mail,* 8 December 1947.

18 Elaine Young, "Being 'Over There': Veterans, Civilians, and the Vimy Pilgrimage of 1936" (Master's thesis: York University, 2008); and John Hundevad (ed.), *Guide Book of the Pilgrimage to Vimy and the Battlefields, July–August, 1936* (Ottawa: Published on behalf of the Vimy Pilgrimage Committee by *The Veteran,* 1936).

19 Arthur Randles, "Overseas Pilgrimages," *The Legionary* (November 1950) 16.

20 "Silver Cross Women Want Pilgrimage," *The Globe and Mail*, 11 May 1956.

21 "Next-of-Kin Pilgrimage," *The Legionary* (March 1962) 14.

22 "Canadians Meet Queen Juliana," *The Globe and Mail*, 3 October 1962.

23 "The Holland Pilgrimage," *Legion* (November 1975) 35.

24 "More Canadians Sample Dutch Hospitality," *The Legionary* (November 1964) 16.

25 Lance Goddard, *Canada and the Liberation of the Netherlands, May 1945* (Toronto: Dundurn Press, 2005) 228.

26 Doug Smith, "What Price Glory?" *Legion* (October 1969) 34.

27 Charles Lynch, "D-Day Got the Headlines but Worst Was to Come," *Ottawa Citizen*, 5 June 1984.

28 John MacFarlane, *Triquet's Cross: A Study of Military Heroism* (Montreal and Kingston: McGill-Queen's University Press, 2009) 140–1.

29 MacFarlane, *Triquet's Cross*, 140–1.

30 Norman DePoe, "Youth Reflect on D-Day in the Vietnam Era," CBC-TV's *Newsmagazine*, 3 June 1969, CBC Digital Archives.

CHAPTER 9

1 Ernest A. Crosthwaite, letter, *The Legionary* (April 1965) 6.

2 E.C. Box, letter, *The Legionary* (April 1965) 6.

3 "Reflections on Remembrance," *Legion* (November 1975) 24.

4 "The Poppy and Remembrance," *Legion* (September 1971) 12.

5 Willis Moogk, letter, *Legion* (January 1970) 3.

6 "Bridging the Generation Gap," *Legion* (September 1971) 8.

7 See John MacFarlane, *Ernest Lapointe and Quebec's Influence on Canada's Foreign Policy* (Toronto: University of Toronto Press, 1999).

8 Daniel Byers, *Zombie Army: The Canadian Army and Conscription in the Second World War* (Vancouver: University of British Columbia Press, 2016) 7.

9 John MacFarlane, *Triquet's Cross: A Study of Military Heroism* (Montreal and Kingston: McGill-Queen's University Press, 2009) 118.

10 J.L. Granatstein, *The Generals: The Canadian Army's Senior Commanders in the Second World War* (Toronto: Stoddart Publishing Co., 1993) 238, 256.

11 Robert Speaight, *Vanier: Soldier, Diplomat & Governor General* (Toronto: Collins & Harvill, 1970).

12 MacFarlane, *Triquet's Cross*, 118.

13 Albert Braz, *The False Traitor: Louis Riel in Canadian Culture* (Toronto: University of Toronto Press, 2003).

14 Ronald Rudin, *Making History in Twentieth-Century Quebec* (Toronto: University of Toronto Press, 1997) 95; Jocelyn Létourneau, *A History for the*

Future: Rewriting Memory and Identity in Quebec (Montreal and Kingston: McGill Queen's University Press, 2004) 4; Mourad Djebabla-Brun, *Se souvenir de la Grande Guerre: La mémoire plurielle de 14–18 au Québec* (Montreal: VLB Éditeur, 2004); and Mourad Djebabla, "Historiographie francophone de la Première Guerre mondiale: Écrire la Grande Guerre de 1914–1918 français au Canada et au Québec," *Canadian Historical Review* 95.3 (September 2014) 407–16.

15 Geoff Keelan, "'Il a bien merité de la Patrie': The 22nd Battalion and the Memory of Courcelette," *Canadian Military History* 19.3 (Summer 2010): 28–40; Jean Provencher, *Québec sous la loi des mesures de guerre 1918* (Montreal: Les Éditions du Boréal, 1971); and John English, *Just Watch Me: The Life of Pierre Elliott Trudeau, 1968–2000* (Toronto: Knopf Canada, 2009) 92.

16 Beatrice Richard, "La mémoire collective de la guerre au Québec: Un espace de résistance politique?" *Canadian Issues/Themes canadiens* (2004) 18–9.

17 Beatrice Richard, "Dieppe: The Making of a Myth," *Canadian Military History* 21.4 (2015) 44.

18 Timothy Balzer, *The Information Front: The Canadian Army and News Management during the Second World War* (Vancouver: University of British Columbia Press, 2010).

19 "Silver Cross Women Take Part in Ceremony," *The Globe and Mail*, 15 August 1959.

20 "Fusiliers Mont Royal Remember," *Montreal Gazette*, 18 August 1947; and "Ship Bombing Recalled," *The Globe and Mail*, 18 August 1944.

21 Mark David Sheftall, *Altered Memories of the Great War: Divergent Narratives of Britain, Australia, New Zealand and Canada* (London: I.B. Tauris, 2009).

22 "Dieppe Fallen Are Honored," *The Globe and Mail*, 23 August 1953.

23 Editorial, *The Legionary* (April 1956) 5.

24 Tim Cook, "Immortalizing the Canadian Soldier: Lord Beaverbrook, the Canadian War Records Office in the First World War," in Briton C. Busch (ed.), *Canada and the Great War: Western Front Association Papers* (Montreal and Kingston: McGill-Queen's University Press, 2003) 46–65.

25 Brian Villa, *Unauthorized Action: Mountbatten and the Dieppe Raid* (Toronto: Oxford University Press, 1989 [1994]); Béatrice Richard, *La mémoire de Dieppe: Radioscopie d'un mythe* (Montreal: VLB Éditeur, 2002); Peter Henshaw, "The Dieppe Raid: A Product of Misplaced Canadian Nationalism?" *Canadian Historical Review* 77.2 (1996) 250–66; Brian Villa and Peter Henshaw, "The Dieppe Raid Debate," *Canadian Historical Review* 79.2 (1998) 304–15; and David O'Keefe, *One Day in August: The Untold Story Behind Canada's Tragedy at Dieppe* (Toronto: Vintage Canada, 2014).

26 H.M. Woffindin, letter, *The Legionary* (June 1956) 6.

27 Milton Shulman, "The Dieppe Raid: Who Bungled It?" *The Legionary* (April 1956) 30.

28 "Veterans Recall Horror on Beach," *The Globe and Mail*, 20 August 1982.

29 Mel Bradshaw, "The Legacy of Ortona," *Canadian Forum* (December 1983) 12.

CHAPTER 10

1 C.P. Stacey, *Canada and the Age of Conflict: A History of Canadian External Policies, vol 1: 1867–1921* (Toronto: Macmillan of Canada, 1977) 238.

2 J.L. Granatstein, *The Generals: The Canadian Army's Senior Commanders in the Second World War* (Calgary: University of Calgary Press, 2005) 112.

3 Terry Copp, "To the Last Canadian? Casualties in 21st Army Group," *Canadian Military History* 18.1 (Winter 2009) 3–6.

4 Terry Copp, "The Approach to Verrières Ridge: Army, Part 25," *Legion Magazine* (1 March 1999).

5 Terry Copp and Robert Vogel, "No Lack of Rational Speed: 1st Canadian Army Operations, September 1944," *Journal of Canadian Studies* 16.3–4 (Fall–Winter 1981) 145; John A. English, *The Canadian Army and the Normandy Campaign: A Study of Failure in High Command* (New York: Praeger, 1991); and J.L. Granatstein, *The Best Little Army in the World: The Canadians in Northwest Europe 1944–1945* (Toronto: HarperCollins, 2015).

6 W.A.B. Douglas, "The Prospects for Naval History," *The Northern Mariner* 1.4 (October 1991) 19; James A. Boutilier (ed.), *The RCN in Retrospect, 1910–1968* (Vancouver: University of British Columbia Press, 1982); and W.A.B. Douglas (ed.), *The RCN in Transition, 1910–1985* (Vancouver: University of British Columbia Press, 1988).

7 For the quote, see Marc Milner, *Canada's Navy: The First Century* (Toronto: University of Toronto Press, 1999) 96.

8 W.A.B. Douglas, "Canadian Naval Historiography," *Mariner's Mirror* LXX.4 (November 1984) 349–362; and W.A.B. Douglas, "The Prospects for Naval History," 19–26.

9 Marc Milner, *North Atlantic Run: The Royal Canadian Navy and the Battle for the Convoys* (Toronto: University of Toronto Press, 1985); and Marc Milner, *The U–boat Hunters: The Royal Canadian Navy and the Offensive against Germany's Submarines* (Toronto: University of Toronto Press, 1994)

10 W.A.B. Douglas et al., *No Higher Purpose: The Official Operational History of the Royal Canadian Navy in the Second World War, 1939–1943, Volume II, Part 1* (St. Catharines: Vanwell, 2002); W.A.B. Douglas et al., *A Blue Water Navy: The Official Operational History of the Royal Canadian Navy in the Second*

World War, 1943–1945, Volume II, Part 2 (St. Catharines: Vanwell, 2007); and William Johnston et al., *The Seabound Coast: The Official History of the Royal Canadian Navy, 1867–1939, Volume I* (Toronto: Dundurn Press, 2010).

11 For a discussion of the British and American ways of war in Normandy, see John Buckley, *Monty's Men: The British Army and the Liberation of Europe* (New Haven and London: Yale University Press, 2013) Introduction.

12 Max Hastings, *Overlord: D-Day and the Battle for Normandy 1944* (New York: HarperCollins, 1984) 211; and Paul Koring, "Book Raps Canadians' Performance in Normandy," *Ottawa Citizen*, 1 June 1984. Also see W.A.B. Douglas, "Two New Histories Take Different Approaches," *Ottawa Citizen*, 9 June 1984; and Noel Taylor, "Overlord," *Ottawa Citizen*, 5 June 1984.

13 Buckley, *Monty's Men*, 5–8; and Carlo D'Este, *Decision in Normandy: The Unwritten Story of Montgomery and the Allied Campaign* (London: Pan, 1984) 457.

14 Colin McCullough, *Creating Canada's Peacekeeping Past* (Vancouver: University of British Columbia Press, 2016) 123.

15 See Norman Hillmer, "Peacekeeping: The Inevitability of Canada's Role," in Michael A. Hennessy and B.J.C. McKercher (eds.), *War in the Twentieth Century: Reflections at Century's End* (Westport and London: Praeger, 2003) 145–65; for the Canadian forces' activities beyond peacekeeping, see Sean Maloney, *Canada and UN Peacekeeping: Cold War by Other Means, 1945–1970* (St. Catharines: Vanwell, 2002).

16 All quotes here from James Hale, "Resolution Follows Long Battle over Memorial," *Legion* (February 1981) 32.

17 Jim Garner, "Memorial's Updating Result of Long Debate," *Ottawa Citizen*, 27 May 1982.

18 John Gardam, *The National War Memorial* (Ottawa: Supply and Services Canada, 1982), 2.

19 Michael Dolski, Sam Edwards, and John Buckley, "Introduction," in Michael Dolski, Sam Edwards, and John Buckley (eds.), *D-Day in History and Memory: The Normandy Landings in International Remembrance and Commemoration* (Denton: University of North Texas Press, 2014) 24.

20 For the meaning of these types of gatherings, see Matthew Graves, "Memorial Diplomacy in Franco-Australian Relations," in Shanti Sumartojo and Ben Wellings (eds.), *Nation, Memory and Great War Commemoration: Mobilizing the Past in Europe, Australia and New Zealand* (Bern: Peter Lang, 2014).

21 Charles Lynch, "Canadians Should Be Told Our Boys Were Heroes Too," *Ottawa Citizen*, 26 May 1984. Alterations in original.

22 *Time* magazine, 28 May 1984.

23 Lynch, "Canadians Should Be Told Our Boys Were Heroes Too."

24 "Networks Plan Special D-Day Programming," *Ottawa Citizen*, 2 June 1984.

25 For Reagan's speech, see Michael R. Dolski, "'Portal of Liberation': D-Day Myth as American Self-Affirmation," in Dolski et al. (eds.), *D-Day in History and Memory*, 61–2; and Douglas Brinkley, *The Boys of Pointe du Hoc: Ronald Reagan, D-Day, and the U.S. Army 2nd Ranger Battalion* (New York: William Morrow, 2005) 186–92.

26 Tyler Marshall, "Germans Still Carry the Heavy Weight of Their History," *Ottawa Citizen*, 31 May 1984.

27 Charles Lynch, "Spirit of D-Day," *Ottawa Citizen*, 7 June 1984.

28 Mark Kennedy, "I Can Still See Us There, Getting Slaughtered," *Ottawa Citizen*, 9 June 1984.

29 Paul Koring, "Non-Combatant Trudeau's Presence Angers Veterans," *Ottawa Citizen*, 7 June 1984; and Mark Kennedy, "French Greet Vets with Hero's Welcome," *Ottawa Citizen*, 4 June 1984.

30 For a critical reading of Trudeau during the war, see Max and Monique Nemni, *Young Trudeau: Son of Quebec, Father of Canada, 1919–1944*, trans. William Johnson (Toronto: Douglas Gibson Books, 2005).

31 Koring, "Non-Combatant Trudeau's Presence Angers Veterans," *Ottawa Citizen*.

32 *Ottawa Citizen*, 9 April 1994.

33 Marci McDonald, "A Memorial Plan," *Maclean's* (11 June 1984) 27.

34 "Vets at D-Day Ceremony Riled by Media," *Ottawa Citizen*, 7 June 1984.

35 McDonald, "A Memorial Plan." *Maclean's*.

36 Kennedy, "French Greet Vets with Hero's Welcome," *Ottawa Citizen*.

37 Michael C.C. Adams, *The Best War Ever: America and World War II*, (Baltimore: John Hopkins University Press, 2015) 15.

CHAPTER 11

1 Kent Fedorowich, "'Cocked Hats and Swords and Small, Little Garrisons': Britain, Canada and the Fall of Hong Kong, 1941," *Modern Asian Studies* 37.1 (February 2003) 111–57; Terry Copp, "The Decision to Reinforce Hong Kong: September 1941," *Canadian Military History* 20.2 (Spring 2011) 11.

2 On the PoW experience, see Nathan M. Greenfield, *The Damned: The Canadians at the Battle of Hong Kong and the POW Experience, 1941–1945* (Toronto: HarperCollins Canada, 2010); and Matthew Schwarzkopf, "The Second Mission: Canadian Survival in Hong Kong Prisoner-of-War Camps, 1941–1945" (Master's thesis: University of Ottawa, 2019).

3 See Bradley St. Croix, "The Omnipresent Threat: Fifth Columnists' Impact on the Battle of Hong Kong, December 1941," in *Close Encounters in War Journal* 1 (2018), 1–18.

4 Order of Council PC 1486, 24 February 1942.

5 J.L. Granatstein, *The Last Good War: An Illustrated History of Canada in the Second World War, 1939–1945* (Vancouver: Douglas & McIntyre, 2005) 63.

6 J.L. Granatstein and Gregory A. Johnson, "The Evacuation of the Japanese Canadians, 1942: A Realist Critique of the Received Version," in Norman Hillmer, Bohdan Kordan, and Lubomyr Luciuk (eds.), *On Guard for Thee: War, Ethnicity, and the Canadian State, 1939–1945* (Ottawa: Canadian Committee for the History of the Second World War, 1988) 103–6.

7 Dave McIntosh, *Hell on Earth: Aging Faster, Dying Sooner: Canadian Prisoners of the Japanese During World War II* (Toronto: McGraw-Hill Ryerson, 1997) 104; and Granatstein and Johnson, "The Evacuation of the Japanese Canadians, 1942," in Hillmer et al., (eds.) *On Guard for Thee,* 103–6.

8 Roy Miki and Cassandra Kobayashi, *Justice in Our Time: The Japanese Canadian Redress Settlement* (Vancouver: Talonbooks, 1991) 37.

9 Library and Archives Canada, Record Group (RG) 117, Records of the Office of the Custodian of Enemy Property.

10 Doug Owram, *The Government Generation: Canadian Intellectuals and the State, 1900–1945* (Toronto: University of Toronto Press, 1986) 263.

11 Lyle Dick, "Sergeant Masumi Mitsui and the Japanese Canadian War Memorial: Intersections of National, Cultural, and Personal Memory," *Canadian Historical Review* 91.3 (September 2010) 435–63.

12 Miki and Kobayashi, *Justice in Our Time,* 49.

13 See Audrey Kobayashi, "The Japanese-Canadian Redress Implications for 'Race Relations,'" *Canadian Ethnic Studies* 24 (1992) 3–4.

14 The Japanese Canadian Centennial Project, *A Dream of Riches: The Japanese Canadians, 1877–1977* (Vancouver: The Japanese Canadian Centennial Project, 1978).

15 Ken Adachi, *The Enemy That Never Was: A History of the Japanese Canadians* (Toronto: McClelland & Stewart, 1976) Preface.

16 Barry Broadfoot, *Years of Sorrow, Years of Shame: The Story of the Japanese Canadians in World War II* (Toronto: Doubleday Canada, 1977); Ann Gomer Sunahara, *The Politics of Racism: The Uprooting of Japanese Canadians during the Second World War* (Toronto: Lorimer, 1981); and The Japanese Canadian Centennial Project, *A Dream of Riches.*

17 Sherrill Grace, *Landscapes of War and Memory: The Two World Wars in Canadian Literature and the Arts, 1977–2007* (Edmonton: University of Alberta Press, 2014).

18 John E. Bodnar, *The "Good War" in American Memory* (Baltimore: Johns Hopkins University Press, 2010) 189–93.

19 Hansard, House of Commons Debates, 2nd Session, 32nd Parliament. V. 4, 29 June 1984, 5306–7.

20 Roy L. Brooks, "The Age of Apology," in Roy L. Brooks (ed.), *When Sorry Isn't Enough: The Controversy over Apologies and Reparations for Human Injustice* (New York: New York University Press, 1999) 3–11; and see W. James Booth, *Communities of Memory: On Witness, Identity, and Justice* (Ithaca: Cornell University Press, 2006).

21 National Association of Japanese Canadians, *Democracy Betrayed: The Case for Redress, November 21, 1984* (Winnipeg: National Association of Japanese Canadians, 1984) 24.

22 Roy Miki, *Redress: Inside the Japanese Canadian Call for Justice* (Vancouver: Raincoast Books, 2004) 236–9.

23 Both polls conducted by Environics Research Group in Toronto.

24 J.L. Granatstein, *Saturday Night* (November 1986) 32–4, 49–50.

25 Interview, J.L. Granatstein, 26 October 2018.

26 Ian Radforth, "Ethnic Minorities and Wartime Injustices: Redress Campaigns and Historical Narratives in Late Twentieth-Century Canada," in Nicole Neatby and Peter Hodgins (eds.), *Settling and Unsettling Memories: Essays in Canadian Public History* (Toronto: University of Toronto Press, 2011) 382.

27 See Lindsay Gibson, "Understanding Ethical Judgments in Secondary School History Classes," (Ph.D. thesis: University of British Columbia, 2014) for a discussion and analysis of the challenges of teaching this charged history.

28 Douglas Fisher, letter, *Legion* (June 1989) 5.

29 Douglas Fisher, letter, *Legion* 5.

30 See the insights in Joan Beaumont, "Australian Prisoners of War in Australian National Memory," in Bob Moore and Barbara Hately-Broad (eds.), *Prisoners of War, Prisoners of Peace: Captivity, Homecoming and Memory in World War II* (New York: Berg Publishers, 2005) 185–94.

31 Julie Summers, *Remembered: The History of the Commonwealth War Graves Commission* (London: Merrell, 2007) 40.

32 McIntosh, *Hell on Earth*, 250.

33 William Allister, *Where Life and Death Hold Hands* (Delta: Retsila Publishing, 2000) 236.

34 Carl Vincent, *No Reason Why: The Canadian Hong Kong Tragedy* (Stittsville: Canada's Wings, 1981) 239.

35 Mark Sweeney, "The Canadian War Crimes Liaison Detachment—Far East and the Prosecution of Japanese 'Minor' War Crimes" (Ph.D. thesis: University of Waterloo, 2013).

36 See Patricia Roy, J.L. Granatstein, Masako Iino, and Hiroko Takamura (eds.), *Mutual Hostages: Canadians and Japanese during the Second World War* (Toronto: University of Toronto Press, 1990) 73.

37 Jonathan Vance, *Objects of Concern: Canadian Prisoners of War through the Twentieth Century* (Vancouver: University of British Columbia Press, 1994) 237.

38 See Clare Makepeace, "For 'ALL Who were Captured'?: The Evolution of National Ex-Prisoner of War Associations in Britain after the Second World War," *Journal of War & Culture Studies* 7.3 (August 2014) 253–68.

39 J.N. Crawford, "A Preliminary Report on a Follow-up Study of Repatriates from Japanese Prisoner of War Camps" (1950), cited in McIntosh, *Hell on Earth*, 251.

40 "The New Pension Legislation," *Legion* (February 1971) 12.

41 Vincent, *No Reason Why*, 203–4; and Tim Cook, *The Necessary War, Volume 1: Canadians Fighting the Second World War: 1939–1943* (Toronto: Allen Lane, 2014) 82–91.

42 See Tim Carew, *Hostages to Fortune* (London: Hamish Hamilton, 1971); and the Legion reaction: "The Truth About Hong Kong?" *Legion* (August 1971) 43; C.P. Stacey, *A Date with History: Memoirs of a Canadian Historian* (Ottawa: Deneau, 1983) 240; Galen Perras, "Defeat Still Cries Aloud for Explanation: Explaining C Force's Dispatch to Hong Kong," *Canadian Military Journal* 11.4 (Autumn 2011) 37–47.

43 Fedorowich, "'Cocked Hats and Swords and Small, Little Garrisons,'" 153.

44 *Calgary Herald*, 1 February 1993; *Calgary Herald*, 2 February 1993; *The Gazette*, 2 February 1993.

45 *Edmonton Journal*, 2 February 1993.

46 Michael Valpy, "Why the Canadians Were in Hong Kong in 1941," *The Globe and Mail*, 3 February 1993.

47 See the argument in McIntosh, *Hell on Earth*.

48 The submission was called "The Sequelae of Inhuman Conditions and Slave Labour Experienced by Members of the Canadian Components of the Hong Kong Forces, 1941–1945, while Prisoners of the Japanese Government."

49 "Memorial Honours Canada's Hong Kong Veterans," Canadian Press, 13 August 2009; "War Amps Acknowledges Importance of Japan Finally

Apologizing to Canada's Hong Kong Veterans," *The War Amps Newsroom Archives,* 8 December 2011; CBC Digital Archives, *Canadians Captured in Hong Kong Receive Compensation,* 1998. Also see the Hong Kong Veterans Commemorative Association website at www.hkvca.ca.

50 See Akiko Hashimoto, *The Long Defeat: Cultural Trauma, Memory, and Identity in Japan* (Oxford: Oxford University Press, 2015).

51 "War Dead Honored," *Star-Phoenix,* 13 November 1990.

52 Hashimoto, *The Long Defeat,* 57–8.

53 Douglas Fisher, "Between Us," *Legion* (September 1995) 4.

54 "Veterans Gather to Unveil Hong Kong Memorial Wall," CTV News, 15 August 2009.

55 "The Monument," Battle of Hong Kong (website dedicated to Major Maurice A. Parker), http://battleofhongkong.com/32.htm.

56 "Canada Accepts Japan's Apology for Hong Kong PoWs," CBC News, 8 December 2011.

57 "Canada Accepts Japan's Apology for Hong Kong PoWs," CBC News.

CHAPTER 12

1 R. Scott Sheffield and Noah Riseman, *Indigenous Peoples and the Second World War: The Politics, Experiences and Legacies of War in the US, Canada, Australia and New Zealand* (Cambridge: Cambridge University Press, 2019) 87.

2 Sheffield and Riseman, *Indigenous Peoples and the Second World War,* 63.

3 On recruitment, see Michael D. Stevenson, "The Mobilization of Native Canadians during the Second World War," *Journal of the Canadian Historical Association* (New Series) 7 (1996) 205–226; and Timothy C. Winegard, *For King and Kanata: Canadian Indians and the First World War* (Winnipeg: University of Manitoba Press, 2012).

4 R. Scott Sheffield, *A Search for Equity: A Study of the Treatment Accorded to First Nations Veterans and Dependents of the Second World War and the Korean Conflict. The Final Report of the National Round Table on First Nations Veterans' Issues* (Ottawa: Assembly of First Nations, 2001) 113.

5 Robert Innes, "'I'm On Home Ground Now. I'm Safe': Saskatchewan Aboriginal Veterans in the Immediate Postwar Years, 1945–1946," *The American Indian Quarterly* 28.3&4 (January 2004) 694.

6 R. Scott Sheffield, "Canadian Aboriginal Veterans and the Veterans Charter after the Second World War," in P. Whitney Lackenbauer, R. Scott Sheffield, and Craig Leslie Mantle (eds.), *Aboriginal Peoples and Military Participation: Canadian and International Perspectives* (Winnipeg: Canadian Defence Academy Press, 2007) 84.

7 Sheffield, "Canadian Aboriginal Veterans and the Veterans Charter after the Second World War," 93.

8 Sheffield, *A Search for Equity*, Executive Summary; Sheffield and Riseman, *Indigenous Peoples and the Second World War*, 260.

9 *The Aboriginal Soldier After the Wars: Report of the Standing Senate Committee on Aboriginal Peoples* (Ottawa: Senate of Canada, March 1995) 21; and Janet Davison, "We Shall Remember Them: Canadian Indians and World War II," (Master's thesis: Trent University, 1992) 157–71.

10 Sheffield, *A Search for Equity*, 53.

11 McKenzie Porter, "Warrior: Tommy Prince," *Maclean's* (1 September 1952).

12 See Ellin Bessner, *Double Threat: Canadian Jews, the Military, and World War II* (Toronto: New Jewish Press, 2018).

13 See Bryan D. Palmer, *Canada's 1960s: The Ironies of Identity in a Rebellious Era* (Toronto: University of Toronto Press, 2008).

14 Innes, "'I'm On Home Ground Now. I'm Safe,'" 711–12.

15 See J.R. Miller, *Skyscrapers Hide the Heavens: A History of Native-Newcomer Relations in Canada*, Fourth Edition (Toronto: University of Toronto Press, 2018).

16 Donna Goodleaf, *Entering the War Zone: A Mohawk Perspective on Resisting Invasions* (Penticton: Theytus Books Ltd., 1995); Timothy C. Winegard, *Oka: A Convergence of Cultures and the Canadian Forces* (Kingston: Canadian Defence Academy Press, 2008); and Robin Philpot, *Oka: dernier alibi du Canada anglais* (Montreal: VLB Éditeur, 1991).

17 Tom MacGregor, "Senate Committee Seeks Apology to Native Veterans," *Legion* (July 1995) 17.

18 MacGregor, "Senate Committee Seeks Apology to Native Veterans," 17.

19 MacGregor, "Senate Committee Seeks Apology to Native Veterans," 17.

20 See Sharon Adams, "Honouring Aboriginal Veterans," *Legion* (19 June 2019); and Pohanna Pyne Feinberg, "Lloyd Pinay and the National Aboriginal Veterans Monument."

21 Sheffield, "Canadian Aboriginal Veterans and the Veterans Charter after the Second World War," 94.

22 Robert G. Halford, *The Unknown Navy: Canada's World War II Merchant Navy* (St. Catharines: Vanwell Publishing, 1995) 243.

23 Patricia Giesler, *Valour at Sea: Canada's Merchant Navy* (Ottawa: Veterans Affairs Canada, 1998) 29.

24 Matt Moore, "'The Kiss of Death Bestowed with Gratitude': The Postwar Treatment of Canada's Second World War Merchant Navy, Redress, and the Negotiation of Veteran Identity" (Master's thesis: Carleton University, 2016) Chapter 1. For a complete list of Canadian merchant ships lost during the war,

including Newfoundland registered ships, see Robert C. Fisher, "Canadian Merchant Shipping Losses, 1939–1945," *Northern Mariner* 5.3 (July 1995) 57–73. For the role of the mariners, see Frederic B. Watt, *In All Respects Ready: The Merchant Navy and the Battle of the Atlantic 1940–1945* (Scarborough: Prentice-Hall Canada, 1985); and Doug Fraser, *Postwar Casualty: Canada's Merchant Navy* (Lawrencetown Beach: Pottersfield Press, 1997).

25 Letter, *Charlottetown Guardian*, 10 October 1945.

26 Halford, *The Unknown Navy*, 241.

27 "D.V.A. Replies to Legion Convention Resolutions," *The Legionary* (June 1957) 32

28 "D.V.A. Replies to Legion Convention Resolutions," *The Legionary*, 29.

29 George Walters, letter, *Legion* (December 1981) 46.

30 Halford, *The Unknown Navy*, 241.

31 Moore, "The Kiss of Death Bestowed with Gratitude," Chapter 3; and Anthony Wilson-Smith and John Demont, "The Unsung Seamen," *Maclean's* (6 July 1992) 77.

32 Bill Fairbairn, "Ex-Merchant Seamen State Their Case," *Legion* (May 1990) 24.

33 Fairbairn, "Ex-Merchant Seamen State Their Case," *Legion*, 24.

34 Douglas Fisher, "Between Ourselves," *Legion* (November 1990) 5.

35 "Treat Merchant Seamen as Veterans, Legion Says," *Legion* (September 1991) 28.

36 "Treat Merchant Seamen as Veterans, Legion Says," *Legion*, 28.

37 Fisher, "Between Ourselves," *Legion*, 50.

38 *It's Almost Too Late: Report of the Subcommittee on Veterans Affairs of the Standing Senate Committee on Social Affairs, Science and Technology* (Ottawa: Senate of Canada, 31 January 1991).

39 "Merchant Navy Veterans," *Legion* (May 1992) 2.

40 Ray Dick, "A Book of Their Own," *Legion* (October 1994) 6.

41 Earle McCrae, "That's One Gem of a Junket," *Ottawa Sun*, 3 October 1998.

42 Earl McCrae, "Merchant Navy Veterans Snubbed," *Ottawa Sun*, 6 October 1998.

43 Barbara Budd and Mary Lou Finlay with guest Ossie MacLean, "Merchant Seamen Stage Hunger Strike on Parliament Hill," CBC Radio's *As It Happens*, 1 October 1998.

44 "Vets," *Ottawa Sun*, 5 October 1998.

CHAPTER 13

1 Tom MacGregor, "Harbor of Remembrance," *Legion* (January 1991) 9.

2 Strome Galloway, "No Sacrifice Greater," *Legion* (May 1990) 10.

3 Bill McNeil, *Voices of a War Remembered: An Oral History of Canadians in World War Two* (Toronto: Doubleday Canada, 1991) 220–1.

4 D. Dunbar, letter, *Legion* (November 1990) 52.

5 "Brown's Books," *Legion* (July/August 1943) 81.

6 Graham Carr, "Rules of Engagement: Public History and the Drama of Legitimation," *Canadian Historical Review* 86.2 (June 2005) 319.

7 For Currie's reputation, see Tim Cook, *The Madman and the Butcher: The Sensational Wars of Sam Hughes and General Arthur Currie* (Toronto: Penguin Canada, 2011).

8 Laura Pratt, "Shaping the Course of History," *Legion* (November 1993) 16.

9 See Richard Overy, *The Bombing War: Europe 1939–1945* (London: Allen Lane, 2013).

10 Tami Davis Biddle, "On the Crest of Fear: V-Weapons, the Battle of the Bulge, and the Last Stages of World War II in Europe," *Journal of Military History* 83.1 (January 2019) 157–94. For Canadians' awareness of bombing, see Laurie Peloquin, "A Conspiracy of Silence? The Popular Press and the Strategic Bombing Campaign in Europe," *Canadian Military History* 3.2 (1994) 22–30.

11 See Sebastian Cox, "The Dresden Raids: Why and How," in Paul Addison and Jeremy Crang (eds.), *Firestorm: The Bombing of Dresden, 1945* (London: Pimlico, 2006) 18–61.

12 Peter Gray, "A Culture of Official Squeamishness? Britain's Air Ministry and the Strategic Air Offensive Against Germany," *Journal of Military History* 77.4 (October 2013) 1349–78.

13 For example, A.C. Grayling, *Among the Dead Cities: Is the Targeting of Civilians in War Ever Justified?* (London: Bloomsbury, 2007); and Eric Markusen and David Kopf, *The Holocaust and Strategic Bombing: Genocide and Total War in the Twentieth Century* (Boulder: Westview Press, 1995). For a discussion of the historiography, see David F. Crew, *Bodies and Ruins: Imagining the Bombing of Germany, 1945 to the Present* (Ann Arbor: University of Michigan Press, 2017); and Jörg Arnold, *The Allied Air War and Urban Memory: The Legacy of Strategic Bombing in Germany* (Cambridge and New York: Cambridge University Press, 2011).

14 Gilad Margalit, *Guilt, Suffering, and Memory: Germany Remembers Its Dead of World War II*, trans. Haim Watzman (Bloomington and Indianapolis: Indiana University Press, 2010) 50.

15 Bas von Benda-Beckmann, *A German Catastrophe? German Historians and the Allied Bombings, 1945–2010* (Amsterdam: Amsterdam University Press, 2010); and Robert G. Moeller, "Germans as Victims? Thoughts on a Post-Cold War History of World War II's Legacies," *History and Memory* 17.1–2 (2005) 147–94.

16 For the scapegoating of Harris, see Peter Lee, "Return from the Wilderness: An Assessment of Arthur Harris' Moral Responsibility for the German City Bombings," *Air Power Review* 16.1 (2013) 85–6.

17 David Hall, "Black, White and Grey: Wartime Arguments For and Against the Strategic Bombing Offensive," *Canadian Military History* 7.1 (Winter 1998) 7.

18 J. Douglas Harvey, *Boys, Bombs and Brussels Sprouts: A Knees-Up, Wheels-Up Chronicle of WW II* (Toronto: McClelland & Stewart, 1981) 11.

19 Henry Probert, *Bomber Harris: His Life and Times: The Biography of Marshal of the Royal Air Force Sir Arthur Harris, the Wartime Chief of Bomber Command* (Mechanicsburg: Stackpole Books, 2001); Sebastian Cox, Introduction to *Sir Arthur T. Harris: Despatch on War Operations: 23rd February to 8th May, 1945* (London: Frank Cass, 1995) xxii; Tami Davis Biddle, "Bombing the Square Yard: Sir Arthur Harris at War, 1942–45," *International History Review* 21 (1999) 626–64.

20 James Hale and Peter Milner, "The Vision and the Revision," *Legion* (June 1992) 7.

21 For reviews, see Monica MacDonald, *Recasting History: How CBC Television Has Shaped Canada's Past* (Montreal and Kingston: McGill University Press, 2019) 137.

22 Willam Cram, letter, *Legion* (August 1992) 71.

23 Douglas Fisher, "Between Ourselves," *Legion* (April 1992) 4–5.

24 Letter cited in Fisher, "Between Ourselves," 5.

25 See David J. Bercuson and S.F. Wise (eds.), *The Valour and the Horror Revisited* (Montreal and Kingston: McGill-Queen's University Press, 1994).

26 James Hale and Peter Milner, "The Vision and the Revision," *Legion* (June 1992) 7.

27 Galafilm press release, "Historians Agree with Filmmakers 'The Valour and the Horror' Is Bullet-Proof," 25 June 1992.

28 See Carr, "Rules of Engagement," 317–54.

29 The book was Merrily Weisbord and Merilyn Simonds Mohr, *The Valour and the Horror* (Toronto: HarperCollins, 1991); the review in *Canadian Historical Review* 74.2 (June 1993).

30 Hale and Milner, "The Vision and the Revision," 8.

31 John A. English, *The Canadian Army and the Normandy Campaign: A Study of Failure in High Command* (New York: Praeger, 1991). Also see J.L. Granatstein, *The Generals: The Canadian Army's Senior Commanders in the Second World War* (Toronto: Stoddart Publishing Co., 1993).

32 "The Inaccurate and the Outrageous," *Legion* (April 1992) 2.

33 "The Inaccurate and the Outrageous," *Legion*, 2.

34 *Production and Distribution of the National Film Board Production* The Kid Who Couldn't Miss: *Report of the Standing Senate Committee on Social Affairs, Science and Technology* (Ottawa: Senate of Canada, 1986) 5.

35 "The CBC Responds Positively," *Legion* (December/January 1992–93) 2.

36 See Ernest J. Dick, "'The Valour and the Horror' Continued: Do We Still Want

Our History on Television?" *Archivaria* 35 (Spring 1993) 263–5; and Carr, "Rules of Engagement."

37 Bill Fairbairn, "Senate Report Blasts TV Mini-Series," *Legion* (April 1993) 29.

38 "CBC Takes Strong Stand," *Legion* (December/January 1992–93) 25.

39 "Back in the News," *Legion* (September 1993) 2.

40 Cited in Douglas Fisher, "Between Ourselves," *Legion* (March 1994) 5.

41 Barney Danson with Curtis Fahey, *Not Bad for a Sergeant: The Memoirs of Barney Danson* (Toronto: Dundurn Press, 2002) 269.

42 Brereton Greenhous, Stephen J. Harris, William C. Johnston, William G.P. Rawling, *The Crucible of War, 1939–1945: The Official History of the Royal Canadian Air Force, vol. 3* (Toronto: University of Toronto Press, 1993).

43 Dave McIntosh, letter, *Legion* (September 1992) 60. He was also author of *Terror in the Starboard Seat* (Don Mills: General Publishing, 1980).

44 Greenhous et al., *The Crucible of War, 1939–1945*, 867.

45 See, for example, Adam Tooze, *The Wages of Destruction: The Making and Breaking of the Nazi Economy* (New York: Viking, 2006); Phillips Payson O'Brien, *How the War Was Won: Air–Sea Power and Allied Victory in World War II* (Cambridge: Cambridge University Press, 2015); David Bashow, *None but the Brave: The Essential Contributions of RAF Bomber Command to Allied Victory during the Second World War* (Kingston: Canadian Defence Academy Press, 2009); and Tim Cook, *Fight to the Finish: Canadians in the Second World War, 1944–1945* (Toronto: Allan Lane, 2015) 370–6.

46 J.L. Granatstein, "Warring Aloft 50 Years On," *Quill and Quire*, June 1994. Also see, David Bercuson and Syd Wise in "*The Valour and the Horror* Controversy and the *Official History of the RCAF*, Volume 3," *Canadian Military History* 3.2 (Autumn 1994) 107–10.

47 Reginald Dixon, letter, *Legion* (September 1994) 68. Also see Douglas Fisher, "The Armchair Generals Rave On," *Toronto Sun*, 22 May 1994.

48 Hale and Milner, "The Vision and the Revision," 6.

CHAPTER 14

1 "A Controversy," *Legion* (December–January 1993–4) 2.

2 Raymond Maguire, letter, *Legion* (October 1944) 67.

3 William Dennis, letter, *Legion* (October 1944) 67.

4 Douglas Fisher, "Between Ourselves," *Legion* (September 1994) 4.

5 James Hale, *Branching Out: The Story of the Royal Canadian Legion* (Ottawa: The Royal Canadian Legion, 1995) 248–51; and "A Controversy," *Legion* (December–January 1993–4) 2.

6 James Cook, letter, *Legion* (February 1994) 52.

7   Ernst Frohloff, letter, *Legion* (August 1994) 84.

8   Dunstan Pasterfield, letter, *Legion* (August 1994) 84.

9   Douglas Fisher, "Between Ourselves," *Legion* (September 1994) 4.

10 Fisher, "Between Ourselves," *Legion*, 4.

11 Paul Koring, "Role as Peacekeepers Now Proudest Tradition of Canadian Military," *The Globe and Mail*, 30 September 1988. For a sustained discussion, see Colin McCullough, *Creating Canada's Peacekeeping Past* (Vancouver: University of British Columbia Press, 2016).

12 J.L. Granatstein and David Bercuson, *War and Peacekeeping: From South Africa to the Gulf—Canada's Limited Wars* (Key Porter Books Ltd., 1991) 249.

13 National Capital Commission and Department of National Defence, *Creating a National Symbol: The Peacekeeping Monument Competition* (Ottawa: National Capital Commission, 1991) 2–3.

14 P. Gough, "'Invicta Pax' Monuments, Memorials and Peace: An analysis of the Canadian Peacekeeping Monument, Ottawa," *International Journal of Heritage Studies* 8.3 (2002) 201–223.

15 For these operations, see Carol Off, *The Ghosts of Medak Pocket: The Story of Canada's Secret War* (Toronto: Random House Canada, 2004); and Lee Windsor, "Professionalism Under Fire: Canadian Implementation of the Medak Pocket Agreement, Croatia 1993," *Canadian Military History* 9.3 (2000).

16 David Bercuson, *Significant Incident: Canada's Army, the Airborne, and the Murder in Somalia* (Toronto: McClelland & Stewart, 1996).

17 Terry Copp, "What the War Was All About," *Legion* (May 1995) 25.

18 Duncan Fraser, "Americans Out to Steal D-Day Anniversary Thunder," *The Chronicle-Herald*, 24 July 1993.

19 *Ottawa Sun*, 15 June 1994.

20 Douglas Porch, *The Path to Victory: The Mediterranean Theatre in World War II* (New York: Farrar, Straus and Giroux, 2004) 656.

21 Henry Rousso, *The Vichy Syndrome: History and Memory in France since 1944* (Cambridge: Harvard University Press, 1991).

22 On the importance of Normandy, see Geoffrey Bird, Sean Claxton, and Keir Reeves (eds.), *Managing and Interpreting D-Day's Sites of Memory: Guardians of Remembrance* (London: Routledge, 2016).

23 "Germany Forced to Swallow Second Defeat Over D-Day Ceremony," *The Times*, 8 March 1994.

24 Matthew Graves, "Memorial Diplomacy in Franco-Australian Relations," in Shanti Sumartojo and Ben Wellings (eds.), *Nation, Memory and Great War Commemoration: Mobilizing the Past in Europe, Australia and New Zealand* (Oxford: Peter Lang, 2014).

25 "Row Over D-Day Triggers French Rebuke for Bonn," *The Times*, 17 March 1994.

26 Michael R. Dolski, "'Portal of Liberation': D-Day Myth as American Self-Affirmation," in Michael Dolski, Sam Edwards, and John Buckley (eds.), *D-Day in History and Memory: The Normandy Landings in International Remembrance and Commemoration* (Denton: University of North Texas Press, 2014) 614.

27 Dan Black, "Merci Canada! Merci," *Legion* (August 1994) 15–16.

28 Terry Copp and Matt Symes, "Canada's D-Day: Politics, Media, and the Fluidity of Memory," in Michael Dolski, Sam Edwards, and John Buckley (eds.), *D-Day in History and Memory: The Normandy Landings in International Remembrance and Commemoration* (Denton: University of North Texas Press, 2014) 147–8.

29 Black, "Merci Canada! Merci," *Legion*, 16.

30 "The Focal Point," *Legion* (December 1994) 2.

31 Fisher, "Between Ourselves," *Legion*, 4.

32 Diane Sims, "A Date with the Dutch," *Legion* (October 1994) 16.

33 J.L. Granatstein, "A Half-Century On: The Veterans' Experience," in Peter Neary and J.L. Granatstein (eds.), *The Veterans Charter and Post–World War II Canada* (Montreal and Kingston: McGill-Queen's University Press, 1999) 226.

34 "Soldiers of the Scheldt," *Legion* (January 1995) 15.

35 "Soldiers of the Scheldt," *Legion*, 15.

CHAPTER 15

1 Tom MacGregor, "Liberation Celebration," *Legion* (August 1995) 6.

2 Tom MacGregor, "Liberation Celebration," *Legion*, 6.

3 On American memory, see Karal Ann Marling and John Wetenhall, *Iwo Jima: Monuments, Memories, and the American Hero* (Cambridge: Harvard University Press, 1991); and Joy Waldron Jasper, James P. Degado, and Jim Adams, *The USS Arizona: The Ship, the Men, the Pearl Harbor Attack, and the Symbols That Aroused America* (New York: St. Martins, 2001).

4 Tom MacGregor, "VJ-Day Events Salute Pacific War Veterans," *Legion* (October 1995) 30.

5 J.N. Roger Cyr, speech, 12 August 1995, in author's possession.

6 MacGregor, "VJ-Day Events Salute Pacific War Veterans," *Legion*, 31.

7 David Bercuson, *Maple Leaf Against the Axis: Canada's Second World War* (Toronto: Stoddart Publishing Co. Ltd., 1995); and W.A.B. Douglas and Brereton Greenhous, *Out of the Shadows: Canada in the Second World War* (Toronto: Oxford University, 1977).

8 Serge Bernier, *La participation des Canadiens français à la Deuxième Guerre mondiale: mythes et réalités* (Montréal: Association québécoise d'histoire politique, 1995).

9 George Blackburn, *The Guns of Normandy: A Soldier's Eye View, France 1944* (Toronto: McClelland & Stewart, 1995).

10 Robert M. Stamp, *Books in Canada* 24.8 (November 1995) 33.

11 John Ward, "Baptism of Fire," *The Ottawa Journal*, 19 January 1997, 10.

12 Blackburn, *The Guns of Normandy*, xiii.

13 *The British Columbia Report* 7.34 (22 April 1996) 42.

14 Farley Mowat, *And No Birds Sang* (Toronto: McClelland & Stewart, 1979).

15 Lance Goddard, *Canada and the Liberation of the Netherlands, May 1945* (Toronto: Dundurn Press, 2005) 220.

16 Naval Officers Association of Canada, *Salty Dips* (Ottawa: privately published, 1979 to 2001) 8 volumes.

17 Fred Langan, "Jean Portugal Chronicled Stories of Canadian Veterans," *The Globe and Mail*, 1 January 2017.

18 Buzz Bourdon, "George Blackburn, Soldier and Author, 1917–2006," *The Globe and Mail*, 15 January 2007.

19 J.L. Granatstein, "Canadian History Textbooks and the Wars," *Canadian Military History* 3.1 (1994) 123–4. For a rebuttal, see Margaret Conrad and Alvin Finkel, "Textbook Wars: Canadian Style," *Canadian Issues* (October 2003) 12–5.

20 Robert Vogel, "Some Reflections on the Teaching of Military History in Canada," *Canadian Military History* 1.1&2 (1992) 101–4.

21 Donald M. Schurman, "Writing About War," in John Schultz (ed.), *Writing About Canada: A Handbook for Modern Canadian History* (Scarborough: Prentice-Hall Canada, 1990) 231.

22 Terry Copp and Matt Symes, "Canada's D-Day: Politics, Media, and the Fluidity of Memory," in Michael Dolski, Sam Edwards, and John Buckley (eds.), *D-Day in History and Memory: The Normandy Landings in International Remembrance and Commemoration* (Denton: University of North Texas Press, 2014) 141.

23 Terry Copp, *Cinderella Army: The Canadians in Northwest Europe, 1944–1945* (Toronto: University of Toronto Press, 2006).

24 "Veterans Snapshot," *Legion* (November/December 1995) 59; and "Membership Concerns Raised in Ontario," *Legion* (August 1995) 28.

25 "Legion Image Needs Improvement," *Legion* (January 1996) 22.

26 Mac Johnston, "Newfoundland Tackles Membership," *Legion* (September 1945) 28.

27 April Bremner, letter, *Legion* (August 1995) 84.

28 See *Canada Remembers, VE-Day Commemorative Events* (pamphlet: Veterans Affairs Canada, 1995).

29 Dave McIntosh, "Our Story of Sacrifice Is Shabby and Shunned," *Legion* (February 1988) 8–9.

30 David Dean and Peter E. Rider, "Museums, Nation and Political History in the Australian National Museum and the Canadian Museum of Civilization," *Museum and Society* 3.1 (2005) 35–50; and John English, "Report: The Canada Hall and the Museum of Civilization," Canadian Museum of Civilization Library (1999).

31 See Peter E. Rider, "Presenting the Public's History to the Public: The Case of the Canadian Museum of Civilization," in Peter E. Rider (ed.), *Studies in History and Museums* (Ottawa: Canadian Museum of Civilization, 1994) 77–101.

32 "Tools Which Finished the Job Last Time, on Display Here," *The Ottawa Journal*, 17 January 1942; "Military Museum Opening in Sussex Street Bldg," *The Evening Citizen*, 17 January 1942; and see John Swettenham, "The Canadian War Museum," *Canadian Defence Quarterly* 4.4 (Spring 1975) 40–4.

33 Canadian War Museum (CWM), 57A, MMB 22, vol. 1, R. Glover to G.G.E. Steele, 9 March 1965; Roger Sarty, "The Nationalization of Military History: Scholarship, Politics and the Canadian War Museum," in Norman Hillmer and Adam Chapnick (eds.), *Canadas of the Mind: The Making and Unmaking of Canadian Nationalisms in the Twentieth Century* (Montreal and Kingston: McGill-Queen's University Press, 2007) 123.

34 Hugh Halliday, "We Shouldn't Just Give Pacifist View of Our History," *Ottawa Citizen*, 23 September 1998.

35 *Task Force on Military History Museum Collections in Canada* (Ottawa: Minister of Supply and Services Canada, 1991) 25–7.

36 Tom MacGregor, "Task Force Urges Museum Autonomy," *Legion* (June 1991) 29.

37 *Task Force on Military History Museum Collections in Canada*, 28–9.

38 MacGregor, "Task Force Urges Museum Autonomy," *Legion*, 29.

39 Norman Hillmer, "The Canadian War Museum and the Military Identity of an Unmilitary People," *Canadian Military History* 19.3 (Summer 2010) 20–1.

40 Edward T. Linenthal, *Preserving Memory: The Struggle to Create America's Holocaust Museum* (New York: Viking, 1995).

41 Donald Bloxham, *Genocide on Trial: War Crimes Trials and the Formation of Holocaust History and Memory* (Oxford: Oxford University Press, 2003).

42 James Young, *The Texture of Memory: Holocaust Memorials and Meaning* (London: Yale University Press, 1993).

43 David F. Crew, *Bodies and Ruins: Imagining the Bombing of Germany, 1945 to the Present* (Ann Arbor: University of Michigan Press, 2017) 49.

44 "Lest We Forget," *Ottawa Citizen*, 6 February 1997.

45 "Lest We Forget," *Ottawa Citizen*, 6 February 1997.

46 Laura Bobak, "Holocaust Wing Hits Home," *Ottawa Sun*, 13 February 1997.

47 Cameron Pulsifer, "The Roots of a Museum Crisis: Exploring the Origins of the Proposal to Put a Holocaust Gallery in the Canadian War Museum" (unpublished article: 4 May 2005) n.p., in author's possession.

48 Victor Suthren, letter, *Ottawa Citizen*, 6 March 1997.

49 Canadian War Museum, "Canadian War Museum Unveils Design for Expansion" (press release: 13 November 1997) in author's possession.

50 The War Amps News Release, 12 November 1997; and Allan Thompson, "Veterans Declare War on Plan for Museum," *Toronto Star*, 30 October 1997.

51 "Museum Turf War," *Winnipeg Free Press*, 17 November 1997.

52 "Museum Turf War," *Winnipeg Free Press*, 17 November 1997.

53 Irving Abella, "Why Do Canadian Veterans Belittle Their Proud Actions Against the Holocaust," *The Globe and Mail*, 22 November 1997.

54 George MacDonald, letter, *Toronto Star*, 28 November 1997.

55 George MacDonald, *The Toronto Star*, 28 November 1997.

56 Suthren left the museum in early October 1997. *Ottawa Citizen*, 23 October 1997.

57 Elizabeth Payne, "The 'Miracle' of LeBreton Flats," *Ottawa Citizen*, 8 May 2005; and The Senate of Canada, Press Release, 14 November 1997.

58 Charles Enman, "Veterans Lambaste Museum," *Ottawa Citizen*, 7 February 1998.

59 "Guarding History: A Study into the Future, Funding, and Independence of the Canadian War Museum," Report of the Subcommittee on Veterans Affairs of the Standing Senate Committee on Social Affairs, Science and Technology (May 1998).

60 Pulsifer, "The Roots of a Museum Crisis," n.p.

61 Cited in Cameron Pulsifer, "The 330 Sussex Drive Years: And the Quest for a New Building, 1967-2005" (unpublished article: 4 May 2005) n.p., in author's possession.

62 Enman, "Veterans Lambaste Museum."

CHAPTER 16

1 See Kate Clarke Lemay, *Triumph of the Dead: American World War II Cemeteries, Monuments, and Diplomacy in France* (Tuscaloosa: The University of Alabama Press, 2018); Edward T. Linenthal, *Sacred Ground: Americans and*

Their Battlefields (Urbana and Chicago: University of Illinois Press, 1991); and Sam Edwards, "War and Collective Memory: American Military Commemoration in Britain and France, 1943 to the Present" (Ph.D. thesis: Lancaster University, 2007).

2   Matt Symes, "The Personality of Memory: The Informal Process of Commemoration in Normandy," in Geoffrey Hayes, Mike Bechthold, and Matt Symes (eds.), *Canada and the Second World War: Essays in Honour of Terry Copp* (Waterloo: Wilfrid Laurier University Press, 2012) 461–77.

3   See Michael Bechthold, "Lessons Learned on the Normandy Battlefields: The Experience of the Canadian Battlefields Foundation Student Study Tours," *Canadian Military History* 15 (2006) 10–6; and Geoffrey Hayes, "Building a Path of Informed Memory: The Work of the Canadian Battlefields Foundation," in Geoffrey Bird, Sean Claxton, and Keir Reeves (eds.), *Managing and Interpreting D-Day's Sites of Memory: Guardians of Remembrance* (London: Routledge, 2016) 153–4.

4   Paul Gough, "A Difficult Path to Tread," *Canadian Military History* 8 (1999) 78–81; and N. Griffiths, "Memory, Monument, and Landscape," *Canadian Military History* 8 (Winter 1999) 75–8.

5   See Geoffrey R. Bird, "Place Identities in the Normandy Landscape of War: Touring the Canadian Sites of Memory," in Leanne White and Elspeth Frew (eds.), *Dark Tourism and Place Identity: Managing and Interpreting Dark Places* (London: Routledge, 2013) 167–185.

6   There is a fine private museum in Adegem, Belgium, the Canada-Poland Museum, created and curated by Gilbert Van Landschoot.

7   Marci McDonald, "A Memorial Plan," *Maclean's* (11 June 1984) 29.

8   Ian J. Campbell, *Murder at the Abbaye: The Story of Twenty Canadian Soldiers Murdered at the Abbaye d'Ardenne* (Ottawa: Golden Dog Press, 1996) 167.

9   Vanessa McMackin, "Rearranged Snowdrops: The Construction of Memory at the Abbaye d'Ardenne," *Canadian Military History* 20 (2011) 31.

10 McMackin, "Rearranged Snowdrops," 38.

11 Albert Auster, "*Saving Private Ryan* and American Triumphalism," in Robert Eberwein (ed.), *The War Film* (New Brunswick: Rutgers University Press, 2005) 205–6, 212.

12 Michael R. Dolski, "'Portal of Liberation': D-Day Myth as American Self-Affirmation," in Michael Dolski, Sam Edwards, and John Buckley (eds.), *D-Day in History and Memory: The Normandy Landings in International Remembrance and Commemoration* (Denton: University of North Texas Press, 2014) 67.

13 Steve Weatherbe, "Saving Private Ryan," *The Globe and Mail*, 24 August 1998.

14 Lyle Dick, "Saving the Nation through National History: The Case of *Canada: A People's History*," in Nicole Neatby and Peter Hodgins (eds.), *Settling and Unsettling Memories: Essays in Canadian Public History* (Toronto: University of Toronto Press, 2012) 188–212; and Margaret Conrad, "My Canada Includes the Atlantic Provinces," *Histoire sociale/Social History* 34.68 (2001) 392–402.

15 See Mark Starowicz, *Making History: The Remarkable Story Behind Canada: A People's History* (Toronto: McClelland & Stewart, 2003).

16 R. Caldwell, "Operation Overkill," *The Globe and Mail*, 4 September 2001.

17 Ted Barris, "This Day in History: Juno–A Beach to Remember," *Zoomer*, 6 June 2018.

18 Terry Copp, "Canada's Own D-Day," *Canadian Issues* (Fall 2015) 33.

19 Anthony Reinhart, "Juno Beach Troops Refuse to Be Forgotten," *The Globe and Mail*, 9 November 2005.

20 Susan Bourette, "Normandy Museum Planned: Facility to Honour Canadian War Effort," *The Globe and Mail*, 7 February 2001.

21 Copp and Symes, "Canada's D-Day: Politics, Media, and the Fluidity of Memory," in Dolski (eds.) *D–Day in History and Memory*, 148–50; and "Canada's D-Day," *National Post*, 6 June 2003.

22 Bruce Wallace, "Soldiers Return to Juno Beach," *Calgary Herald*, 7 July 2003.

23 Reinhart, "Juno Beach Troops Refuse to Be Forgotten."

24 Copp and Symes, "Canada's D-Day: Politics, Media, and the Fluidity of Memory," in Dolski (eds.) *D–Day in History and Memory*, 152.

25 J.L. Granatstein, *National Post*, 18 June 2004.

26 Diane Kenny, letter, *National Post*, 10 June 2003.

27 See Serge Durflinger, "How We've Remembered D-Day Over the Years," *Ottawa Citizen*, 5 June 2019.

28 Thomas S. Axworthy, "Veterans Have Taught Us a Lesson," *National Post*, 10 June 2003.

CHAPTER 17

1 Dave Brown, "Pull Out Attack Manual," *Ottawa Citizen*, 1 October 1999.

2 "Recovering Memory," *Ottawa Citizen*, 3 October 1998.

3 Barney Danson, with Curtis Fahey, *Not Bad for a Sergeant: The Memoirs of Barney Danson* (Toronto: Dundurn Press, 2002) 273; and Elizabeth Payne, "The 'Miracle' of LeBreton Flats," *Ottawa Citizen*, 8 May 2005.

4 "The Museum that Jack Built," *Ottawa Citizen*, 5 October 1998.

5 J.L. Granatstein, *Who Killed Canadian History?* (Toronto: HarperCollins, 1998).

6 Linda Williamson, "A Worthy Place for Memories," *The Ottawa Sun*, 12 November 1999.

7   Williamson, "A Worthy Place for Memories."

8   J.L. Granatstein, "At Play in the Field of the Museologists: Two Years at the Canadian War Museum" (Ross Ellis Memorial Lecture: University of Calgary, 19 January 2001).

9   Graham Fraser, "Copps Recruits a War-Museum Fundraiser," *The Globe and Mail*, 12 November 1999.

10 "After What They Paid," *Ottawa Citizen*, 13 September 1999.

11 See Laura Brandon, *Art or Memorial?: The Forgotten History of Canada's War Art* (Calgary: University of Calgary Press, 2006) 61–3; and Laura Brandon and Dean F. Oliver, *Canvas of War: Painting the Canadian Experience* (Douglas & McIntyre, 2000).

12 Laura Brandon, "'A Unique and Important Asset?' The Transfer of the War Art Collections from the National Gallery of Canada to the Canadian War Museum," *Material History Review* 42 (Fall 1995) 67–74.

13 K.S. Inglis, "Entombing Unknown Soldiers: From London to Paris to Baghdad," *History & Memory* 5.2 (1993) 7–31.

14 Dan Black, "The Tomb of the Unknown Soldier," *Legion* (1 September 2000); and Katrina Bormanis, "What Remains: Repatriating and Entombing a Canadian Unknown Soldier of the Great War in the Nation's Capital," *War & Society* 35.3 (August 2016) 219–40.

15 Black, "The Tomb of the Unknown Soldier."

16 Robert Klara, *The Devil's Mercedes: The Bizarre and Disturbing Adventures of Hitler's Limousine in America* (New York: Thomas Dunne Books/St. Martin's Press, 2017); Interview with J.L. Granatstein, 10 June 2019.

17 Chris Cobb, "Callers Urge War Museum Not to Sell Hitler's Car," *The Ottawa Citizen*, 3 February 2000.

18 Chris Cobb, "Callers Urge War Museum Not to Sell Hitler's Car."

19 "War Museum Keeps Hitler's Car," CBC News, 8 February 2000.

20 David Anido, "Rockcliffe Is Brilliant," *Ottawa Citizen*, 20 March 2001.

21 Chris Cobb, "War Museum Pledge 'Keeps Faith' with Dead," *Ottawa Citizen*, 17 March 2000.

22 Cobb, "War Museum Pledge 'Keeps Faith' with Dead."

23 "Granatstein to Leave War Museum," *The Globe and Mail*, 13 March 2000; and "He Saved History," *Ottawa Citizen*, 14 March 2000.

24 "Joe Geurts to Head War Museum," *Ottawa Citizen*, 17 May 2000.

25 Michael Prentice, "Vets Outraged by Museum Site Switch," *Ottawa Citizen*, 8 March 2001.

26 Prentice, "Vets Outraged by Museum Site Switch."

27 M. Gordon Foster, "LeBreton Flats Site Won't Satisfy War Museum's Needs,"

Ottawa Citizen, 9 March 2001; and William Barclay, "Legion Is Puzzled Why Beautiful Site for War Museum Is Being Rejected," *Ottawa Citizen*, 14 March 2001.

28 Cameron Pulsifer, "The 330 Sussex Drive Years: And the Quest for a New Building, 1967–2005" (unpublished article: 4 May 2005) n.p., in author's possession.

29 Raymond Moriyama, *In Search of a Soul: Designing and Realizing the New Canadian War Museum* (Vancouver: Douglas & McIntyre, 2006).

30 Maria Cook, "War Museum Won't Be 'Old Wine in New Bottles,'" *Ottawa Citizen*, 14 April 2001; also see Roger Sarty, "The Nationalization of Military History: Scholarship, Politics, and the Canadian War Museum," in Norman Hillmer and Adam Chapnick (eds.), *Canadas of the Mind: The Making and Unmaking of Canadian Nationalisms in the Twentieth Century* (Montreal and Kingston: McGill-Queen's University Press, 2007).

31 *Windsor Star*, 25 November 2006.

32 "Those Who Paid the Price," *Ottawa Sun*, 8 May 2005.

33 "War Museum Lacks Gallery on Holocaust," *Winnipeg Free Press*, 8 May 2005.

34 Bruce Campion-Smith, "Veterans Vow to Pass Torch to Canada's Youth," *Toronto Star*, 8 May 2005.

35 Patrick Dare, "Crowds Flock to Museum Opening," *CanWest News Service*, 8 May 2005.

36 Dare, "Crowds Flock to Museum Opening."

37 Victor Rabinovitch, "Narrating Public History and the Bomber Command Controversy, (2005–07)" (presentation to the Canadian Historical Association: Vancouver, 2008).

38 See Edward T. Linenthal and Tom Engelhardt (eds.), *History Wars: The Enola Gay and Other Battles for the American Past* (New York: Holt Paperbacks, 1996); and Martin Harwit, *An Exhibit Denied: Lobbying the History of Enola Gay* (New York: Copernicus, 1996).

39 *Ottawa Citizen*, 29 November 2006.

40 Val Ross, "Fighting Words Rile Historians," *The Globe and Mail*, 29 August 2007.

41 There is overwhelming evidence. See, for example, Richard Overy, *The Bombing War: Europe 1939–1945* (London: Allen Lane, 2013); Paul Addison and Jeremy Crang (eds.), *Firestorm: The Bombing of Dresden, 1945* (London: Pimlico, 2006); and Jörg Arnold, *The Allied Air War and Urban Memory: The Legacy of Strategic Bombing in Germany* (Cambridge: Cambridge University Press, 2011).

42 *Ottawa Citizen*, 29 September 2006.

43 *Ottawa Citizen*, 29 September 2006.

44 *Montreal Gazette*, 10 October 2006

45 *Ottawa Citizen*, 1 December 2006

46 *National Post*, 27 November 2006.

47 For the best accounts of Canadian involvement in Afghanistan, see Murray Brewster, *The Savage War: The Untold Battles of Afghanistan* (Toronto: John Wiley and Sons Canada, 2011); and Jean-Christophe Boucher and Kim Richard Nossal, *The Politics of War: Canada's Afghanistan Mission, 2001–14* (Vancouver: University of British Columbia Press, 2017).

48 See Brooke Jeffrey, *Dismantling Canada: Stephen Harper's New Conservative Agenda* (Montreal and Kingston: McGill-Queen's University Press, 2015); and Michael Eamon, "The War Against Public Forgetfulness: Commemorating 1812 in Canada," *London Journal of Canadian Studies*, 29.1 (November 2014) 134–185.

49 *National Post*, 28 November 2006.

50 See David J. Bercuson, "The Canadian War Museum and Bomber Command: My Perspective," *Canadian Military History* 20.3 (2011) 55–62.

51 Paul Manson, "A Poor Display of Canada's Military History," *The Globe and Mail*, 9 January 2007.

52 Robert Bothwell, Randall Hansen, and Margaret MacMillan, "Controversy, Commemoration, and Capitulation: The Canadian War Museum and Bomber Command," *Queen's Quarterly* 115.3 (Fall 2008) 370; and David Dean, "Museums as Conflict Zones: The Canadian War Museum and Bomber Command," *Museum & Society* 7.1 (2009) 5–6.

53 J.L. Granatstein and Dean Oliver, *The Oxford Companion to Canadian Military History* (Don Mills: Oxford University Press and the Canadian War Museum, 2011) 58.

CONCLUSION

1 Interview with Wayne Shantz, 25 January 2019. An eighth Book of Remembrance, for the War of 1812, was unveiled in February 2019.

2 Angela Duffett, "Memory, Myth and Memorials: Newfoundland's Public Memory of the First World War," (Master's thesis: Carleton University, 2010); and Tim Cook, *Vimy: The Battle and the Legend* (Toronto: Allen Lane, 2017).

3 Jack Jedwab, "Knowledge About War Is a Must—But What We Must Know Is Less Certain," *Canadian Issues* (Fall 2015) 16–7.

4 Lance Goddard, *Canada and the Liberation of the Netherlands, May 1945* (Toronto: Dundurn Press, 2005) 226.

5 Douglas Brinkley (ed.), *The World War II Memorial: A Grateful Nation Remembers* (Washington: Smithsonian Books, 2004).

6 See John E. Bodnar, *The "Good War" in American Memory* (Baltimore: The John Hopkins University Press, 2010).

7 See Travis Tomchuk and Jodi Giesbrecht, *Redress Movements in Canada* (Ottawa: Canadian Historical Association, 2018).

8 The War Amps website, "Our History / 1985: *NEVER AGAIN!* video series debuts."

9 Doug Saunders, "Memories 'Very, Very Hard to Face,'" *The Globe and Mail*, 7 June 2004.

10 "Vets Go Online to Recall Battle," *Edmonton Journal*, 7 June 2003.

11 "Des centaines de vétérans Canadiens sur les plages du débarquement," *Le Devoir*, 7 June 2004.

12 Blake Heathcote, *Testaments of Honour: Personal Histories from Canada's War Veterans* (Toronto: Doubleday Canada, 2002) 28.

13 Greg Buium, "Veterans Remember Sights, Sounds of Battle," *Edmonton Journal*, 7 June 2003.

ACKNOWLEDGMENTS

This book sent me off into much unchartered territory, although I had some guides, and the many sources in the endnotes reveal my debt to other scholars, veterans, and commentators.

I was lucky to call upon friends to read the manuscript at various stages. I am grateful for the insight, questions, and observations from Dr. Mike Bechthold, Dr. Andrew Burtch, Eric Brown, Sarah Cook, Robert Fisher, Dr. J.L. Granatstein, Dr. Steve Harris, Dr. Mark Humphries, Dr. John Macfarlane, Dr. Bill Stewart, and Dr. Bill Waiser. Special thanks go to my colleagues at the Canadian War Museum. I had many informal discussions with curators, archivists, librarians, creative developers, learning specialists, collections specialists, and historians. While it has been my privilege to work at the CWM since 2002, the analysis and conclusions drawn in the book about the museum are mine alone.

I would like to thank Eric Storey at Wilfrid Laurier University, who conducted newspaper research that aided in rounding out several stories in the book. I gratefully acknowledge the support from the Laurier Centre for Military Strategic and Disarmament Studies, where I am lucky to be a research fellow. Sarah Cook, an expert researcher and historian, also carried out important research.

I would like to thank my friend and agent, Rick Broadhead, who is always on the look-out for me. In our ninth book together, I'd like to thank my editor at Penguin Random House Canada, Diane Turbide, who continues to champion my work. Providing her fastidious and skilled line and copy editing, Tara Tovell guided the writing forward, as she has done since we first worked together in 2006. Tara, Diane, and many others work hard to make my books better. I am grateful for their support and skill.

Sharon Cook listened to some of the stories I told in the book and we both commented more than once that my father, Terry, would have enjoyed it. My wife, Sarah, was with me the whole way on this book, as she has been on all the others. She has a great passion for history, archives, remembrance, and memory studies, and I am a lucky man to share my life with her. And Chloe, Emma, and Paige remain our bright stars. They have grown up in a house of history and with much talk about the past, but Sarah and I see them as our future. They inspire and amaze us every day. Perhaps this book will give them greater insight into the Second World War and their great-great grandfather who served in it. Gordon Cook, a bomber pilot, died decades before they were born. And they lost their grandfather, Terry, five years ago, a gentle and brilliant man of archives, history, and stories. But both the presence of Gordon and Terry remain strong in our home and in our hearts.

INDEX

Note: Italicized numbers refer to illustrations.

CREDITS

The Author has been collecting images from multiple sources for two decades. All of the images here are his own unless otherwise stated.

Page 11: Canadian Expeditionary Force official photograph, O-1005
Page 21: Library and Archives Canada (LAC), PA-140881
Page 48: LAC, C-049434
Page 60: LAC, PA-119733
Page 67: LAC, Mikan 4167359
Page 72: Courtesy of Sarah Cook
Page 75: LAC, PA-1332441
Page 83: Courtesy of Chloe Cook
Page 93: LAC, 999909132
Page 95: LAC, 025107
Page 98: Courtesy of Emma Cook
Page 103: LAC, 135956
Page 106: LAC, 131504
Page 114: LAC, 136201
Page 133: LAC, 162648
Page 177: Courtesy of Paige Cook
Page 187: LAC, 163403
Page 210: Courtesy of Chloe Cook
Page 283: Courtesy of Paige Cook
Page 309: LAC, PA-129124